Baedeker's

CYPRUS

Aphrodite's Island

Cyprus (Greek Kypros), so named in antiquity on account of its flourishing copper mines, appears in classical mythology as the island of Aphrodite, goddess of love and fertility. A wave-lapped rock, the famous Pétra tou Romioú, is said to mark the spot where the spume-born goddess rose from the sea. Not far away at Palaía Páphos (now Koúklia) are the remains of one of the largest temples to Aphrodite in the ancient world, to which devotees of the goddess once flocked.

Today the great attraction of this friendly island is the wide variety of leisure opportunities. There is plentiful evidence of Cyprus's 9000-year history, much of it spent under the hegemony of various foreign powers. The Ptolemies left the Tombs of the Kings cut into the rock at Páphos and the Romans bequeathed colourful mosaic pavements. In the Middle Ages the Knights of St John built the great castle at Kolóssi, which for a time was the headquarters of the Order and produced the celebrated Commandaria, one of the world's first branded wines.

Visitors for whom a good holiday means, first and foremost, the beach will not be alone in appreciating the island's varied coastal scenery and its generally high standard of hotels.

Famagusta/ Gazimağusa
View from the walls over the Old Town

Ayía Nápa
monastery in south-eastern Cyprus

Since the occupation of northern Cyprus by Turkish forces in 1974, and the ensuing partition of the island, holidaymakers have been slow to visit what today is the Turkish Republic of North Cyprus. However, tourism has shown signs of hesitant recovery, chiefly in the idyllic little town of Kyrenia and in Famagusta, formerly the island's principal port.

Ramblers will relish the nature trails around Mount Ólympos, the highest peak in the Tróodos range where impassable mountainsides – like those in the vicinity of the mysterious Cedar Valley – once offered hermits the seclusion they sought, and where in the Middle Ages Byzantine and Western monasteries and barn-roofed churches were built. Unique to Cyprus, every single one of these small churches, their walls embellished with murals still for the most part well preserved, appears on UNESCO's list of World Heritage Sites.

Tróodos
Some of the most delightful scenery in Cyprus

Definitely not to be missed is a visit to Nicosia, the island's divided capital, a city with a distinctly oriental character. In the Old Town, still encircled by its Venetian walls, Laiki Yitoniá (the people's quarter), where traffic is now restricted, forms an oasis of peace. Nicosia is as typically Cypriot as the remotest mountain village. Here, in homely tavernas, you can drink good wine and sample delicious *meze* – a selection of 20 or so appetising starters illustrating the full variety of Cypriot cuisine, or enjoy folk music and dancing in one of the bouzouki bars.

CONTENTS

Introduction 8–75

Sights from A to Z 77–222

Practical Information from A to Z 224–265

Principal Sights

South Cyprus

★★

Asinou

Kakopetriá

Koúrion

Lagoudherá

Nicosia

Páphos

★

Ayía Nápa

Chala Sultan Tekke

Galáta

Kalophanayiótis

Khirokitía

Kolóssi Castle

Koúklia/Palaia Páphos

Kykko Monastery

Lárnaca

Léfkara

Limassol

Neóphytos Monastery

Peristeróna

Platanistása

Tamassós

Tróodos Massif

Yeroskípos

North Cyprus

★★

Bellapais

Famagusta

Salamís

★

Kantara

Karpasía Peninsula

Kyrenia

Nikosia – North

St Hilarion

Following the tradition established by Karl Baedeker in 1846, buildings, places of natural beauty and sights of particular interest are distinguished by one ★ or two ★★ stars. The places listed above are merely a selection of the principal sights – there are of course many other sights in Cyprus, to which attention is drawn in the guide by the Baedeker stars.

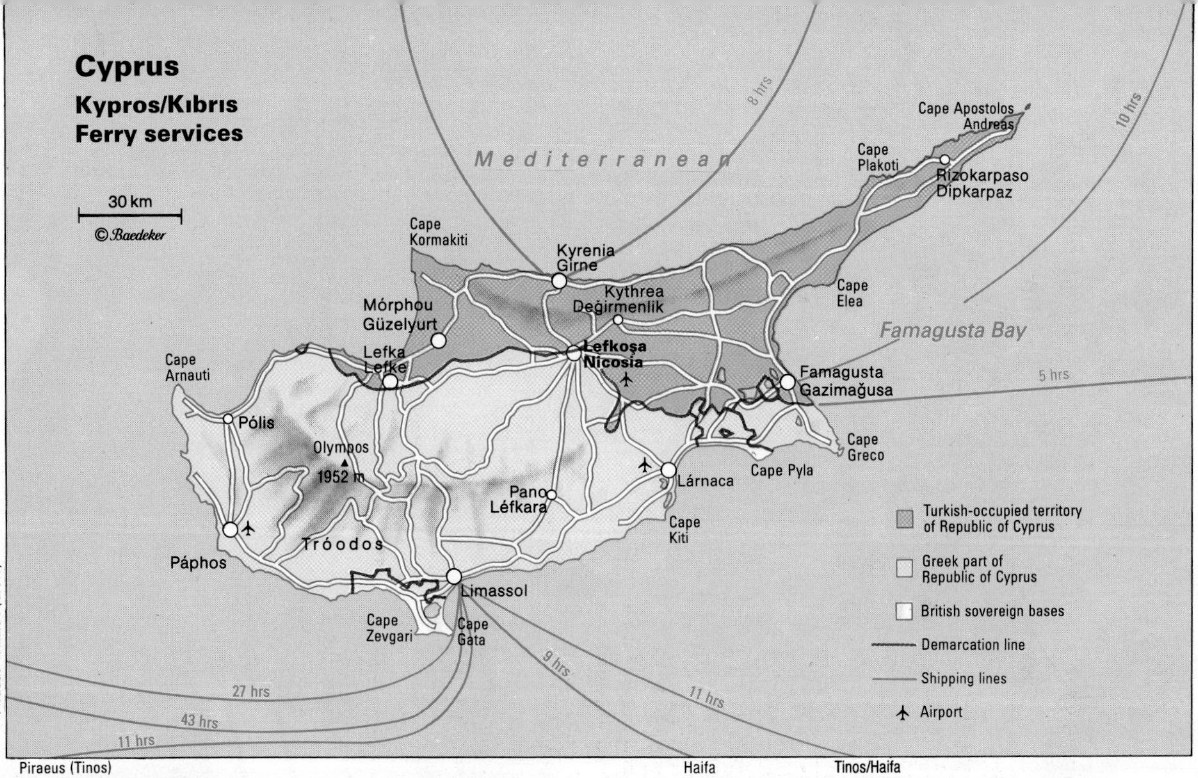
Cyprus
Kypros/Kıbrıs
Ferry services
30 km
© Baedeker
Mediterranean
Famagusta Bay
Cape Apostolos Andreas
Cape Plakoti
Rizokarpaso
Dipkarpaz
Cape Kormakiti
Kyrenia
Girne
Kythrea
Değirmenlik
Cape Elea
Mórphou
Güzelyurt
Lefka
Lefke
Lefkoşa
Nicosia
Famagusta
Gazimağusa
Cape Arnauti
Pólis
Olympos
1952 m
Cape Greco
Cape Pyla
Lárnaca
Pano
Léfkara
Cape Kiti
Páphos
Tróodos
Limassol
Cape Zevgari
Cape Gata
8 hrs
10 hrs
5 hrs
9 hrs
11 hrs
27 hrs
43 hrs
11 hrs
Turkish-occupied territory of Republic of Cyprus
Greek part of Republic of Cyprus
British sovereign bases
Demarcation line
Shipping lines
Airport
Piraeus (Tinos)
Haifa
Tinos/Haifa
Haifa (Israel)
Piraeus Iraklion (Crete)

Introduction

Facts and Figures

Only the introductory section of this guide deals with the island as a whole. The greater part of the gazetteer section (Sights from A to Z) is concerned with the Greek Cypriot Republic of Cyprus, which is internationally recognised as the legitimate authority over the whole island. The Turkish Republic of Northern Cyprus, unilaterally proclaimed in 1983 and recognised only by Turkey, is treated separately.

On February 16th 1995 it was agreed that the Cypriot capital Nicosia should officially be named Lefkosia. Both names are used in this guide.

General

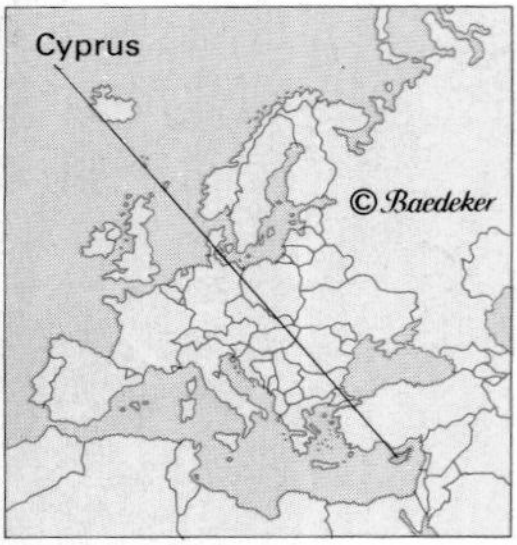

Cyprus, the third largest Mediterranean island, lies between latitude 34°33′ and 35°40′ N and between longitude 32°17′ and 34°36′ E.

Situated in the eastern Mediterranean at the meeting of the continents of Europe, Asia and Africa, Cyprus lies 65 km off the coast of Turkey, 95 km from Syria, 173 km from Lebanon and 380 km from Egypt. The Greek island of Crete lies 553 km west of Cyprus.

Area
With a total area of 9251 sq km, Cyprus is the third largest island in the Mediterranean, after Sicily (25,462 sq km) and Sardinia (24,090 sq km). Its greatest extent from west to east is 224 km and from north to south 96 km, and it has a total coastline of 780 km.

Foreign rule
As a result of its central position between East and West, a focal point of many different interests, Cyprus has been since prehistoric times the scene of conflict between neighbouring powers. Successive periods of foreign rule have left their mark on the culture and mentality of the Cypriots, who despite this have been able to preserve their identity. It was only in 1960, after thousands of years of foreign domination, that the island achieved independence; and only 14 years later, in 1974, Turkish troops invaded the northern part of the island, which they still occupy.

A divided island
Since 1974 some 38 per cent of the island's area has been under Turkish occupation. The Turkish Republic of Northern Cyprus, which was proclaimed in 1983 by its self-appointed president Rauf Denktash is internationally outlawed and recognised only by Turkey.

The Greek Cypriot southern part of the island occupies 62 per cent of its total area and forms the Republic of Cyprus, which in international law represents the whole island. The two parts of Cyprus are separated by a buffer zone, the Green Line, established in 1974 and controlled by United Nations forces. It begins near Lefke in the north-west, cuts through Nicosia and ends to the south of Famagusta.

Districts
The island is divided into the six districts of Nicosia, Limassol, Lárnaca, Páphos, Famagusta and Kyrenia – the last two of which have been separately administered since 1974.

Topography

Although in history and culture closely connected with Europe, Cyprus is geographically part of Asia. The two main ranges of hills, the Kyrenia (Pentadáktylos) range and the Tróodos

◄ Wall paintings in St John's Cathedral, Nicosia (south)

Coastal scenery on the Akámas peninsula ►

massif, run parallel to the Taurus in Asia Minor.

Some 60 million years ago, an arm of the sea divided the island into two parts, corresponding broadly to the Kyrenia range in the north and the Tróodos massif in the south. In the late Tertiary era earthquakes and a rise in the level of the sea bed created the Mesaória plain, which lies between the two early Tertiary ranges of hills.

Landscapes

The characteristic outline of Cyprus, with the long and narrow Karpasía peninsula reaching north-east, was seen in antiquity as resembling a deer skin. This green Mediterranean island is also remarkable for the variety of its topography, with a series of sand and shingle beaches, wide bays and rugged cliffs round the coasts, steep volcanic hills, forest-covered up to the highest peaks, upland regions with gently rounded hills and deep valleys, and fertile plains.

Five different landscape zones can be distinguished in Cyprus: the coastal regions, the ranges of hills (Kyrenia and Tróodos) which run parallel to them, the foothills of the Tróodos and the large central plain, the Mesaória, which lies between the two ranges of hills.

Coastal regions

The coastal regions show great variety of scenery. On the east coast are beautiful bays, the finest sandy beaches being at Famagusta and Ayía Nápa. On the south coast are the large towns of Lárnaca and Limassol and many tourist centres developed since 1974 which have reduced the natural charm of this coastal region. The north and west coasts have a varied pattern of long, lonely sandy beaches alternating with sheer cliffs and beautiful bays with stony beaches.

Kyrenia range

The Kyrenia range in the north of the island – a rugged and sparsely wooded chain of hills 128 km long – consists of limestones, marbles, phyllites and serpentines. The highest point, which extends eastward to the narrow Karpasía peninsula, is Kyparissóvouno (1024 m). The hills fall steeply to the north coast.

The Kyrenia hills are also known as Pentadáktylos (five-fingered) after the lower Pentadáktylos range (730 m), whose five peaks rise up like the fingers of a hand.

Tróodos massif

The volcanic Tróodos massif in south-western Cyprus, extending from west to east for a distance of 80 km and rising to 1951 m in Mount Ólympos (also known

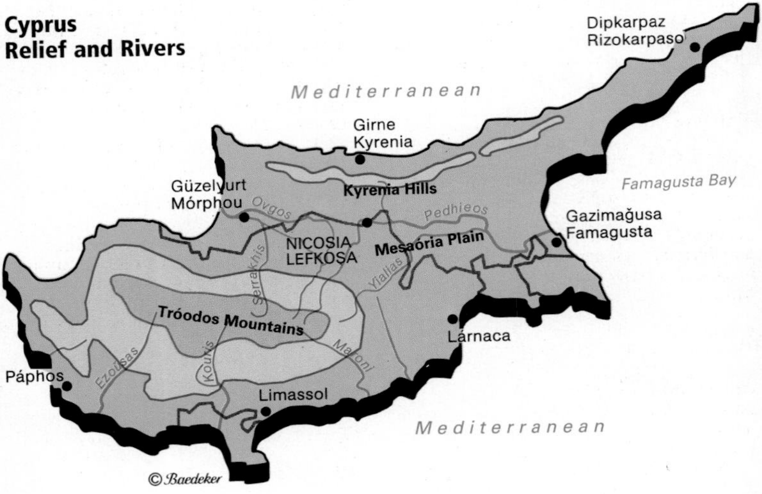

The rugged and sparsely wooded Kyrenia range

as Khionístra, snow-capped), occupies, including its foothills, almost a third of the island's area. Unlike the Kyrenia range, it is densely wooded up to its highest peaks. With its mild and agreeable climate and its refreshing coolness it is a popular recreation area in the hot summer months and offers skiing in winter.

Mesaória plain

The Mesaória plain lying between the two ranges is an important agricultural region. It extends from Mórphou Bay in the north-west to Famagusta Bay in the east, and now lies mainly in Turkish-occupied Cyprus. The plain consists of late Tertiary sediments and fertile alluvial soils and is broken up by dry valleys and hills.

Towns

The largest town in Cyprus is Nicosia (pop. 203,000), the island's capital, which lies in the Mesaória plain. It is now cut in two by the boundary between the Greek and Turkish parts of the island.

Second to Nicosia is Limassol (pop. 150,000), on the south coast, the largest port and tourist centre. To the east of Limassol, in a wide bay, is Lárnaca (pop. 54,000), which has increased in importance since 1974 following the construction of a new airport. Páphos (pop. 23,000), on the west coast, offers the attraction of its extensive ancient remains and in recent years has also developed into a popular seaside resort.

At the eastern end of the island is the town of Famagusta (Turkish Gazimağusa; pop. 20,000). Until 1974 it was Cyprus's largest port and principal tourist centre, but since the division of the island has declined in importance. On the Turkish-occupied north coast is the picturesque small port of Kyrenia (Turkish Girne; pop. 7000), one of the most charming towns on the island.

Climate

Cyprus has a typical Mediterranean climate, with hot dry summers and mild wet winters. This seasonal

View from Stavrovoúni over the Tróodos foothills to the coast

variation results from the fact that in summer the subtropical zone of high pressure and aridity moves northward and influences weather conditions in the Mediterranean, while in winter the low-pressure zone of the temperate latitudes moves south over the Mediterranean.

Climatic regions

The climate in Cyprus is fairly uniform, with local variations resulting from:

- situation (on the coast or inland). On the coast, due to the moderating influence of the sea, temperature variations over the day and over the year are less than in the interior of the island, with its more continental climate. On hot summer days winds blowing off the sea bring a degree of coolness lacking in the interior.
- the alignment of the hills in relation to the prevailing winds. On the windward side of a range the air masses rise and cool down, leading to the formation of clouds and in extreme cases to rain, while on the leeward side the clouds break up and there is less rain.
- altitude. With increasing height temperatures fall by between 0.5°C and almost 1°C per 100 m depending on season and humidity. Rainfall increases with height.

Climatic charts

The climatic characteristics of different parts of Cyprus are shown in the climatic charts opposite based on data from six typical weather stations: Kyrenia for the north coast; Nicosia for the Mesaória plain in the interior of the island; Famagusta for the east coast; Limassol for the south coast; Páphos for the west coast; and Trikoukkia (1341 m) for the Tróodos massif.

In the climatic charts the blue columns show annual rainfall in millimetres month by month. Temperatures are shown in the orange band, the upper edge of which shows average maximum day temperatures and the lower edge average minimum night temperatures.

On the basis of these charts it is possible to estimate rainfall and temperatures for areas between the selected weather stations.

Six typical weather stations in Cyprus

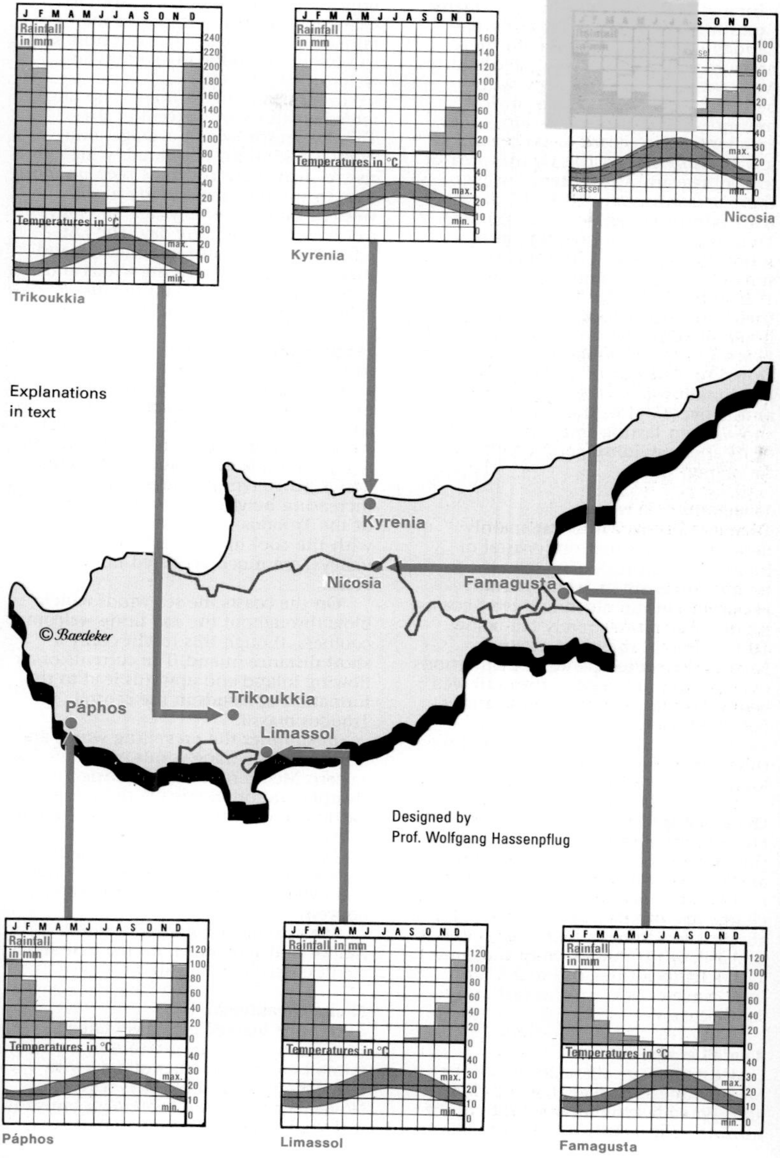

Rainfall in winter
The highest levels of rainfall are in winter (December and January), many times higher than in central Europe. Periods influenced by areas of high pressure coming from the mainland of Asia, without rain, alternate with periods influenced by areas of low pressure, accompanied by rain. Frequently the centre of such areas of low pressure lies in the Cyprus area or in the Aegean. Altogether, however, there are only some 10 to 12 days with rain in December and January. The other days are predominantly sunny. Nicosia has 170 hours of sunshine in each month, Famagusta 195 and 180. In the Tróodos massif there is heavier cloud cover, with 120 hours of sunshine in each month and 225 mm of precipitation in January. Down to a height of 1000 m the precipitation is in the form of snow, and above 1500 m there are 2–3 m of snow, often lasting until the end of April and providing good conditions for skiing.

Temperatures in winter
Temperatures in winter are mainly determined by situation (coastal or inland) and altitude. The lowest temperatures are in January and February. On the north and west coasts night temperatures rarely fall below 10°C, while in the plain around Nicosia, where temperature fluctuations over the day are greater, they fall well below that level. Water temperatures fall to 18–19°C in December and 16–17°C in January to April, reaching their lowest level in February and March.

Climate in spring
From February monthly rainfall and the number of days with rain decline and temperatures increase. Levels of rainfall are shown in the climatic charts; the number of days with rain is about 9 in February, 5 in March and 3 in April, with none in May and June. Water temperatures rise to 22°C by June, and to 23°C on the east and south coasts.

Rainfall in summer
Dry summers are characteristic of the Mediterranean climate. Between May and September the number of hours of sunshine per month is well over 300. In July Nicosia has some 398 hours of sunshine, and the Tróodos massif have only seven hours less. From April to October evaporation is greater than the rainfall. The drought increases from May to September, and many springs and watercourses dry up.

In July and August there is no rain anywhere in Cyprus except in the Tróodos massif, which averages one rainy day (5 mm). The clouds which give rise to such showers can be seen on most days in summer, particularly in the western hills. In some years June may not have a single rainy day. The rain returns, however, in September. Inland there may be dust-carrying winds and sudden showers which fill the dry valleys.

Temperatures in summer
In July and August, and on the south and east coasts also in September, maximum day temperatures are consistently above 30°C. The highest summer temperatures are in the inland regions (at Nicosia in July and August 36°C). Since temperatures fall with increasing height, the southern slopes of the Tróodos massif in particular, with the cool upper reaches of the valleys, are much favoured holiday areas.

On the coasts the sea winds which blow throughout the day bring welcome coolness, though this reaches only a short distance inland. The currents of air flowing inland and upwards lead to the formation of clouds in the central Tróodos massif.

In summer the prevailing winds are northerly (the trade winds of the eastern Mediterranean), blowing steadily and often gustily, though in particular areas they may be diverted by hills.

More frequent in spring and autumn are sirocco winds from the south – hot and, when saturated with water vapour, oppressively sultry.

Water temperatures are about 26°C in August and September, on the east and south coasts 27°C in August.

Climate in autumn
Autumn is marked by slowly falling temperatures and an increase in monthly rainfall and the number of days with rain. October has three days with rain, November five. From September onwards it is warmer at night on the coast,

Aloes

Mesembryanthemum

particularly on the west and north coasts, than in the interior – a result of the gradual fall in water temperatures (from 26°C in September to 21°C in November).

Nature

Flora

Cyprus's mild and equable Mediterranean climate allows a rich variety of flora, with some 1900 different species of plants, including 100 endemic species found only on the island.

Spring
The flora of Cyprus is at its finest in March and April, when the island is covered by a multicoloured sea of blossom. In addition to various species of orchids there are tulips, gladioli, irises, wild poppies, great fields of strongly perfumed rape, blossoming fruit trees and various decorative trees.

Summer
Since the water courses soon dry up after the snow melt and the brief rainy season in spring, Cyprus is rather barren and arid in summer; the plains of the interior and the coastal regions are burned up by the sun, and the golden grain gives way to various shades of brown. Only the blossoms of the oleanders add small touches of colour. In the hills, however, the coniferous and deciduous trees remain green.

Autumn
With the first autumn rains Cyprus is transformed once again into a green and blooming island, with crocuses, narcissi, anemones, hyacinths and lilies.

Forests
The felling of the island's great expanses of forest began in ancient times, when the sea powers of the eastern Mediterranean used the timber for the construction of their fleets. In addition to the uncontrolled felling which continued down the centuries

Tróodos massif – black pines …

and Star of Bethlehem (May/June)

further losses have resulted from grazing by goats, forest fires and Turkish incendiary bombs in 1974, reducing the forest cover of this once green Mediterranean island to barely 20 per cent. Most of the forests are state-owned, mainly on the slopes of the Tróodos massif, where an intensive programme of re/afforestation has been under way since 1982. Measures to limit the danger of forest fires include the installation of forest telephones for emergency calls and the formation of special firefighting forces. Forest reserves and national parks such as the one at Kyrenia (Girne) also contribute to the protection of the island's forests.

Species of trees
Almost 90 per cent of Cyprus's forests consist of Aleppo pines, which grow at lower altitudes. Above 1200 m the black pine, sometimes bizarrely shaped, is common. The native forest of the Tróodos massif also includes cypresses, oaks and cedars, and in the foothills there are eucalyptus and olive trees.

Because of the island's mild climate apples, cherries, pears, almonds and walnuts can be grown up to a height of 1200 m. The annual show of cherry blossom in the little town of Pedhoulás, to the north of Plátres, has given rise to a regular festival.

Vegetation in the plains
In the plains, in addition to the trees growing in the foothills of the main ranges, there are carob trees, laurels, vines, citrus fruits and bananas. Grain and vegetables are grown in the Mesaória plain and in the coastal regions. Large areas of the island are covered with dark green *macchia*, a scrub of spiny bushes and shrubs.

Fauna

Moufflon
The fauna of Cyprus is less varied than its flora. Its best known animal, now a protected species, is the moufflon (Greek *agrinon*), a shy mountain sheep distinguished by the powerful curved

Moufflon (wild sheep) – now a protected species

horns of the male. These agile creatures, good climbers, live in small numbers in the Tróodos massif, but are rarely to be seen in the wild. The island's stock of moufflon, which numbered many thousands in ancient times, was decimated in the Middle Ages, when Cyprus was held by the French Lusignan dynasty, and more recently by British sportsmen. Nowadays visitors are likely to see them in the moufflon enclosure at the Stavrós tis Psókas forestry station (north-west of Cedar Valley), at Platanía (near Kakopetriá) and in Limassol's small zoo.

Other animals

Accounts by medieval travellers refer to leopards, deer and wild asses, but these have long since been exterminated. Domestic animals such as donkeys, sheep, goats and cats, however, are common all over Cyprus.

In the forests of Cyprus there are numerous small animals including hares, rabbits, foxes, squirrels and weasels. Reptiles include lizards, chameleons, turtles and two feared poisonous snakes, the *koúfi* (green, with black spots) and the adder. When walking in the country, therefore, it is advisable to have stout footwear in case you happen to tread on a snake.

Birds

Cyprus's 300 species of birds include partridges, Cetti's warblers, wild pigeons and great tits. Birds of prey including falcons, vultures and imperial eagles are found in the hills. In marshy regions there are herons and snipe.

Cyprus is also a stop for large numbers of migrant birds on their journeys between continents. Up to a thousand flamingos winter on the salt lakes of Lárnaca and Akrotíri. Coming from the Caspian Sea, they spend the winter months until March in the island's mild climate.

Population

Of Cyprus's population of about 840,000, 77 per cent are Greek and

22 per cent Turkish; the remaining 1 per cent is made up of Armenian, Maronite, Latin and British minorities. The southern part of the island has a population of 640,000 (80 inhabitants per sq kilometre), the Turkish-occupied northern part 200,000 after a massive wave of immigration by Anatolian settlers. These figures do not include 17,000 British troops stationed in the military bases at Akrotíri and Dhekélia, 1200 United Nations soldiers, and a few thousand refugees from Lebanon in the south.

Population movements since 1974
The movement of refugees and the separation of the Greek and Turkish communities in 1974 led to over-population in the southern part of the island and under-population in the northern part – later made good by the immigration of an estimated 70,000 Turks from mainland Turkey (Anatolia). Some 1600 Greeks who were unable to get out of the Turkish-occupied areas are still unaccounted for.

Since the 1974 invasion the Turkish Cypriot population has steadily fallen, some 70,000 people having left the country because of the desperate economic situation.

In the Greek southern part of the island the influx of refugees made it necessary to establish refugee camps and organise other accommodation hastily, and refugees from the occupied areas still enjoy special government assistance, including in some cases rent-free accommodation. Considerable numbers of Cypriots emigrated to the United States, Canada and Australia – mainly Turkish Cypriots who did not like the new political situation.

The large numbers of unemployed in the Greek part of the island in the first few years after partition were soon absorbed by the considerable investment in building projects and the gradually recovering tourist trade. Turkish refugees in the north found plenty of accommodation available in houses abandoned by Greeks who had fled to the south.

Coexistence
In spite of the separation of the two communities since 1974 there are still Greeks and Turks who have stayed in their old homes. Thus on the Karpasía peninsula in North Cyprus there are still some 550 Greeks (with another 220 on Kyrenia), mainly old, who are able with the agreement of the Turkish administration to visit their relatives in the southern part of the island. In the Greek part of the island, in the little frontier village of Pýla near Lárnaca, some 300 Turks live in peace with their Greek neighbours. The United Nations peace keeping forces look after the interests of these minorities.

Language
The two official languages of Cyprus are Greek and Turkish; and since the British colonial period English has been the language of culture and commerce in both parts of the island, spoken fluently by most of the Greek and many of the Turkish Cypriots.

Urbanisation
Almost half the population live in the towns of Nicosia, Limassol, Lárnaca, Páphos, Famagusta and Kyrenia. The largest concentrations of population are in the Mesaória plain and in and around Limassol. The economic prosperity of the towns has led to an increasing flight from the land. This has not, however, endangered the established Cypriot family traditions. In spite of increasing urbanisation and the beginnings of female emancipation the male head of the family is still, among both Greeks and Turks, the focal point of the Cypriot sense of community.

Religion

Orthodox Church

Beginnings of Christianity
The religious allegiance of the Cypriot population matches their ethnic composition, with some 73 per cent belonging to the Greek Orthodox faith. Cyprus can claim to be one of the world's oldest Christian countries, for the apostles Paul and Barnabas preached Christianity here as early as the year 46. It was only at the end of the 4th c., however, under Byzantine rule, that Christianity became firmly established on the island. The old pagan temples, destroyed in violent earthquakes, were replaced in the course of the century by Christian basilicas (for example at Sálamis and Páphos).

In the early years of Christianity the Orthodox Church consisted of the five patriarchates of Rome, Jerusalem, Constantinople, Alexandria and Antioch. Cyprus belonged to the patriarchate of Antioch, but sought from an early stage to become independent.

Autocephaly of the Cypriot Church

In 477 Anthemios, archbishop of Cyprus, saw in a vision the tomb of the apostle Barnabas, and duly discovered a tomb containing the saint's remains near Sálamis. The apostle was found holding in his hand a manuscript of the Gospel of St Matthew. This enabled the Cypriot Church to prove that it was an apostolic foundation, and a synod held in 478 recognised the autocephaly (i.e. the independence, with the power to appoint its own head) of the Cypriot Church. This first autocephalous Church was followed by others – in the 7th c. the Georgian Church, in the 10th c. the Bulgarian Church, and thereafter the Russian, Serbian and Romanian Churches. The Greek Church became independent only in 1850.

The grant of autocephaly gave the archbishop of Cyprus the right to wear purple robes on feast days, to sign documents in red ink and to carry a sceptre.

Orthodox priest

Development

The independent Cypriot Church was little affected by the Great Schism of 1054, the split between the Western and Eastern Churches.

In the Middle Ages Cyprus was ruled by a French noble family, the Lusignans, who declared the Roman Catholic faith as the state religion, oppressed Orthodox believers and confiscated church property.

The Orthodox church recovered its ancient rights only under Ottoman rule. The archbishop of Cyprus then became the official representative of the Cypriot people and gained political influence.

Between 1960 and 1977 Cyprus was the only state apart from the Vatican to be ruled by a prince of the church, Archbishop Makarios III.

Priests

In the Orthodox church the ordinary priests may be married provided that they have taken a wife before being ordained; they are, however, excluded from higher office in the church. Bishops, like monks, are celibate.

Islam

Some 22 per cent of the population of Cyprus – living predominantly in the Turkish-occupied part of the island – are Muslims. The first Muslims came to the island when it was conquered by the Turkish Pasha Lala Mustafa in 1571.

The Muslims of Cyprus are Sunnis, who, unlike the Shiites, recognise the first four caliphs and accept the authority, in addition to the Koran, of the Sunnah, a collection of the Prophet Mohammed's sayings compiled in the 9th c.

Muslim duties

The five pillars of Islam laid down by Mohammed are the five duties of the Muslim: to believe in Allah as the one God and Mohammed as his Prophet, to pray five times daily, to give alms, to fast for the mouth of Ramadan and to make the pilgrimage to Mecca if his health and his means permit.

The main source of the Muslim faith is the Koran, which consists of 115 suras

IC·XC

(chapters). The consumption of pork, alcohol and drugs is prohibited to Muslims, as is gambling. The head of the Cypriot Muslim community is the mufti, a man learned in Islamic law.

The mosque
The Muslim place of worship is the mosque, from the minaret of which the muezzin issues the call to prayer five times daily. Before entering the mosque believers must take off their shoes and perform a ritual purification. In Muslim belief water is Allah's highest gift to man, and accordingly in front of every mosque there is an ablutions fountain at which worshippers wash their face, hands, forearms and feet.

Inside the mosque is a *mihrab* (prayer niche) marking the direction of Mecca, and close to it is the *minbar*, the pulpit from which the imam leads the prayers.

Other denominations

Armenian Church
Armenian Christians from Eastern Anatolia and Cilicia came to Cyprus in successive waves of refugees from the 6th c. There are now some 5000 Armenians on the island.

The head of the Armenian Church, which looks back to St Gregory the Enlightener as the founder of Christianity in Armenia, is the *katholikos*, whose seat is in the Armenian town of Etchmiadzin. The Armenians differ from the Roman Catholic and Orthodox Churches in ascribing a divine, but not a human, nature to Christ. The head of the Armenian community in Cyprus (now exclusively in the southern part of the island), which has its own schools and other organisations, is a bishop with his seat in Nicosia.

Maronite Church
There are some 4000 Greek-speaking Maronites – a sect which originally came from Lebanon – on Cyprus, including small numbers in the Turkish-occupied north of the island. The Maronites maintain a close relationship with the Roman Catholic Church and recognise the Pope as supreme head of the Church. The founder of the Maronite community was St Maro, who founded a monastery on the river Orontes in the 5th c. The first Maronites came to Cyprus in the 9th c., and in the Middle Ages there were 80,000 of them on the island. The head of the Maronite community in Cyprus is a bishop, whose church is in the Greek part of Nicosia, near the partition.

Others
There are also small Roman Catholic and Anglican minorities with their own churches.

Society

The independent Republic of Cyprus was established in 1960. The Turkish intervention of 1974 led to the division of the island into the (Greek) Republic of Cyprus and the Turkish Republic of Northern Cyprus, which is not recognised internationally and is still occupied by Turkish military forces. The Republic of Cyprus is recognised as the sole legitimate representative of the whole of Cyprus, although since 1974 it has, *de facto*, administered only the Greek-speaking southern part of the island.

Society – South Cyprus

The Republic of Cyprus is a presidential democracy based on the constitution of 1960. It is a non-aligned state, a member of the United Nations and of the Council of Europe. It is also associated with the (former British) Commonwealth and the European Union.

◄ The Mother of God with Christ: an icon from Troodhítissa monastery

Cyprus

Flag
The national flag of Cyprus, with a gold outline of the island on a white background, symbolises its non-aligned status. The two crossed olive branches below the island symbolise the striving for peace of the Cypriots, who have had from time immemorial to defend themselves against the expansionism of other peoples.

Coat of arms
The coat of arms adopted in 1960 shows a white dove carrying a sprig of olive surrounded by an olive branch, symbolising the desire for the peaceful coexistence of Cypriot Turks and Greeks.

National anthem
As its national anthem Cyprus adopted the Greek national anthem. The music was composed in 1828 by Nikolaos Mantzaros (1795–1872). The words (beginning 'Se gnorízo apó tin kópsi tou spathioú', I recognise you by the cut of your sword) come from the *Hymn to Freedom* by Dionysos Solomos (1798–1857), the first major Greek lyric poet of modern times.

Government
The president of the Republic of Cyprus (at present the conservative Glafkos Klerides, who was re-elected in 1998) is directly elected by the population for a five-year term. He appoints and presides over the cabinet, which consists of 11 ministers. The office of vice-president is at present vacant, since under the 1960 constitution it must be held by a representative of the Turkish population.

Parliament
Since 1974 only 56 of the 80 seats in the house of representatives have been occupied, since under the constitution 24 of them are reserved for representatives of the Turkish community. Representatives are elected every five years.
At present the following parties are represented in the house of representatives:
DISY, the Democratic Assembly, a conservative party;
DIKO, the Democratic Party, a party of the centre;
AKEL, the Communist Progressive Party; and
EDEK, the Democratic Union, a liberal socialist party.

Armed forces
All male citizens are liable for military service, which lasts 26 months. The Greek Cypriot National Guard has a strength of 13,000, and in addition there are 3000 armed police officers.

Since 1964 a United Nations peace keeping force formed from troops of five countries has been stationed on Cyprus. Originally numbering more than 6000, it has now been reduced to about 1200 men. The force (UNFICYP, United Nations Force in Cyprus), the members of which serve for six months at a time, controls the demarcation line between the two parts of the island (representing about 3 per cent of the area of the country). Since the cost of stationing the peace keeping forces on Cyprus is borne not by the United Nations but mainly by the countries concerned (now only Britain and Austria), the gradual withdrawal of the blue-helmeted troops has begun.

There are also two British sovereign bases at Akrotíri and Dhekélia.

Social and health services

Social insurance

The social insurance system covers almost all employed persons and provides unemployment, health, pregnancy and accident insurance, old age and widows' pensions and disability insurance. It is financed mainly by contributions from employers and employed persons amounting to 15.5 per cent of gross wages – 6 per cent each from employers and employed persons and 3.5 per cent from the state. The social welfare service is concerned with the care of children, young people and families.

Hospitals

The health services have been considerably developed since 1986. In addition to municipal hospitals (general hospitals) in all the larger towns there are health centres in rural areas (all providing treatment free of charge) as well as private institutions, mostly specialist clinics, in which there are charges for treatment. The Mining Institute runs its own hospitals. Since there is no medical school in Cyprus all the island's doctors have been trained in other countries.

Education

Schools

There is an obligatory nine-year period of schooling. Six years in primary school (*dimotikon skholion*) are followed by three years of general education in a secondary school (*gymnasion*), after which pupils can go on to a lyceum (*lykion*) or vocational school. The lyceum provides specialist training, with both compulsory and optional subjects. After successful completion of a course at a vocational school, which 80 per cent of all children take, pupils are entitled to go on to higher education.

In the last two years of primary school English is a compulsory subject. The school system is controlled by the ministry of education. Schoolbooks and curricula come from Greece, but the system shows marked British influence.

Vocational schools

There are the following specialised training establishments: hotel school, child care school, agricultural college, forestry college.

Cyprus International University

The creation of a Pan-Cypriot university which had been under discussion for many years was long frustrated by the division of the island, but finally a university on the British model, open equally to Greeks and Turks, was founded at the end of 1992 in Nicosia. Cyprus International University began teaching in 1997 with the aim of providing students with the skills and knowledge necessary for a career in a modern and technically advanced society. It therefore has courses in communication and marketing, economics and international relations, and computer and information technology among others. Previously students had to go to universities in other countries. The most popular foreign universities are in Greece, Britain and Germany.

Cyprus also has two teacher training colleges and a college of technology.

Media

Newspapers and periodicals

The 1960 constitution guarantees the freedom of the press, subject to possible restrictions in exceptional cases. Cyprus has 11 daily newspapers, 10 in Greek and one in English, the *Cyprus Mail*. The Greek dailies with the largest circulations are *Philephtero*, *Apogevmatini* and *Haravgi*.

There are also 18 weeklies, including the English-language *Cyprus Weekly*, and 19 magazines. *Cyprus Time Out*, a tourist and shopping guide, is published monthly.

Radio and television
The Cyprus Broadcasting Corporation (CyBC), founded in 1952, transmits radio programmes in Greek, Turkish and English and also has two Greek and Turkish television channels. The directors of the CyBC are appointed by the government. British forces stationed in Cyprus have their own broadcasting system, the British Forces Broadcasting Service (BFBS), which is on the air 24 hours a day.

Society – North Cyprus

State

A year after the Turkish invasion of 1974 Rauf Denktash (Denktas), spokesman for the Turkish Cypriot community, declared the Turkish-occupied territories to be the Turkish Federal State of Cyprus. On November 15th 1983 he proclaimed the Turkish Republic of Northern Cyprus (Kuzey Kíbrís Türk Cumhuriyeti, KKTC), and in 1985 amended the constitution introduced only 10 years before. For postal purposes North Cyprus is part of the Turkish town of Mersin.

Flag
The Turkish Cypriot flag, following the model of the Turkish flag, has a red

crescent and star between two red bands on a white background.

Coat of arms
Like the Greek Cypriot arms, the Turkish Cypriot coat of arms has a white dove holding a sprig of olive in its beak, encircled by olive branches, with the addition of a red crescent and star and the date 1983 (the year of foundation of the Turkish Republic of Northern Cyprus).

National anthem
The Turkish Republic of Northern Cyprus adopted the Turkish national anthem, *Istiklal Marší* (Independence March). The tune was composed by Ali Rifat àağatay, the words by Lof Ersoy. The anthem begins 'Korkma sönmez bu safak' (Fear not, be not afraid).

Government
The self-appointed and internationally unrecognised president of the Turkish-occupied part of the island since 1976 has been Rauf Denktash, who has been re-elected every five years (most recently in 1995) with an overwhelming majority. He has power to call a general election, to impose martial law and to declare a state of emergency. The president appoints the prime minister (at present Dervis Eroglu), and the president and prime minister together appoint the 10 members of the Cabinet.

Parliament
The parliament of North Cyprus, which met for the first time in 1985, is elected for a five-year term. The following four parties are at present represented in it:
UBP, the Party of National Unity (conservative), founded by Rauf Denktash in 1975
CTP, the Turkish Republican Party, the main opposition party (left' wing)
TKP, the Communal Liberation Party (centre left)
YDP, the Party of Rebirth (liberal).

Trade union
The Kíbrís Türk Išái Sendikalarí Federasyonu, a large trade union founded in 1954, has 15,000 members. 15 other trade unions are affiliated to it.

Armed forces
Turkish Cypriots are subject to a two-year period of military service. In addition there are some 30,000 Turkish troops from mainland Turkey stationed in the northern part of the island. As in the Greek part of the island, there are United Nations peace keeping forces monitoring the situation.

Social and health services

All employed persons are covered by

View over the Green Line into north Nicosia

social security, most of the insurance contributions being paid by employers. In the larger towns there are social service offices and kindergartens.

Health services fall far short of those in the Greek part of the island. There are two large government hospitals, two district hospitals and a psychiatric clinic, as well as national health centres and a number of private establishments. The doctors have all been trained outside Cyprus, mostly at British and Turkish universities.

Education

Schools

There is an obligatory nine-year period of schooling. In the primary school (six years) and secondary school (three years) education is free. Thereafter pupils can go on to three years of further education in a lyceum, technical school or vocational school (nursing, midwifery, agriculture, hotel management).

Higher education

In addition to a teacher training college and a college of technology, North Cyprus has several private universities which are very popular with students from mainland Turkey, with some 8000 registered. These include the Eastern Mediterranean University in Famagusta, founded in 1986, with faculties of mechanical and electrical engineering, and the University College of North Cyprus (UCNC) in Kyrenia, an expensive private institution teaching administration and languages. There is also a branch of the University of Anatolia, with departments of administration and economics. Most students, however, go to universities outside Cyprus, mainly in Turkey, Britain and the United States.

Economy

Independence to partition

When Cyprus became independent in 1960 it was a mainly agricultural country, with just under 50 per cent of the population working on the land. The economy, dependent on foreign trade, was backward, and the widespread unemployment led to mass emigration. In order to make good the country's major structural deficiencies – limited mineral and other natural resources, flight of capital – the government sought to promote entrepreneurial initiatives in a series of five-year plans. As a result the growth rate of the economy rose to 7 per cent between 1960 and 1973 (in 1995 4.2 per cent). Agricultural production was doubled, there was a threefold increase in industrial production and tourism became the largest earner of foreign currency (in 1995 C£813 million). Over half of the country's exports go to the countries of the European Union (mainly agricultural produce).

The Turkish invasion and its consequences
The Turkish invasion of northern Cyprus (38 per cent of the island's area) in 1974 brought a previously flourishing economy to a standstill. The Turks now occupied the best agricultural areas – much of the Mesaória plain, the main wheat-, barley- and potato-growing area, which before partition produced almost 80 per cent of the island's grain, and Mórphou Bay, still the principal area for the growing of citrus fruits and other fruit and vegetables.

Some 70 per cent of the island's total economic potential was in the occupied territory: the principal tourist centres, Famagusta and Kyrenia, and most of the industrial installations. Famagusta, Cyprus's largest port, was now closed to the Greek Cypriots. In 1994 the European Union countries decided that goods from North Cyprus could only be imported if they had export documents from the Republic of Cyprus. This amounts to a virtual economic embargo.

Economy – South Cyprus

The economic miracle
The Republic of Cyprus made a rapid economic recovery after the Turkish invasion of 1974: so much so that it has been termed an economic miracle. In the early years after partition the unemployment rate rose to 35 per cent as a result of the huge influx of refugees, and war damage was estimated at US$1.5 billion. By 1980, however, the economy had stabilised; by 1996 inflation had been brought down to 3 per cent and the unemployment rate was 3.2 per cent. Income per capita is US$9640 in the south as opposed to US$3000 in the occupied north. The Republic of Cyprus now enjoys a relatively high level of prosperity.

Financial support from the West made a major contribution to this recovery, and an additional boost was given to the economy when the war in Lebanon brought wealthy Lebanese businessmen and firms to Cyprus. Agricultural production was intensified; additional land was brought into cultivation and new factories processing agricultural produce were established. Foreign firms were attracted by tax concessions, and the establishment of new industries was promoted by government assistance. A new airport was built at Lárnaca and the port of Limassol was enlarged and developed to make up for the loss of Famagusta to the Turks.

Agriculture

Just under 20 per cent of the Greek Cypriot population work in agriculture, forestry and fisheries, compared with 25 per cent in Greece. New agricultural centres have been created and the cultivation of agricultural produce has been intensified in the coastal plains between Lárnaca and Pólis. The main crops in these areas are groundnuts, bananas, almonds, olives, potatoes (with two harvests a year), vegetables, carob beans, tobacco and wine. The Tróodos area produces abundant crops of apples, pears, cherries and almonds. Other crops such as sugar cane (which has been grown in Cyprus since the Middle Ages), cotton and silk are now of only subordinate importance.

The most important crops are wine, vegetables, potatoes and olives. South Cyprus now has over 90 per cent of the island's wine-growing areas, 80 per cent of the area devoted to vegetables and 74 per cent of the area producing olives and potatoes.

The principal exports are fruit, potatoes, vegetables, wine and tobacco. The main customers are the EU countries, the former Soviet Union and the Arab countries.

Livestock farming
The most important types of livestock are sheep and goats. There are some 900,000 fatty-tailed sheep in Cyprus, reared both for their meat and their wool. There are now practically no cattle as a result of the increasing conversion of pasture to arable land. Poultry farming is also important, and birds and eggs are exported.

Forestry
In antiquity Cyprus was one of the most densely wooded countries in the Mediterranean area, but over the centuries the island's forests have been decimated

by the felling of timber for the construction of ships and houses, mining, forest fires and over grazing. Only about a fifth of the island's area is now covered by forests. The most important species are pines and cypresses. Until a few years ago some 80,000 cu m of timber were felled annually, including 71,000 cu m of softwood. Most of it was for timber, only a third being used as firewood (which is now increasingly being imported in order to preserve the country's timber resources).

Fisheries
The fisheries of Cyprus are underdeveloped, since unfavourable environmental conditions and the agencies of man have hindered the growth of fish stocks. Efforts are being made to promote freshwater fisheries by the development of trout and carp farms.

Minerals, water and energy

Cyprus's mineral resources are now largely exhausted. The rich deposits of copper which were worked in antiquity are now recalled only by the island's name (*kypros*, copper). In the early years of the 20th c. the British authorities tried to revive the copper mining industry, but with little success; the last copper mine closed down in 1980 after many years of uneconomic working.

Until recently asbestos was mined by opencast methods at Amíandos, north-east of the hill town of Tróodos. Small quantities of chromium are still worked near Mount Ólympos. At Pólis, in north-western Cyprus, there is also some small-scale mining of sulphur, iron pyrites and iron ore. The various minerals are almost exclusively exported.

Water supply
The supply of water has long been one of the central problems of Cypriot agriculture. The difficulty is not a shortage of water but the uneven distribution of rain over the year. The loss of large areas of irrigated land in the Mesaória plain after the Turkish invasion further aggravated the situation. In 1997 the first desalination plant came into operation.

Irrigation projects
The construction of reservoirs to store rainwater and snow melt in spring had

Orange tree

Lemons

Windmills at Ayía Nápa

begun before 1974, and the irrigation projects which they made possible have increased the yield of important agricultural products. The Páphos irrigation scheme, completed in 1983, provides irrigation for 5000 ha of land in the south-western coastal region. The Vasilikos-Pendaskinos scheme, completed in 1987, with two dams at Léfkara and Kalavasós, has the capacity to irrigate 2200 ha. One of the most important projects is the Southern Supply Scheme. Under this scheme the water of three rivers will be held back by the Koúrris Dam and conveyed in a 110 km pipeline to the towns on the coast, as well as irrigating 7200 ha of arable land. The Akhna Dam will provide irrigation for the area around Ayía Nápa. There are today more than 90 reservoirs in the southern part of the island.

Energy

Since Cyprus has no rivers flowing throughout the year there is no possibility of hydroelectric power, and energy production therefore depends on the import of oil from the Middle Eastern countries. There is a large oil refinery near Lárnaca.

Cyprus has three power stations, run by the partially state-owned Electricity Authority (established 1952), which also supplies power free to Turkish-occupied North Cyprus; the Moní station at Limassol; the Dhekélia station near Lárnaca (old and new stations).

A further source of power is solar energy, though this is used only in the private sector. Many households now get their supplies of hot water from solar heating installations.

Industry

Some 28 per cent of the population work in the manufacturing industry, which since 1978 has overtaken agricultural production. In the 1960s only about 15 per cent of the population was employed in industry: the increase was largely due to government measures to promote the development of industry. Increasing numbers of foreign firms have been attracted to Cyprus by tax concessions and relatively low wage levels. Since the great majority of firms in Cyprus are small or medium-sized enterprises, government planning has made a useful contribution to the development of the country's economic life.

Industrial centres
Almost 50 per cent of manufacturing firms are in and around Nicosia, and around 25 per cent in the Limassol district. Nicosia is the centre for shoe manufacture, textiles, paper making and chemical industries, Limassol for cement manufacture and the production of soft drinks. The main industries in the Páphos district are textiles and clothing.

Industrial sectors
The leading branch of industry, employing 30 per cent of the industrial labour force, is textile production, which has been intensively promoted with the help of modern technology – though most of the raw materials have to be imported. The principal customers are Libya, Britain and Germany. In second place are the foodstuff and tobacco industries, followed by building and civil engineering, which enjoyed a great boom after 1974 when large numbers of new dwellings had to be built for refugees.

Offshore companies
Between 1975 and 1999 the Central Bank of Cyprus has issued more than 30,000 licences for offshore companies (that is, businesses which operate and earn income outside Cyprus), of which only a small proportion have been established in Cyprus. They include western European, American and Arab companies in the fields of commerce, sales, shipping, banking, insurance and culture (press agencies). Whereas in the 1980s the majority of firms came from Beirut, today there is an increasing number of Russian companies. The government took this initiative after the partition of the island in order to prevent the emigration of highly qualified employees, of which there were above-average numbers in Cyprus.

Foreign companies were attracted by the offer of tax incentives, their net profit being taxed at the rate of only 4.25 per cent. In addition foreign employees of offshore companies pay only half the normal rates of income tax and benefit from generous currency and customs regulations. Firms managed outside Cyprus pay no tax at all. The Central Bank guarantees complete confidentiality on the management and accounts of offshore firms, which has led to occasional criticisms that this facilitates the laundering of illicitly acquired money.

Financial and commercial centre
Due to its geographical situation among three continents and to its links with the Middle East, eastern Europe and the European Union, Cyprus is becoming an important financial and commercial centre. The growth of this new branch of the economy is also promoted by the high educational level of the population and the country's modern telecommunications system.

Transportation

Roads
South Cyprus has some 5000 km of surfaced roads and 6000 km of unsurfaced roads. The Turkish invasion of 1974 had a devastating effect on the island's road network. Since then important traffic arteries such as the Nicosia–Lárnaca and Nicosia–Astromerítis roads have had to be re-routed to avoid Turkish-occupied territory. Other important projects are the new Nicosia–Limassol and Nicosia–Lárnaca motorways; and a new stretch between Limassol and Páphos is under construction. There are still, however, considerable numbers of dusty unsurfaced roads, particularly in the Tróodos massif, and drivers in these areas should allow plenty of time for their journeys.

Railways
There are no railways on the island.

Air services
Since the closure of Nicosia's international airport in 1974 new international airports have been opened first at Lárnaca and then at Páphos. Over 30 airlines now fly to Cyprus from Europe, Africa, the Middle East and the Gulf region. Increasing air traffic has forced the government to agree to extend Lárnaca airport with a new terminal.

Shipping
Soon after 1974 the ports of Lárnaca and Limassol were able to make good the loss of Famagusta. Due to Cyprus's increasing

importance as an entrepôt for more than a hundred shipping lines sailing among the three continents it now takes sixth place among the world's shipping nations. The transition from traditional methods of handling freight to the container system began in the late 1970s, and the new container terminals in Limassol free port are designed to handle modern cargo vessels. Lárnaca freeport has facilities for the servicing of heavy equipment used in the oil industry of the Near and Middle East.

Ferry services: see map p. 7.

Tourism

A significant proportion of the Cypriot economy is occupied by the services sector, in which some 40 per cent of the working population are employed. From the early days of independence the government gave particular attention to the development of the tourist trade. In spite of the loss of 65 per cent of the island's hotel capacity in the Turkish-occupied towns of Famagusta and Kyrenia tourism quickly recovered and enjoyed a fresh period of prosperity only a few years after partition.

Tourist infrastructure
New hotel developments mushroomed in the coastal towns of Limassol and Lárnaca, providing employment for the thousands of refugees. Just under a quarter of the employed population now work in the tourist trade, which accounts for some 40 per cent of the country's total earnings of foreign currency. In 1998 more than 2 million holidaymakers and business travellers visited Cyprus. The high standard of service provided is illustrated by the fact that 40 per cent of visitors return.

A third of all visitors come from Britain, followed by Lebanese, Scandinavians and Germans. Some 90 per cent of visitors come for a beach holiday, the remainder for the island's cultural attractions. The most popular destination for sun lovers is Ayía Nápa, in the south-east of the island. The major tourist centres offer visitors not only large and comfortable hotels, but discos, nightclubs and *bouzoúki* bars. Cyprus's season lasts throughout the year, for the mild winter months are equally suitable for a visit.

Cyprus Tourism Organisation (CTO)
The Cyprus Tourism Organisation (CTO) runs 10 tourist offices throughout the country. The CTO also fixes the categories and tariffs of hotels. Increased attention has been given to the promotion of hotels in the higher price categories, the winter holiday trade and business tourism in order to avoid the further development of mass tourism. There are now more than 84,000 hotel beds available for visitors. The rehabilitation of old Tróodos villages has been promoted by government subsidies in order to attract visitors away from the built-up coastal areas. The establishment of new guest houses and the preservation of village structures provide jobs and thus counteract the continuing flight from the country.

Economy – North Cyprus

After the Turkish invasion in 1974 the economic situation of North Cyprus was no less catastrophic than that of the southern part of the island. Although the north had the best agricultural land, the most interesting tourist centres and many industrial plants, the departure of some 200,000 Greek Cypriots left it seriously underpopulated.

Lack of skilled workers
In addition North Cyprus lacked the skilled workers needed in the factories and tourist facilities. In the years before the Turkish invasion the Turkish Cypriot population – mostly peasants, shopkeepers and craftsmen – had lived apart from the Greek population in their own enclaves and were thus frequently excluded from the country's prosperity and economic progress. After the partition of the island some 70 per cent of its economic potential was in Turkish hands, and the villages abandoned by Greek Cypriots were reoccupied by 70,000 peasants from Anatolia, whose educational level was far below that of the Turkish Cypriots.

Economic boycott
Since Turkish-occupied North Cyprus was boycotted by nations throughout the world, international markets were closed to the new Turkish state. Its

Sheep and goats – a common sight in North Cyprus

economy has still not recovered and only survived with massive support from Turkey.

Agriculture
About 23 per cent of the population are employed in agriculture, and three-quarters of the country's area is used for farming.

The main agricultural crops are citrus fruits (Mórphou Bay), grain and potatoes (Mesaória plain) and tobacco (Karpasía peninsula); 72 per cent of the island's total citrus fruit and tobacco growing areas are in North Cyprus. Vegetables, carob nuts, fruit and walnuts are mainly grown for domestic consumption. Wine production (Pentadáktylos range and Karpasía peninsula) is of only minor importance.

Among the principal exports are citrus fruits, tobacco, vegetables and carob nuts, which mainly go to Turkey. Before the 1994 trade restriction Britain and Germany were also important customers.

Water supply
North Cyprus has limited water resources, with only a quarter of the island's springs. In recent years reservoirs have been constructed for the storage of water.

Livestock farming
Livestock farming brings in a third of the total revenue from agriculture. In addition to sheep and goats there are cattle and poultry. Products such as poultry, eggs and meat are exported.

Forestry
Some 18 per cent of the total area of North Cyprus is covered by forest. Aleppo pines and cypresses grow in the Pentadáktylos range. Reafforestation began in 1976.

Fisheries
Stocks of fish are low, and accordingly fisheries play a very minor role in the economy. Three-quarters of the fishermen still have small boats suitable only for inshore waters.

Industry
Industry provides employment for 24 per cent of the working population. Most

industrial firms are small, producing consumer goods and electrical appliances. An important branch of industry is textiles, centred in Nicosia. The soft drinks industry has developed in Mórphou Bay. In view of the surplus of housing and industrial sites in North Cyprus after partition the construction industry is of only limited importance in the economy.

Mining
The importance of mining also declined after 1974. The large mines at Karavostási/Gemikonağí (Morphoú Bay), which formerly yielded iron ore and pyrites, were closed down by the Cyprus Mines Corporation.

Shipping
The only commercial port in North Cyprus – now mainly used by military traffic – is Famagusta. Before partition it was the only port with loading and discharging facilities, handling most of Cyprus's foreign trade.

Ferry services: see map p. 7.

Tourism
Tourism has begun to develop again in North Cyprus only in the last few years. The Cyprus Turkish Enterprise, founded in 1975, controls all hotels and private accommodation. After the division of the island North Cyprus was left with 65 per cent of the island's hotel beds, but the development of the tourist trade was inhibited by lack of skilled staff and the international economic boycott.

Nowadays 80 per cent of visitors come from mainland Turkey, spending Turkish liras and bringing in no foreign currency. Second place is taken by British visitors, followed by Germans.

History

Mythology

The island of Aphrodite

Cyprus featured in ancient mythology as the island of Aphrodite. The celebrated Rock of Aphrodite, the Pétra tou Romioú, between Páphos and Limassol marks the spot where the goddess of love and fertility, spume-born (*aphros*, foam), is supposed to have risen out of the sea. The name Pétra tou Romioú literally means rock of the Roman (the Byzantines, inheritors of the Eastern Roman Empire, referred to themselves as Romaioi, which came simply to mean Greeks).

Archaeological finds at Koúklia, near Páphos, show that this was the site of one of the largest shrines of Aphrodite in antiquity.

Hesiod's account of the birth of Aphrodite

The poet Hesiod (ca 700 BC) gives an account in his *Theogony* of the birth of Aphrodite off the coast of Cyprus. He tells us that Aphrodite was the daughter of Gaia (the Earth) and Uranos (the Sky), the primal Greek deities who emerged from Chaos (the Void). They had numerous children, the Cyclopes, the Hecatoncheires (Hundred-Armed) and the Titans. Uranos exiled the Hecatoncheires and the Cyclopes to Tartaros (the Underworld), whereupon Gaia, angered, urged their son Kronos, one of the Titans, to take revenge on his father. Kronos hid in his parents' bedroom, cut off Uranos's testicles with a sickle and threw them into the sea. They were carried by currents to Cyprus, where Aphrodite then rose from the surf. In Hesiod's words:

'And even as he cut off the privy parts with the sickle and hurled them from the mainland into the foaming sea, even so were they borne over the sea for a long time, and from the immortal flesh a white foam arose round it, and therein a maiden grew. And first she came nigh unto holy Kythera, whence next she came to sea-girt Kypros. And she came forth as a fair goddess to be revered by men, and around her the grass grew under her tender feet. Her do gods and men call Aphrodite.' (After the translation by AW Mair)

As goddess of beauty, of love, of fertility and of marriage Aphrodite was one of the most revered of the divinities of Olympus. She married the lame god Hephaistos, but did not remain faithful to him.

Oriental origin of Aphrodite

When the Greeks came to Cyprus about 1000 BC they encountered the fertility cult of an oriental mother goddess, reflecting a matriarchal society. The islanders worshipped the Babylonian love goddess Ishtar, who was identified with the Palestinian and Syrian goddess of fertility and war, Astarte. With the Hellenisation of the island this mother goddess was in turn identified with Aphrodite, the goddess of a patriarchal society.

According to Pausanias (2nd c. AD) the first Greek to set foot on the island was King Agapenor of Tegea in Arcadia, who landed in Cyprus on his way back from Troy and founded the first temple to Aphrodite at Páphos.

Cypriot legend

Cypriot legend is closely bound up with the goddess of love, whose myth was blended with historical events.

According to one legend **Pygmalion** was king of the city state of Amáthous. Aphrodite had laid down a law that all women before being married must yield themselves to a stranger in the goddess's temple: a myth reflecting an old matriarchal tradition of temple prostitution, of which there is evidence in Cyprus. Since this law was not observed Aphrodite punished all women by giving them insatiable sexual desire. Horrified by this, Pygmalion withdrew into solitude and devoted himself to sculpture. He created a marble statue of Aphrodite, with which he then fell desperately in love. Aphrodite took pity on him and breathed life into the statue, creating Galatea, who bore Pygmalion a son called Paphos; hence the name of the town of Páphos.

Paphos in turn lay with his sister Metharme and had a son named **Kinyras** who, according to Homer, was the first priest-king of the temple of Aphrodite at Páphos.

Apollodoros (2nd c. BC) tells the story of Kinyras. His wife claimed to be fairer than Aphrodite who took her revenge by causing Paphos's daughter Myrrha to form a violent passion for her father. One night, having made him drunk, she crept into his bed. When Paphos realised that he was the father of the child conceived by Myrrha he was about to kill her, but at the last moment Aphrodite transformed her into a myrtle bush, from which nine months later Adonis was born.

Transition to a patriarchal society
The legends of Paphos, who married his own sister, and Kinyras reflect the transition from the hypothetical matriarchy to a patriarchal society. In a matriarchy royal authority was passed down through the female line, and a king could maintain that authority in his family only by marrying his sister or his daughter. The change from matrilinear to patrilinear succession also finds expression in the story of the birth of Aphrodite, born of the sperm of a male divinity.

Chronology

Prehistory and early history

7000–3000 BC The first traces of human occupation on Cyprus occur in Neolithic settlements of small round houses at Khirokitía, Sotíra and Kalavasós, dated to the 9th and 8th millennia BC, in the early Neolithic period. Mainly nomadic hunters, with some sedentary farmers, the occupants came from the Syrian and Mesopotamia and worshipped the mother goddesses Ishtar and Astarte. The most important object of trade was obsidian from Anatolia.

3000–2300 BC In the Chalcolithic (Copper/Stone Age) copper is worked for the manufacture of jewellery and implements. The existing village communities are fortified and new settlements are established, like Erími to the west of Limassol. An active trade develops with the Near East, Egypt and Phoenicia.

2300–1900 BC In the early Bronze Age copper is worked on an increasing scale and bronze begins to be produced. The copper-mining areas of Cyprus are densely populated. The technique of making bronze from copper and tin is brought to Cyprus by immigrants from Anatolia. Evidence of this period is provided by finds at Alámbra (south of Nicosia) and Vounoús (near Bellapais).

1900–1550 BC In the middle Bronze Age Cyprus has trading contacts with Sicily and Crete: Bronze displaces copper. A large village settlement is established at Enkomi (near Famagusta). Copper and pottery are exported.

1550–1050 BC The Cypro-Mycenaean syllabic script is evolved about 1500. The process of Hellenisation begins in the late Bronze Age. From 1400 Mycenaean and Minoan traders visit the island. Around 1000 the Achaeans, fleeing from the advancing Dorians, seek a new home on Cyprus, bringing the patriarchal system. The working of copper brings prosperity to Cyprus. Foundation of the first urban centres at Enkomi, Kítion (Lárnaca), Márion (Pólis) and Tamassós.

1050–709 BC On Cyprus as in the Aegean the early Iron Age is a Dark Age. The population declines, as does the working of copper. Iron becomes increasingly important. The first city-kingdoms develop on the island. Phoenician traders, arriving about 800, establish a kingdom at Kítion, though their interest in Cyprus is purely commercial.

709–663 BC The Assyrians conquer Cyprus. The city-kingdoms survive, but for the next 40 years are obliged to pay tribute to Assyria.

663–560 BC The city-kingdoms of Cyprus regain their independence.

560–525 BC Cyprus under Egyptian rule.

525–333 BC Persia gains control of the island, which is obliged to pay tribute. The city-kingdoms, however, preserve their independence, prosper and enter into rivalry with one another.

499/498 BC During the rebellion of the Ionian Greeks, led by King Onesilos of Sálamis, there is also resistance in

Cyprus. Only the city-kingdom of Amáthous remains loyal to the Persians. The rebellion is crushed by the Persians with the help of their Phoenician allies.

478–477 BC A Greek fleet commanded by Pausanias, a Spartan, liberates Cyprus from the Persians. A year later, however, the Persians regain control of the island.

450–449 BC Cyprus is still involved in the conflict between the Greeks and the Persians. It has increasingly close cultural relations with Greece. Kimon of Athens attacks the Persians with a Greek fleet but dies of plague off the coast of Cyprus; the fleet then withdraws.

392–379 BC Euagoras of Sálamis, one of the principal city-kingdoms on the island, conquers the other kingdoms and unifies Cyprus under his rule. Soon afterwards, however, he is defeated by the Persians.

333–331 BC Alexander the Great defeats Darius III's Persian army at Issos in 333; Cyprus is granted independence in 331.

325–294 BC After Alexander's death in 323 Cyprus is involved in the conflict between his successors, the Diadochoi. Ptolemy I and Antigonos fight for control of the Persian empire; both are anxious to secure Cyprus for the sake of its rich resources of copper and timber.

In 310 Zeno of Kítion founds his school of Stoic philosophy in the Stoa in Athens.

294 BC Ptolemy I of Egypt becomes the new ruler of Cyprus. The city-kingdoms lose their political power, and Cyprus is ruled from Alexandria. The island is governed by a *strategos* (governor), with Páphos as capital. Much building activity.

From 168 BC Rome becomes involved for the first time in the conflicts in the eastern Mediterranean and supports the Ptolemies in their military operations. In return Rome is promised possession of Cyprus.

Cyprus under Roman rule (58 BC–AD 395)

58 BC Rome gains control of Cyprus. A Roman governor is appointed.

51/50 BC Cicero is the Roman governor of Cyprus.

47 BC After his victory over Pompey Caesar returns the island to Egypt. Cyprus is now ruled by Cleopatra.

31 BC Augustus defeats Antony and Cleopatra in the battle of Actium, and Cyprus returns to Roman control.

AD 1 Much building activity; new temples and other buildings erected in Koúrion, Sálamis and other towns.

AD 45/46 The apostles Paul and Barnabas come to Cyprus on their first missionary journey and convert Sergius Paulus, the Roman proconsul.

116 A large Jewish rising, said to have resulted in over 200,000 dead. The Jews are expelled from Cyprus.

327 St Helen, mother of Constantine the Great, lands in Cyprus on her way back from the Holy Land with the True Cross and founds the monastery of Stavrovoúni.

332–42 The island is devastated by violent earthquakes and famine. The town of Sálamis is rebuilt under the name of Constantia. Basilicas are erected at Páphos, Koúrion and Sálamis on the ruins of ancient buildings.

395 Division of the Roman Empire. For the next eight centuries Cyprus is part of the Byzantine Empire.

Cyprus under Byzantine rule (395–1191)

478 After the finding of the remains of St Barnabas the Church of Cyprus is granted autocephaly (independence).

7th–10th c. Cyprus is ravaged by Arab raids. The first large Arab campaign is launched by Muawiyah in 647–9. During this campaign Hala Sultan, said to be a relative of Mohammed, dies and is commemorated by the Hala Sultan Tekke, a mosque built in her honour. For a time the island is obliged to pay tribute to the Arabs. Constantia is destroyed. The Byzantine Empire is weakened by the iconoclastic conflict between 726 and 843.

Historic map of Cyprus (17th c.)

965 The Byzantine emperor, Nicephorus Phocas II, finally liberates Cyprus from Arab rule.

10th–11th c. A period of economic prosperity in the Byzantine Empire. Many monasteries are founded in Cyprus; some of them still exist (Chrysorroyiátissa, Makherás, St Neóphytos, Kýkko).

The fortresses of St Hilarion, Buffavento and Kantara in the Kyrenia hills are built to provide protection against Arab raids.

1054 The Great Schism, the final split between the Eastern and Western Churches, has both political and religious causes.

Cyprus under the Lusignans (1192–1489)

1185–91 Cyprus is ruled by the Byzantine general Isaac Comnenus. He breaks away from the Byzantine Empire and reigns in cyprus de facto as an independent Emperor.

1191 During the Third Crusade Richard I, king of England, conquers Cyprus on his way to the Holy Land. He marries Berengaria of Navarre in Limassol. Before continuing on his way to the Holy Land he sells Cyprus to the Templars for 100,000 gold bezants.

1192–1489 After a rising against the Templars in 1192 Cyprus is sold to a French noble, Guy de Lusignan. Thereafter, for 300 years, Cyprus is a Frankish kingdom. Roman Catholicism is declared the state religion.

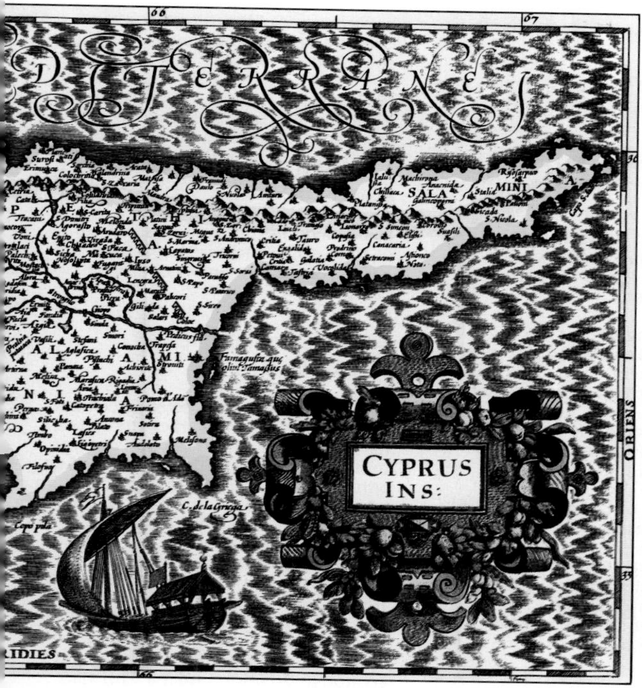

1228 The German emperor, Frederick II, lands in Cyprus during the Fifth Crusade and tries to seize control of the island. His troops occupy part of Cyprus.

1233 The Lusignans defeat the imperial forces.

1291 With the fall of Acre the last Christian stronghold in the Holy Land is lost. The Knights of St John withdraw to Cyprus (Kolóssi).

1359–69 The Frankish king Peter I is the most brilliant of the Lusignans. During his reign there is much building activity. On his initiative a crusade is launched against Alexandria.

1372–4 A conflict between the Genoese and the Venetians at Peter II's coronation ends in the predominance of Genoa in Cyprus. The Genoese gain control of Famagusta, Páphos and Nicosia and take Peter prisoner; he regains his freedom only on payment of a ransom.

1374 Peace treaty between Peter II and the Genoese; Famagusta remains in Genoese hands.

1426 Egyptian Mamelukes invade Cyprus. Battle of Khirokitía. King Janus is taken prisoner and carried off to Cairo, but is freed on payment of a ransom and an annual tribute.

1453 Constantinople falls to the Turks.

Cyprus under Venetian rule (1489–1571)

1489 The widow of the last Lusignan king, Caterina Cornaro, hands over Cyprus to the Venetians, who appoint a governor to rule the island. The population is oppressed by high taxation. The Turks invade the Karpasía peninsula.

1517 Egypt falls to the Turks. Cyprus now has to pay its annual tribute to the Turks.

1539–40 The Turks destroy Limassol. In 1540 the Venetians sign a peace treaty with the Sultan.

From 1544 To meet the continuing threat from the Turks the Venetians begin to strengthen the defences of Famagusta, Nicosia and Kyrenia.

1562 Popular rising against the Venetians, provoked by high taxation and tribute payments. The rebellion is crushed and the ringleaders executed.

1566 Sultan Suleiman the Magnificent dies and is succeeded by Selim, who shows increased interest in Cyprus.

1570–1 Conquest of Cyprus by the Turks, led by Mustafa Pasha. The siege of Nicosia begins on July 25th, and after its conquest on November 9th Kyrenia also surrenders. The siege of Famagusta lasts 10 months; it surrenders in 1571 and the Venetian commandant, Bragadino, is executed. Cyprus becomes a Turkish province.

Cyprus under Ottoman rule (1571–1878)

1573 Venice surrenders all rights in the island to Turkey. Orthodox worship is again permitted. Economic and cultural decline. The population suffers from heavy taxation.

From 1660 The archbishop of Cyprus is recognised by the Turks as the representative and spokesman of the Greek Cypriots.

1703 Cyprus becomes a fief of the Turkish grand vizier, who auctions it each year to the highest bidder. The tax burden on the population becomes steadily heavier. There are frequent popular risings.

1754 The archbishop of Cyprus becomes ethnarch: leader of the Greek Cypriot community. The dragoman (originally an interpreter) becomes the intermediary between the Sublime Porte and the Greeks and is also responsible for the collection of taxes.

1821 Beginning of the Greek war of independence on the mainland. As a deterrent to action by the Cypriots the Turkish governor, Küçük Mehmed, has Archbishop Kyprianos and his supporters executed in Nicosia.

Mid-19th c. The Turks establish a council of state which includes the archbishop and three Greek members as well as Turkish representatives.

British Colonial rule (1878–1960)

June 4th 1878 Under a secret agreement between Britain and Turkey the sultan hands over the administration of Cyprus to Britain, subject to the payment of an annual rent of £92,799. In return Britain guarantees Turkey military protection against the advance of Russian troops in the Balkans. Britain is interested in Cyprus because of its convenient situation on the way to the Suez Canal, which had come into service in 1869 and opened up a new route to India.

The people of Cyprus look forward to an improvement in their political and economic situation under a Christian power with a parliamentary system of government. The return of the Ionian Islands, a British colony, to Greece in 1864 encourages Cypriot confidence in Britain as a power friendly to Greece.

Britain appoints a high commissioner, with supreme judicial authority, to govern the island. A Cypriot parliament of six British, nine Greek and three Turkish members is established. The health services and the legal system are reformed and the tax system altered in favour of the taxpayers. But Britain shows no sign of being prepared to hand over Cyprus to Greece. This leads to unrest among the Greek population, and the call for enosis (union with Greece) becomes increasingly insistent. Archbishop Sophronios comes out in favour of enosis and travels to Britain with a delegation to press for it.

1914 When Turkey enters the first world war on the side of Germany Britain annexes Cyprus, and the Turkish inhabitants of the island (who represent some 25 per cent of the population) are declared to be British citizens.

1916 Britain seeks to induce Greece to enter the war on the side of the Allies, offering in return the union of Cyprus with Greece. Because of its military weakness Greece decides not to enter the war. The British offer to return Cyprus to Greece is not again repeated.

1921–2 The Greco-Turkish war ensues from the Greek occupation of Smyrna, given to Greece by the 1920 Treaty of Sèvres. The Turkish victory is confirmed in the Treaty of Lausanne.

1925 Turkey recognises the British annexation of Cyprus, which becomes a Crown Colony.

1931 The British authorities repress widespread riots by supporters of the enosis movement. Political associations are forbidden, press censorship introduced and the election of an archbishop prohibited.

1940 Cyprus enters the second world war on the side of the Allies, which leads to an improvement in the political climate on the island. Britain introduces new measures of democratisation. In 1943 local government elections are again permitted.

1950 Makarios III becomes archbishop. He raises the question of enosis (union with Greece) to an international level and brings it before the United Nations. In a referendum organised by the Orthodox Church 96 per cent of Cypriots vote for enosis. Britain still resists the idea.

1952–3 Makarios visits the United States, Britain and France, but makes no progress towards achieving enosis.

1954 Britain again rejects the idea of enosis. Makarios publicly declares his support for it in Troodhítissa monastery.

1955 Colonel Grivas and his EOKA (Epanastatiki Organosis Kypriakou Agonos), an underground movement fighting for enosis, enters the struggle against British rule, carrying out bomb attacks on leading British figures and institutions.

1956 Makarios and his principal associates are exiled to the Seychelles.

The Turks step up their opposition to enosis. As a counterpart to EOKA they found TMOUNT, an organisation for the defence of the rights of the Turkish minority on Cyprus. TMOUNT advocates the division of the island according to ethnic groups.

1957 Makarios returns from exile. Discussions begin on the granting of independence to Cyprus.

Independence

1960 Cyprus becomes an independent republic, with Archbishop Makarios as president and the Turkish Cypriot leader Fazíl Küçük as vice-president. The new Cypriot parliament has 35 Greek and 15 Turkish members. Under the agreed constitution the vice-president has a right of veto – a provision which was one of the factors in the failure of the young republic. Greece, Turkey and Britain guarantee the sovereignty of Cyprus, which becomes a member of the Commonwealth, the United Nations and the Council of Europe.

Britain retains two sovereign military bases. The movement for enosis continues.

1963 A constitutional crisis leads to disturbances. General Grivas founds EOKA/B, a radical right-wing organisation. There are violent clashes between Greeks and Turks. The Turkish representatives leave the government.

1964 The United Nations send a peace-keeping force of over 6000 men to Cyprus. The Turkish population withdraw into Turkish enclaves. Violence between the two population groups continues.

1967 A military junta led by Yeoryios Papadopoulos seizes power in Greece. Makarios no longer advocates enosis and his violent criticism of the Greek junta leads to increasing tension with Greece. He also alienates the United States with his neutralist, pro-Soviet policy.

July 15th 1974 After a number of unsuccessful attempts on Makarios's life earlier in 1974 he is overthrown on July 15th. The Presidential Palace is

bombed, but Makarios escapes to Páphos and from there to Britain. Nikos Sampson, a former EOKA fighter noted for his anti-Turkish views, assumes power.

July 20th 1974 Turkish forces land on the north coast of Cyprus and within 10 days occupy Kyrenia, part of Nicosia and a strip of land between the two towns. By mid-August a third of the island is in Turkish hands. Turkey claims to have intervened for the protection of the Turkish minority. By its intervention it has achieved its objective of separating the population of the island on an ethnic basis.

July 24th 1974 The Greek military junta, which was involved in the failed coup against Makarios, is compelled to resign. In Cyprus there is a panic movement of refugees: some 200,000 Greek Cypriots flee from Turkish-occupied North Cyprus into the southern part of the island, while 45,000 Turks flee from the south into the north.

December 8th 1974 Makarios returns from Britain to Cyprus. He remains president of the republic and continues to press for the abolition of the frontier between the two parts of the island, now controlled by United Nations troops.

June 20th 1975 Rauf Denktash proclaims the Turkish Federal State of Cyprus, with himself as president. The new state is not recognised by the international community.

1977 Death of Makarios. He is succeeded by Spyros Kyprianou as president and by Chrysostomos as archbishop.

1983 Rauf Denktash is elected president of the Turkish Republic of North Cyprus, which is recognised only by Turkey.

1990 Further discussions in New York under United Nations auspices. In July the Republic of Cyprus applies for full membership of the European Community.

◀ Statue of Archbishop Makarios III

1991 The Gulf War has catastrophic effects on the economy of Cyprus, with a steep fall in the number of visitors. A general election is held in the Republic of Cyprus in May. In August Greece and Turkey declare themselves ready to take part in a conference on Cyprus under United Nations chairmanship.

1992 The first university in Cyprus is opened in Nicosia (South). Under the aegis of Boutros-Ghali, United Nations secretary-general, an agreement is reached on a considerable reduction in the Turkish-occupied area, under which the Turks would give up Famagusta and Mórphou and 34 villages near Nicosia. Once again, however, the negotiations collapse.

1993 In a parliamentary election in March the opposition candidate, Glafkos Klerides, leader of the Democratic Assembly (DISY), is elected president.

1994 Measures aimed at restoring confidence are proposed by the United Nations, of which the most important are the reopening of Nicosia Airport (in the occupied sector) and the return of the former Greek resort of Varosha to the Greek south.

Goods from North Cyprus can be imported into the European Union only if accompanied by Republic of Cyprus export papers (July).

1996 A demonstrator is shot by Turkish soldiers when youths from South Cyprus attempt to cross the demarcation line.

1998 Formal negotiations on the Republic of Cyprus's entry to the European Union begin. President Glafkos Klerides is re-elected for another period in office. The plan to station Russian surface-to-air missiles in the south of the island is abandoned in the face of NATO opposition.

1999 The European Union is only willing to accept Cyprus as a member when the first steps have been taken towards settling the conflict between Greeks and Turks over the division of the island. The American president, Bill Clinton, joins in the pressure for a solution to the Cyprus question.

Nicosia, capital of Cyprus

Cyprus Divided

Island in crisis
When the island became independent in 1960 Turkey, Greece and Britain, as guarantor powers, retained the right to intervene if the status of the new republic should be threatened. Britain also had the right, under the London agreement, to maintain two sovereign air and naval bases at Dhekélia and Akrotíri.

Origins of the conflict
The origins of the Cyprus crisis go back to the Ottoman conquest in 1571, when the Turkish general, Lala Mustafa Pasha, settled soldiers of the Ottoman army and peasants from Anatolia on the island. The 300 years of Turkish rule, however, left undiminished the power of the Orthodox Church, which maintained traditions inherited from Byzantine times. From 1754 to 1821, under Ottoman rule, the archbishop of Cyprus, as ethnarch, represented the interests of the Greek ethnic group, which made up four-fifths of the population of the island.

Enosis
The establishment of an independent state of Greece in 1830 raised for the first time the question of enosis: that is, the union of all Greek-speaking territories – among them Cyprus – with the Greek motherland.

Escalation of the conflict
Britain promised the Ottoman Empire military protection against the Russian thrust in the Balkans, and in return the Turks ceded Cyprus to Britain in 1878. In 1925 the island became a British Crown Colony. After the first violent clashes between Greek Cypriot supporters of enosis and the British colonial authorities in 1931 Britain encouraged the idea of Turkish claims on Cyprus, since it had no interest in an independent Cyprus, which would have threatened its essential base on the route to the Suez Canal.

During the campaign of violence mounted against the British from 1955 onwards by the Greek-Cypriot independence movement EOKA led by Giorgios Grivas, Britain supported the Turkish underground organisation TMT (founded to protect the Turkish minority in Cyprus), and agreed in 1959 to grant

Cyprus independence only under international pressure.

Under the 1960 constitution President Makarios had a Turkish Cypriot vice-president with an unlimited right of veto. The disproportionate representation of Turks in the Cypriot parliament was resented by the Greeks, and in 1963–4 there were further violent conflicts between the two populations, which were settled by the stationing in Cyprus of the United Nations peacekeeping force.

1974 – fateful year

In 1974 the Greek military junta led by Dimitrios Ioannides, with the help of Cypriot fanatics, sought to overthrow Archbishop Makarios, who was concerned to maintain the independence and unity of Cyprus, and bring about union with Greece by violent means. Turkey, claiming to act under its rights as a guarantor power, sent in troops (under the code name Operation Attila) to protect the Turkish Cypriot population against possible attacks by Greek extremists. According to official Greek statements almost 200,000 Greeks were expelled from the Turkish-occupied areas, and some 1600 are still recorded as missing. At the same time the Turkish Cypriots who had hitherto been living in separate enclaves, were called on by the Turks to move into the northern part of the island.

Since a third of the population of the Republic of Cyprus consists of refugees from the north the partition of the island is unlikely in future to be acceptable to Greek Cypriots.

Demarcation zone

The 180 km long demarcation zone, often several kilometres wide, is guarded by the Greek Cypriot National Guard, Turkish troops and the United Nations peacekeeping force. The Green Line (or Attila Line) – so called because in 1953 a British colonial official drew a partition line on a plan of Nicosia with a green pencil – cannot be crossed by Greek Cypriots. Foreign visitors are allowed through on foot at the crossing point by the former Ledra Palace Hotel for a day visit.

Proposed solutions

Since 1974 attitudes have hardened. In spite of repeated attempts by representatives of the two ethnic groups, with United Nations mediation, to establish a dialogue no progress was made. After Yeoryios Vassiliou became President of the Republic of Cyprus in 1988 further attempts were made to break the deadlock. So far, however, discussions on the proposals put forward by the United Nations to bring the two parts of the island together either in a federal state on the Swiss model or in a loose confederation have produced no results. Glafkos Klerides, elected president in 1993, rejected the plan in part.

The Greek Cypriot position

In the event of the reunion of the two parts of the island the flourishing Greek south would have to share its recently won prosperity with the economically backward north. The main demands of the Greek Cypriots are the withdrawal of all foreign troops, freedom of movement for all Cypriots, freedom of settlement for all those expelled from their homes and an unlimited right of ownership (involving the return of abandoned houses and businesses to their original owners).

The Turkish Cypriot position

In the event of reunion the Turkish Cypriots are apprehensive about the revival of the idea of enosis, since the Greeks are superior to them not only in numbers but also in economic strength. They are in two minds about the relationship with mainland Turkey. On the one hand they want a close link with Turkey and regard the stationing of Turkish troops in Cyprus as a protection against the Greek majority; on the other hand they are concerned about the burden of the Turkish military presence.

According to official Greek estimates the Turkish Cypriot leader Rauf Denktash has brought in some 70,000 mainland Turks from Anatolia in order to make good the loss of population from northern Cyprus. Most of Denktash's political support, indeed, comes from the mainland Turks. Many Turkish Cypriots are unhappy about their new neighbours, since they regard themselves as better educated, more cosmopolitan and more law-abiding than their Anatolian fellow citizens. They are also concerned that the large numbers of incomers will swamp the Turkish Cypriot community, the character of which is gradually being changed by the Anatolians. Resentment at the loss of their cultural identity has led tens of thousands of Turkish Cypriots to emigrate since 1974.

The Turkish position

In spite of the high cost of maintaining troops in Cyprus and providing financial help for the Turkish Republic of Northern Cyprus, which economically is wholly dependent on Turkey, the Turkish government has shown no signs of being ready to yield any ground.

The success of Turkey's application for full membership of the European Union will depend in part at least on the solution of the problem of Cyprus.

Famous People

This section contains brief biographies, in alphabetical order, of notable Cypriots or people connected with the island.

Alexander the Great (356–323 BC)
Alexander was born in Pella (north-western Greece), the son of King Philip II of Macedon and his wife Olympias, daughter of King Neoptolemos. From 342 to 340 BC his tutor was the great Greek philosopher Aristotle. He distinguished himself at an early age in the battle of Chaironeia in 338 BC, and two years later, after his father's murder, made good his claim to the throne after eliminating his rivals. After being appointed general-in-chief of the Confederacy of Corinth he led campaigns against the Thracians and Illyrians and repressed a rebellion by Thebes (335 BC). Then, as supreme commander of the Greek forces, he set out in 334 BC with an army of 35,000 men on a pan-Hellenic campaign of vengeance against the Persians. Thrusting through the Taurus Mountains into Cilicia, he defeated Darius III in November 333 in the cavalry battle of Issos (north of present-day Iskenderun, Turkey). His victory over the Persians brought Persian rule in Cyprus to an end, and in 332 the Cypriot city-kingdoms took part in the campaign which led to the capture of Tyre and thereafter continued to support Alexander. The victory at Issos opened up the road to Egypt, where Alexander founded the city of Alexandria and consulted the oracle of Zeus Amun in the Siwa oasis, which confirmed his divine descent and claim to royal power.

From Egypt Alexander led his army on to Babylonia and after decisively defeating Darius at Gaugamela in the plain of Mosul (now in Iraq) in 331 BC pushed on to Persia and finally India (327–325 BC) in a campaign which took him to the Hyphasis river (Beas; now in the northern Indian state of the Punjab), where his exhausted army compelled him to turn back. After marching down the Indus valley part of the Greek army took ship down the Persian Gulf, while Alexander himself, with the rest of the army, followed a gruelling route through the Gedrosian desert and returned by way of Persia to Babylon, where Alexander died while planning a campaign against Arabia.

Alexander's declared – and in some respects partly realised – policy of unifying and consolidating his newly established empire, made up of so many heterogeneous elements, was doomed to failure, and his death was followed by conflicts between his successors, the Diadochoi.

Rauf Rašit Denktaš (b. 1924)
Rauf Rašit Denktaš (Denktash), self-appointed President of the Turkish Republic of Northern Cyprus, was born in Páphos, the son of a judge. After studying law in London he became a solicitor in Nicosia and from the outset fought strenuously for the rights of the Turks in Cyprus. He was a close associate of Fazíl Küçük, first vice-president of the newly established republic and leader of the Turkish Cypriots, and from 1958 to 1960 was chairman of various Turkish Cypriot institutions.

After Cyprus became independent in 1960 there were violent clashes between Turkish and Greek nationalists. An inflammatory speech by Denktash to the United Nations in New York led to a ban on his entry into Cyprus. In 1963 Denktash and other Turkish representatives withdrew from the government, but during the troubles of the 1960s he remained leader of the Turkish Cypriots. In 1968 he headed the Turkish delegation in negotiations with Archbishop Makarios and advocated the partition of Cyprus into separate Greek and Turkish areas. In 1973 he succeeded Fazíl Küçük as vice-president of the Republic of Cyprus.

After the Turkish invasion in 1974 Denktash ran the Turkish Cypriot part of the island, and was elected president in 1983 when he proclaimed the Turkish Republic of Northern Cyprus, a state recognised only by Turkey. After various unsuccessful attempts to solve the problem of Cyprus Denktash declared in 1989 that he was ready to consider a federal Turco-Greek state. So far, however, no progress has been made in achieving this.

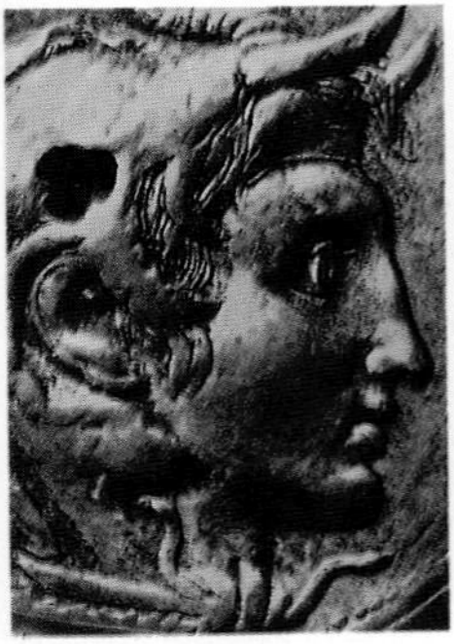
Alexander the Great

Archbishop Makarios III

Zeno of Kítion

Lawrence Durrell (1912–90)
The Anglo-Irish poet, novelist and dramatist Lawrence Durrell was born at Jullundur in northern India, at the foot of the Himalayas, and went to school in Darjeeling and in Britain. Thereafter he spent many years travelling in Athens, Corfu, Egypt and Cyprus. While in Paris he became a close friend of Henry Miller. From 1941 onwards he was a press attaché in Cairo, Alexandria, Rhodes and Belgrade. From 1953 to 1956 he lived in Cyprus, first as a teacher in the Pancyprian Gymnasium in Nicosia and then as press attaché in the diplomatic service. He now bought a house in Bellapais. His book *Bitter Lemons* was based on his experiences in Cyprus against the background of the struggle for independence which was then developing. Durrell's last years were spent in Nîmes (southern France).

Durrell's works included novels, essays, travel impressions, satirical sketches, lyric poetry and verse dramas, but his main preoccupation was with man's quest for an identity. One of his finest works is the *Alexandria Quartet*, in which, in a series of changing perspectives and periods influenced by the theory of relativity, he demonstrates the variety of human truths.

Euagoras I (ca 435–373 BC)
Euagoras was one of the outstanding rulers of ancient Cyprus. He was a scion of the Teucrian dynasty which for generations had been kings of Sálamis. In the 5th c. BC, however, the Teucrians were expelled by the Phoenicians, who were allied with the Persians, and in 415 Euagoras fled to Soli in Cilicia. In 411 he returned and overthrew Abdemon, a Phoenician who had been appointed king of Sálamis. In 394 BC he took part in a campaign, together with the Persians and Athenians, against the Spartans, which ended in a victory at Knidos. Thereafter Euagoras embarked on a campaign of expansion, securing the submission of other city-kingdoms on Cyprus in 392 and conquering Tyre (Lebanon). In 382 the Persians sent a fleet against Sálamis, and a treaty was concluded under which Euagoras remained king of Sálamis until ca 373 BC but was compelled to pay tribute to Persia. Soon afterwards, however, he fell victim to an intrigue at his own court.

Yeoryios Grivas (1898–1974)
Yeoryios (George) Grivas was born in Tríkomo/Iskele, near Famagusta. He attended the Cadet School in Athens and in 1919 was granted Greek nationality. In 1920–2 he fought in the Greco-Turkish War as an infantry officer. In 1928 he was promoted to staff officer and entered the French Military Academy in Paris. Returning to Greece, he joined the teaching staff of the Officers' School in Salonica and then the Military Academy in Athens. In 1940 he was appointed to the operational staff of the Greek army and became chief of staff. During the Italian and German occupation of Greece he founded an underground organisation known simply as X.

In 1951 Grivas, then a colonel, retired and returned to Cyprus, where he founded EOKA, an underground organisation which began to operate against the British occupying forces in 1955. Under the pseudonym of Dighenis he organised a partisan war aimed at securing enosis (union with Greece). EOKA now became the main driving force in the struggle against British rule. Grivas's objective of securing enosis, however, was frustrated by the establishment of an independent Republic of Cyprus in 1960. He returned to Greece, where he was promoted to general and awarded high decorations. In 1961 he published the first part of his memoirs.

In the late 1960s Grivas, who in the 1950s had fought for enosis along with Makarios, turned against him, disappointed by his new anti-enosis policy, and from 1970 began to work for his overthrow. In 1971 he founded EOKA/B, which organised demonstrations and bomb attacks with the aim of securing enosis. He died in January 1974 and was buried in a friend's garden in Limassol.

Namík Kemal
(1840–88)

Namík Kemal was one of the great Turkish popular poets. The son of an aristocratic family in Tekirdağ in European Turkey, in 1857 he became an official in Istanbul. A fierce opponent of the despotic sultans from an early age, he published strongly critical articles in newspapers and periodicals and in 1867 fled to Paris and from there to London, where he ran an anti-government newspaper. He returned to Turkey in 1870, but after the performance of his play *Vatan yahud Silistre* (Home or Silistria) led to riots he was exiled to Cyprus. From 1873 to 1876 he was confined in Famagusta prison, which occupied a wing of the Palazzo del Provveditore. He is commemorated by a bust erected in 1953 opposite the Palazzo, in front of the Lala Mustafa Mosque (formerly St Nicholas's Cathedral). After his release he left Cyprus and went to Paris, where he founded the Young Turks party in 1876. He died of tuberculosis on Chios.

By awakening the spirit of Ottoman patriotism Namík Kemal's works prepared the way for Atatürk's revolution.

Kimon of Athens
(ca 510–ca 449 BC)

Kimon, son of Miltiades, victor over the Persians in the battle of Marathon (490 BC), was one of Athens' leading statesmen, a conservative aristocrat belonging to the Athenian nobility. He gained a great reputation with his military successes, particularly against the Persians. In 468 he launched a large campaign in Cyprus but failed to recapture it from the Persians. Between 469 and 466, however, he won a double victory over the Persians on the Eurymedon river. Well disposed towards the Spartans, he was overthrown in 461 by the democratic and anti-Spartan party in Athens and was exiled from Attica for 10 years. In 450 BC he distinguished himself as a general in the Athenian fleet sent to reconquer Cyprus from the Persians. Landing at Márion (now Pólis), he took Sálamis, but during the siege of Kítion (Lárnaca) died of plague. The Greek army thereupon abandoned the siege and left Cyprus, which remained under Persian sovereignty.

Spyros Kyprianou
(b. 1932)

Spyros Kyprianou, ex-President of the Republic of Cyprus, was born in Limassol. After studying economics and law in Britain he became in 1950 a close associate of Archbishop Makarios, promoting and defending his policy in Britain and Greece and at the United Nations. From 1960 to 1972, as foreign minister of the Republic of Cyprus, he pursued a policy of neutrality. Thereafter he founded the Democratic Front (later the Democratic Party), which won an election in 1976, when Kyprianou became speaker of the Cypriot Parliament. In 1977 he was elected president of the Republic. In spite of repeated conflicts with parliament he remained in power, surviving a vote of no confidence moved in 1985. He rejected a proposal by Rauf Denktash to form a federation of two separate Cypriot states. In 1985 he took part in discussions with Denktash in New York under the chairmanship of United Nations Secretary-General Pérez de Cuéllar, but these made no progress. In 1988 Kyprianou was replaced as president by Yeoryios Vassiliou.

Hadjigeorgákis Kornésios
(1779–1809)

Hadjigeorgákis Kornésios was the son of a wealthy Christian cloth merchant. He received an excellent education, learned Turkish at an early age and took an active part in the intellectual life of Cyprus. In 1779 the Sultan appointed him dragoman of the Seraglio for Cyprus.

The dragoman was a paid official responsible for acting as an intermediary between the Sultan and his Christian subjects and also for the collection of taxes. Hadjigeorgákis held the post for almost 30 years. All public and private business passed through his hands. As dragoman he acquired great possessions, but his wealth and his role as tax collector made him many enemies. In 1804 the oppressive burden of taxation and a period of famine led to rioting by Turkish Cypriots, in the course of which the dragoman's house was looted. The dragoman himself had already gone to seek help from the Sultan, who sent an army to Cyprus to crush the rising. Hadjigeorgákis spent the last years of his life in Istanbul, where he became involved in intrigues at the Sultan's court and was executed in 1809.

Archbishop Makarios III (1913–77)

Archbishop Makarios was one of the outstanding personalities of modern times in Cyprus. As archbishop and as president of the Republic of Cyprus he played a major part in the political development of the island.

Makarios was born Michalis Christodoulou Mouskos in Páno Panayiá, near Páphos. After the death of his mother he entered Kýkko monastery as a novice at the age of 13. Three years later the monastery arranged for him to attend the Pancyprian Gymnasium in Nicosia. In 1938 he was ordained as a deacon. With the help of a scholarship from Kýkko monastery he went to Athens to study theology. He was ordained as a priest in 1946, taking the name of Makarios, and then went to Boston for two years' study with a bursary from the World Council of Churches. In 1948 he became bishop of Kítion and in 1950 archbishop of Cyprus.

Makarios supported the Greek Cypriots in their desire for union with Greece, and repeatedly raised the question of Cyprus in the United Nations, in the United States and in Greece. When all efforts to achieve a peaceful solution failed he supported Colonel Grivas's underground activities. As a result he was exiled to the Seychelles in March 1956. In 1957 he returned to Cyprus, and in 1960 he agreed to the proposals for Cypriot independence and became president of the new Republic of Cyprus.

In the late 1960s, when Makarios increasingly turned away from the idea of union with Greece, his relations with the Greek military junta deteriorated. In 1974 the Greek government was involved in a *coup d'état* by the National Guard and EOKA/B against Makarios, who managed to flee to Páphos and from there to London. After the failure of the coup he returned to Cyprus and remained president of the Republic until his death in August 1977.

Yeoryios Vassiliou (b. 1931)

Yeoryios (George) Vassiliou, until March 1993 the president of the Republic of Cyprus, was born in Famagusta, the son of a doctor who was one of the founding members of the communist party AKEL. After studying economics in Genoa, Vienna and Budapest he specialised in marketing and market research in London. In 1962, after his return to Cyprus, he founded the largest market research business in the Third World, with offices in 11 countries. Although without any political experience and with no party allegiance but with the support of the communist AKEL and the socialist party EDEK, he won a surprising victory over Spyros Kyprianou and the conservative candidate Glafkos Klerides in the presidential election of 1988. In line with his undertaking during the election campaign to make a fresh start in seeking a solution to the problem of Cyprus, he initiated negotiations with the leader of the Turkish Cypriots, Rauf Denktash, meeting him for the first time in 1988 in the buffer zone occupied by the United Nations peace keeping force and discussing the possible establishment of a federation of two largely independent states. So far, however, the discussions have led to no concrete results.

Zeno of Kítion (Zeno the Younger; ca 333–262 BC)

Zeno, founder of the Stoic school of philosophy, was born in Kítion (Lárnaca) to a family of Phoenician origin. At the age of 22 he went to Athens and became a disciple of the Cynic philosopher Krates of Thebes. About 300 BC he began to teach in the Stoa Poikile, the Painted Hall (with paintings by Polygnotos), in the agora of Athens, from which the Stoic school took its name.

Stoicism was a complete philosophical system, consisting of logic (including grammar, rhetoric and dialectic), physics and ethics. In the Stoic view the cosmos is governed by reason and rigid determinism. Accordingly ethics is based on the maxims of reason, which alone leads to perception and to good fortune. Virtues like courage, self-control, humanity and justice help the wise man to achieve harmony with himself and with nature. But since each man bears reason within himself there can in principle be only one law, one right and one state. Zeno conceived a universal state in which men could live in peace with one another and with equal rights.

Zeno developed his philosophy in a time of change in Greece. The city-kingdoms were beginning to fall apart and people were in a state of uncertainty. Against this social background it is easy to understand the wide appeal of Zeno's philosophy, which looks forward to a happy state independent of external circumstances – a happiness people can find within themselves, unaffected by government or politics. Zeno died by his own hand about 262 BC.

Culture

Art and Architecture

Neolithic (7000–3000 BC)

The oldest traces of human life on Cyprus date from the Neolithic period: for example the settlement at Khirokitía of the 6th millennium BC. Under the earth floors of the semi-underground circular dwellings the dead were buried in a tightly contracted foetal position, perhaps in the expectation of later rebirth. The inhabitants of this village community were farmers, and on the evidence of bones found on the site had domesticated wild sheep and goats. Needles and pointed implements made from shells point to the beginnings of spinning and weaving.

Towards the end of the Neolithic period the first pottery vessels appear alongside domestic utensils and implements made from stone and bone. With the help of a comb-like instrument made from shell or bone the pottery was decorated with incised ornament (combed ornament). The vessels, mostly shaped like gourds, were covered with a reddish-brown glaze. Necklaces of carnelian beads and obsidian blades are evidence of trading contacts with Asia Minor and Syria. Violin-shaped stone idols also begin to appear.

Chalcolithic (3000–2300 BC)

In the Chalcolithic period Cyprus has trading contacts with Asia Minor and the Levant. Settlements are established at Erími, Lápithos, Kythréa and other sites. The round dwellings of the Neolithic period increasingly give place to rectangular houses. The dead are now buried outside the village.

Different types of pottery are now produced. The predominant type is Erími ware (red-on-white ware), named after the principal site where it was found. Decoration is mainly linear and geometric. Cross-shaped idols in steatite or clay are increasingly common. They now show female sexual characteristics, pointing to the cult of a mother goddess, predecessor of Aphrodite. Jewellery and implements of beaten copper are thought still to be imports.

Towards the end of the Chalcolithic period occasional alabaster vases begin to appear, showing Egyptian influence. The pottery shows great variety of form, with geometric and plant ornament. Red and black polished ware with incised decoration is now predominant.

Bronze Age (2300–1050 BC)

In the Early Bronze Age settlements are established at Vounoús, Politikó, Tamassós and other sites. Copper mining provides the raw material for metal weapons and domestic requisites and jewellery of copper and silver. The villages are now increasingly fortified, and the dead are buried in dromos (entrance passage) tombs outside the settlement.

The red polished ware of this period has incised decoration in the form of wavy lines, bands of zigzags or circles.

Middle Bronze Age

In the middle Bronze Age the technique of bronze production is brought to Cyprus by Anatolian merchants. Red polished ware is produced in a great range of forms; the rims and handles of jars are decorated with animal protomes (the upper parts of animals' bodies). Pottery models of cult ceremonies are now found, for example a walled shrine from Vounoús (Archaeological Museum, Nicosia). There are also models of scenes from everyday life such as ploughing and baking bread.

The range of pottery forms is extended by the production of composite vessels, combining several different types. Narrow-neck vases appear for the first time, trading relations with Egypt and Palestine having brought new wares including oils and luxury ointments to Cyprus. Towards the end of the middle Bronze Age red polished ware begins to give place to white painted ware and black slip ware.

Also characteristic of this period are flat-bodied 'plank idols' in red pottery with incised decoration and necklaces formed from imported beads of glass paste or faience.

◄ Doorway of Ayía Nápa Monastery church, built ca 1570

Late Bronze Age

The late Bronze Age is a period of trading contacts with Minoans, Mycenaeans and Achaeans. Settlements such as Énkomi, Kítion and Márion are established as a result of the increasing importance of copper working. The most important house type in this period is the megaron house with an antechamber. Settlements are now laid out on a regular plan. The dead are buried in chamber tombs with a long dromos and several chambers. Gold jewellery now appears, often made from beaten gold foil and decorated with spiral ornament or animal motifs. Mycenaean influence can be detected in the forms of the jewellery.

Mycenaean influence also appears in the white slip and black slip ware, which, like the Zeus Crater in the Archaeological Museum in Nicosia, is decorated with mythological scenes and representations of cult ceremonies.

The extraordinary variety of pottery forms in the late Bronze Age includes full-bodied craters (wide-mouthed jars for mixing water and wine), small decorative vases, jars imitating metal (at this period still very precious) and bird-headed mother figures holding a child. Carved ivories with oriental motifs such as griffins or lions reflect the close links between Aegean and oriental cultures. Representations of the Egyptian god Bes become increasingly common. A valuable and magnificently decorated rhyton (drinking vessel) from Kítion (Archaeological Museum, Nicosia) shows that vases were now much more than utility objects. Bronze statuettes such as the horned god from Énkomi (Archaeological Museum, Nicosia) point to an active metal-working industry in the final stages of the Bronze Age.

Cypro-Minoan syllabic script

In the 16th c. BC the first forms of writing appear in Cyprus. The Cypro-Minoan syllabic script shows close affinities with the Minoan Linear A script. The hundred or so characters of the syllabary have not yet been deciphered. Inscribed on everyday objects, they may have indicated the contents of a vessel or the name of the owner.

Geometric period (1050–725 BC)

After the coming of the Achaeans, bringing with them their beliefs and cults, the Hellenisation of the island begins.

Archaic wine jar

In Cyprus as in Greece a certain cultural stagnation can be observed at the beginning of the Geometric period. A fresh cultural flowering occurs only from the 10th c. onwards, influenced by the island's close connections with Phoenicia. Phoenician traders introduce the technique of iron working and found the first Phoenician city, Kítion. The Achaeans build a number of towns, including Koúrion, Márion, Sóloi. Tombs now have a long narrow dromos with a pointed roof.

In pottery the predominant types are red slip ware and black-on-red ware. The decoration consists of both geometric patterns and pictorial scenes. The neck and rim of vases are now also decorated. Occasional gold, silver and bronze dishes are found.

Archaic period (725–475 BC)

Assyrian, Egyptian and Persian influences now make themselves felt. City-kingdoms such as Sálamis and Amathoús flourish. Richly furnished tombs at Sálamis and Tamassós bear witness to a period of cultural flowering. The grave goods show oriental influence, while the architecture of the tombs comes from Greece. The dead are no longer buried in a tightly contracted position but lie on their backs in stone sarcophagi. Stelae begin to appear as grave markers.

In view of the lack of marble on Cyprus large sculpture is mainly in limestone. The dress and hair styles of the statues show Oriental influence. At Ayía Iríni more than 2000 terracotta figures were found, including many small figures of bulls – suggesting that the old mother goddess had been displaced by male fertility symbols. In spite of the Assyrian and Egyptian influences Cypriot sculpture shows affinities with the Archaic sculpture of mainland Greece in its intense concern with the human body.

The powerful influence of the city-kingdoms leads to the formation of local styles and the emergence of distinctive artistic personalities. Bichrome vases decorated with flower and plant motifs now appear. The oriental style, which had come to the fore in mainland Greece at the end of the Geometric period, begins to establish itself in Cyprus. The free-field style also develops. Polychrome decoration with figures of animals and fabulous beasts is found principally on bulbous vases. The rich painted decoration spreads freely over the vessels with no frames to confine it, and the painting of the figures is more concerned with decorative effect than with anatomical accuracy.

Towards the end of the Archaic period black-figured vases imported from Greece begin to appear.

Egyptian glassware, faience and scarabs are common during the period of Egyptian rule.

Classical period (475–325 BC)

The Classical period is also the period of the conflict with Persia, but even under Persian rule Cyprus establishes increasingly close cultural relations with Greece. The magnificent palace at Vouní (5th c. BC) shows a mingling of oriental and Greek elements.

Imports of Attic black-figured and red-figured vases increase, but vase painting in Cyprus itself also follows Greek styles. In the reign of King Euagoras of Sálamis Greek artists and scholars come to the island.

From the middle of the 5th c. Cypriot sculpture shows Ionian and Attic influences. Fine bronze sculpture is produced, for example the figure of a cow from Vouní (Archaeological Museum, Nicosia).

Hellenistic period (325–58 BC)

After the death of Alexander the Great Cyprus is held by Ptolemy I of Egypt. The city-kingdoms are dissolved and the island is ruled from Alexandria. At Páphos large peristyle tombs with a colonnaded inner courtyard are built, showing Egyptian influence; the architectural decoration, however, is still Greek. The island's close political and cultural links with Egypt do not displace Greek cultural influence. Increasing prosperity and ostentation lead to the building of new temples at Páphos and Sálamis.

Pottery continues to be imported from Greece or is modelled on Greek products. The so-called Hadra vases – mass-produced ware in their country of origin – are imported from Egypt. Valuable pieces of small sculpture reflect the island's prosperity. One of the few surviving marble statues, the Aphrodite of Sóloi, can be seen in the

The Hellenistic Tombs of the Kings at Páphos

Early Christian Basilica Koúrion

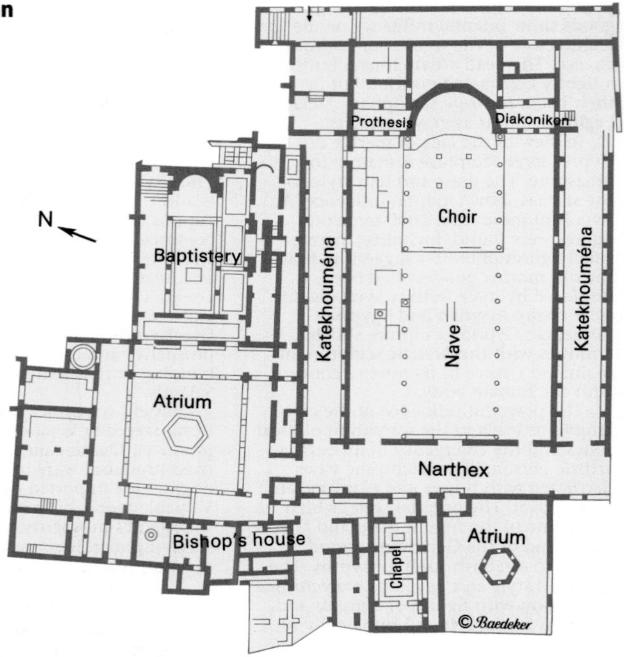

Archaeological Museum in Nicosia. Glassware begins to be produced in Cyprus, and pressed glass is used in the manufacture of honey-coloured and sea-green drinking glasses.

Roman period (58 BC–AD 395)

As a Roman province Cyprus continues Hellenistic traditions. Towns such as Páphos, Sálamis and Sóloi grow in size and are embellished with Roman temples. After a great earthquake in the 4th c. many towns are rebuilt. Theatres, gymnasia and palaestras are erected. Under the Ptolemies the peristyle house comes to Cyprus. The peristyle, a colonnaded courtyard, frequently has a colourful mosaic pavement (fine examples found at Páphos and Koúrion), an ornamental pool and flower beds.

Sálamis now becomes the cultural centre of Cyprus. Public buildings and private houses are decorated with sculpture, strongly influenced by Roman models. There are portraits and statues of emperors, leading citizens, gods and heroes (e.g. the statue of the Emperor Septimius Severus from Kythréa, now in the Archaeological Museum, Nicosia).

The pottery consists mostly of undecorated ware for everyday use, showing Syrian and Cilician influence. Terra sigillata, a red ware with moulded decoration bearing the potter's stamp (*sigilla*), becomes popular in Cyprus.

In the 2nd c. AD the scale of glass production increases. Undecorated glass for everyday use is manufactured on the island, but glassware is also imported from Syria.

Byzantine art (AD 330–1191)

When Constantinople became capital of the Roman Empire in 330 this multi-territorial state faced the difficulties involved in seeking to create a unified Roman nation. An

Church of Ayia Paraskevi Yeroskípos

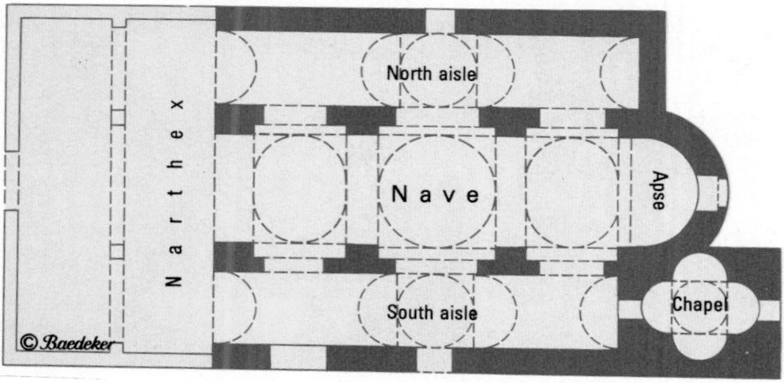

effective means to this end was Christianity, which was granted toleration by Constantine the Great in the Edict of Milan in 313 and was made the state religion by Theodosius the Great at the end of the 4th c. Thereafter there was much building activity.

Byzantine church types

Early Christian basilica The first Christian basilicas in Cyprus were built at Koúrion, Páphos, Amathoús and Sálamis in the 4th c., some 300 years after Paul and Barnabas's missionary work on the island. This type of church was derived from the secular basilicas of the Roman world, which served as market halls and law courts. It had a central aisle (nave) with its own windows which was higher than the lateral aisles and separated from them by columns or pillars.

The basilicas found on Cyprus are long buildings of three to five aisles with one or more apses at the east end. Behind the altar, on a higher level, is the bishop's throne (*kathedra*). The apse and the area containing the altar form the sanctuary (*bema*), which only the officiating clergy can enter. It is separated from the body of the church (*naos*) by a low screen, the templon.

On either side of the sanctuary there are usually two small rooms, the diakonikon or sacristy to the right and the prothesis, in which the eucharist is prepared, to the left. In addition to the lateral aisles some churches have outer aisles (*katekhouména*), separated from the church itself, which are occupied by catechumens (members of the congregation who have not yet been baptised). At the west end of the church is a kind of antechamber, the narthex, and beyond it the atrium, with a fountain (*kántharos*) for ablutions. The baptismal font is in the baptistery, outside the church.

The interior of the church is decorated with mosaics and wall paintings.

Domed cruciform church In the 9th and 10th c. the basilican type of church increasingly gives way throughout the Byzantine Empire to the domed cruciform type, a church on a centralised plan of the same type as Hagia Sophia in Istanbul. The immediate prototype of the Cypriot churches is the basilica of St John at Ephesus, a hybrid of the basilican and the centralised plan. There are usually three domes over the nave and two more over the arms of the cross (Peristeróna, Yeroskípos, St Barnabas's Monastery). The sanctuary has one or more apses.

The sanctuary is separated from the main part of the church by the templon, a marble screen. In the 13th c. this develops into the iconostasis, a tall wooden screen bearing tiers of icons.

Barn-roofed church A type of church peculiar to Cyprus is the barn-roofed church, a long, single-aisled church

Wall painting in the church of Ayia Paraskeví, Yeroskípos

which is particularly favoured in the Tróodos massif. These medieval churches in the upland regions were given pitched roofs in the crusader period; if the church had a dome this was covered by a tiled pitched roof. With its deep overhanging eaves the roof, borne on a supporting wall, provides protection from snow and rain. The ambulatory between the church and the supporting wall provides constant ventilation and thus helps to conserve the walls with their rich decoration of paintings.

Byzantine wall paintings
Byzantine churches are usually decorated with magnificent frescos, which were painted on the fresh, wet plaster (Italian *al fresco*). The pigments thus penetrate into the plaster ground, which acts as a binding medium and makes the painting more durable.

The veneration of images is based on the belief that the likeness of God or of a saint is a representation of the archetypical conception of God or the saint; and in order to approach as closely as possible to the archetype the form of representation must be fixed and unchanging. The flat linear composition of the iconography disregards normal principles of scale and spatial relationship and sets the figures in a false perspective.

Wall paintings also served as a graphic Bible for those who could not read the Biblical story; they depicted Biblical events and parables and thus symbolised the teachings of the Church.

The Byzantine religious art of Cyprus can be divided into early, middle, late and post-Byzantine periods. It incorporates Hellenistic, Roman, Syrian and oriental (Persian) elements.

Early Byzantine period In the early Byzantine period (6th–8th c.) the wall paintings depict only scenes from the

An elongated figure of St Peter in the ➤
Comene style, Laghouderá

Ὁ ΑΠ(ΟΣΤΟΛΟΣ) ΠΕΤΡ(ΟΣ)

ΑΓΑΠΗΤΟΙ
ΠΑΡΑΚΑΛѠ ѠС
ΠΑΡΟΙΚΟΥС ΚΑΙ
ΠΑΡΕΠΙΔΗΜΟΥС
ΑΠΕΧΕСΘΕ ΤѠΝ
СΑΡΚΙΚѠΝ ΕΠΙ
ΘΥΜΙѠΝ ΑΤΙΝΕС
СΤΡΑΤΕΥΟΝΤ(ΑΙ)

life of Christ. The style is lively and expressive.

Iconoclasm The iconoclastic conflict between 726 and 843 turned on the meaning and veneration of sacred images. The iconoclasts (destroyers of images) opposed any pictorial representation of Christ or any other sacred persons, citing the third commandment: 'Thou shalt not make unto thee any graven image, or any likeness of any thing that is in heaven above ...' This view was influenced by religions like Judaism and Islam which were also hostile to images.

Those who believed in the power of images – mainly monks and the ordinary people – saw Christ, who took on human form, as an image of God and thus as a justification for the representation of other sacred persons and saints. It was also believed that Luke the Evangelist had himself painted the first likeness of Mary, the Mother of God.

Mandílion and Keramídion A historical basis for the veneration of images was also seen in the existence of the Mandílion and the Keramídion, explained by the story in apocryphal writings that the king of Edessa in Syria sent a painter to Christ to paint his likeness. Christ did not agree to the painting of his portrait, but pressed his face into a cloth, which he gave to the painter. The cloth, now imprinted with the likeness of Christ's face, was then hung on the city gate of Edessa, where it left an impression on a tile. In the 9th c. the Holy Cloth (Mandílion) and Holy Tile (Keramídion) were taken to Constantinople, where they were the subject of great veneration.

The iconoclastic controversy ended in victory for the supporters of images, and the view of St John of Damascus that images should be regarded only as intermediaries between man and the divine became orthodox doctrine.

The **middle Byzantine period** (870–1204) followed the period of iconoclasm, after which the theological content and form of representation of images were precisely defined. The decoration of churches with wall paintings now followed an established iconographic programme. The paintings depicted figures in a rigidly frontal position, and perspectives were based on relative importance, the principal figures being shown larger than the subsidiary ones. The paintings covered a wide range of scenes of theological significance. The paintings of the Macedonian Renaissance (9th–11th c.), which developed after the end of the iconoclastic controversy in the reign of the Emperor Basil I, are distinguished by delicate draughtsmanship and the elongated representation of the figures. Under the Comnene dynasty (1081–1185) there was a return to Hellenistic models, with gently flowing movement, elaborately folded draperies and delicate chiaroscuro effects.

The oldest surviving wall paintings in Cyprus are in the church of Ayios Nikólaos tis Stéyis at Kakopetriá (11th c.).

Late Byzantine period In the late Byzantine period (1204–1453), also known as the Palaeologue period after the Palaeologue imperial dynasty, the paintings are full of contrasts, tensions and richly contrasting colours. During the period of Frankish rule western elements are incorporated in the traditional style.

Post-Byzantine period The post-Byzantine period (15th–19th c.), which begins with the conquest of Constantinople by the Turks in 1453, is characterised by a profusion of figures, the representation of subsidiary persons and genre scenes, the introduction of central perspective and the painting of detailed backgrounds.

Iconograph

After the end of the iconoclastic period the arrangement of paintings in a church is determined by a strict canon. The painters' artistic intentions do not count: what is important is the theological message of the paintings.

The paintings are arranged in accordance with a horizontal and a vertical hierarchy. There may be minor variations in content and style, usually attributable to the donors of the paintings.

The **horizontal hierarchy** begins in the sanctuary (*bema*), which is regarded as the point of contact between heaven and earth. In the apse is the Mother of

God with the Infant Christ, and below this are the Communion of the Apostles, symbolising the Last Supper, and the fathers of the Church, representing the timelessness of the Church. In the body of the church (*naos*) are scenes from the legends of saints, the life of the Virgin and the life of Christ, based on the 12 great festivals of the Orthodox Church (the Annunciation, the Nativity of Christ, the Presentation in the Temple, the Baptism, the Transfiguration, the Raising of Lazarus, the Entry into Jerusalem, the Crucifixion, the Descent into Hades, the Ascension, Pentecost and the Dormition of the Mother of God).

At the west end of the church, over the doorway or in the narthex, is the Last Judgment.

The **vertical hierarchy** begins in the dome, which represents heaven, with the figure of Christ Pantokrator (Ruler of All), surrounded by angels. In the pendentives are prophets or the four Evangelists, forming a transition to the earthly sphere, in which are scenes from the life of the Virgin or of Christ. In the lowest register are saints and representatives of the ecclesiastical and secular hierarchies.

In a sociological interpretation the rigid iconographic programme can be seen as representing the unshakeable order of the Byzantine Empire, in which the emperor was supreme head of the Church as well as of the state.

Icons

Like the wall paintings, icons also serve for the instruction of the worshippers. An icon (Greek *eikon*, image) is a likeness of Christ, the Mother of God or a saint. During the iconoclastic conflict of the 8th and 9th c. conflict icons were destroyed by the iconoclasts. Others were hidden away, and their rediscovery in later times led to the foundation of monasteries (Makherás, Kýkko).

Icon painting, like wall painting, was subject to strict **rules**. Painters' handbooks laid down not only the subjects but also the technique and the treatment. The representation, frequently on a gold ground, was flat and without central perspective. The emphasis was on the theological message: the background was left blank, since otherwise it might divert attention from the main figure. The flat, two-dimensional effect of the icon was deliberate, not the result of any lack of artistic skill.

Frankish and Venetian art (1191–1571)

Cypriot Gothic

The conquest of Cyprus by Richard I, king of England, in 1191 brought in western influences. Thereafter the island was ruled by a French noble family, the Lusignans, who initiated an active building programme. Masons were brought in from the West and palaces and churches were built by the king, the bishops and wealthy citizens. The first large Gothic cathedrals were erected in Nicosia and Famagusta (St Sophia, St Nicholas). In the Pentadáktylos range the castles of St Hilarion, Buffavento and Kantara were built to protect the island from foreign attacks.

Cypriot Gothic lacks the lightness and upward movement of French Gothic. Heavy, squat forms predominate. The long nave and aisles often have flat roofs rather than the pitched roofs usual in France, and the interiors of the churches are bare in comparison with the sumptuous decoration of French churches. They lack galleries above the aisles; there are no chapels round the choir and no transepts. Most churches have a choir with three apses at the east end; usually there is no ambulatory round the choir (though the cathedral of St Sophia in Nicosia is an exception).

Barn-roofed churches

The small churches in the hills have a special type of barn roof. The churches, usually barrel-vaulted or domed, have an additional steeply pitched roof with deep overhanging eaves which provides protection from rain and snow.

Pottery

The predominant type of medieval pottery – mainly dishes and drinking vessels – is brownish-green, with rich and imaginative sgraffito decoration.

The barn-roofed church of the Panayía tou Arákou, Laghouderá

Ottoman art (1571–1878)

After the conquest of Cyprus the Turks converted abandoned Catholic churches into mosques. The cathedral of St Sophia in Nicosia became the Selimiye Mosque, St Nicholas's Church in Famagusta the Lala Mustafa Pasha Mosque. Minarets were built on the stumps of church towers, and the Gothic decoration of the interiors was removed. New mosques were built were in classical Ottoman style, with a square ground plan and a dome.

Mosques

The mosque was not only the Muslim house of God and a meeting place for prayer and the Friday sermon, it was also used as a place for teaching, for legal proceedings and for political meetings.

The layout of the mosque was originally derived from the plan of an Arab dwelling, out of which developed the courtyard mosque on the model of Medina (e.g. the Omayyad Mosque in Damascus). The large inner courtyard (*sahn*) with the fountain for ritual ablutions is surrounded by galleries (*riwaks*) and a long multi-aisled prayer hall facing in the direction of Mecca. Also oriented towards Mecca are the *mihrab* (prayer niche) and the *minbar*, the high pulpit for the Friday sermon. From the Omayyad period (666–750) onwards the minaret from which the muezzin issued the five daily calls to prayer became an essential element in the structure of the mosque.

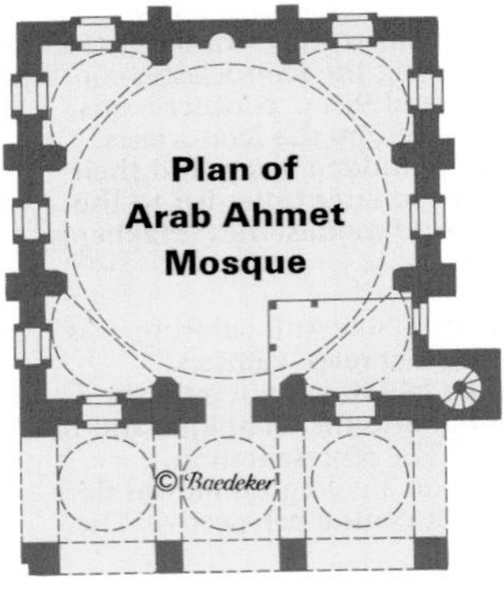

In the 11th c. a new element stemming from the palace architecture of the pre-Islamic period, the *iwan* – a barrel-vaulted hall open on one side and preceded by a courtyard – was introduced. From the 12th c. the mosque may have four *iwans* axially related to one another. The *iwans* were frequently used as *medreses* (theological schools).

Domed mosques The domed mosque, modelled on domed Byzantine churches, developed in the Ottoman Empire from the 13th c. onwards. The type of the square domed building on a centralised plan (e.g. the Suleimaniye Mosque in Istanbul) now became established. Most of the mosques built in Cyprus followed this pattern, for example the Hala Sultan Tekke near Lárnaca and the Arab Ahmet Mosque in Nicosia.

Rectangular mosques In the 19th c. the rectangular type of mosque without a dome, entered through a columned narthex, came to Cyprus. Examples of this type are found in Lefke and Nicosia (Sarayönü Mosque).

Secular buildings
In addition to mosques numbers of secular buildings were also erected in the Ottoman period, such as the two *hans* (caravanserais) in Nicosia and various bath houses, including the Büyük Hamam with its domed hot bath in the Turkish-occupied part of Nicosia (still open to the public). Other examples of Ottoman architecture are a library, a fountain and a number of dwellings in the Turkish part of Nicosia and the aqueduct at Lárnaca.

Glossary

Abacus The upper part of the capital of a Doric column, a square slab above the echinus (☛66).

Acropolis The highest part of a Greek city, usually its religious centre.

Cathedral of St Sophia, Nicosia – now the Selimiye Mosque

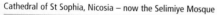

Temple of Apollo, Koúrion (reconstructed)

Agorá The market place of a Greek city, the main centre of public life; the equivalent of the Roman forum.

Ayía, Ayios Holy; (prefixed to a name) Saint.

Amphitheatre An oval arena surrounded by tiers of seating.

Anástasis Christ's Descent into Hades: the usual representation of the Resurrection in the Eastern church.

Apocrypha Biblical writings not recognised by the Western church as canonical.

Archaic art Greek art of the 7th and 6th c. BC.

Architrave A horizontal stone lintel resting on the columns of a temple.

Archivolt The under surface of an arch.

Asklepieion Sanctuary of Asklepios, the Greek god of healing.

Atrium An open courtyard in the centre of a Roman house; the forecourt of an Early Christian basilica.

Basilica A type of church with three or more aisles in which the central aisle (nave) is higher than the lateral aisles and has its own windows.

Bema The sanctuary of a Byzantine church.

Blacherniótissa A representation of the Mother of God standing in the attitude of prayer, without the Child.

Bothros A pit for offerings.

Caldarium The hot room of a Roman bath house.

Capital The moulded or carved top of a column or pillar, supporting the entablature (☛66).

Cavea The auditorium of a Roman theatre (Greek *koilon*).

Corinthian columns in the Gymnasium, Sálamis ➤

Cella The inner chamber of a temple, the holy of holies.

Chalcolithic A period transitional between the Stone and Bronze Ages (on Cyprus 3000–2300 BC).

Cippus A monumental stone or pillar.

Console A projecting bracket supporting a cornice.

Corinthian order See Orders, p. 68.

Crater A large open bowl or jar for mixing wine.

Crepidoma The three-stepped platform of a temple. See below.

Déesis In Byzantine painting, a representation of Christ between the

Doric Order | **Ionic Order** | **Corinthian Order**

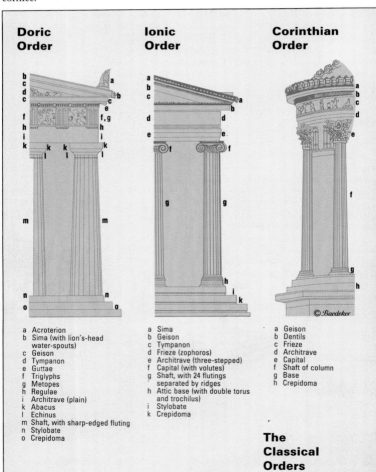

Doric Order

a Acroterion
b Sima (with lion's-head water-spouts)
c Geison
d Tympanon
e Guttae
f Triglyphs
g Metopes
h Regulae
i Architrave (plain)
k Abacus
l Echinus
m Shaft, with sharp-edged fluting
n Stylobate
o Crepidoma

Ionic Order

a Sima
b Geison
c Tympanon
d Frieze (zophoros)
e Architrave (three-stepped)
f Capital (with volutes)
g Shaft, with 24 flutings separated by ridges
h Attic base (with double torus and trochilus)
i Stylobate
k Crepidoma

Corinthian Order

a Geison
b Dentils
c Frieze
d Architrave
e Capital
f Shaft of column
g Base
h Crepidoma

The Classical Orders

Virgin and St John interceding for mankind.

Diakonikon A room on the south side of the sanctuary in an Orthodox church; sacristy.

Doric order See Orders, p. 68.

Dromos The corridor or passage leading to a tomb (on Cyprus frequently stepped).

Echinus A convex moulding under the abacus of a Doric capital (☛66).

Encaustic An ancient method of painting in which wax colours were fused to the surface.

Enkleistra Hermitage.

Entablature The superstructure carried by columns.

Forum The Roman market place and place of assembly; the equivalent of the Greek agorá.

Frieze A decorative band above the architrave of a temple; in the Doric order made up of metopes and triglyphs, in the Ionic order plain or with continuous carved decoration (☛66).

Frigidarium The cold room in a Roman bath house.

Geometric art Greek art 1050–720 BC.

Hammam Turkish bath.

Han A Turkish caravanserai or hostelry.

Hellenistic art Greek art 325–58 BC.

Hippodrome An elliptical course for chariot races.

Hodigitria A type of representation of the Mother of God as 'She who shows the Way', with the Child on her left arm.

Hypocaust An underfloor heating system in Roman houses and baths.

Hypogeum An underground vault, especially one used for burials.

Iconoclasm A movement in the Eastern church 8th and 9th c. opposed to the veneration of images.

Iconostasis A screen in a Byzantine church between the sanctuary and the main part of the church, bearing tiers of icons.

Impluvium A basin for collecting rainwater in the atrium of a Roman house.

Ionic order See Orders, p. 68.

Kantharos A fountain in the forecourt of an early Christian basilica.

Katekhoumenon A room for catechumens (unbaptised members of the congregation) in an Early Christian basilica.

Keramidion The Holy Tile (☛60).

Koimisis The Dormition (Falling Asleep) or Death of the Mother of God; the equivalent in the Eastern church of the Assumption of the Virgin.

Kore Maiden; statue of a girl.

Kouros Statue of a naked youth, characteristic of the Archaic period.

Mandílion The Holy Cloth (☛60).

Metope A rectangular panel between the triglyphs in the frieze of a Doric temple, either plain or with relief decoration (☛66).

Mihrab The prayer niche in a mosque, indicating the direction of Mecca.

Minaret The tower of a mosque, from which the muezzin issues the call to prayer.

Minbar The high pulpit in a mosque.

Muezzin The official in a mosque who calls the faithful to prayer.

Naos The enclosed chamber of a temple (the Greek equivalent of the Roman *cella*).

Narthex A rectangular entrance hall preceding the nave of a church, occupied by the unbaptised (catechumens) during services.

Nestorians Adherents of a heresy attributed to Patriarch Nestorius of Constantinople which was condemned by the Church in the 5th c.

Nymphaeum A Roman fountain house with a facade like that of a temple.

Odeion A hall (usually roofed) for musical performances.

Orchestra A circular or semicircular area between the stage and auditorium of a Greek theatre in which the chorus danced.

Orders The different styles of classical architecture, characterised by the type of columns and entablature.

1. Doric order: column without a base; shaft with (usually 20) sharp-edged flutings; capital consisting of echinus and abacus; entablature with frieze of metopes.

2. Ionic order: column standing on base; 20 flutings separated by ridges; capital with spiral volutes; architrave made up of three sections, each projecting over the one below; frieze continuous, without triglyphs.

3. Corinthian order: column base and shaft as in Ionic order; capital consisting of two rows of acanthus leaves.

The composite capital developed in Roman times, with a combination of Ionic and Corinthian elements.

Palaestra A courtyard surrounded by colonnades, a training school for physical exercises.

Panayía All Holy: the Mother of God, the Virgin.

Pantokrator Christ as the Ruler of All.

Pastophoria The rooms to left and right of the sanctuary in an Orthodox church, the diakonikon and prothesis.

Peristyle A colonnade surrounding a courtyard.

Pithos A large storage jar.

Portico A colonnade, usually in front of a building.

Propylon Gateway.

Prostyle Temple with columned portico in front.

Prothesis A room on the north side of the sanctuary in an Orthodox church in which liturgical utensils and vestments are kept.

Protome A figure used as decoration on a vase.

Pyxis A cylindrical vase.

Rhyton A drinking vessel, often in the form of an animal's head.

Scriptorium A room in a monastery for the writing or copying of manuscripts.

Sgraffito A type of ceramic or mural decoration in which the top layer of glaze or plaster is incised with a design to reveal parts of the ground.

Skene The stage building of a Greek theatre.

Stadion 1. An ancient measure of length (183 m).

2. A running track 183 m long.

3. A stadium, with a running track and embankments or benches for spectators.

Stele An upright stone slab (often a tombstone), usually with an inscription and frequently with relief carving.

Stoa A portico; a hall with columns along the front.

Stylobate The uppermost step of a temple platform (☛66).

Sudatorium The sweat bath in a Roman bath house.

Tekke The Muslim equivalent of a monastery.

Temenos A sacred precinct bounded by a wall.

Tholos A circular building, rotunda.

Triglyph A projecting member, with two vertical channels, between the metopes of the Doric order (☛66).

Volute The spiral scroll of an Ionic capital (☛66).

Heritage under Threat

The looting of Greek Orthodox churches, excavation sites and museums in Turkish-occupied Cyprus was not the first threat to Cypriot culture. The destruction began with the Ottoman conquest in 1571.

Ottoman rule

In the 16th c. the Ottoman rulers of Cyprus, who in general were tolerant of Christianity in their empire, converted the Gothic churches built during the Lusignan and Venetian periods into mosques, complete with minarets. The Cathedral of St Sophia in Nicosia became the Selimiye Mosque, St Nicholas's Cathedral in Famagusta the Lala Mustafa Pasha Mosque.

19th century

With the increasing interest in antiquities in the 19th c. the export of excavation finds began. Thus the former American consul in Cyprus, Luigi Palma di Cesnola, assembled a private collection of antiquities which was displayed in the newly founded Metropolitan Museum of Art in New York in 1872.

North Cyprus since 1974

After the invasion by Turkish troops in 1974 the occupying forces began systematically to obliterate all traces of Greek settlement; the Greek language, Greek philosophers and Greek books were banned. Apart from the historic archaeological sites of Sóloi, Vouní, Énkomi and Sálamis all Greek place names were replaced by Turkish names.

The gravest loss, and one which is irreparable, is the indiscriminate destruction of material from Greek churches, some of which has found its way on to the international art market. Hardly a single Orthodox chapel has been left unscathed, and many Greek cemeteries have been desecrated. Churches have fallen into disrepair, been used for housing sheep or goats or converted into mosques. The crosses on the roofs of churches have been torn

The ravaged church of the Panayía Kanakaría, Lythrángomi

down, the ropes for ringing the bells cut off. The monastery of St John Chrysostom at Koutsovéndis, below Buffavento Castle, is now a military post, since it affords wide views extending as far as Nicosia and the Tróodos massif. Cycles of frescos of incalculable value have been torn off the walls; icons, altars and liturgical utensils have disappeared.

One notorious instance was the sale in New York of a cycle of frescos, broken up into innumerable parts, from the former church of St Thermionaros, Famagusta. Six of the 6th c. mosaics which disappeared from the church of Panayía Kanakariá, Lythrángomi – among the finest examples of Early Christian art in the territory of the former Byzantine Empire – were rediscovered in 1989 and recovered by the Republic of Cyprus. They can now be seen in the Icon Museum in Nicosia. Only two other churches with valuable mosaics survived the iconoclastic conflict unscathed, thanks to the 300 years of Arab rule in the turmoil of the 7th–9th c.: the Panayía Kerá at Livádia (North Cyprus; looted by the Turks) and the Panayía Angelóktistos at Kíti (in the Greek Republic of Cyprus).

Folk Traditions

Religious festivals

Easter

Cypriot popular culture still holds to the old traditions. Thus Easter, the principal Orthodox church festival, has traditionally been celebrated in country areas with particular ceremony. The fast begins 50 days before Easter. In the week before Easter houses are whitewashed and spring cleaned, the *flaoúna*, a special Easter cheese pastry, is baked and on the Thursday eggs are dyed red. On Good Friday the *epitaphion*, a reproduction of Christ's shroud, is laid out under a portable canopy which is decorated by young girls with flowers and fine fabrics. The icons in the churches are covered with black cloths, and after the evening service the *epitaphion* is carried about the village.

On Easter Saturday the church is decked with flowers and the black cloths are removed from the icons. At 11pm the congregation, carrying candles, gather for the Easter night service; then at midnight the priest comes out from behind the iconostasis and pronounces the words 'Christos anesti' (Christ has risen) and lights the first candle. Outside the church a large bonfire is lit and a doll symbolising Judas is burned. Then the children announce the glad news of Christ's resurrection with noisy fire crackers. People then go home and eat the traditional Easter soup (*maryeiritsa*) made from lambs' entrails. On Easter Day families eat the Easter lamb.

Since the Orthodox Easter is determined according to the Julian calendar and that of other Christian Churches by the Gregorian calendar the two coincide only every three years.

Kurban Bayramí

Kurban Bayramí, the four-day Feast of the Sacrifice, is an important Islamic festival, celebrating God's goodness to and care for his people. The origin of this custom goes back to the Old Testament story of Abraham's sacrifice: God calls on Abraham to sacrifice his only son, Isaac, but while he is preparing to do so God intervenes again and through an angel tells him to sacrifice a lamb instead of his son. This Islamic reference to an Old Testament story reflects the common origin of the two religions in Arab territory.

At Kurban Bayramí families eat a roast sheep in accordance with a religious rite, and what is left over is given to the poor, the sick or a social welfare institution. Wealthy families, after praying in the mosque, give presents of money to charitable institutions and poor families.

Circumcision ceremony

One of the most important events in the life of male Muslims is the circumcision ceremony, which symbolises a boy's admission to the Islamic community. The reasons for the continuation of this tradition are religious, social, hygienic and sexual. About two weeks before the ceremony invitations are sent out to relations and acquaintances. Then, just before the actual ceremony, the boy is taken round the village in special garb with a red scarf, to the accompaniment of music and dancing. The circumcision itself is performed by an official circumciser (*sünnetái*). After the ceremony the boy is put to bed in a specially made nightshirt, and the celebrations continue round him. He has now been accepted into the community of men.

Crafts

In spite of changing cultural influences Cypriot folk art has preserved its own distinctive character. Traditional crafts are still practised in many villages. The folk museums of Nicosia, Yeroskípos and Páphos offer visitors an overview of the island's arts and crafts. In Nicosia, Lárnaca, Limassol and Páphos there are state handicraft centres, which give demonstrations of a great variety of crafts and also sell the products. The object of these centres is to preserve and promote the island's native arts and crafts, the raw materials for which (wood, clay, cotton, linen, silk) are all found locally.

Symbols as decoration

The elements used in the decoration of wooden chests and stands, in embroidery and in pottery decoration originally had symbolic and magical significance in the everyday life of Cypriot people; they gave expression to their view of the world and their religious beliefs. For example cypresses (as in the catacombs in Rome) and cedars were symbols of death, while a rosette symbolised the sun, and thus life. Wavy lines represented eternity, birds announced coming events and a snake meant temptation.

Wood carving

Wood carving was formerly an important craft in Cyprus, as is demonstrated by the sumptuous carved iconostases in Cypriot churches. The chapter house of Ómodhos Monastery has a magnificent carved cedarwood ceiling. Everyday household objects were made of walnut or pine. In villages such as Moutoullás wooden troughs and bread boards are still made in traditional style, and carved chests and presses remain part of the equipment of every Cypriot bride.

Textiles

Old traditions of textile manufacture are carried on in the production of woven cloths of the highest quality in geometric patterns.

In Lápithos and Karavás the culture of silkworms provides the raw material for beautiful silk fabrics. Silkworm culture was brought to Cyprus by the crusaders.

The village of Léfkara is famed for its embroidery and lace. The craft of hemstitch embroidery (*lefkarítika*), which dates back to Venetian times, is still handed down from mother to daughter.

The little village of Phití (Páphos district) is noted for its brightly patterned woven fabrics (*phithkiótika*).

Pottery

Pottery has been an important Cypriot craft since ancient times and is today produced manually in traditional style at Phiní, Kórnos and Lápithos. In the villages of Kórnos and Phiní the potters are mainly women. Phiní is noted for its large wine jars, still based on ancient types.

Basketwork

In the Páphos area and in the village of Liopétri flat baskets with brightly coloured geometric patterns are made in traditional fashion. The materials used are reeds and palm fronds.

Icon painting

Even during the period of Ottoman rule the tradition of icon painting was maintained, and the craft has been preserved in its authentic form down to the present day. The nuns in the convent of Ayios Minás (Léfkara) make a contribution to the cost of running the convent with their icon painting. The Chrysorroyiátissa and Ayios Alemános monasteries are also famed for their icons.

Metalwork

The origins of metalworking on Cyprus can be traced back to the Chalcolithic period. Traditional goldsmiths' and silversmiths' work is mainly produced nowadays in Léfkara, Limassol and Nicosia. The Orthodox churches of Cyprus have fine silver lamps and richly decorated metal candlesticks.

Costumes

Cypriots now wear ordinary European dress, and traditional costumes are seen only in folk performances, on major festivals and occasionally in villages.

The traditional women's dress consists of a cotton or silk undergarment and baggy trousers, over which is worn a cotton dress (*sayia*), in colours and patterns which vary from village to village. The dress is drawn in by a diagonally folded square of cloth by way of a belt. On their head the village women wear a headscarf (*mantíla*). The dress in towns is different, usually consisting of a long skirt, a short low-necked bodice over a white blouse, a short jacket and a fez.

The men's costume consists of baggy black trousers (*vraka*) reaching down to the knee and held up by a woven belt (*sostra*) – still common in the villages – with a white shirt, an embroidered waistcoat and high black boots.

Folk dances

Cypriot folk dances are generally similar to Greek dances. Men and women dance separately. Two types of dance can be distinguished – the measured tread of the *syrtós* dances and the vigorous movements of the *pidik* dances. The *syrtáki*, the best known Greek dance, is also performed in Cyprus.

Greek costumes

One typical Cypriot dance is the *potíri*, which is performed in every bouzouki taverna. Great skill is required for this as the dancer balances anything up to 20 glasses on his head.

In the *syrtós antikristós* men and women dance opposite one another. The men's steps show agility, strength and courage; the women's movements are restrained and graceful.

In the *zeibékkiko* dance the women balance water jars on their heads and are courted by the men. At first they are coy, but later show themselves ready to flirt with the men.

The *drépani* is danced by men carrying scythes, in a simulation of harvesting wheat.

The *Nikolís* dance tells the story of Nikolís, a great lady's man, who is made fun of by his friends. They stick a newspaper in his belt and try to set light to it, while Nikolís eludes them by his skill and agility.

The *soústa* is a round dance for both sexes in which each performer in turn must dance solo in the centre of the ring.

Folk music

As early as the 10th c. wandering minstrels such as the ballad singers of Europe were travelling round Cyprus and passing on the latest news in their songs. These *poietárides*, who came from the villages of south-eastern Cyprus, have continued to influence Cypriot poetry.

The folk music of the present day takes as its themes both historical events and topics of current interest. The singer is accompanied by the bouzouki (an instrument resembling a lute), the *sandoúri* (a kind of dulcimer), the violin and the flute.

The folk music of the Turkish Cypriots comes from the little villages of Anatolia but is accompanied by instruments similar to those which accompany the Greek singers – the *bozuk* (a stringed instrument) and the *kaval* (flute). Western influences began to arrive in the 19th c.

Literature

Ancient Greek poetry

The Cypriots have maintained since ancient times that Cyprus was the home

The *potíri* dance

of Greece's great epic poet Homer. Euklos, a Cypriot poet of the 8th/7th c. BC, claims that Homer was born in Sálamis and concludes therefore that Cyprus was the cradle of Greek literature. An ancient epic poem, which is preserved only in fragments, the Kypria, is attributed either to Homer or to the Cypriot poet Stasinos (8th/7th c.); it deals with events preceding those described in the *Iliad*. The Cypriot king Kinyras, who according to Homer was the first priest-king of Páphos, is said to have been a great lyric poet.

Folk poetry

From the Middle Ages onwards folk poems were written on historic themes and love poems in the Cypriot dialect. In the 19th c. folk poetry took on a new lease of life in Cyprus. Vassilis Mikhailides and Dimitris Lipertis wrote in Cypriot dialect.

Greek Cypriot literature

Modern Cypriot literature is closely associated with the literature of mainland Greece, and the Cypriot dialect has given place to modern Greek. The best known representative of modern Cypriot writing is Costas Mondis, who after serving as director of the Cyprus Tourism Organisation founded Cyprus's first professional theatre, the Lyriko. The most important contemporary prose writer is Ikonomides Iannis Stavrinos.

Turkish Cypriot literature

Turkish Cypriots have had a number of notable writers, including Aziz Ibrahim and Yasin Mehmet. The poems of Yasin Nese have been set to music as nursery rhymes.

Quotations

Herodotus
Greek historian (5th c. BC)
Onesilus, being now king of Sálamis, sought to bring about a revolt of the whole of Cyprus. All were prevailed on except the Amathusians, who refused to listen to him; whereupon Onesilus sate down before Amathûs and laid siege to it . . .

Tidings came to Onesilus, the Sálaminian, who was still besieging Amathûs, that a certain Artybius, a Persian, was looked for to arrive in Cyprus with a great Persian armament. So Onesilus, when the news reached him, sent off heralds to all parts of Ionia and besought the Ionians to give him aid. After brief deliberation these last in full force passed over into the island; and the Persians about the same time crossed in their ships from Cilicia and proceeded by land to attack Sálamis; while the Phoenicians, with the fleet, sailed round the promontory which goes by the name of the Keys of Cyprus . . .

By sea the Ionians, who that day fought as they have never done either before or since, defeated the Phoenicians, the Samians especially distinguishing themselves. Meanwhile the combat had begun on land, and the two armies were engaged in a sharp struggle, when thus it fell out in the matter of the generals. Artybius, astride upon his horse, charged down upon Onesilus, who, as he had agreed with his shield-bearer, aimed his blow at the rider; the horse reared and placed his fore feet upon the shield of Onesilus, when the Carian cut at him with a reaping-hook and severed the two legs from the body. The horse fell upon the spot, and Artybius, the Persian general, with him.
Book V of Herodotus' *History* (translation by George Rawlinson, 1858)

Wilbrand von Oldenburg
German pilgrim (13th c.)
The island is extremely fertile and produces excellent wine. It lies near the Cyclades but is not one of them. Its length is four days' journey, its breadth more than two. It has high mountains. There is one archbishop, who has three suffragans. These are Latins; but the Greeks, over whom throughout this land the Latins have dominion, have thirteen bishops, of whom one is an archbishop. They all obey the Franks and pay tribute like slaves. Whence you can see that the Franks are lords of this land, whom the Greeks and Armenians obey as serfs. They are rude in all their habits, and shabby in their dress, sacrificing chiefly to their lusts. We shall ascribe this to the wine of the country, which provokes to luxury, or rather to those who drink it. It is for this reason that Venus was said to be worshipped in Cyprus . . . For the wines of this island are so thick and rich that they are sometimes specially prepared to be eaten like honey with bread. Cyprus rears many wild asses and rams, stags and hinds; but it has no lions, bears or wolves, or other dangerous beasts.
The journal of a pilgimage in 1211 (first published 1653)

Sir John Mandeville
English writer (d 1372?)
Cipres is a good yle and a great, and there are many good cities, and there is an Archbishoppe at Nichosy, and foure other Bishops in the lande. And at Famagost is one of the best havens on the sea that is in the worlde, and there are christen men and Sarasins and men of all nations. In Cipres is the hill of the holy crosse, and there is the crosse of the good thefe Dismas, as I sayd before, and some wene that there is halfe of the crosse of our lord, but it is not so, and they do wrong that make men to believe so. In Cipres lieth S Simeon, of whome the men of the countrey make a great solempnitie, and in the Castell of Amours lyeth the body of Saint Hillarion, and men kepe it worshipfully, and beside Famagost was sainct Barnarde [Barnabas] borne.
The Voiage and Travayle of Syr John Maundeville Knight (a compilation based on earlier travellers' accounts)

John Locke
English pilgrim (16th c.)
The second of October we returned to Arnacho (Lárnaca), where we rested untill the sixth day. This towne is a pretie village, there are thereby toward the sea divers monuments, that that there hath bene great overthrow of

buildings, for to this day there is no yere when they finde not, digging under ground, either coines, caves, and sepulchres of antiquities, as we walking, did see many, so that in effect, all alongst the seacoast, throughout the whole Island, there is much ruine and overthrow of buildings; for, as they say, it was disinhabited sixe and thirtie yeres before Saint Helens time for lacke of water. And since that time it hath bene ruinated and overthrowen by Richard the first of that name, king of England, which he did in revenge of his sisters ravagement comming to Jerusalem, the which inforcement was done to her by the king of Famagusta.

The sixt day we rid to Nicosia, which is from Arnacho seven Cyprus miles, which are one and twentie Italian miles. This is the ancientest citie of the Island and is walled about, but it is not strong neither of walles nor of situation. It is by report three Cyprus miles about, it is not thoroughly inhabited, but hath many great gardens in it, and also very many Date trees, and plentie of Pomegranates and other fruites. There dwell all the Gentilitie of the Island, and there hath every Cavallier and Conte of the Island an habitation ... The streetes of the citie are not paived, which maketh it, with the quantitie of the gardens, to seeme but a rurall habitation. But there be many faire buildings in the Citie, there be also monasteries both of Frank and Greekes.

An account of a visit to Cyprus in 1553, included in Richard Hakluyt's *Principal Navigations Voyages and Discoveries of the English Nation* (1589).

Nikos Kazantzákis
Greek writer (1885–1957)

Cyprus is the true home of Aphrodite. Never have I seen an island with such a feminine character; never have I breathed an air so full of dangerous, most sweet temptations. I feel slightly dazed, sleepy and well content, and towards evening, when the sun goes down and the wind blows in from the sea, and to right and left the sailing cutters begin to pitch and toss and the children with their bunches of jasmine flock on to the quay, my heart looses its girdle and yields itself up like Pandemos Aphrodite. What elsewhere you sense only in moments of enchantment you sense here all the time; you feel the fragrance of jasmine slowly permeating your being.

Descriptions of Palestine and Cyprus

Sights from A to Z

Suggested Routes

The following routes – all day trips – are intended as suggestions to guide visitors in planning a visit to Cyprus, leaving them free to select and vary the routes in accordance with their particular interests. Except where otherwise indicated, all the routes are on asphalt roads.

The suggested routes take in all the main tourist sights in Cyprus; but not all the places of interest described in this guide lie directly on the routes, and to see some of them it will be necessary to make detours from the main route.

The suggested routes can be followed on the map enclosed with this guide, which will help with detailed planning.

North and South Cyprus
Since the Green Line between North and South Cyprus can be crossed only in Nicosia, the suggested routes are described separately for the two parts of the island. Visitors taking a day trip from the Greek part of the island into the Turkish-occupied north must be back by 6pm at latest. It is advisable, therefore, to make Nicosia the base for trips into North Cyprus.

In these routes the names of places which are the subject of a separate entry in the Sights from A to Z of the guide are given in **bold** type.

The distances given in brackets at the head of each route are approximate figures for the main route, taking no account of detours or alternatives.

South Cyprus

1. Nicosia to Asínou and Kakopetriá and back (140 km)

Leave **Nicosia** on the road which runs west to **Peristeróna** (28 km) with the important five-domed church of SS Hilarion and Barnabas. From there continue on the main road into the **Tróodos massif** and then, 4 km beyond Astromerítis, take a narrow road on the left which leads south to Nikitári and Asínou. After passing the little barn-roofed church of Vizakiá it comes to Nikitári. Ask in the *kafeníon* for the local priest (*papas*), who has the key of the church of **Asínou** (4 km from the village), with its magnificently restored frescos of the 12th and 14th c.

From Nikitári return to the main road by way of Páno Koutraphás and turn left. 18 km beyond the junction is **Galáta**, which once had seven churches. Particularly worth seeing are two adjoining barn-roofed churches, the Panayía tis Podíthou, with unusually well preserved frescos, and the church of the Archangel Michael.

Beyond Galáta is **Kakopetriá**, the old part of which is protected as a national monument (restaurants and coffee houses). 5 km south-west is the church of Ayios Nikólaos tis Stéyis, St Nicholas of the Roof.

The return to Nicosia is on the main road. From the road, which runs close to the border with North Cyprus, guard posts can be seen on the hills.

2. Nicosia to Tamassós and Makherás and back (70 km)

Leave Nicosia on the road which runs south-west to Palekhóri. At Káto Dhefterá, in a rock face to the right of the road, is the cave church of the Panayía Chrysospiliótissa, which is well worth a visit.

From Káto Dhefterá the road goes south to Péra, near which can be found the site of ancient **Tamassós**, with tombs and the remains of temples dating from the 7th c. BC 1.5 km west of Péra, in the village of Politikó, stands the convent of Ayios Iraklidhios (St Heraclidius).

From Péra a road runs south by way of Kambiá and Kapédhes to the monastery of **Makherás** (16 km), picturesquely situated in the foothills (800 m) of the Tróodos massif. The monastery was founded in the 12th c. after the discovery of a legendary icon of the Mother of God.

The return to Nicosia is either on the same route as on the outward journey or on a road west via Lazaniá to Goúrri

◄ Evening at the Sanctuary of Apollo Hylátes, Koúrion

Pétra tou Romioú, the birthplace of Aphrodite ►

(partly unsurfaced) to rejoin the main road from Palekhóri to Nicosia.

Detour
From Lazaniá it is worth making a short detour (unsurfaced road) to the village of **Phikárdhou**. Recently restored, it displays typical 18th c. village architecture.

3. Nicosia to Limassol (140 km)

Leave Nicosia either on the ordinary road or on the motorway to **Limassol**. In 17 km there is an exit from the motorway to the village of Perakhório, with a small church containing 12th c. frescos. From Perakhório the motorway continues south to the exit for **Stavrovoúni**. Commandingly situated on its hill, the monastery of Stavrovoúni, the oldest and strictest (women not admitted) in Cyprus, can be seen from far away. In clear weather there is a magnificent view from the summit of the hill, extending over terraced slopes to the coast. 14 km further down the motorway a road goes off to **Léfkara**, famed for its handmade lace and embroidery. From Léfkara the road continues south-west by way of Vávla to **Khirokitía**, where excavations have brought to light the remains of one of the oldest Neolithic settlements on the island. From here the motorway continues to Limassol, Cyprus's second largest town. Shortly before reaching the town it is well worth while making a detour to the remains of Amathoús, one of the city-kingdoms of ancient Cyprus.

4. Lárnaca via Ayía Nápa to Dherínia and back (110 km)

From **Lárnaca**, the point of arrival for most visitors flying to Cyprus, the coast road runs east to **Ayía Nápa** (37 km), a former fishing village which is now the most popular seaside resort on the island. From the beach of fine golden sand can be seen, 8 km away, Cape Gréco, the imposing crag which rises out of the sea at the south-easterly tip of Cyprus. The coast road continues to the hotel town of Protarás and Paralímni, passing innumerable windmills, which draw up water to irrigate the extensive fields of grain and vegetables. From Dherínia, near the border with Turkish-occupied territory, there is a view of the ghost town of Varósha, only a few kilometres away. It was the hotel district of **Famagusta** before the Turkish invasion in 1974.

The return route to Lárnaca is by way of Sotíra and Liopétri, famed for its basketwork.

Alternative
If the round trip is done from Ayía Nápa the distance is 55 km.

5. Lárnaca to Pyrgá, Khirokitía and Kíti and back (140 km)

Leave Lárnaca on the motorway to Limassol and at Kalókhorio turn off into a road on the right which runs via Ayía Anna to the village of **Pyrgá** (21 km), with the historic Royal Chapel. From here the route continues south on the old Nicosia–Limassol road. A detour can be made on a steep hill road (10 km) to the monastery of **Stavrovoúni** (see Route 3).

In another 14 km take a road on the right to **Léfkara**, famed for its hand-made lace and embroidery.

From Léfkara the route continues by way of Vávla to **Khirokitía**, the oldest settlement on Cyprus. Then back to the motorway, and in a few kilometres take the exit for Lárnaca. In 4 km take a road on the right signposted to Menoyía, which runs through beautiful scenery via Alaminós and Mazotós to **Kíti** (short stretch of unsurfaced road), with the church of the Panayía Angelóktistos and its magnificent 6th c. mosaic. From Kíti it is a short distance to the Salt Lake of Lárnaca, on the shores of which is the **Hala Sultan Tekke**, attractively situated amid palms and cypresses. Just beyond this is Lárnaca.

Alternative: Lárnaca to Limassol
Leave Lárnaca on the road signposted to the airport, Hala Sultan Tekke and Kíti; then back to the main Limassol road, from which detours can be made to Léfkara, Khirokitía and, shortly before reaching Limassol, the site of ancient Amathoús. Distance about 110 km.

6. Limassol to Plátres and Ólympos and back (130 km)

From **Limassol** take the bypass to the Tróodos/Ypsonas exit, from which a road leads 40 km north through beautiful scenery to the hill resort of Páno Plátres in the **Tróodos massif** with its inviting tavernas and coffee houses. 7 km higher up is Tróodos, the highest village on the island, well equipped with hotels and tavernas and pleasantly cool in the hot summer months, a good base for walks and climbs in the hills (Sights from A to Z, Tróodos massif). From here take the road to Pródhromos and turn off into a side road on the left which leads to the highest peak in the Tróodos massif, Mount Ólympos (1951 m). From here there are magnificent views of the whole mountain range, extending in clear weather as far as the coast.

On the way back a detour can be made to the legendary monastery of Troodhítissa, a place of pilgrimage for childless couples.

Soon after Páno Plátres take the road to Ómodhos, with another interesting monastery. From Ómodhos the route continues through extensive vineyards by way of Kissoúsa, Ayios Amvrósios and Káto Kivídhes to join the coast road. On the way back to Limassol a visit to the medieval castle of **Kolóssi**, once held by the Knights of St John, is recommended.

Alternative: Limassol to Asínou and back
Follow the road into the Tróodos massif, described above, as far as **Kakopetriá**, with its picturesque old town and the church of Ayios Nikólaos tis Stéyis (fine frescos). Further north is **Galáta** with its barn-roofed churches. 4 km beyond this take a road on the right, signposted to Nikitári, which leads to the early medieval church of **Asínou** with its fine Byzantine wall paintings. Distance about 180 km.

7. Limassol to Kolóssi and Koúrion and back (36 km)

This route takes in the most interesting sights around Limassol.

Leave Limassol by way of Archbishop Makarios Avenue or Franklin Roosevelt Street, on the road to **Páphos**. The road runs through large citrus plantations and comes in 10 km to **Kolóssi**, with the medieval castle of the Knights of St John.

6 km beyond this, on a plateau to the left of the road, are the excavated remains of ancient **Koúrion**.

A few kilometres further west on the Páphos road are the remains of the ancient sanctuary of Apollo.

On the way back the interesting Koúrion Museum in Episkopí can be visited. There is a good beach at Koúrion.

Alternative: Limassol to Páphos
From Limassol take the road to Kolóssi and Koúrion, and from there continue on the coast road, passing Pétra tou Romioú, the legendary rock marking the spot where Aphrodite emerged from the foam. A few kilometres further west is **Koúklia**, with the most important shrine of Aphrodite in the ancient world. Beyond this are **Yeroskípos**, with the domed church of Ayía Paraskeví, and Páphos, with its many ancient remains. Distance about 70 km.

8. Round trip from Páno Plátres through the Tróodos massif (100 km)

Leave Páno Plátres on the road to Tróodos and from there continue on the Nicosia road, passing **Kakopetriá** and **Galáta**. At Káto Koutraphás take a road on the right to Nikitári and ask for the priest (*papas*), who takes visitors to the church of **Asínou**, outside the little town.

On the way back it is worth making a detour to Vizakiá, which has a small barn-roofed church. Then back to the Tróodos–Nicosia road, which leads to Kakopetriá.

Galáta and Kakopetriá have interesting barn-roofed churches with wall paintings. From Kakopetriá the road returns to Páno Plátres.

Alternative: into the eastern Tróodos
This route passes through beautiful scenery; the roads are narrow, with many bends.

From Páno Plátres take the road running up to Tróodos and from there continue on the road to Kakopetriá, turning off in 7 km onto the road to Kyperoúnda and Khandriá. From here the road continues to **Lagoudherá**, a well situated old mountain village with a notable monastic church. Then back to Khandriá, passing vineyards and fruit orchards, and from there via Polystipos to **Platanistása**, where the custodian of the barn-roofed church of Stavrós tou Ayiasmáti can be picked up. From Platanistása a narrow road runs via Alona and Askás to Palekhóri (fine wall paintings); then back to Khandriá and Páno Plátres.

From Limassol
From Limassol take the main road into the Tróodos massif by way of Káto Amíandos. Distance about 180 km.

9. Páphos to the Akámas peninsula and back (110 km)

Leave **Páphos** on the Pólis road (Tombs of the Kings Street), which runs past the Tombs of the Kings and comes to Emba, with an interesting little church. 10 km from Páphos, on higher ground, is St **Neóphytos** Monastery (16th c.), with the 12th c. cave hermitage (Enkleistra) of Neóphytos.

From here return to Emba and follow the coast road (rewarding detour to picturesque Coral Bay) to Péyia and the basilicas of Ayios Yeóryios. Near the basilicas is an attractive taverna from which there are fine views of the little port of Péyia and the coast. From here a detour can be made to Lara Bay (beautiful beach; protected area for turtles), on the unsurfaced road to the Akámas peninsula.

From Péyia the route continues via Káthikas and Droúsha to **Pólis**, on a beautiful road with fine views of the vineyards, the sea and the Tróodos massif. The quiet little town of Pólis, unlike other coastal towns, has remained unspoiled by tourism; it has no large hotels and is patronised mainly by backpackers. From here the route continues by way of the little port of Lakhí to the Baths of Aphrodite (6 km), amid rocky coastal scenery. There is an attractive walk along the promontory to the Fontana Amorosa, Aphrodite's Fountain of Love. Then return to Páphos on the main road.

10. Walks in the Tróodos massif

See Sights from A to Z South Cyprus, Tróodos massif.

North Cyprus

1. Nicosia to Kyrenia and back (70 km)

From **Nicosia** a new road cuts through the Pentadáktylos hills to the north coast. 20 km from Nicosia, just beyond a pass, take a road on the left which runs through a military area to **St Hilarion**, the best preserved castle in the Pentadáktylos hills. From the hill on which it stands there are fine views of the idyllically situated small town of Kyrenia and the surrounding hills. After visiting Kyrenia, until 1974 a flourishing tourist resort, with a picturesque harbour and castle, take the road signposted to **Bellapais** (6 km south-east), where many British people still have houses. Bellapais Abbey is the finest Gothic monastic ruin in the Mediterranean area. From here a narrow road leads west to join the main road back to Nicosia.

From Famagusta
Leave Famagusta on the Nicosia road and at Trakhóni/Demirhan turn right into a road which runs north to Kyrenia. Distance ca 180 km.

From Kyrenia
The round trip from Kyrenia to St Hilarion Castle and Bellapais Abbey is about 30 km.

2. Nicosia to Famagusta and Sálamis and back (120 km)

From Nicosia take the expressway that runs east to the port of **Famagusta** (61 km), with its old town surrounded by Venetian walls. From here the coast road runs 8 km north to the world-famous excavations of ancient **Sálamis**, once the most powerful of the city-kingdoms of Cyprus. A few kilometres west of the necropolis of Sálamis, the largest cemetery area on the island, is the abandoned monastery of St Barnabas, which is well worth a visit. Before returning to Nicosia on the more northerly of the two main roads from Famagusta a visit should be made to the site of ancient Enkomi, near Tuzla.

From Famagusta
Kantara Castle in the Pentadáktylos hills. Distance about 90 km.

From Kyrenia
From Kyrenia take the coast road running east, which in 10 km turns south through the Pentadáktylos hills to join the more northerly Nikosia–Famagusta road at Trakhóni/Demirhan. Then as described above. Distance ca 150 km.

3. Nicosia to Mórphou, Sóloi and Vouní and back (120 km)

Take the road which goes west from Nicosia and at Skylloúra/Yílmazköy turn into a road on the left to Philiá/Serhadköy. (An alternative route is to continue on the main road to Myrtou/Camlíbel and from there take a road on the left to Mórphou). The road runs south-west via Káto Kopiá/Zümrütköy to the little town of Mórphou, with the abandoned church of St Mamas and an interesting small museum. 12 km west on the coast road is Karavostási/Gemikonagí. Above the village is the site of ancient **Sóloi**, with a restored Roman theatre and the remains of an Early Christian basilica. From here a road ascends, with many bends, to the palace of **Vouní** (5 km), on a hill (250 m) from which in clear weather the view reaches to the coast of Turkey. The return to Nicosia is by way of Mórphou and then on the new expressway.

From Kyrenia
Leave **Kyrenia** on the coast road to the west, which in 8 km passes the Peace Monument, commemorating the Turkish landings in 1974. At Myrtou/Camlíbel turn right into the road to Mórphou/Güzelyurt. Then as described above. Distance ca 120 km.

4: Tour of the Karpasía peninsula from Famagusta (230 km)

Leave **Famagusta** on the road which leads north past the remains of ancient **Sálamis** to Tríkomo/Iskele. From here there is an attractive detour (30 km there and back) to **Kantara Castle** on a winding road that runs up into the Pentadáktylos hills, passing endless olive groves and lonely hill villages. The romantic ruins of Kantara Castle (signposted) lie on the summit of a hill, overgrown by grass and trees. From here there is a superb view of the long, narrow Karpasía peninsula with its cliff coast and idyllic coves.

From Tríkomo/Iskele the route continues on the coast road and then turns inland by way of Livádhia/Sazlíköy to Lythrángomi/Boltaslí. It then continues via Ayía Triás to the largest place on the peninsula, Rizokárpaso/Dipkarpaz (30 km). From here there is an attractive detour to Cape Andréas, with beautiful bathing beaches. On the way back there is another possible detour from Rizokárpaso/Dipkarpaz to the church of Ayios Phílon and the ancient site of Aphéndrika. Then back to Famagusta on the main road.

Sights from A to Z South Cyprus

To make it easier to locate the places listed in the Sights from A to Z section of the guide, their coordinates on the fold-out map are shown at the head of each entry.

Asínou E 5/6

Ασίνου
Altitude: 450 m

Halfway between Nicosia and Tróodos a road goes off on the left to the village of Nikitári, 4 km south of which is the isolated barn-roofed church of Asínou, with magnificent wall paintings; the key is held by the village priest in Nikitári. On Sundays and public holidays this is a very popular resort with the people of Cyprus.

Until the medieval period there was a small town called Asínou here, thought to have been founded in the 11th c. BC by settlers from the ancient city of Asine in the Argolid (Peloponnese).

★★Church of the Panayía Phorviótissa

The church, built in the early 12th c., belonged to the monastery of Phorvia, which survived until the 16th c. The name Phorvia comes from the euphorbias (spurges) which are common in this area. After the destruction of the monastery the name was transferred to the church.

The barrel-vaulted church has an apse at the east end. The narthex, added at the end of the 12th c., has apsidal projections on each side. While the church itself is built of undressed stone, the narthex has walls of ashlar.

Inscriptions and portrait of donor
An inscription under the painting of

The church at Asínou, with restored wall paintings inside

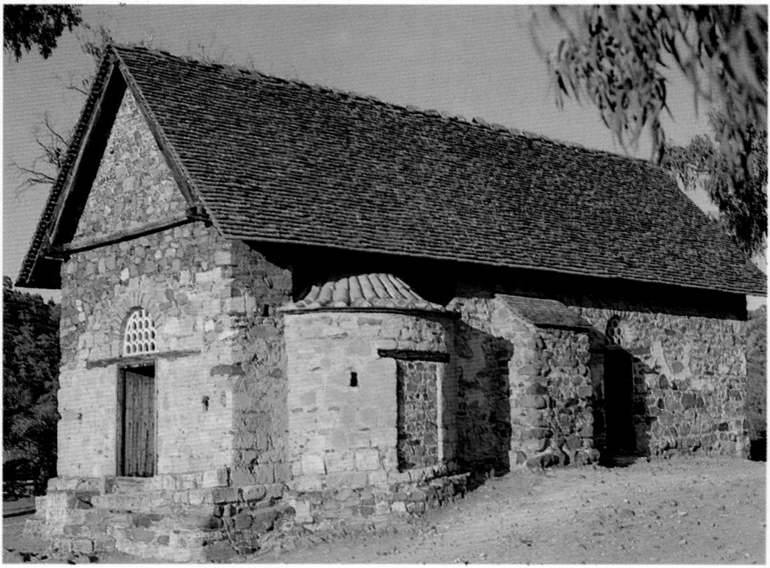

SS Constantine and Helen records that the church was built and the walls painted at the expense of Nikephoros Magistros in 1105/6. The Byzantine title of *magistros* was borne by a high official or judge.

Under the painting of St George is another inscription giving the donor's name as Nikephoros, owner of a racing stable. A third inscription over the doorway of the narthex gives the date 1333, with Theophilos as donor; at that time the paintings in the church and narthex were renewed.

A painting of the early 14th c. over the south doorway of the church shows Nikephoros Magistros presenting the church to the Mother of God.

Wall paintings

The wall paintings have been excellently restored by the Dumbarton Oaks Institute of Harvard University. Two main phases can be distinguished, the early 12th c. and the 14th c.

Early 12th c. The paintings of this period, which date from about 1105/6, are in the sanctuary and the western part of the naos. In the vault of the apse, in accordance with Byzantine tradition, is the Mother of God as Theotokos (God-Bearer), with arms raised in prayer, flanked by the Archangels Michael and Gabriel (overpainted in 14th c.). Under her is the Communion of the Apostles (a reference to the Last Supper), in which Christ gives bread and wine to the apostles, with Judas turning his back on Christ and taking the bread out of his mouth.

In the lowest zone are six Fathers of the Church, symbolising the timelessness of the Church. In niches flanking the apse are the Birth of the Virgin and the Presentation of the Virgin in the Temple.

The west bay of the church, separated off by rectangular piers, also has 12th c. paintings. In the vault is the Descent of the Holy Ghost (Pentecost). On the south wall is the Raising of Lazarus. Below the painting of Constantine and Helen (who were canonised by the Eastern Church) are other Orthodox saints.

On the west wall are the Entry into Jerusalem, the Last Supper and the Dormition of the Mother of God (Koimisis). On the north wall, below the Washing of the Feet, are the 40 Martyrs of Sebaste, frozen to death on an ice-covered lake.

14th c. The rest of the church has 14th c. paintings. On the vaulting above the south doorway are the Nativity of Christ, the Presentation in the Temple, the Baptism and the Transfiguration. On the opposite side are the Betrayal (Judas's Kiss), the Bearing of the Cross, the Crucifixion and the Entombment. In the lowest zone are various Orthodox saints. On the piers between the central and west bays are Peter and Paul, the Princes of the Apostles.

In the narthex are St George, St Mamas on his lion and St Anastasia. In the dome is Christ Pantokrator surrounded by angels. Below him are scenes from the Last Judgment.

Surroundings

Vizakiá

6 km north of Asínou on the road to Nicosia is the small village church of Vizakiá (key in house next to church), with 16th c. wall paintings which are of interest for their naive but impressive style. The paintings, which date from the Venetian period and show clear western influence, depict scenes from the life of Christ.

On the south wall are the Annunciation, the Nativity, the Presentation in the Temple, the Baptism and the Raising of Lazarus. The central painting on the west wall is the Crucifixion; the soldier who is piercing Christ's side with his spear is dressed in the style of a Venetian noble. Below this are the Washing of the Feet, the Last Supper, the Betrayal and the Descent from the Cross.

An example of the naive and very lively narrative style of the paintings is the Last Supper, in which the disciples are holding forks. In the representation of the Betrayal the soldiers have Venetian swords.

★Ayía Nápa F 11/12

Αγία Νάπα
Altitude: sea level
Population: 2000

The popular seaside resort of Ayía Nápa lies 40 km east of Lárnaca in a bay bounded on the south-east by Cape

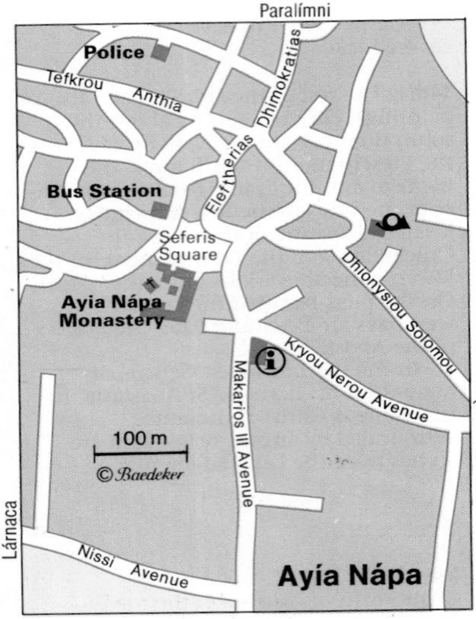

Gréco and on the west by Cape Pýla. Beyond the Green Line between the Greek and the Turkish-occupied parts of the island is the former hotel town of Varósha, now a ghost town (☛Sights from A to Z North Cyprus, Famagusta).

Ayía Nápa, formerly a small fishing village, takes its name from the monastery of Ayía Nápa, the town's principal tourist sight. It lies in one of the most fertile agricultural areas on the island (fruit and vegetables). The area is also known Kokkinokhoria (red villages) on account of the reddish-brown soil.

★Resort
After the Turkish invasion of 1974, which left the Famagusta hotel district of Varósha in Turkish hands, Ayía Nápa developed in a very short time into the most popular seaside resort in southern Cyprus. Numerous new hotel complexes mushroomed, and the town now has more than 10,000 beds available for visitors. With its beautiful sandy beaches – a rarity on the island – its varied coastal scenery and its facilities for all kinds of water sports it offers everything the holidaymaker can wish for. The tourist facilities – tavernas, bars, souvenir shops, discos and other

Beautifully decorated well in the monastery of Ayía Nápa

entertainment – cater for most needs. Only the harbour with its old tavernas still recalls the former fishing village.

★Monastery of Ayía Nápa

In the centre of the town, on Makarios III Avenue, is the monastery of Ayía Nápa, now an ecumenical conference centre for the World Council of Churches.

The monastery is dated by an inscription to the year 1530, during the period of Venetian rule. According to legend the church was built on the spot where a hunter found the legendary icon of the Mother of God in a grotto. Situated in a densely wooded area, the monastery was dedicated to Our Lady of the Forests, Ayía Nápa. The present buildings date mainly from the Venetian period; the bell tower is modern.

In the centre of the monastery courtyard, in a domed fountain house, there is an octagonal fountain basin decorated with garlands and Cupids, and with the heads of a man and a woman, presumed to be the founders of the monastery. Round the courtyard are the conventual buildings, with pointed arcades – a feature characteristic of crusader Gothic. Facing the south entrance is a two-storey gatehouse with Renaissance-style windows. Steps lead down to the cave church below, the grotto in which the icon of the Mother of God is believed to have been found.

In front of the monastery stands a centuries-old mulberry fig tree, a tree of North African origin which is thought to have been planted during the period of Lusignan rule. The fruit is edible.

Surroundings

Cape Gréco
8 km east of Ayía Nápa is Cape Gréco, the south-eastern tip of the island. Many ships have been wrecked on this rugged crag rising sheer out of the sea. At the tip of the cape is a radar station. There is good walking along the cliff coastline.

Paralímni and Protarás
Paralímni and Protarás have developed

Cape Gréco – the south-eastern tip of Cyprus

Chrysorroyiátissa Monastery

in recent years into popular holiday resorts. Between the two villages is the Valley of Windmills. The windmills (which are still there) used to draw up the ground water needed for the irrigation of the fields of potatoes and other vegetables. Since the water table has fallen considerably as a result of years of drought, the irrigation is now performed by power pumps.

Dherínia
From a viewing terrace in the village of Dherínia, which lies just inside the border with North Cyprus, there is a view over the Green Line of Famagusta and the abandoned and dilapidated hotels of Varósha.

Liopétri
The village of Liopétri, a little way inland, is famed for its basketry. The octagonal-domed church of Ayios Andrónikos dates from the 15th c.

Potamós
14 km west of Ayía Nápa is the harbour of Potamós, with small tavernas which serve excellent fish. It is reached on a road which runs down to the coast from **Xylophágou**.

Dhekélia
The British Sovereign Base of Dhekélia lies to the west of Ayía Nápa.

Chrysorroyiátissa Monastery F 3

Μονή Χρυσορρωγιατίσσης
Altitude: 850 m

From the Páphos–Pólis road, just before Stroumbí, the road to Polémi goes off on the right and climbs through the Tróodos massif to the Chrysorroyiátissa Monastery (40 km), the present buildings of which date from the 18th and 20th c. From here there are fine views of the gently sloping vineyards in the surrounding area.

Foundation legends
The origins of the monastery go back to 1152, when, in a cave near Yeroskípos, a monk named Ignatius is said to have salvaged an icon, unscathed, from a blazing fire.

Another story relates that during the iconoclastic conflict of the 8th and 9th c. a woman threw the icon into the sea at Constantinople, from where it was carried by the sea to Cyprus and washed ashore. There it was found by a fisherman, who hid it in a cave. Later a monastery was founded to house the icon, which was believed to have been painted by Luke the Evangelist, and dedicated to Our Lady of the Hill of the Golden Pomegranate.

History
During the period of Turkish rule the monastery was impoverished and fell into ruin, until in the 18th c. the bishop of Páphos built a new monastery. When the abbot supported the Greek struggle for independence in 1821 the Turkish authorities sent troops who destroyed much of the site.

Church
In the church, which is surrounded by a two-storey range of cells, is the wonder-working icon of the Mother of God, which is credited with the power of healing the sick and protecting criminals. Every year on August 15th (by the Julian calendar) the feast of the Dormition of the Mother of God is

celebrated with great splendour. The carved iconostasis dates from the 18th c. The church has a fine silver-plated cross, discovered by a local shepherd in 1970.

Winery
In the cellars visitors can see the monastery's own winemaking establishment with its huge oak casks. Excellent wine (☛Practical Information, South Cyprus, Wine) is made here by traditional methods, using Cypriot types of grape which were not attacked by phylloxera (Xynisteri white grapes and Ophthalmo, Mavron and Maratheftiko red grapes).

Surroundings

Ayía Moní
3 km south stands the Ayía Moní, a small daughter house of Chrysorroyiátissa which is no longer occupied by monks and is used as a guest house. The monastery is claimed to have been built in the 4th c. on the site of an ancient temple of Hera. Stones from ancient buildings are incorporated in the structure of the monastery, which was renovated in the 17th and 19th c.

Páno Panayiá
3 km north of Chrysorroyiátissa lies the village of Páno Panayiá. Here, in 1913, the future archbishop and president Makarios was born in a house (now a museum) which had just two rooms where the family lived, ate and slept, with a stall to the rear for the livestock. Photographs illustrate Makarios's life, while the simple household objects show how modestly the future archbishop's family lived.

Galáta E/F 5

Γαλάτα
Altitude: 600–620 m

55 km south-west of Nicosia on the main road to Tróodos, in the valley of the Karyótis river, is the hill village of Galáta. Like nearby Kakopetriá (see entry), it is a popular holiday resort during the hotter months of the year. Of Galáta's churches, originally seven in number, four remain. The most notable are the churches of the Panayía tis Podíthou and the Archangel Michael, to the north of the village, while the other two, the Church of Ayios Sozómenos stands in the middle of the old village, and the smaller Church of Ayía Paraskevi lies on the old Galáta to Kakopetriá road. The keys for the churches can be obtained from the village priest (on the road to the Panayía tis Podíthou, opposite the Gymnasium).

★Church of the Panayía tis Podíthou

The church of the Mother of God Eleousa (the Compassionate), originally belonging to the monastery of the Panayía tis Podíthou, was built in the early 16th c. It has a pitched roof supported on a wall surrounding the church. Thanks to the circulation of air in the ambulatory thus formed round the church the wall paintings are unusually well preserved. (☛Culture, Art and Architecture, Byzantine art).

The paintings show the influence of the Italian Renaissance, which reached Cyprus towards the end of the 15th c. The strictly prescribed Byzantine style of painting is relaxed in the sharply individualised representation of the figures.

Inscription and portraits of donors
An inscription on the west front of the church gives the date of building as 1502, and there are portraits of the donors, a French nobleman named Demetre de Coron and his wife Helen. The donor, an old man, is shown presenting a model of the church to the Mother of God. To the left of this scene are the figures of other donors.

Wall paintings
In the apse is a painting of the Mother of God enthroned holding the Child, flanked by two angels. The style of the painting is reminiscent of the paintings in Kalopanayiótis Monastery (see entry). Below this is the Communion of the Apostles, in which the handsome, classically formed faces of the disciples show clear western influence. On the east gable Moses is depicted receiving the Tables of the Law and seeing the burning bush. On the north and south walls of the sanctuary (bema) are scenes from the story of Joachim and Anne. On the west wall of the church is a dynamic

The church of the Panayía Podíthou – Galáta

representation of the Crucifixion, with a use of perspective which is the clearest indication of the influence of the Italian Renaissance.

★Church of the Archangel Michael

100 m south of the Panayía tis Podíthou stands the church of the Panayía Theotókos (the God-Bearer), previously a family chapel. Some years ago it was given a new roof in order to protect the wall paintings.

Portraits of donors

An inscription over the north doorway gives the foundation date as 1514. There are portraits of the donors of the church, Stefano Zacharia and his wife, and the donors of the paintings, Polos Zacharia, his wife Madelena and their children. These last are below the representation of the Déesis – Christ enthroned with the Mother of God and St John, who are interceding for mankind. Madelena is holding a rosary, which suggests that she was a Roman Catholic. The daughter kneeling behind her is holding an open book with the verses of the Acathist Hymn, an Orthodox hymn to the Mother of God – indicating that the children were brought up in the Orthodox faith. The lion in the family coat of arms suggests that Madelena belonged to the Lusignan family, kings of Cyprus, and had married a Venetian. The name of the painter is given as Symeon Axentes, who was also responsible for the paintings in the church of Ayios Sozómenos (see below).

Wall paintings

The wall paintings inside the church show western influence. On the south wall is a cycle of New Testament scenes, beginning with the Annunciation and continuing with the Nativity, the Presentation in the Temple, the Raising of Lazarus, the Entry into Jerusalem, the Transfiguration and the Last Supper.

On the west wall are the Bearing of the Cross, the Crucifixion and the Descent from the Cross. Next to these are the Washing of the Feet, Christ on the Mount of Olives, the Betrayal, Christ before Annas and Caiaphas, Christ before Pilate and Peter's Denial. On the north wall are the Mocking of Christ, the Flagellation, the Lamentation, the Resurrection, Christ with Mary Magdalene and the Descent into Hades. After these are scenes from the life of the Virgin. In the sanctuary are the Ascension, the Descent of the Holy Ghost (Pentecost), the Hospitality of Abraham and the Sacrifice of Isaac.

Church of Ayios Sozómenos

Above the old road from Galáta to Kakopetriá, to the right of the new church, is the church of Ayios Sozómenos (key held by the village priest), which has a fine cycle of wall paintings (not yet restored). An inscription over the west doorway records that the church was built by 13 inhabitants of the village and that the donor of the paintings was one Ioannis.

Wall paintings
Along the upper part of the walls are New Testament scenes, beginning over the south doorway with the Annunciation. On the lower half of the walls are various saints, notable among them St Mamas and St George. The figure of St George has an inscription naming the donor of the paintings and the painter, Symeon. Under this painting are scenes from the life of St George, and adjoining these are scenes from the life of the Virgin. On the north wall are military saints.

The outer walls of the church also have paintings. On the north wall are the Last Judgment and the seven ecumenical councils, including the Triumph of Orthodoxy. The representations of the councils show the emperor in the middle, flanked by prelates, with the condemned heretics crouching in front of them.

Hala Sultan Tekke F 9

Τεκκες Χαλα Σουλταν
Altitude: sea level

On the road from Lárnaca to the airport, beyond the Salt Lake, can be seen, surrounded by palms, cypresses and lemon trees, the burial mosque of Hala Sultan (Honoured Mother), foster mother or aunt of the Prophet Mohammed, or according to another version of the legend the aunt of one of Mohammed's close associates. Soon after the turning for the airport a road branches off on the right to the Tekke (the Muslim equivalent of a monastery), the fourth most-important Islamic place of pilgrimage after the Kaaba in Mecca, the tomb of the Prophet in Medina and al-Aqsa mosque in Jerusalem.

History
Hala Sultan, whose Arabic name was Umm Haram, was the wife of the governor of Palestine and came to Cyprus in 647 in the Sultan's suite during the victorious advance of the Muslim forces. While in Cyprus in 649 she was killed by falling from her mule. Thereafter, during the period of Turkish rule, Turkish ships sailing past her tomb dipped their flags in her honour.

The present mosque was built by Seyyit Emir Effendi, the Turkish governor of Cyprus, in 1816.

Mosque
In the gardens in front of the mosque is the usual ablutions fountain. The mosque itself, in the classical manner of

Hala Sultan Tekke

mosque architecture (☛Culture, Art and Architecture, Ottoman art), has a square plan and a domed roof. The dome is borne on four pillars with relief decoration, on which are inscriptions with the names of the caliphs. The sparse furnishings of the mosque, which is whitewashed and has mats and carpets on the floor, consist of the mihrab (prayer niche) marking the direction of Mecca and the minbar (pulpit).

The tomb
Beside the mihrab a doorway leads to the tomb chamber. The tomb is screened by curtains, but with the aid of a torch it is possible to see, above the sarcophagus, a large stone on two timber supports. According to the legend the stone flew from Mecca to Cyprus on the day Umm Haram died and hovered over her tomb.

Another legend has it that on the day before Umm Haram's death three stones sailed over the sea from Jerusalem; and according to still another version the stone was transported from Sinai by angels.

In a side room are the sarcophagi of important Muslim figures, including the grandmother of King Hussein of Jordan.

Surroundings

Excavations
500 m west on the unsurfaced road which passes the Hala Sultan Tekke is the fenced excavation site of a late Bronze Age settlement on which work is still in progress. The excavators have discovered a large town of about the same size as Kítion, laid out on a rectangular plan, the name of which is unknown. The grave goods found in tombs included objects in gold, silver and faience. The most interesting find was a bath of dressed stone, similar to Minoan baths on Crete. Objects recovered in the excavations are displayed in the Turkish fort in Lárnaca.

Salt lake of Lárnaca
The salt lake of Lárnaca has an area of some 5 sq km and a circumference of 11.5 km. Between November and March this is the home of flamingos from the Caspian Sea and other migrant birds. The existence of the salt lake is explained by a popular legend. It is said that Lazarus one day passed a large vineyard in which the vines were heavy with grapes and, being hungry and thirsty, asked the woman who owned it for a few grapes. She refused to give him any, saying that all her grapes were dried up, whereupon Lazarus cursed the vineyard and it turned into a salt lake.

The **extraction of salt** from the lake began in ancient times, and from the Middle Ages until the beginning of the 20th c. salt was an important export, sold in large quantities to Europe and neighbouring countries. Accordingly during the period of Lusignan rule Lárnaca was known as Salines. Since the lake lies some 2.5 cm below sea level it is thought to be fed by sea water seeping through the dunes. Additional water had to be brought in from the sea by pipeline.

During the rain-free months of August and September, when the lake is covered with a layer of salt 3 cm thick, the salt was extracted with the aid of donkeys and small tractors and piled in great mounds on the shores of the lake. Since 1992, however, owing to increasing air pollution from nearby Lárnaca airport, salt is no longer extracted here or from the larger salt lake of Akrotíri.

Kakopetriá F 5

Κακοπετριά
Altitude: 670 m

60 km south-west of Nicosia and 15 km north of the little town of Tróodos in the Tróodos massif (see entry) is Kakopetriá (bad stones), now a popular holiday resort whose hotels, tavernas and coffee houses attract large numbers of Cypriots, particularly from Nicosia. It lies near the neighbouring village of Galáta (see entry) in the beautiful and fertile Karyótis valley with its large plantations of poplars, apple trees and walnut trees. Kakopetriá is an important apple-growing centre famed for its preserved fruit (*glykó*).

The old centre of the village, built on a ridge above the river, is now a protected national monument, and the houses, mostly dating from the 18th and 19th c., have been restored with the help of state grants. They are built of sun-dried brick – with a rendering – on stone foundations. The other main sight is the

Church of St Nicholas tis Stéyis, Kakopetriá

church of Ayios Nikólaos, 5 km south-west of the village.

★★Church of Ayios Nikólaos tis Stéyis

To reach the church leave the village on the Tróodos road and turn right into a narrow road signposted to the church.

The church of Ayios Nikólaos tis Stéyis (St Nicholas of the roof), on a site which now belongs to the archbishop of Cyprus, is attached to a holiday home for schoolchildren. It was originally the church of a monastery founded in the 9th c. of which no trace survives.

As the name 'of the roof' indicates, this is one of the characteristic Cypriot barn-roofed churches (☛Culture, Art and Architecture, Byzantine art). The original domed cruciform church of the 11th c. was given an additional saddle roof and a narthex was built on to the west end in the 12th c.

🕲 *Tue.–Sat. 9am–4pm, Sun. 11am–4pm.*

Wall paintings

The wall paintings (well restored) are the work of six centuries, from the early 11th c. – among the earliest wall paintings in Cyprus – to the 17th c.

11th c. The paintings at the west end of the naos date from the early 11th c. On the north side are the Transfiguration and the Raising of Lazarus, on the south side the Entry into Jerusalem. The fragments of the Dormition of the Mother of God also date from this period. In the bema other 11th c. paintings were discovered under 14th c. paintings, including the Mother of God flanked by angels, the Ascension and the Descent of the Holy Ghost (Pentecost). The paintings are in the style characteristic of the art of Constantinople in the 11th c.

12th c. On the south-west wall of the church are paintings of the early 12th c., including a scene from the life of the Virgin and the Forty Martyrs of Sebaste. Near the bema is St Nicholas with a small figure of the donor, a work of outstanding quality. In the narthex is a representation of the Last Judgment. Like the frescos in the church at Asínou (see entry), these

The Forty Martyrs of Sebaste

paintings belong to the middle Byzantine period.

14th c. Other paintings were added during the period of Lusignan rule. The Crucifixion and the Resurrection on the north side of the church date from the early 14th c. In the dome is Christ Pantokrator, and in the south arm of the church are the Nativity, the Presentation in the Temple and the Annunciation. The Nativity is depicted in an unusual form – probably reflecting oriental influence – with the Mother of God sitting up rather than in the usual reclining position, in the type of the Galaktotrophoúsa (suckling the Child).

Church of the Ayía Theotókos

On the outskirts of Kakopetriá, on the right of the old road to Galáta (near the filling station), stands the modest little 16th c. barn-roofed church of the Ayía Theotókos (key in the house next the filling station). The church is built of sun-dried brick on a stone foundation.

Portraits of donors
About half of the original wall paintings have been preserved. Over the entrance is a painting of the donors, who are named as Leontius and his wife Lucretia, with an inscription giving the date of construction as 1520. The names of the donors and their dress show that Leontius was a Greek and his wife a Venetian. In the foreground is another man in a black tunic, probably the donor of the wall paintings.

Wall paintings
On the north wall are the Entombment, the Holy Women at the Tomb, the Resurrection, the Descent of the Holy Ghost (Pentecost) and the Dormition of the Mother of God. In the Dormition, note the small figure of the Jew Jephonias who according to an apocryphal gospel tried to touch the bier and had his hands cut off by an angel.

In the bema are the Sacrifice of Isaac, the Hospitality of Abraham, the Ascension and figures of prophets. The Hospitality of Abraham (entertaining the three angels unawares) is seen in the Orthodox church as a symbol of the

Trinity. On the vault of the apse is the Mother of God with arms raised in prayer, in the type known as Blacherniótissa, flanked by the Archangels Michael and Gabriel. Below this are the Communion of the Apostles and six fathers of the Church.

Kalopanayiótis F 4

Καλοπαναγιώτης
Altitude: 720 m

In the Marathása valley on the northern slopes of the Tróodos massif, 20 km from the little town of Tróodos, is the hill village of Kalopanayiótis, famed for its sulphur springs.

Near the springs is a complex of three churches (keys obtainable from the village priest) which belonged to the former monastery of Ayios Ioannis Lampadistís (St John Lampadistes). The churches have wall paintings of different periods.

Monastery of Ayios Ioannis Lampadistís

The three churches are covered by a common roof. The most southerly of the three, an 11th c. domed cruciform church, is dedicated to St Heraclidius. The second church, dedicated to St John Lampadistes, was rebuilt in the 18th c. The two churches have a common 15th c. narthex at the west end. On the north side is the small 15th c. Latin Chapel.

Church of St Heraclidius
The church of St Heraclidius has wall paintings of the early 13th and the early 15th c. Heraclidius was appointed by Paul as the first bishop of Tamassós. He is buried in the monastery of St Heraclidius at Tamassós (see entry).

13th c. wall paintings The paintings in the dome and the west and south arms of the church date from the 13th c. The paintings, in a reversion to an earlier Comnene style, show oriental influence.

In the dome is Christ Pantokrator, surrounded by angels and prophets. In the pendentives are the four Evangelists. In the western arm of the church are the Entry into Jerusalem, the Raising of Lazarus, the Sacrifice of Isaac and the Crucifixion. The Entry into Jerusalem is a painting of particular quality. An unusual but realistic feature is that the children cutting palm branches are wearing black leather gloves. Unusual too is the placing of the Sacrifice of Isaac (normally found in the bema) on the west wall. On the vaulting of the south arm of the church is the Ascension.

15th c. wall paintings The second series of paintings – in a late Byzantine style of an individual character – dates from the early 15th c. Over 30 New Testament scenes are depicted on the remaining vaults of the church.

The cycle of scenes from the life of Christ begins on the east wall above the altar with the Annunciation and continues with the Nativity, the Adoration of the Kings, the Presentation in the Temple, Christ dispatching his disciples to fetch the colt, the Entry into Jerusalem, Mary, sister of Lazarus, meeting Christ on his way to Bethany and the Raising of Lazarus.

In the northern vault are Christ before Annas and Caiaphas, Christ before Pilate, the Mocking, the Bearing of the Cross and, in the lunette, the Dormition of the Mother of God.

In the south-west of the naos are another representation of Christ before Annas and Caiaphas, various healing miracles by Christ, the appearance of Christ after his Resurrection and Doubting Thomas.

On the other walls are the Entombment, the Descent into Hades (Anástasis), the Tree of Jesse and various saints. In the vault of the apse is the Mother of God Blacherniótissa, standing between the Archangels Michael and Gabriel with her hands raised in prayer.

Church of St John Lampadistes
The barrel-vaulted church of St John Lampadistes was built in the early 18th c., probably replacing an earlier church of the 15th c. The skull of this local saint is preserved in a silver casket above his tomb. According to his legend St John Lampadistes lived in a village in the Tróodos in the 11th c. He was engaged to be married, but renounced matrimony in favour of the monastic life, whereupon his bride's parents caused him by enchantments to go blind. Heraclidius died at the age of 22 and was buried in the monastery which bears his name; but his grave remained

Monastery of Ayios Ioannis Lampadistís

unknown until an epileptic was cured by accidentally touching it. In the 12th c. a church was built in his honour, and thousands of people came in pilgrimage to seek healing at his tomb. His feast day is October 4th.

Narthex
In the 15th c. the great numbers of pilgrims necessitated the construction of the narthex which serves the two churches. The walls are covered with paintings of that period, on themes related to the hopes of the pilgrims (healing miracles, Christ's appearances after the Resurrection). Until quite recently sick people used to bring their bedding and lodge in the narthex. An inscription over the south entrance records that the paintings were the work of a painter from Constantinople – probably a refugee who had come to Cyprus after the fall of Constantinople in 1453.

Wall paintings At the south end of the east wall is a representation of the Last Judgment, with four figures of donors. Above the doorway in the south wall are the Three Youths in the Fiery Furnace and Daniel in the Lions' Den. On the upper part of the east wall is Christ with the woman of Samaria, followed by a series of his miracles of healing, beginning with the healing of the paralytic at the pool of Bethesda and continuing with the healing of the man with dropsy, in which Christ is shown touching the man's swollen belly, and the healing of the man born blind. The middle zone shows Mary Magdalene telling Peter and John about the empty tomb and the two disciples at the tomb, seeing for themselves. Beyond this are Mary Magdalene at the empty tomb, her encounter with Christ (Touch me not), Doubting Thomas and the Miraculous Draught of Fishes.

Latin chapel
The paintings in the Latin chapel, which date from the 15th and 16th c., show a mingling of Italian and Byzantine elements. The iconographic programme still follows the Byzantine scheme, but the artist's conception of space, his use of perspective and the physical form of his figures point to his training in Italy.

The main theme of the paintings is the **Acathist Hymn**, the famous Orthodox hymn in honour of the Virgin, which was sung standing (*akáthistos*). The hymn, based on apocryphal narratives of the Nativity, consists of 24 verses, each beginning with one of the 24 letters of the Greek alphabet. The cycle of scenes begins on the south wall with the Annunciation and ends on the north wall with the Mother of God enthroned, holding out her hand to two popes – a clear indication of western influence.

In the apse, in accordance with the Byzantine canon, is the Mother of God with the Child. On the left-hand wall Moses is depicted receiving the tablets of stone, on the right-hand wall seeing the burning bush. In the lunette of the apse is the Hospitality of Abraham.

Surroundings

Moutoullás

2 km south of Kalopanayiótis is the hill village of Moutoullás (alt. 760 m), whose clear spring water is bottled and sold all over Cyprus. The village also produces large quantities of a Cypriot speciality, *soutzoúko*, strings of almonds soaked in grape juice. The pears grown here are particularly esteemed. Moutoullás is also noted for its traditional craft of making *vournes* (troughs for kneading dough and washing clothes) and *sanides* (bread-boards with round cavities for shaping loaves) from pine trunks.

At the far end of the village is a little barn-roofed church.

Church of Panayía tou Moutoullá This little church (key from the adjacent house) was built in 1280 and is believed to be the oldest surviving saddle-roofed church in Cyprus. The wall paintings are dated to the same year in an inscription on the north wall of the bema. Below the inscription are the figures of the donors, John and his wife Irene.

The paintings follow the usual Byzantine iconographic programme, with figures of saints in the lower zone and scenes from the life of Christ in the upper zone.

In the vault of the apse is the Mother of God Blacherniótissa, with six fathers of the Church in the lower zone. On the south wall are the Nativity and the Presentation in the Temple (the latter dating from the 15th c.); on the west wall the Raising of Lazarus, the Entry into Jerusalem and the Crucifixion; and on the north wall the Descent into Hades (Anástasis) and the Dormition of the Mother of God. On the outside of the north wall is the Last Judgment (15th c.).

Pedhoulás

Situated 8 km south of Kalopanayiótis at an altitude of 1100 m above the beautiful Marathása valley, Pedhoulás is a popular summer resort with small hotels and tavernas. It is famed for its cherry blossom, and hosts of visitors are attracted to the village in spring when its 100,000 cherry trees are in flower.

Also of interest is the church of the Archangel Michael with its 15th c. wall paintings.

Church of the Archangel Michael This small saddle-roofed church can be found in the lower part of the village (key in the house to the right of the church). An inscription over the north doorway names the donor as Basileos and gives the date of construction as 1474. Above the inscription the donor, accompanied by his family, is shown presenting the church to the Archangel Michael. The women's dresses have embroidery of a type similar to that made in Léfkara today. The painting is in a rustic style. Western influence is evident in the dress of the soldiers in the Betrayal scene.

On the iconostasis are the arms of the Lusignan family, suggesting that the site for the church was donated by the Lusignan rulers of Cyprus.

Wall paintings In accordance with Byzantine practice, the paintings in the naos are in two zones, with figures of saints in the lower zone and New Testament scenes in the upper one.

The cycle begins on the south wall with the Birth of the Virgin and continues with the Presentation of the Virgin, the Annunciation, the Nativity of Christ, the Presentation in the Temple, the Baptism, the Entry into Jerusalem and the Betrayal. In the pediment of the west wall is the Crucifixion, badly defaced by rain water. On the north wall are the Lamentation, the Descent into Hades and the Dormition of the Mother of God. In the conch of the apse is the Mother of God Blacherniótissa, standing with her hands raised in prayer, with six

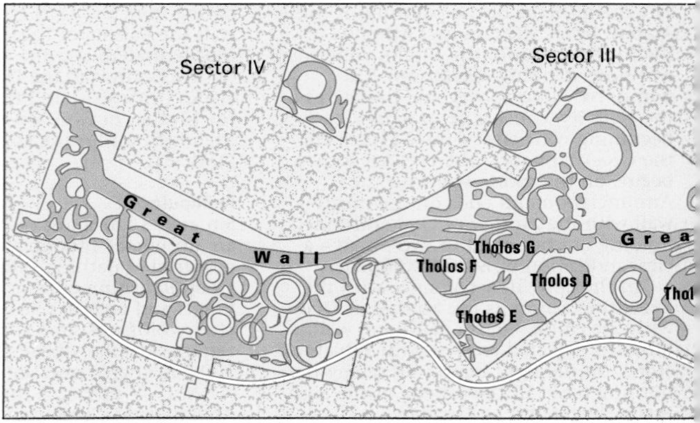

fathers of the Church below. In the vaulting is the Ascension, on the north wall the Sacrifice of Isaac.

★Khirokitía G 7/8

Χοιροκοιτία
Altitude: 100–200 m

Halfway between Lárnaca and Limassol, 7 km from the coast, just off the motorway (junction 14), is the site of Khirokitía. Dating from the sixth millennium BC, this is one of the oldest settlements on the island and its most important Neolithic site (☛Culture, Art and Architecture).
Daily 7.30am–5.30pm, summer to 7.30pm.

Neolithic settlements
In the Neolithic period people gradually began to give up their nomadic life as hunter-gatherers and to change to a sedentary life, farming and domesticating wild animals (as evidenced by finds of the bones of sheep and goats). The first settlers on Cyprus came from Syria and Cilicia and established themselves in the well-watered foothills of the mountains. In 1999 UNESCO made Khirokitía a World Heritage Site. Other Neolithic settlements have been identified at Kalavasós/Tenta near Khirokitía, Pétra tou Limniti on the north coast and Sotíra, near Koúrion.

Excavations

Excavation of the site began in 1936 under the direction of Porphyrios Dikaios, and the work is being continued by French archaeologists. The water supply of the settlement was provided by the Maroni river, at the foot of the south-facing slope on which it was built.

Thóloi
On both sides of a wall running up the steep hill from the river are a series of round houses (*thóloi*) similar to those of the Thessalian Sesklo culture (near Vólos in mainland Greece). The largest of the houses have an external diameter of some 10 m and an internal diameter of 5 m and could accommodate two or three people. The smaller houses, with a diameter of only 2–3 m, could accommodate only a single individual, or may have been animal stalls or store rooms. Families presumably occupied several houses, forming a kind of homestead.

The beehive-shaped houses stood on 50 cm thick foundations of river boulders (still preserved), on which was erected a superstructure of sun-dried brick. Some of the houses had pillar-like supports in the middle, presumably bearing an upper storey of the roof. The floor was of beaten earth. The only furnishings were a stone bench, tables and a hearth.

Burials
Neolithic people buried the dead under the floors of their houses. Several generations might be buried in the same house, and up to 26 skeletons were

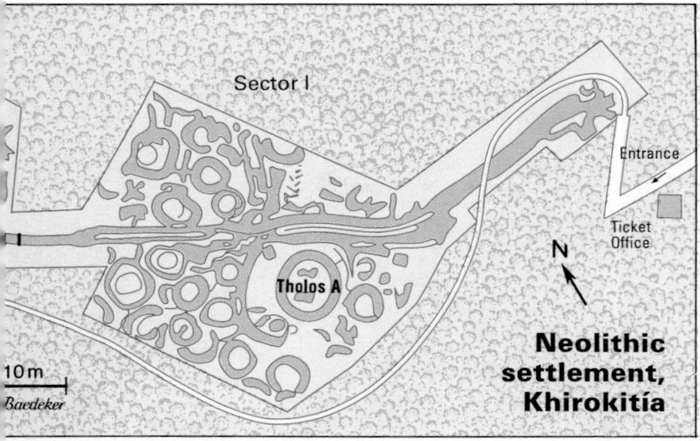

found in some houses. The dead were buried in a crouching position, lying on their sides. Since Neolithic people seem to have believed in a life after death, the bodies were covered with heavy stones to prevent them returning.

Among the commonest grave goods were food jars, offering dishes, jewellery, tools and weapons – further evidence of a belief in an afterlife. The graves of women were more richly furnished than those of men; the grave goods included necklaces of carnelian beads and obsidian knives. The average age of the dead was 33–35.

The wall

A great wall 2 m wide and 3 m high runs between the houses, following a winding

Neolithic houses, Khirokitía

Church of the Panayía Angelóktistos, Kíti

course from the river up the slope of the hill and down again to the river at the other end. The first excavators took this to be the main street of the village, but recent investigations have shown that it was originally a defensive wall. When new settlers came to the village in the 4th millennium BC further *thóloi* were built outside the wall and a new defensive wall was later constructed.

The wall thus yields evidence of two phases of settlement, a phase beginning in the 6th millennium BC in which pottery was unknown and, after an unexplained hiatus of 1500 years, a new culture in the 4th millennium BC using comb-decorated pottery. No material of a later period has been found, and it is not known why Khirokitía was not occupied after the 4th millennium BC.

Surroundings

Kalavasós
8 km west of Khirokitía on the road from Lárnaca, just before Kalavasós, an unsurfaced road goes off on the left to the Neolithic site of Kalavasós/Tenta. Here too were found round houses with burials under the floors. The most interesting find was a complete preserved child's skeleton of the 7th millennium BC. Excavation of the site is continuing.

A few hundred metres nearer the motorway is the Bronze Age site of Kalavasós/Ayios Dhimitrios, which shows longer continuity of settlement than Khirokitía. On this site was found a rectangular structure of unknown function built round a central courtyard with an area of 10 sq m. A few metres away were two chamber tombs with rich grave goods, including fine gold jewellery, of the 14th c. BC.

Léfkara
See entry

Kíti F 9

Κίτι
Altitude: 50 m

11 km south-west of Lárnaca on the road running past the airport and Hala Sultan Tekke is the village of Kíti, which takes its

name from ancient Kítion (now Lárnaca). The inhabitants of the ancient port moved inland in the 7th c. AD, presumably for safety from Arab raids, and settled in this area, as is shown by the fragments of late antique masonry, Corinthian capitals and remains of architraves built into the old walls of the settlement. The church of the Panayía Angelóktistos is notable for an early Christian apse mosaic (6th c.) which is unique in Cyprus (☛Culture, Heritage under Threat).

★Church of the Panayía Angelóktistos

The present church of the Panayía Angelóktistos (built by angels) contains elements from different periods. The apse at the east end with its mosaic decoration dates from the original 6th c. building. The church was rebuilt as a domed cruciform church in the 11th c. after its destruction in Arab raids; then in the 12th c. the extension on the north side was built, and in the 13th c. the annexe on the south side that now serves as a narthex was added; and finally in the 20th c. the west end was extended. Below the bell tower are the arms of the Gibelin family who built the south annexe as a private chapel. The vaulting in the interior points to the Frankish origin of the donors. On the west wall of the chapel is the gravestone of Simone, wife of Renier de Gibelet.
Mon.–Sat. 8am–4pm, Sun. 9am–noon, 2–4pm.

★Mosaic
In the apse of the church can be seen a 6th c. mosaic of the Mother of God of the Hodigitría type (She who shows the Way) with the Child on her left arm, flanked by the Archangels Michael and Gabriel. The mosaic is the only surviving pre-iconoclastic example of the Hodigitría type. An inscription above the Mother of God refers to her as Hagia Maria. The mosaic is notable for the lively representation of the archangels and the lifelike figure of the Child. Round the mosaic is a frieze of animal figures – parrots, ducks and stags – between acanthus leaves.

Terebinth tree
Outside the church is a 300-year-old terebinth, with fragrant branches and edible fruits. An aromatic substance resembling turpentine is made from its bark.

Surroundings

Tersephánou
2 km north-east of Kíti, near the dam on the Tremithos river (turn right just beyond the bridge), stands the small church of Ayios Yeóryios of Arpera (key in the farmhouse beside the church). This 18th c. church of St George preserves remains of wall paintings. There is a fine portrait of the donor, the Greek dragoman (an intermediary between the sultan and his Christian subjects) Christophakis. On the iconostasis is an icon of the dog-headed St Christopher (who according to his legend was a man-eating creature with a dog's head before his conversion to the Christian faith).

Kolóssi G 5

Κολόσσι
Altitude: sea level

10 km west of Limassol on a road flanked by cypresses lies the village of Kolóssi, with the massive castle of the Knights of St John. The castle lies in an intensively cultivated area, with large citrus plantations established in 1933 by a co-operative of Cypriot and Israeli agricultural specialists. In this area too are grown the vines – originally planted by the Knights – that produce Commandaria, a sweet dessert wine named after the commandery of the Order of St John (☛Practical Information, South, Wine).
Daily 7.30am–5pm, summer to 7pm.

★Kolóssi Castle

History
Around 1210 the Frankish king Hugo I presented a fertile territory around Kolóssi to the Knights of St John. The castle that they built in this area was held for a time by the Templars; but even after the Knights of St John transferred their main base from Cyprus to Rhodes between 1291 and 1310 Kolóssi remained a commandery of their order. The fertile soil of the region

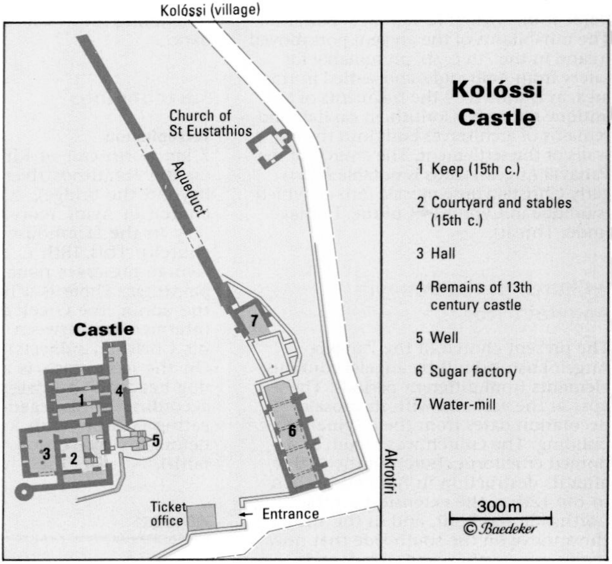

produced large yields of wheat, grapes for wine (Commandaria), cotton, oil and cane sugar.

In 1373 the Genoese attacked the castle but were repelled. In the mid-15th c. Grand Commander Louis de Magnac began the renovation of the castle, then much dilapidated, which gave it its present form.

Keep

Of the castle built in the mid-15th c. only the high keep, 16 m square, remains intact. On the east side of the outer wall, at first floor level, can be seen four coats of arms – in the middle the arms of the Lusignan kingdoms of Jerusalem, Cyprus and Armenia, below this the arms of Louis de Magnac and to right and left the arms of grand masters Jean de Lastic and Jacques de Milli.

First floor The keep is entered by a modern drawbridge leading to the first floor. Above the entrance is an elaborate machicolation. In one of the two rooms on the first floor, which were presumably the kitchen and living quarters (with store rooms and cisterns on the ground floor), is a fireplace. To the left of the entrance is a painting of the Crucifixion, with the arms of Louis de Magnac.

Second floor A spiral staircase leads up to the second floor, with the commander's state apartments. Large cavities for beams in the upper part of the walls show that there was originally an intermediate timber floor, no doubt with sleeping accommodation. On the fireplaces are the arms of Louis de Magnac. From the battlements there are fine views over the vineyards to Limassol.

Relics of 13th c. castle

East of the keep is a semicircular structure with a well, a relic of an older 13th c. castle. To the south of the keep are the remains of stables.

Sugar factory

To the east of the castle are the remains of an old sugar factory, consisting of a rectangular barrel-vaulted main building and other structures, probably a watermill, to the north. The necessary water supply was provided by an aqueduct. (On sugar manufacture see Koúklia/Palaía Páphos.)

Kolóssi Castle

Machaeron tree
Near the aqueduct is a tipa tree a member of the *Papilionaceae* family, originally from North America) over 150 years old. Named after its razor-sharp seed pods (Greek *makhaira*, knife), it stands 27 m high.

Ayios Eustathios
100 m north of the castle is the little Byzantine church of Ayios Eustathios (key in house next door). Eustathius, one of the great military saints and martyrs of the Orthodox Church, was a Roman officer in the reign of Trajan (AD 98–117) who according to his legend was converted to the Christian faith when he encountered a stag bearing a white cross between its antlers.

This domed cruciform church with an apse at the east end, built in the 12th c. and restored in the 15th, was presumably a church of the Knights of St John. There are scanty remains of a painting of St Eustathius in full armour mounted on a horse, and in the dome is Christ Pantokrator with the four Evangelists below him.

Koúklia – Palaía Páphos G 3

Κούκλια Παλαία Πάφος
Altitude: 100 m

Some 15 km south-east of Páphos is the old village of Koúklia, whose inhabitants live mainly by growing and processing groundnuts. It takes its name from the Frankish castle of Covocle. This was the site of Old Páphos (Palaía Páphos), with the most celebrated shrine of Aphrodite in the ancient Greek world, the Sanctuary of Aphrodite. Excavations have also found remains of temples of the Bronze Age and Roman period. Outside the village are the scanty remains of a mound built by the Persians during a siege of the town in the 5th c. BC

The castle of Covocle (Manor House), built by the Lusignans to protect their sugar-cane plantations, now houses a small museum displaying finds from the surrounding area. Below the castle are remains of a medieval sugar factory.

Daily 7.30am–5pm, summer to 7pm.

The Knights of St John

The Order of the Knights of St John or Knights Hospitallers, the oldest of the Crusading orders, has survived in altered form until the present day. It was founded in the 11th c., when a pilgrim hospice dedicated to St John the Baptist was established in Jerusalem. After its recognition by the Pope in 1113 the Order began to found daughter houses along the pilgrim roads. Originally a charitable order, it soon developed into a military order of chivalry which fought against the infidel in the Holy Land. To distinguish themselves from the Templars, who wore a white habit with a red cross, the Knights of St John wore a black habit with a white cross.

After the fall of Acre in 1291 the Knights of St John were obliged, like the other Crusading orders, to leave this last Christian stronghold in the Holy Land. Their headquarters were moved to Cyprus and remained there for 19 years before being transferred to Rhodes. The head of the Order was the Grand Master, who while on Rhodes was also ruler of a secular state.

After withstanding a six months' siege on Rhodes the Knights were compelled in 1522 to surrender to overwhelmingly superior Turkish forces and moved to Malta, which had been granted to the Order by the Emperor Charles V. There they successfully defended the island against a siege by Sultan Suleiman the Magnificent in 1565.

Thereafter the Order increasingly devoted itself to caring for the sick. At the Reformation it split into two – the Protestant Order of St John and the Catholic order of the Knights of Malta. During the French Revolution the Order was expelled from Malta and its property confiscated. Its headquarters were then moved to St Petersburg, where Tsar Paul I illegitimately declared himself Grand Master. After Paul's death the Order moved to Catania in Sicily, then to Ferrara and finally to Rome, where it still has its headquarters. After reorganisation in the 19th c. the Order was usually known as the Order of the Knights of Malta.

The Order has national associations in many countries, including Britain. There is also in Britain a Grand Priory of the Order of St John which is independent of the Roman Catholic Order.

★Sanctuary of Aphrodite

Palaía Páphos (Old Páphos) was so called in the 4th c. BC to distinguish it from Nea Páphos (New Páphos), the new foundation on the coast. The importance of Palaía Páphos was based on its status as the religious centre of Cyprus, only a short distance from Pétra tou Romioú, where Aphrodite was believed to have risen from the sea (☛Surroundings; also History, Mythology).

History

According to the Greek traveller Pausanias (2nd c. AD) the shrine of Aphrodite was founded by Agapenor, king of Tegea in Arcadia, who landed here during his return from Troy. According to another account the temple was founded by the legendary priest-king Kinyras, son of Páphos.

There is evidence of a settlement on the site in the 15th c. BC. During the Hellenisation of Cyprus, in the 12th c. BC, Achaean settlers established themselves in Páphos, where they encountered a cult of Ishtar/Astarte, who was worshipped in the form of a conical black stone. In the course of centuries this Great Mother (Magna Mater) developed into the Greek goddess Aphrodite.

There are remains of a temple and tombs of the late Bronze Age. The earliest king of Páphos known to us by name was Eteandros, who is recorded as having paid tribute to the Persians in the 7th c. BC The kings of Páphos were both political and religious heads of their state. In 499 BC Páphos joined the Ionian rising against the Persians, but was compelled to surrender when the city was besieged in the following year.

The heyday of Páphos was in the Archaic and Classical periods. Nikokles, the last independent priest-king of Páphos, moved his capital to the coast, founding Nea Páphos at the end of the 4th c. When, soon afterwards, the city-kingdoms of Cyprus were incorporated in the Ptolemaic empire the kings of Palaía Páphos became chief priests of Aphrodite. Nea Páphos took over the political and economic role of Palaía Páphos, whose importance now depended solely on the sanctuary of Aphrodite.

In Roman times the shrine continued to draw pilgrims from all over the Roman world, among them emperor Titus.

Palaía Páphos continued to flourish into the 4th c. AD, but the spread of Christianity led to the decline of the cult of Aphrodite. In Byzantine times Palaía Páphos was an insignificant village. In the 13th c. the Franks built the castle of Covocle near the ancient shrine to protect their sugar-cane plantations. Later it was taken over by the Turks.

Cult of Aphrodite

Every spring the great festival of Aphrodite, the Aphrodisiae, was celebrated in Palaía Páphos. Pilgrims came from all over the ancient world to take part in a great procession through the Sacred Gardens to Palaía Páphos, and young trees were planted in front of the temple of Aphrodite as votive offerings to the goddess.

The celebration of the mysteries lasted several days. The votaries began by taking a ritual bath in the sea in honour of the goddess, and offerings (not involving the effusion of blood) were made to her. This was followed by various contests between the worshippers. The Aphrodisiae also incorporated the cult of Adonis, Aphrodite's handsome lover. The culmination of the ceremonies was the Sacred Marriage of the priest-king with the goddess in the form of a priestess. The sacred stone was anointed with oil and offerings of incense were made to Aphrodite.

An important element in the cult of Aphrodite was **temple prostitution**, a practice described by Herodotus (5th c. BC). Before their marriage all brides were required to give themselves to a stranger near the temple precinct. 'When a woman has come here she may not return home until a stranger has thrown

Massive stone blocks in the sanctuary of Aphrodite

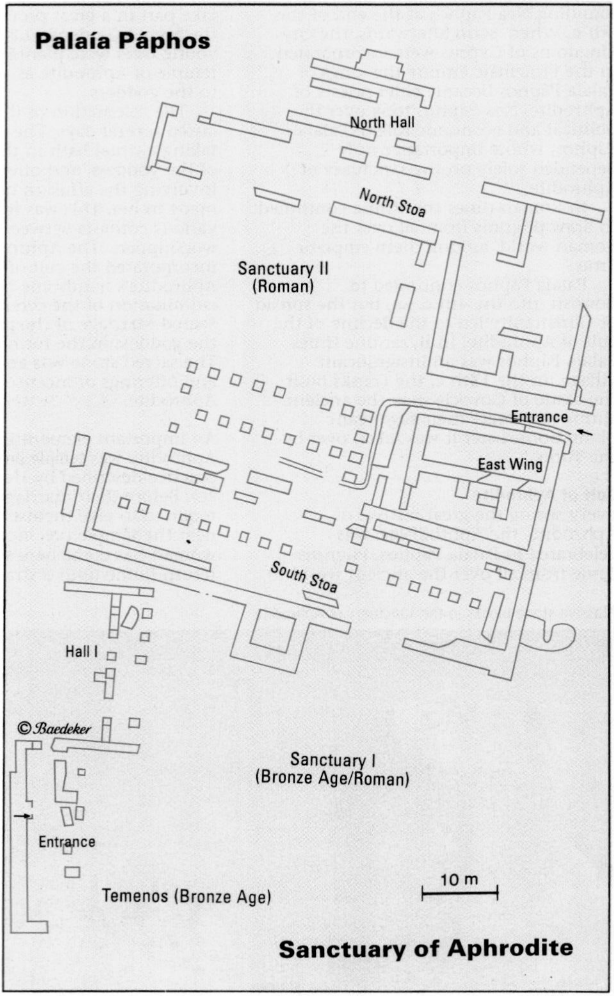

gold into her lap and has lain with her outside the sanctuary' (Herodotus I,119). This custom was presumably a rite of initiation for men and the virginity of the woman an offering to Aphrodite. It was also an important source of income for the temple.

In Roman times there was said to be an **oracle** here. The shrine was also a place of sanctuary for those pursued by their enemies.

Sanctuary

Two complexes of buildings, one dating

from the Bronze Age and the other from the Roman period, are all that remains of a sanctuary which was used from the 13th c. BC to the 4th c. AD.

Earlier sanctuary At the south end of the site, aligned north–south, is the earlier sanctuary, which dates from the late Bronze Age. There are only a few remains of the cyclopean wall round the sacred precinct which enclosed the temple containing the goddess's sacred cult stone. Within the precinct were a small chamber and a basin for ritual ablutions, and no doubt also an altar and various votive offerings. The function of the round holes in the cyclopean walls is not known.

Later sanctuary The sanctuary of the Roman period, covering an area 79 × 67 m, is thought to have been built after an earthquake in the 1st c. AD. At the north end were two colonnaded porticoes fronting a courtyard. Roman coins depict the large black sacred stone under a tripartite canopy.
Daily 7.30am–5pm, summer to 7pm.

Roman peristyle house
40 m west of the sanctuary, on the far side of the road, are the remains of a Roman peristyle house, presumably the dwelling of the priestesses.

Other sights

Manor House (Château de Covocle)
The inner courtyard of the Manor House or what used to be known as Château de Covocle, built in the 13th c. as the headquarters of the sugar industry, is entered under a large gate tower. The sugar-cane plantations were royal domains, a major source of revenue in the 15th and 16th c. The castle still preserves Frankish structures on the south and east sides, notably the large hall with Gothic buttresses below the museum. The rest of the castle was rebuilt and restored in the Turkish period.

Museum
The museum is housed in the upper range of buildings. In the first room is the black cult stone of Aphrodite; other exhibits include a large Bronze Age jar and a small Iron Age bath.

The second room contains material ranging in date from the Chalcolithic period to the Middle Ages. Of particular interest are ivories of the Bronze Age, fragments of sculpture of the Archaic period and a reconstruction of the Persian siege mound at Palaía Páphos.

Katholiki Church
To the east of the later sanctuary of Aphrodite is the small Katholiki Church, which at the beginning of the 20th c. still bore the name Panayía Aphrodítissa. It is thought to have been built in the 12th c. and altered in the 14th. It originally belonged to a monastery and is still surrounded by the ruined precinct wall of the monastery, with pointed archways. The courtyard round the church was used as a cemetery. The cruciform church has a barrel vault, with a dome over the crossing. Only a few 15th c. paintings survive. In the dome is Christ Pantokrator surrounded by angels, and on the west wall is a representation of the Last Judgment in which the Euphrates and Tigris rivers are represented by masks from whose mouths water is flowing.

Sugar refinery
The remains of medieval foundations probably represent a sugar refinery built by the Lusignans on the site of the ancient sanctuary. Part of the water supply system can still be identified. In a vaulted underground chamber was the mill wheel, turned by animal power, which crushed the sugar cane. The fibre was then crushed for a second time in a watermill, driven by water from a mill race with a narrow end which directed a powerful jet of water against the horizontal wheel. Thereafter the juice was boiled several times in large copper boilers and then fed into funnel-shaped vessels with a hole at the bottom through which dripped the residual liquid from the sugar crystallising in the vessel.

North-east gate and town walls
600 m from Koúklia on the road signposted to Arkhimandríta is an enclosed site on the right of the road containing the remains of the town walls of Palaía Páphos and its north-east gate, prominently situated on Marcello Hill above the town. The wall was built of

sun-dried brick – the usual material of the period – about 700 BC, but in later periods was given an additional stone facing. By the end of the 6th c. BC it was 6.3 m thick.

Siege mound

Of particular interest is the siege mound built by the Persians in 498 BC, when they took the city. They began by filling in part of the 10 m wide ditch round the city with tree trunks, earth and stones, and then built up a mound against the town walls on which they could set up their timber siege tower and so gain entry to the city. The defenders dug mines under the mound, supporting the roofs of their tunnels on timber props, which they then set on fire, so that the mound fell in. Despite these efforts they were unable to hold out against the Persians and soon afterwards surrendered.

Some of the tunnels can still be seen. In them were found small niches with oil lamps of the Archaic period which provided light for the diggers. The excavators removed the Persian siege mound, which was found to contain numerous fragments of sculpture, columns and inscriptions.

Surroundings

★Pétra tou Romioú

7 km from Koúklia and 21 km south-east of Páphos, just off the west coast of Cyprus, is Pétra tou Romioú, the rock marking the spot where Aphrodite was believed to have emerged from the sea (☛History, Mythology). The name means Stone of the Roman, for the Greeks of the Byzantine (East Roman) Empire were still described as Romans (*Romaioi*).

Roman road to Páphos

7 km from Pétra tou Romioú on the expressway to Limassol, at the turn-off for Pissoúri, a road goes off on the left to Alékhtora. Just before the village a dusty unsurfaced road crosses a bridge and runs between vineyards and olive groves. In the 1st c. this was the main east–west Roman road between Koúrion and Páphos, used throughout the Middle

Pétra tou Romioú, where Aphrodite rose from the sea

Bizarre rock formations east of Koúklia

Ages and into modern times, when it was remade by the British authorities. The Roman paving can still be seen at Yermános.

Lakko Franko
A few kilometres along the road lies the picturesque abandoned hamlet of Lakko Franko (not shown on maps), which during the Frankish period (13th–14th c.) was a feudal stronghold of some importance. There are also the ruins of an old village *han* (caravanserai) of the Turkish period. Better preserved is the fine old farmhouse and steading.

Yermanós
From here the road leads west, climbing to the hill of Yermanós (1 km), on which a late 19th c. German amateur archaeologist, Max Ohnefalsch-Richter, discovered ancient tombs and a Hellenistic shrine of Aphrodite. Some traces of his excavations can be seen.

Asprokremnos
On the road to Páphos, soon after the turn-off for the airport, a road goes off to the huge Asprokremnos dam.

★★Koúrion — G 5

Κούριον
Altitude: 70–80 m

Some 16 km west of Limassol, on a crag rising high above the sea, are the remains of the ancient city of Koúrion (Roman Curium), an extensive site with a theatre, handsome villas and a basilica dating from Hellenistic, Roman and Early Christian times. The first investigation of the site was carried out by the American consul, Luigi Palma di Cesnola, in 1873. Systematic excavation began in 1933 and still continues. An area to the east destroyed by violent earthquakes during the 4th c. AD, including an imposing nymphaeum dedicated to water nymphs, is currently under excavation. To the west are the remains of a sanctuary of Apollo and a Roman stadium.
7.30am–5pm, summer to 7.30pm.

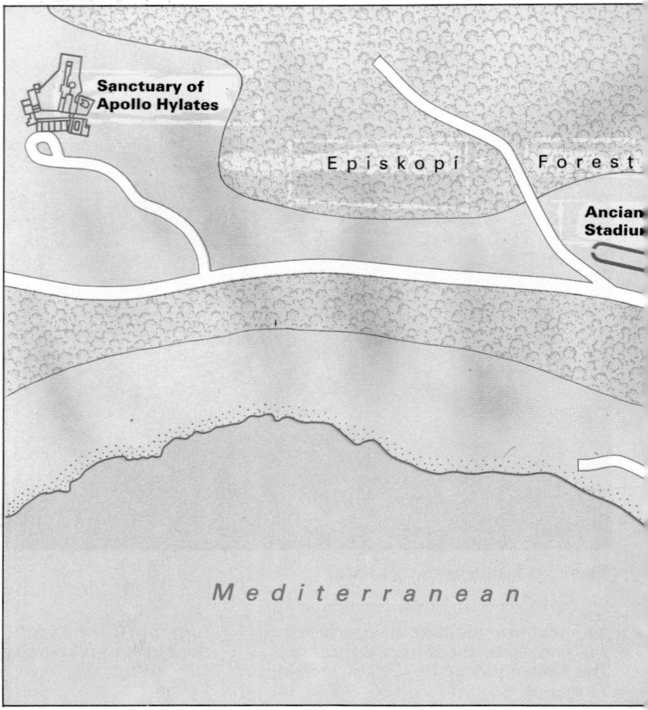

History

Foundation The Koúrion area has been continuously occupied since Neolithic times (finds at Sotíra). According to a legend reported by Herodotus in the 5th c. BC Koúrion was founded by warriors from Argos in the Peloponnese on their way back from the Trojan War. Finds from the immediate vicinity of Koúrion show that there was an Achaean settlement here in the 12th c. BC.

City-kingdom There was a sanctuary of Apollo near the city from the 8th c. BC. In the 7th c. Koúrion is mentioned as one of the city-kingdoms that paid tribute to the Persians. During the rebellion of the Greek cities against Persian rule in the 5th c. BC under the leadership of Onésilos of Sálamis, the king of Koúrion, Stásanor, went over to the Persian side during the battle of Sálamis and contributed to their victory. Under Ptolemaic and Roman rule Koúrion was a place of considerable importance. New temples, theatres and sporting facilities were now built. In the 4th c AD. the town was ravaged by violent earthquakes and razed to the ground.

Episcopal see At this period Christianity had already come to Koúrion, and in the following century it was firmly established; the town, partly rebuilt, became the see of a bishop. Arab raids in the 7th c. led to the transfer of the episcopal see to Episkopí (from *epískopos*, bishop). Under Frankish rule Koúrion passed into the hands of the Cornaro family. The area was then famed for its sugar plantations, which gave place in the 16th c. to fields of cotton.

Sights

Theatre

Entering the site of ancient Koúrion at the foot of the hill, you come first to the theatre, at the southern tip of the hill. It

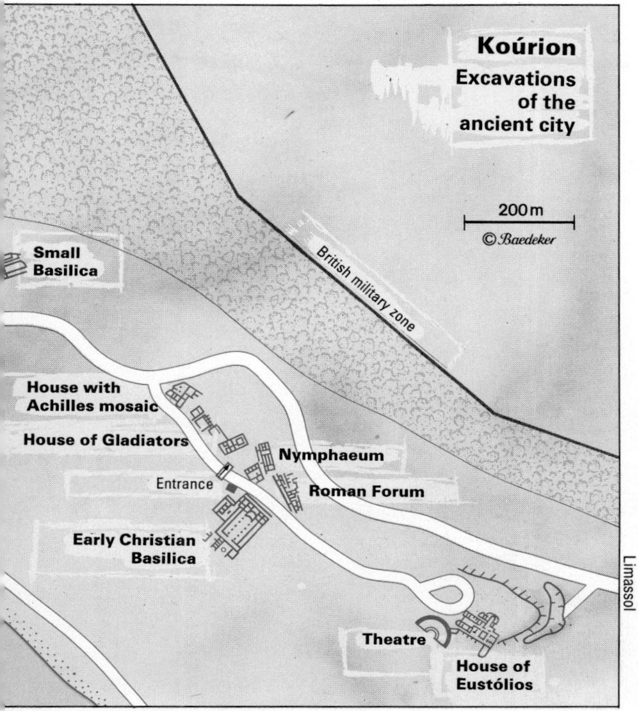

was excavated by American archaeologists, who in 1961 rebuilt part of the structure (which had suffered severe destruction). In summer performances of ancient plays are given in the theatre. The theatre was built in the 2nd c. AD on the site of an earlier Hellenistic theatre of the 2nd c. BC – a rather smaller building which had a circular orchestra and a cavea.

The orchestra of the present semicircular theatre is surrounded by a cavea which could accommodate 3500 spectators. The stage wall originally stood as high as the top of the cavea. A vaulted corridor to the rear of the theatre gave access by way of five passages to the tiers of seating. Over the top rows was a colonnade. At the beginning of the 3rd c. the lowest tiers of seating were removed and replaced by a metal barrier – suggesting that the arena was used for the fights with wild beasts which were popular in that period. The earthquakes of the 4th c. left the theatre in ruins.

House of Eustólios

Adjoining the theatre is a peristyle house of the Early Christian period (4th–5th c.), with its own baths, which later were probably given over to public use. In the entrance hall at the west end of the house is a mosaic with the welcoming inscription 'Enter ... Good fortune to the house'. This leads into an inner courtyard surrounded by columns, in the centre of which is an impluvium (water basin).

To the left, higher up, is the bath house. The large central room, probably the frigidarium, is decorated with mosaics (with a representation of the Ktisis, the personification of the creative spirit, holding a measure of the Roman foot). To the west is the hypocaust that provided heating for the baths, to the north a semicircular basin.

From here you enter the peristyle round the courtyard with its mosaics. A fragmentary inscription names Eustólios as the builder of this 'cool, sheltered

Theatre and House of Eustólios

1 Orchestra
2 Cavea
3 Skene
4 Staircase tower
5 Forecourt
6 Corridor
7 Frigidarium, with Ktisis mosaic
8 Peristyle courtyard with impluvium
9 Inscription naming Eustólios
10 Christian inscription
11 Triclinium

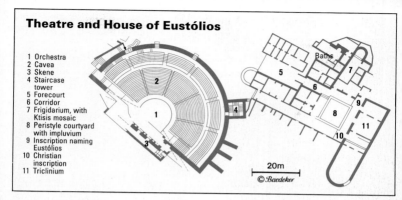

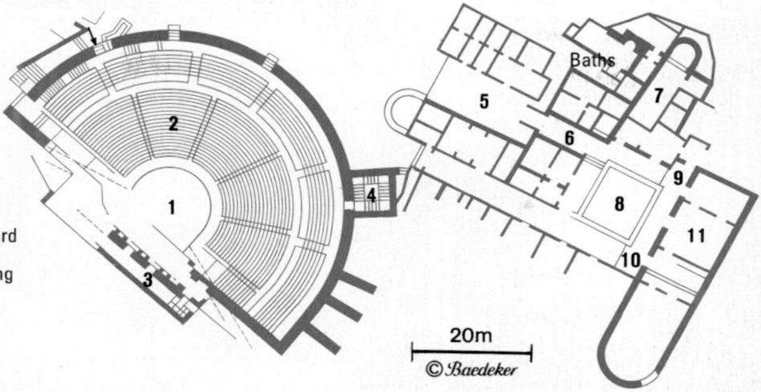

retreat'. Another inscription in front of a mosaic with Christian animal motifs says: 'In place of great stones and solid iron, gleaming bronze and diamonds this house is girt by the much venerated symbols of Christ.' There are also two representations of a fish, a common symbol of Christ in the Early Christian period.

Acropolis
Following the road north, made on the right there is an area under excavation. A large stoa with monolithic columns and Corinthian capitals probably belonged to the Roman forum. Excavation has also revealed the walls of Hellenistic buildings of unknown purpose. Adjoining the stoa on the east is a Roman building, presumably a dwelling. A nymphaeum of the 1st c. AD probably served as a reservoir for the town's water supply; it is still under excavation.

The most recent excavations in the acropolis area have found remains of the city destroyed by the 4th c. earthquakes. and have thrown fresh light on the way of life of the citizens of ancient Koúrion. Since the catastrophe occurred in the early morning most people were at home. In the Koúrion Archaeological Museum at Episkopí (☛Limassol, Surroundings) can be seen the skeletons of a young family buried in the ruins of their home.

House of the Gladiators
The House of the Gladiators, an atrium house belonging to a wealthy patrician family of the 3rd c. AD, takes its name from the mosaics of fights between gladiators in the inner courtyard. The mosaic to the north depicts two fully armed gladiators with blunted swords engaged in a practice bout, giving their names as Margareitis and Ellinikos. The second mosaic shows a heavily armed gladiator named Lytras with a curved dagger advancing on his opponent (mosaic damaged), while between them an unarmed figure named Dareios wearing a white toga, probably a referee, appears to be trying to calm them.

◀ The theatre of ancient Koúrion

Achilles mosaic
Near the Páphos motorway are remains of a Roman building of the 4th c. AD, with a courtyard flanked by rooms and a portico containing a mosaic of Achilles.

In the ancient myth Achilles was sent by his mother Thetis to the court of King Lykomedes of Skyros to be brought up among his daughters. By this means Thetis sought to prevent her son being killed at Troy as had been destined by fate. But since Troy could be captured only with the help of Achilles the wily Odysseus had recourse to a stratagem. He appeared before the king of Skyros laden with gifts, among which were weapons; then he caused the war trumpet to be blown, whereupon Achilles seized the weapons and thus revealed his presence. This is the moment depicted in the mosaic.

Ganymede mosaic
In the adjoining building is a richly ornamented mosaic pavement preserving fragments of a scene depicting Ganymede being carried off by Zeus in the guise of an eagle.

Early Christian basilica
Opposite the Roman forum is an Early

House of the Gladiators

Christian basilica, which bears witness to the reoccupation of Koúrion after the great earthquakes of the 4th c. The foundations of the church show that it was a three-aisled basilica with an apse flanked by two pastophoria. Over the altar was a canopy borne on four columns, the foundations of which can still be seen. Between the sanctuary and the naos was a screen, its position marked by cavities in the floor. Flanking the lateral aisles were *katekhouména*, long corridors with benches for the catechumens, the unbaptised members of the congregation, who were confined to these areas and the narthex. At the west end of the church was an atrium with a hexagonal fountain for ablutions. To the north of this was the bishop's house.

On the north side of the basilica was the **baptistery**, which, like the church, had three aisles and was preceded by a narthex and an atrium with a fountain for ablutions. The large font on the east side was designed for the adult baptisms by immersion which were then normal. To left and right were two rooms in which those about to be baptised were undressed and anointed.

Surroundings

Stadium

1 km west of the Koúrion excavations on the road to Páphos there is a stadium of the 2nd c. AD, in which the city of Koúrion staged contents until the 5th c. – races between eight to ten runners, discus throwing, ball games – in honour of military victories or on the occasion of Christian festivals. The name stadium was derived from a Greek measure of length normally equivalent to 192 m but in Koúrion to only 186 m. The stadium, the foundations of which survive, was a U-planned structure 229 m × 24 m planned, with seven tiers of seating, which could accommodate 7000 spectators, and three entrances. At the east end are traces of the starting line.

Small basilica

150 m east of the stadium are the foundations of a three-aisled basilica of the late 5th c., with a narthex and an atrium containing a fountain for ablutions. On the north side is a small chapel.

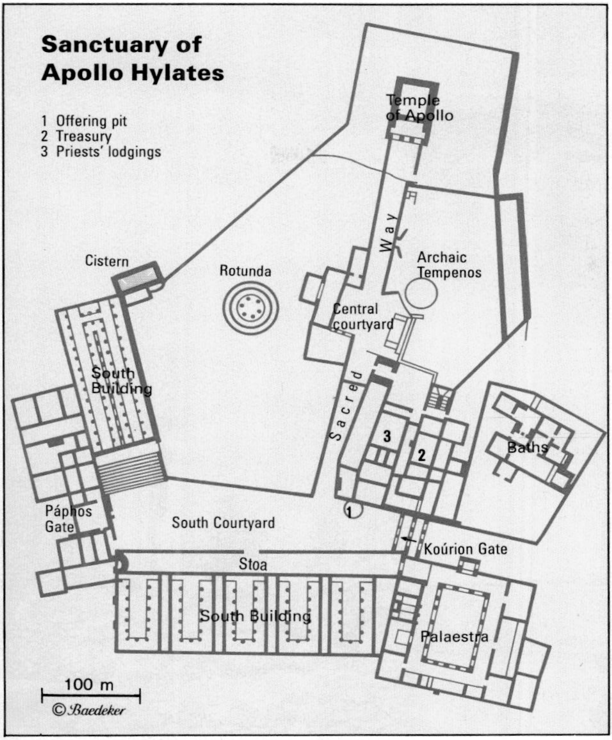

★Sanctuary of Apollo Hylátes

2 km further along the Páphos road is the shrine of Apollo Hylátes. Here Apollo was worshipped as the protector of the forest (Hylátes) and of animals – which were numerous in this area in antiquity. In its present form the sanctuary dates from Roman times, but excavation has revealed remains of an earlier sanctuary of the 6th c. BC.

The sacred precinct was entered by two doorways – to the west the Páphos Gate and to the east the Koúrion Gate, which is the present entrance.

Daily 7.30am–5pm, summer to 7pm.

Palaestra

Outside the sacred precinct, in front of the Koúrion Gate, is a palaestra of the 1st c. AD, the scene of wrestling contests and ball games. The large sand-floored courtyard is surrounded by colonnades, with seven rooms to the rear in which the athletes changed, oiled themselves and washed. At the north-east corner of the courtyard is a large stone pithos that contained water for the refreshment of the athletes.

Baths

Also outside the sacred precinct, in a bath house of the time of Trajan, (AD 98–117) can be seen the hypocaust which provided underfloor heating for the baths.

Sanctuary

The sacred precinct is entered through the Koúrion Gate. To the left stands the large South Building, with five rectangular rooms opening off a long Doric stoa (portico) in which pilgrims to the shrine presumably rested and set up their votive offerings. Each room is surrounded on three sides by a raised Doric colonnade.

An inscription over one of the doors records that two of the rooms were built by the Emperor Trajan in AD 101. Facing the South Building is the North-west Building, with a similar function, which consists of two long rooms surrounded by raised Doric colonnades.

Sacred Way
From the courtyard in front of the South Building a long paved Sacred Way runs north past lodgings for priests and the temple treasury to the temple of Apollo. A stone altar of the Archaic period (7th c. BC) is the oldest feature in the sanctuary.

Temple of Apollo
The temple of Apollo Hylátes of the 1st c. AD (reconstructed) was built on the foundations of an earlier temple of the late Classical or Hellenistic period. A broad flight of steps leads up to this prostyle temple, standing on a podium preceded by four columns with Nabataean capitals.

Rotunda
One of the oldest parts of the sanctuary is the rotunda of the Archaic period (6th c. BC), a circular temple surrounded by a gravel path, round which passed processions in honour of Apollo, lord of the forests. Seven cavities in the rock were once occupied by trees, which played a central part in the ritual of worship.

Offering pit
At the south end of the Sacred Way is a small semicircular pit (bothros) in which over hundreds of years the priests deposited offerings to Apollo, which must not be destroyed. The oldest material found here dated from the 5th c. BC.

Episkopí
See Limassol, Surroundings

Kolóssi
See entry

★Kýkko Monastery F 4

Μονή Κύκκου
Altitude: 1140 m

30 km north-west of the small town of Tróodos, in a lonely mountain setting, stands the monastery of Kýkko, which is famed throughout the Orthodox world. Its name seems to be derived from the *koukous* (ebony) trees which once grew here. The wealthiest and most powerful monastery in Cyprus, it owes its great reputation to its possession of an icon of the Mother of God which is believed to have been painted by Luke the Evangelist.

The monastery formerly owned property in Asia Minor and Russia and it still has large possessions in Cyprus, including numerous farms, which are administered centrally from Nicosia. The monastery runs various social institutions such as hospitals, schools and museums and wields considerable political influence on the island. It is a scene of great activity on Sundays and public holidays (religious fairs take place on 15th August and 8th September) and on the occasion of christenings and marriages, and is well equipped to cater for large numbers of people, with its long ranges of guest rooms, its large restaurants and its snack bars.
⌚ *Daily.*

◄ Koúrion – a pithos in the palaestra, with the temple of Apollo in the distance

Tomb of Archbishop Makarios
Archbishop Makarios III spent several years as a novice in Kýkko, and later built a chapel on the hill at Throni 3 km west of the monastery, near which he is now buried. Two soldiers form a guard of honour at his tomb day and night. During Cyprus's struggle for independence in the 1950s Kýkko Monastery supported the underground movement EOKA, and the hiding place of the EOKA leader Colonel Grivas was only some 2 km from the monastery.

Foundation and legend
The monastery was founded at the end of the 11th c. by a hermit monk named Isaias. According to legend the Byzantine governor of Cyprus, Manuel Voutoumetes, intruded on Isaias's solitude when he lost his way while hunting in the Tróodos massif. When Isaias refused to show him the way the governor kicked him; but when he got home he fell gravely ill and, pricked by conscience, begged Isaias to forgive him and cure him of his illness. At the behest of the Mother of God, who appeared to him in a dream, Isaias healed the governor and in recompense received from the emperor in Constantinople the icon of the Mother of God painted by Luke the Evangelist.

Sights
The present buildings of the monastery date only from the 19th and 20th c.,

Kýkko Monastry, the wealthiest and most powerful in Cyprus

since the older buildings were repeatedly destroyed by fire. As a result the mosaics and wall paintings in the church and monastic buildings show all the colour and skill of Orthodox painting but lack the patina of age.

The monastery's greatest treasure is the precious **icon of the Mother of God**, which is covered by a silver gilt plate and preserved in a special shrine. The icon, which is believed to have been painted by Luke in the Virgin's lifetime and is therefore regarded by the Orthodox Church as the authentic portrait of the Mother of God, has been the model for many later icons. It is credited with the power of bringing rain.

Near the icon is a black **bronze arm**, the presence of which is explained by a local legend. It is said that a negro impiously tried to light a cigarette at the oil lamp in front of the icon, whereupon the Mother of God caused his arm to wither and turn into metal.

Also of interest is the sword of a swordfish, presented by a seaman who was saved from drowning by the intervention of the Mother of God.

Surroundings

★Cedar valley

18 km west of Kýkko on an unsurfaced road with many bends is Cedar valley (alt. 1100 m), a secluded valley on the southern slopes of Mount Trípylos (1408 m). A labyrinthine track, little used, ascends through an unspoiled tract of country which has an almost eerie aspect. The impression of a primeval forest is not belied by the facts. The cedars which grow here, some 40,000 in number, belong to a species unique to Cyprus (*cedrus brevifolia*) which is believed to have covered the whole island in ancient times, when it was much used in the construction of ships and houses.

Very occasionally seen in Cedar valley and the forests to the north is the moufflon, a species of wild sheep which is in danger of extinction (☛Facts and Figures, Nature).

The rugged slopes of Cedar valley

Stavrós tis Psókas
The road continues through forests of cedar, pine, cypress and oak to the lonely forestry station of Stavrós tis Psókas (alt. 800 m), surrounded by volcanic peaks which are used as fire-watching points and afford magnificent panoramic views of the forests of Páphos.

Features of particular interest here are the small forestry museum, the tree nursery and especially the moufflon enclosure, where visitors can see these shy mountain creatures. The forestry station also offers accommodation and a simple restaurant.

Lagoudherá F 5/6

Λαγουδερά
Altitude: 1000 m

The remote mountain village of Lagoudherá lies 25 km east of the little town of Tróodos and 65 km north of Limassol. Above the village is a modest little barn-roofed church which originally belonged to a monastery (key from the village priest, who lives in the former monastic buildings next to the church).

★★Church of the Panayía tou Arákou (Arakiótissa)

As at Asínou (see entry), the designation of the Mother of God is taken from a plant, in this case from *arakás*, the pea. This church, built at the end of the 12th c., has a dome which was later covered by a pitched roof borne on supporting walls. The west end of the church, which has no paintings, was also a later addition (☛62, picture).

Wall paintings
The surviving wall paintings are among the finest in Cyprus, and since restoration in 1973 are resplendent in glowing colour. An inscription dates them to 1192: immediately after the conquest of Cyprus by the crusaders in 1191. Dating from the middle Byzantine period (☛Culture, Art and Architecture), the paintings were probably the work of artists from Constantinople. They are in the classical style of the Comnene period

Wall painting of the Nativity, Lagoudherá

and have a powerful dynamic effect, the elongated figures being depicted with great expression.

On the north wall of the church, below a representation of the Holy Tile (Keramídion), is an inscription naming the donor as a man named Leon.

In the vault of the apse is the Mother of God enthroned with the Child on her lap, attended by the Archangels Michael and Gabriel. Below this are seven busts of Cypriot prelates and eight fathers of the Church. On the side walls of the bema are two stylite saints, the solitary ascetics who sought solitude on the top of a pillar. In the vaulting is a representation of the Ascension.

In the dome of the church is Christ Pantokrator, surrounded by angels. Between the windows in the drum of the dome are Old Testament prophets. On the western pendentives are the four Evangelists, on the eastern pendentives the Annunciation.

In a lunette on the north wall of the church, below the dome, is the Presentation of the Virgin in the Temple. According to an apocryphal gospel Mary was taken by her parents to serve God in the Temple in fulfilment of a vow, accompanied by seven virgins of the house of Judah. Below this scene are a figure of St Nicholas, the Keramídion (Holy Tile) and the Presentation of Jesus in the Temple, which depicts the aged priest Simeon with the Child on his arm and John the Baptist pointing upward.

In the vaulting of the naos are the Descent into Hades (Anástasis) and below this the Baptism of Christ. On the south wall, in a niche below the dome, are the Dormition of the Mother of God and below this the slender figure of the Panayía tou Arákou with the Child on her arm, flanked by an over-life-size figure of the Archangel Michael. Opposite the Descent into Hades is a particularly fine representation of the Nativity. In the lower zone are figures of saints.

★Lárnaca/Lárnax F 9

Λάρναξ
Altitude: sea level
Population: 54,000

Lárnaca (Greek Lárnax, sarcophagus),

Cyprus's third-largest town, lies in a wide bay in the south-east of the island on the site of ancient Kítion. During the period of Turkish rule it was an important trading town. Foreign consuls were stationed in Lárnaca, and it grew to become the island's second-largest town. In the early 20th c. it declined into a provincial town of little consequence.

Post-1974 boom
Lárnaca's rise began after the Turkish invasion of 1974, when the island's principal port, Famagusta, fell to the Turks. This gave a great boost to Lárnaca, which became Cyprus's second-largest export port and now handles almost all the oil imports from the Middle East.

On the northern outskirts of Lárnaca various industries have been established, in particular an oil refinery, and a number of western European firms have factories in this area. The division of the island has given Lárnaca an increased share in international trade, and it has become an important traffic junction. It also has a modern marina with moorings for over 200 boats.

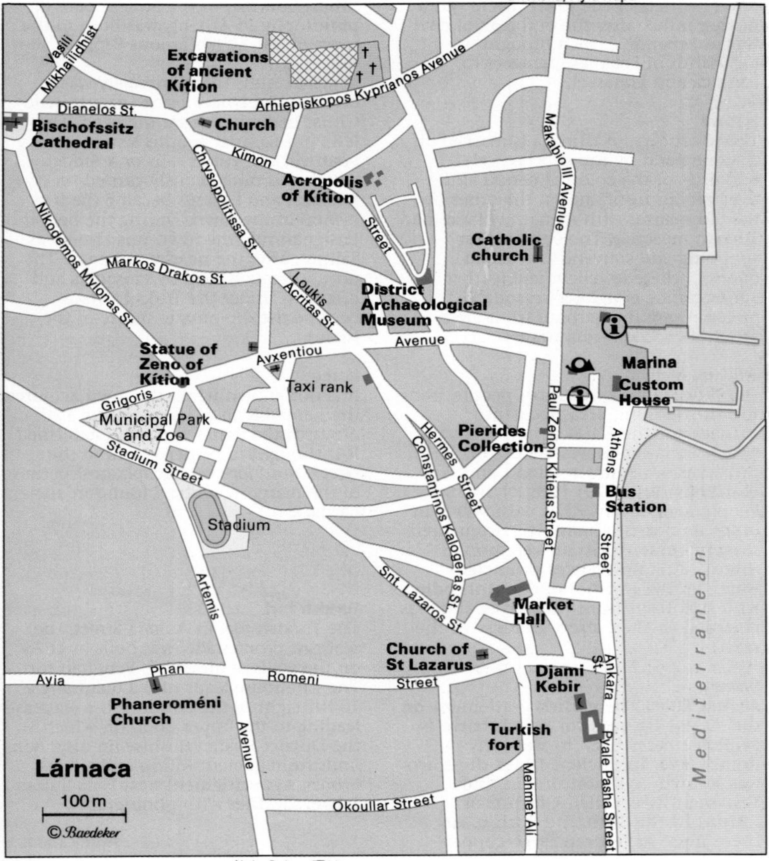

Airport
After the closure of Nicosia airport in 1974 a new international airport was established at Lárnaca, which is now the point of arrival for most foreign visitors (there is also an airport at Páphos). Bathing beaches have been built up with imported sand, and hotels, restaurants and bars have proliferated.

Population
With the great influx of refugees in 1974 the population of Lárnaca more than doubled. New housing schemes were built in great haste, and these developments still set the pattern in the outer districts of the town. There was a further influx after the outbreak of civil war in Lebanon, which brought thousands of Lebanese refugees to Lárnaca and Limassol.

★Town
The townscape of Lárnaca is marked on the one hand by the neoclassical buildings of the colonial period along the harbour front and on the other by the old quarter with its narrow lanes and Turkish mosques. The best area for shopping and souvenirs is the old quarter, where jewellery and leather goods can be bought at reasonable prices. Along the harbour front are a series of excellent restaurants.

Whitsun festival
On Whit Monday country people from the surrounding area flock into Lárnaca for the Kataklysmós festival, which commemorates Noah's preservation from the Flood and is a thanksgiving to Our Lady of the Sea. People spray each other with water in order to cleanse themselves from their sins. In these Christian ceremonies there are reminiscences of ancient water festivals in honour of Aphrodite, who had risen from the waves and was regarded as the patron goddess of the sea.

History
Ancient Kítion The earliest settlement on the site of Lárnaca for which there is evidence dates back to the early Bronze Age. In ancient times the town was known as Kítion; in the Old Testament it is called Chittim or Kittim. In the 14th and 13th c. BC there must have been large copper-working sites and a harbour for exporting the copper. At the end of the 13th c. the area was settled by Achaeans driven out of mainland Greece by Doric incomers. In the 11th c. BC the town was ravaged by an earthquake. Around 800 BC the abandoned site was reoccupied by Phoenicians, who remained there until 312 BC, rebuilding the old temples and founding a sanctuary of Astarte. Lárnaca now became one of the leading city-kingdoms on the island. An alliance with Persia saved it from the conquest suffered by other city-kingdoms.

The famous philosopher Zeno of Kítion, founder of the Stoic school of philosophy in Athens, was born in the town in 336 BC (☛Famous People).

Legend claims that **Christianity** was brought to Lárnaca by St Lazarus, who Christ had raised from the dead. The Jews put Lazarus and his sisters into a boat without either sails or a rudder, which was miraculously carried to Lárnaca, and Lazarus became the first bishop of the town. During the period of Lusignan rule the town was known as Salines, after the nearby salt pans. The port was much used by crusaders and pilgrims. Under the Turks Lárnaca became the diplomatic centre of the island.

Name
It is not known when the town acquired the name Lárnaca, but from the 17th c. onwards the name was well established. It is thought to be derived from the Greek word *lárnax* (sarcophagus) because of the many sarcophagi found in ancient Lárnaca.

Sights

Turkish fort
The Turkish fort in Ankara Street, the seafront promenade, was built in 1625 on the walls of an earlier Venetian fort. The gatehouse leads into a quadrangle. To the right of the entrance is a staircase leading to the upper floor, on which is the District Medieval Museum displaying finds from ancient Kítion and a late Bronze Age settlement near Hala Sultan Tekke, together with photographs

Ayios Lázaros ➤

Pierides Museum – Chalcolithic figure

documenting the excavations. To the left of the gatehouse is the sea wall of the fort. An open hall here contains ancient anchors from Kítion. Steps lead up to the wall walk, from where there are fine views of the harbour. During the Turkish period passing ships were greeted by a cannon shot from here. Under British rule the fort was used as a prison, and later as a store for finds from ancient Kítion. Today part of the fort operates as the Lárnaca Municipal Cultural Centre. *Mon.–Fri. 8am–5pm.*

Mosque

The mosque opposite the fort, the Djami Kebir, is dated by an inscription to 1835/6. The ablutions fountain is 18th c. The mosque is still used by Arab visitors to Cyprus.

★ Ayios Lázaros

From the fort, St Lazaros Street leads to the church of St Lazarus. This multi-domed church was built in the 10th c. on the site where a sarcophagus bearing the name Lazarus was found in 890. This was believed to be the tomb of St Lazarus, first bishop of Kítion. The relics of the saint were taken to Constantinople, but in 1204 were stolen by crusaders and carried off to Marseilles. They are now in the Church of St-Lazare in Autun (Burgundy).

After the building of the church the tomb of St Lazarus attracted large numbers of pilgrims. In the Middle Ages the church was served by Benedictines and later by Armenians. It was taken over by the Turks but in 1589 was sold back to the Christian community. Thereafter it was used both by Orthodox and Catholic worshippers. In the 19th c. the domes collapsed and were rebuilt. The bell tower and the loggia on the south side of the church also date from the 19th c.

The three-aisled basilican church has three domes over the nave. Corinthian capitals from ancient Kítion are built into the pillars at the crossing. The iconostasis, one of the finest in Cyprus, dates from the 18th c. On a pillar near the south doorway is a 17th c. icon of the Raising of Lazarus which eight days before Easter is paraded through the streets of Lárnaca. To the right of the iconostasis are steps leading down to the saint's empty sarcophagus.

Apr.–Aug. Mon.–Fri. 8am–12.30pm, 3.30–5.30pm; Sep.–Mar. Mon., Tue., Thu., Fri. 8.30am–12.30pm, 2.30–5pm, Sat. 8.30am–12.30pm.

Museum

There is a new museum next to the church with venerable old icons.

Ayía Phaneroméni

From here Phane Roméni Street leads west to the new church of Ayía Phaneroméni. In front of it, set into the ground, is a pre-Hellenistic chamber tomb which in Christian times was converted into a small church. The low, barrel-vaulted interior contains a number of icons. The icon of Ayía Phaneroméni (Revelation) is credited locally with the power to heal serious diseases.

★ Pierides Museum

In Zenon Kitieus Street is the small Pierides Museum, with a collection of finds dating from the Chalcolithic period to the Middle Ages. The museum occupies a house which belonged to the diplomat and merchant Dhimitrios Pierides (b 1811), who was a great art collector and saved much archaeological material from being exported from Cyprus. Later generations of the family shared his interest in archaeology and added to the collection, which now contains valuable antiquities from many different periods.

The first room on the left displays material of the Chalcolithic era, the Bronze Age and the Geometric and Archaic periods. In addition to numerous idols the most notable items are the examples of Bronze Age pottery. Particularly interesting (in the case in the centre of the room) is a terracotta figure from Soúskiou (Chalcolithic, 4th millennium BC) representing a naked man sitting on a chair with his hands to his ears and his mouth wide open. Two holes, one in his head and the other in his penis, suggest that it may have been a rhyton (libation vessel). In the same case is a pyxis (small casket) in the form of a sarcophagus (Geometric period).

The next room contains pottery of the Geometric and Archaic periods. Among the finest items are the beautifully decorated vases in the free field style.

In the third room are black-figured and red-figured vases and terracotta figures.

The last room shows glass from different periods and medieval pottery with sgraffito decoration.
Mon.–Sat. 9am–1pm.

Lárnaca District Archaeological Museum
The Lárnaca District Archaeological Museum in Lord Byron Street has a collection of artefacts ranging from the Neolithic period to the Middle Ages. The most notable items in the room to the right are the Neolithic objects from Khirokitía and Kalavasós, together with Bronze Age metal implements, pottery from Kítion and Arsos and Mycenaean and Bronze Age pottery. The second room contains sculpture, torsos and funerary stelae of different periods and an Egyptian sarcophagus of the 7th c. BC
Mon.–Wed., Fri. 7.30am–2.30pm, Thu. 3–6pm.

From here Kimon Street runs north-west to the excavations of ancient Kítion, passing on the right the remains of the ancient acropolis.

Excavations of ancient Kítion

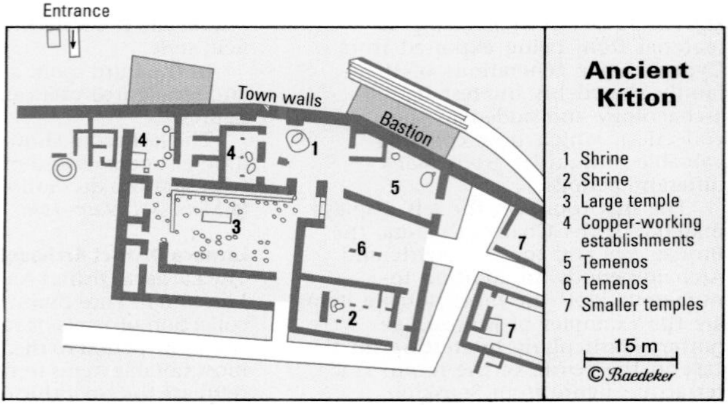

Ancient Kítion

Kimon Street joins Archiepiskopos Kyprianos Avenue, to the north of which are scanty remains of ancient Kítion. The city lay in the wide sheltered Bay of Lárnaca, with a harbour which was partly natural and partly artificial. It was bounded on the south by the salt lake of Lárnaca, and salt working was an important source of revenue from its earliest times. The section of the site known as Area II contains the city's sacred precinct, which was enclosed by a wall. Excavations have shown that there was a sanctuary here in the 2nd millennium BC, probably in the form of a sacred garden containing plants and two small shrines, each with a courtyard at the east end and a chamber containing an altar at the west end.

At the end of the 13th c. BC this first sanctuary was destroyed, and ca 1200 BC was replaced by a new one, which incorporated the old sacred garden. Most of the remains date from this period. The sacred precinct had a large temple on the west side.

Mon.–Fri. 7.30am–2.30pm.

Copper works
From the large temple an opening in the walls led to the copper works immediately north of the sacred precinct – pointing to the close association between the religious cult and copper. In the workshop area, which was open to the sky, were wells and smelting furnaces.

Other temples
On the south side of the sacred precinct one of the two earlier temples was rebuilt. At the east end were built smaller temples, in which a hoard of ivories, including a figure of the Egyptian god Bes, was found.

In the 9th c. BC Kítion was occupied by the Phoenicians, who did much building in the sacred precinct and altered the large western temple. In the 7th c. the temple was divided into three aisles. Finally in 312 BC the whole area was destroyed by fire.

Surroundings

Kamares aqueduct
On the road to Limassol an aqueduct (Kamares means the arches), built by the Turkish governor in 1745, brought water to Lárnaca from the Trémithos river, 10 km south-west. The aqueduct remained in use until 1939.

Kelliá
7 km north-east of Lárnaca lies the village of Kelliá, which was established in the Middle Ages and burned down by the Mamelukes in 1425. On a low hill is the church of **Ayios Antónios** (key in coffee house), which incorporates work from the 11th to the 15th c. Nothing remains of an earlier 9th c. church. The church has wall paintings dating from the early 11th to the 13th c., which are among the earliest paintings on the island. Particularly fine is a representation of the Sacrifice of Isaac on the south-western pillar, in a style similar

to the paintings in Ayios Nikólaos tis Stéyis at Kakopetriá (see entry).

Pýla
From the coast road east of Lárnaca a side road runs north-east to the little village of Pýla. United Nations troops are on duty in the village square, which has a Greek taverna on one side and a Turkish coffee house on the other. Pýla lies on the Green Line, the buffer zone between the Greek and Turkish parts of the island, and is one of the few places in the Republic of Cyprus where Greeks and Turks live together. Of the 1000 or so inhabitants of the village some 300 are Turks. Although the two communities live peaceably together they each have their own mayor and their own school. The Turkish inhabitants have freedom of movement both in the Republic of Cyprus and in the Turkish-occupied part of the island, but the Greek villagers cannot enter Turkish territory.

Hala Sultan Tekke
See entry

Kíti
See entry

Stavrovoúni
See entry

★Léfkara F 7/8

Λέυκαρα
Altitude: 600–650 m

The picturesque village of Páno Léfkara (Upper Léfkara), part of which is now protected as a historic site, lies in the southern foothills of the Tróodos massif between Limassol and Lárnaca, 18 km north of the Neolithic settlement of Khirokitía. It is a pretty little place with traditional houses, with red tiled roofs and whitewashed walls (originally light blue). The elaborately decorated wooden balconies and oriels on the upper floors give welcome shade during the hotter months of the year.

★Léfkara lace
The village is mainly famed for its traditional lace (known as Léfkaritika) and embroidery, the making of which can be traced back to Venetian times. In those times this cool hill village was a favourite summer retreat for noble

Léfkara lace

Street scene in Limassol

Venetian ladies, who spent their time working hemstitch embroidery; and their example was imitated by the local women who worked in their households. It is said that Leonardo da Vinci came here in 1481 to buy an altar cloth for Milan Cathedral. There are now numerous souvenir shops selling Léfkara lace and also the gold and silver jewellery which is made here by hand following ancient styles.

Surroundings

Convent of Ayios Minás
8 km south-west of Léfkara in Kato Léfkara stands the Convent of Ayios Minás, one of the few nunneries in Cyprus. Originally founded in 1670 it had remained empty for many years and was only recently reoccupied. The nuns maintain the convent largely by the sale of the icons that are painted here.

The church (1754) has a beautiful 18th c. carved iconostasis. The principal icon depicts Ayios Minás (St Menas), a military saint who served in the Roman army in Phrygia (Asia Minor), became a convert to the Christian faith and was martyred in the reign of Diocletian (AD 284–305).

Closed 12–3pm.

★Limassol/Lemesós G/H 6

Λεμεσός
Altitude: sea level
Population: 150,000

Limassol (Greek Lemesós; recently the official name), Cyprus's second-largest city and since the partition of the island in 1974 its principal port (☛Facts and Figures, Economy), lies on the south coast, to the east of the Akrotíri peninsula. Following the loss of Famagusta (see entry) Limassol developed into the island's principal port and is a rising commercial and industrial town. On the western outskirts of the town are a range of industrial sites. The large Keo, Etko, Sodap and Loel wineries have made Limassol the centre of the island's wine trade. In addition to table wines sherry, brandy, liqueurs and ouzo are produced here. The Keo winery makes a local brand of beer.

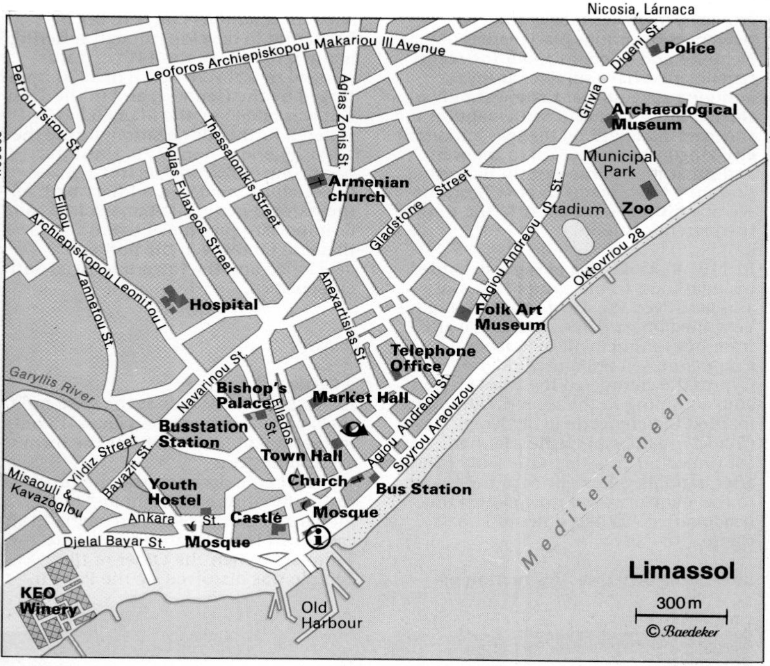

★Holiday resort
After the partition of the island the population of Limassol increased rapidly as a result of the influx of refugees. Tourism now developed into a major source of revenue and created new jobs. Something like a third of all visitors to Cyprus now spend their holiday in Limassol, which has taken over the role of Varósha, the hotel district of Famagusta. Along the coast to the east of the town are a range of high-rise hotels, and the seafront road is lined with restaurants, bars and shops.

Town
After the outbreak of civil war in Lebanon many Lebanese fled to Limassol and established businesses and banks there. These Arab immigrants have left their mark on the streets and many shops and bars draw attention to their wares in Arabic. Limassol now consists of two very different parts, the hotel district to the east and the old town to the west. The old town has preserved an oriental air, with craftsmen's shops huddled round the market square. Since in the past Limassol had many Turkish inhabitants it has preserved a number of mosques and a Turkish bathhouse. The old town is a good shopping area, in which leather goods and gold and silver jewellery can be found at reasonable prices.

Limassol also offers a varied nightlife, with discos and nightclubs as well as numerous bars and restaurants.

Festivals
In summer Limassol offers the attractions of various festivals – flower and fruit festivals as well as cultural events. In spring there is a large and colourful carnival parade. Other major occasions are the International Arts Festival in June/July and the Wine Festival in September.

History
Limassol was a place of no particular importance until the time of the

crusades. In ancient times there are references to various place names like Nemesos and Theodosia, but the scanty remains that have survived from antiquity suggest that there was only a small and insignificant settlement on the site, overshadowed by the two important city-kingdoms of Koúrion to the west and Amáthous to the east. In Byzantine times the town seems to have been the see of a bishop, with a fort to the west of the present castle.

In 1191 **Richard I, king of England,** landed in Amathoús, to the east of Limassol, and destroyed the town. After freeing his betrothed bride, Berengaria of Navarre, from her confinement by Isaac Comnenus, self-appointed ruler of Cyprus, he conquered the whole island and, according to the local tradition, was married to Berengaria in St George's Chapel in Limassol Castle. He then continued on crusade to the Holy Land, after handing over control of the island to the Templars, who now moved the headquarters of their order to Limassol Castle.

Later history After the destruction of ancient Amathoús Limassol began hesitantly to develop, though suffering many setbacks. In the 14th c. it was ravaged by a severe flood; in 1330 it was sacked by the Genoese; and in the 15th c. it was raided by the Mamelukes. It suffered further devastation during the Turkish conquest in 1570. Until the beginning of British rule in 1878 and the establishment of a military base on the Akrotíri peninsula Limassol was an unimportant provincial town; thereafter, however, the port was developed and the town improved and embellished.

Sights

★Castle

Limassol Castle stands at the west end of the seafront promenade. Limassol's only medieval building, it reflects the town's eventful history.

The castle occupies the site of an earlier Byzantine stronghold. Soon after Richard I's marriage to Berengaria in the castle in 1191 he handed it over to the Templars. When the Order of the Temple was dissolved by the Pope in

Limassol Castle

the 14th c. the castle passed into the hands of the Lusignan kings of Cyprus and later to the Knights of St John, whose headquarters were in Kolóssi Castle.

On the west side of the castle is a Gothic hall, built by the Knights of St John, which was used as a church. From here a spiral staircase leads up to the roof. St George's Chapel was later converted into a prison. The Venetians strengthened the castle, but were unable to hold out against the Turkish attack. The tower at the entrance to the castle was built by the Turks. During the period of British rule the castle was used as a prison.

The castle now houses the Cyprus Medieval Museum, whose collection includes part of a hoard of silver found at Lamboúsa and a variety of medieval artefacts – architectural fragments, gravestones of the 14th and 16th c., copper domestic articles, arms and armour. There is a collection of coins ranging from Byzantine times to the Turkish period, and pottery of the 13th to 19th c. In front of the castle is a reconstruction of a Byzantine oil press.

Daily 7.30am–5pm, summer to 7pm.

Reptile House

At the entrance to the Old Harbour, at the end of the promenade, is the Reptile House, with an unusual collection of boas, pythons, cobras, adders, rattlesnakes, lizards and crocodiles. Visitors are allowed, if they wish, to handle the creatures under the supervision of the owner.

Daily 9am–7pm.

Folk Art Museum

In Ayios Andreas Street is the little Folk Art Museum, which illustrates the folk art of the 19th and early 20th c. The exhibits in its seven rooms include embroidery and other types of needlework, traditional costumes, weaving looms and spinning wheels, beds and presses, and an elaborate bride's headdress in wax.

Mon.–Sat. 8.30am–1pm, 3–5pm; closed Tue. and Thu. afternoon.

District Archaeological Museum

Near the Municipal Gardens in Lord Byron Street is the District Archaeological Museum, with a wide range of exhibits from the Neolithic period to the Middle Ages. In the courtyard are mosaics from Alássa, including a fine representation of Aphrodite bathing.

Of particular note is the Chalcolithic material from Erími (the Erími culture) and Sotíra in the first room, including needles, arrowheads and stone axes. There is also a collection of pottery from the Bronze Age to the Roman period.

The second room is mainly devoted to finds from Amathoús, including small sculpture of the Archaic and Roman periods, bronze objects of various dates, seals and jewellery.

The third room contains sculpture and sarcophagi. Among the items from Amathoús are a large statue of the Egyptian god Bes (2nd/3rd c. AD), a huge capital with a female head and a sarcophagus with a recumbent figure on the lid. Other exhibits include Hellenistic sculpture from Koúrion and a small statue of the god Bes (5th c.).

Daily 7.30am–5pm, Thu. to 6pm.

Other sights

Also in the Municipal Gardens is a small zoo, including some moufflon, the rare wild sheep which is now a protected species. In a side street opening off Ayios Andreas Street is a Turkish bathhouse which is still in use. On the western outskirts of the town is the Keo winery, which can be visited.

Surroundings

Akrotíri peninsula

To the west of Limassol extends the Akrotíri peninsula, which culminates in Cape Gáta, the most southerly point on Cyprus. This is one of the British Sovereign Bases and much of the area is closed to the public. The vegetation is rich and luxuriant, with extensive citrus plantations and vineyards. The plantations were laid out in 1933 by the Cyprus Palestine Plantation Society, a cooperative of Cypriot and Israeli agricultural experts.

The salt lake of Akrotíri is no longer used for the extraction of salt. It is possible to drive along its shores for some 8 km to a point just beyond the village of Akrotíri where the road is closed by a barrier manned by British troops.

Kolóssi
See entry

Erími
14 km west of Limassol on the road to Páphos is Erími, one of the most important Chalcolithic sites on Cyprus. The excavations lie to the south of the village, but the scanty remains are likely to be of interest only to specialists. Pottery from the site can be seen in the archaeological museums of Limassol and Nicosia.

Episkopí
1.5 km west of Erími is Episkopí (the name derived from Greek *epískopos*, bishop), to the north of which is the Episkopí Cantonment, a large residential area for the families of the British forces, with British-style houses, schools, sports facilities, a shopping centre and a hospital.

It is worth looking into Episkopí, however, for the sake of the small **Koúrion Archaeological Museum**, which occupies a house opposite the church. The museum displays finds from Koúrion and the surrounding area – sculpture, inscriptions, coins, pottery – bearing witness to human settlement in this area from the Neolithic to the Early Christian period.

The most remarkable exhibit is the group of skeletons of a young family killed in an earthquake in the 4th c. AD which buried the town in mounds of debris. Since the earthquake occurred in the early morning most of the inhabitants were at home; and the attitudes of these skeletons, discovered some years ago, show that the family were huddled together on a bed, with the man trying to protect his wife and children from the catastrophe.
Mon.–Fri. 8am–2pm, Sat. 8am–1pm.

Koúrion
See entry

Sotíra
Just beyond Erími a road goes off on the right to Tróodos. From this road, soon after Kandoú, a minor road on the left leads north-west to Sotíra (8 km from Erími), where excavations on the hill of Teppes found one of the oldest settlements on the island.

A short way outside Sotíra it is worth visiting the church of Ayios Georgios where many icons, including a 15th c. Virgin and Child, are on display in a museum.

Amathoús

8 km east of Limassol on the coast road to Lárnaca with its many holiday hotels, just beyond the Amathus Beach Hotel, the remains of the town walls of the ancient city-kingdom of Amathoús (Roman Amathus; alt. 0–150 m) lie on the right. To the left of the road are the remains of the lower town, part of which, including dwellings as well as the harbour, has been swallowed up by the sea. Only slight remains of the upper town – the acropolis, with the city's temples – have so far been discovered.

Legends
The origins of this powerful city-kingdom are the subject of various myths. One legend makes Amathusa, mother of King Kinyras, the founder of the city. According to Plutarch (1st/2nd c. AD) Theseus put Ariadne, then heavily pregnant, ashore here because of a storm at sea but was then driven away by the storm. Discovering on his return that she had died in childbirth, he founded a shrine in her honour. A third version has it that Pygmalion was the founder and first king of the city. It is known, at any rate, that Eteo-Cypriot (i.e. non-Greek) cults were practised in Amathoús, which was notorious in ancient times for its human sacrifices and temple prostitution (☛Koúklia).

History
Human settlement in this area is thought to have begun in the Iron Age. With its numerous copper mines Amathoús, like Kítion, prospered as a centre of the copper trade, and the proud, independent city at an early stage to minted its own coins. In the conflict between the Greeks and the Persians Amathoús frequently changed sides, and in the 5th c. it was the only city-kingdom on Cyprus not to rebel against Persian rule.

In the 4th c., however, Amathoús sent ships to support Alexander the Great against the Persians. The city continued to flourish in Roman and Early Christian times, but its decline began with the Arab raids of the 7th and 8th c. The city was finally destroyed by Richard I, king of England, in 1191 (☛Limassol). Looting by tomb robbers and the use of stone from ancient buildings in the

Excavations of ancient Amathoús

construction of the Suez Canal did further damage to the ancient site.

Excavations
Excavations by French and Cypriot archaeologists since 1980 have brought to light the scanty remains of the acropolis on the hill, where there once stood a late Hellenistic temple of Aphrodite. So far the foundations of the temple and part of a pediment have been found. At the foot of the hill is the agora, which is better preserved. Tombs dating from the 7th–2nd c. BC have also been discovered.

Convent of Ayios Yeóryios Alemános

15 km east of Limassol (leave on the old road to the east and just after the Moni power station take a road on the left) is the convent of Ayios Yeóryios Alemános, standing amid vineyards and orchards in a valley running down to the sea.

The convent, which is little visited by tourists, was originally founded in the 12th c. and is occupied by nuns who, besides their religious duties, are mainly engaged in icon painting and flower and herb cultivation. After the partition of the island in 1974 the convent offered a home to the last of the three famous icon painters from the monastery of St Barnabas, near Famagusta.

Louvarás F/G 6

Λουβαράς

The little village of Louvarás lies in the Tróodos massif 22 km north of Limassol.

Church of St Mamas

Louvarás is notable only for the church of St Mamas. Built in 1455, it has well preserved wall paintings of 1495; the narthex is a later addition. It is dedicated to St Mamas, a saint much venerated in Cyprus (☛Sights from A to Z North Cyprus, Mórphou).
Key in the house immediately in front of the church.

Portraits of donors
An inscription over the west doorway gives the dates of construction and painting of the church. To left and right of the inscription are the kneeling figures of the donors, Constantine (the building) and John (the paintings), accompanied by their wives. The paintings were the work of Philip Goul, who was also responsible for the paintings in the church of the Stavrós tou Ayiasmáti at Platanistása.

Wall paintings
The paintings are arranged in three zones: various saints in the lowest zone and 27 New Testament scenes in the two upper zones.

Naos The narrative begins on the south wall of the church with the Nativity of Christ and continues with the Presentation in the Temple, the Baptism, the Transfiguration, the Raising of Lazarus, the Entry into Jerusalem, the Holy Women at the empty tomb, the healing of the paralytic at the Pool of Bethesda, Christ preaching to the Jews, Christ and the woman of Samaria, the healing of the man born blind and the healing of Peter's mother-in-law.

On the west wall, under the Crucifixion, are the Last Supper, the Washing of the Feet, the Betrayal, Christ before Annas and Caiaphas, Christ casting out devils, the foundation inscription and the Descent from the Cross.

On the north wall are Pilate washing his hands, the Mocking, the Bearing of the Cross, the Descent of the Holy Ghost (Pentecost), the Descent into Hades (Anástasis), the Ascension and the Dormition of the Mother of God.

Bema In the vault of the apse is the Mother of God Blacherniótissa, standing with her arms raised in prayer between the Archangels Michael and Gabriel. Below this are six fathers of the Church. On the north wall is the Sacrifice of Isaac, on the south wall the Hospitality of Abraham.

Makherás Monastery F 7

Μονή Μαχαίρα
Altitude: 800 m

Makherás Monastery (Greek Moní Machaíra) lies 36 km from Nicosia in the eastern foothills of the Tróodos massif. It is reached on a road which runs south-west from Nicosia, passing the site of ancient Tamassós (see entry). The last few kilometres are on a hill road which climbs, with many bends, to the monastery, picturesquely situated at the foot of Mount Makherás.

Foundation
As with other monasteries in Cyprus, the foundation of Makherás followed the discovery of a wonder-working icon in the 12th c. During the iconoclastic conflict of the 8th and 9th c. (☛Culture, Art and Architecture) many icons were hidden to save them from destruction by iconoclasts, and their rediscovery in the Middle Ages led to the foundation of monasteries.

The monastery was rebuilt in the 19th c. after a devastating fire.

Legends
According to legend two 12th c. hermits, Ignatios and Neóphytos, discovered an icon of the Mother of God in a cave under the present monastery, together with a mysterious knife (*makhaíra*) which later gave the monastery its name. Thereupon the Byzantine emperor Manuel Comnenus gave the two hermits land and money for the foundation of a monastery.

In the early 14th c. Alice d'Ibelin, wife of King Hugo IV of the Lusignan dynasty, is said to have forced her way into the monastery church, which women were forbidden to enter: whereupon the Mother of God punished her by striking her dumb.

Also in the 14th c. King James I and his family sought refuge in Makherás to escape the plague which was then raging.

Icon of the Mother of God
On the large iconostasis of the church is the much venerated icon of the Mother of God, almost entirely concealed under a silver cover. It is credited with the power to heal wounds and bring rain. Miraculously, it survived the fire which destroyed the monastery.

Afxentíou memorial
In a small room in the monastery are displayed photographs and mementos of Grigóris Afxentíou, Grivas's second-in-command in the EOKA movement, who died near here. During the uprising he sought refuge in the monastery but his presence was betrayed by a local peasant. He then withdrew to a cave below the monastery, where he was burned to death in March 1957 in an attack by British forces.

Below the monastery is a memorial to Afxentíou, now a national hero. From here there is an attractive footpath (14 km) to Politikó.

Nicosia/Lefkosía D/E 7/8

Λευκοσία
Altitude: 165 m
Population: 203,000

Nicosia (Greek Lefkosía, Turkish Lefkoša, now officially Lefkosía), the largest city in Cyprus, lies in the wide Mesaória plain, within easy reach of Limassol and Lárnaca by motorway. Since the Turkish invasion in 1974 the demarcation line between Greek and Turkish-occupied Cyprus runs through the centre of the city, which is the capital of both the Republic of Cyprus and Turkish-occupied North Cyprus (☛History, Cyprus Divided).

In contrast to the Greek part of the city, which has continued to grow and now has a population of ca 165,000, the population of the Turkish part has stagnated at ca 45,000.

Nicosia is the seat of the government, foreign embassies, all national organisations and the country's leading businesses. In order to avoid the economic stagnation with which the city was threatened after the closure of Nicosia's international airport in 1974 a motorway was built between Nicosia and Limassol (see entry), providing the essential link with the largest port in Cyprus.

Green Line
Along Hermes Street, once the heart of the Old Town, runs the Green Line, at some points only a few metres wide, between the two parts of Cyprus. It is so called because a line of separation

Makherás Monastry, in the foothills of the Tróodos massif

was drawn on a map with a green pencil in the 1960s, when there were already secret plans for a possible division of Cyprus. Although the frontier is marked only by sandbags, barbed wire and old oil drums, it is nevertheless impenetrable. In the buffer zone between the two territories, in which everything must remain unchanged, there are constant patrols by the United Nations peacekeeping force, which also maintains peace and order in the border area.

Frontier crossing: Ledra Palace Hotel
The only crossing point between the two sides is at the Ledra Palace Hotel, once one of Cyprus's most renowned hotels. Only Armenians and Maronites can cross the frontier without restriction. Visitors to the Republic of Cyprus can get a visa for a day trip (8am–6pm) into Turkish-occupied North Cyprus (though this is frowned on by the government); but visitors to North Cyprus cannot cross the frontier in the reverse direction, since the Greek Cypriot authorities regard entry into the Turkish 'pseudo-state' as illegal. By the same token Greek Cypriots are not allowed to enter North Cyprus; exceptions are made only in cases of particular hardship (e.g. a family funeral) through the intermediary of the United Nations peacekeeping force. The frontier is also closed to Turkish Cypriots wishing to enter South Cyprus (☛Practical Information South Cyprus, Frontier Crossing).

★Old Town
The Old Town of Nicosia is still enclosed within the circuit of its Venetian walls. Here visitors can encounter the authentic daily life: the blaring of car horns in narrow labyrinthine streets, the clamour of Greek folk music, people dozing outside their open front doors in a summer temperature of 40° C in the shade; the relaxed and undemanding Mediterranean way of life, combined with an unconcerned tolerance of a noise level which for visitors from more northerly latitudes may be harder to bear.

An oasis of peace is the Laïkí Yitoniá (People's Neighbourhood) quarter, in which traffic is restricted. This district, now an essential item of any sightseeing tour of the city, has been under renovation in recent years and new houses have been built in traditional style, so that the area now gives a very fair impression of Nicosia as it used to be. The city's principal shopping streets are Ledra Street and Onaságoras Street.

New Town
While in the evening the Old Town empties – many houses are unoccupied and the tourists return to their hotels on the coast – the newer parts of the town continue to hum with activity; for in contrast to the Turkish part of the city, where life seems to have stood still, the Greek part has acquired new apartment blocks suburbs with banks, hotels, shops and entertainment districts.

Because of the city's location in the Mesaória plain there are no natural boundaries to its expansion, and many new businesses have been established within the Nicosia conurbation.

After the removal of the tented camps in which Greek Cypriots from the Turkish-occupied territories were originally housed new accommodation was provided with remarkable speed in settlements on the outskirts of the city in which many refugees still live rent free.

History
Although the Mesaória plain was occupied as early as the Neolithic period the first traces of settlement within the area of Nicosia date only from the Bronze Age. Nicosia first appears in the records in the 7th c. BC, when it is mentioned in Assyrian documents under its then name of Ledra, as one of the ten city-kingdoms paying tribute to Assyria. In the 6th c. the little town of Ledra was incorporated in the powerful city-kingdom of Sálamis.

In the 3rd c. BC Leukos, son of the Egyptian ruler Ptolemy Soter I, founded a city which he called Leukosía on the site of Ledra. In later centuries the town was frequently ravaged by earthquakes. In Roman times Leukosía was a place of little importance, since the Romans preferred the coastal towns.

Middle Ages The town gained in

A Venetian bastion on the perimeter of the old town

importance in the 4th c. AD, under Byzantine rule, when it became the see of a bishop. During Arab raids in the 7th c. many inhabitants of the coastal towns sought refuge in Lefkosía. In the 10th c., after the expulsion of the Arabs, the town flourished. During a rebellion against the Templars (who had bought Cyprus from Richard I for 100,000 gold bezants) in 1192 the Latin name Nicosia was used for the first time.

The town enjoyed its greatest period of prosperity from the end of the 12th c. under Frankish rule (the Lusignan dynasty). It became capital of the kingdom of Cyprus and the see of a Roman Catholic archbishop. In the Middle Ages it had more than 250 churches as well as a royal palace and splendid aristocratic mansions.

From Venetian to British rule When the Venetians gained control of Cyprus at the end of the 15th c. they developed Nicosia still further. In the 16th c., anticipating attack from the Turks, they built new town walls which enclosed a smaller area than the old walls but were much stronger. The construction of the walls involved the demolition of considerable areas of the town.

In 1570 Nicosia was taken by the Turks after a seven-week siege and became the seat of the Turkish governor. During the period of British colonial rule (1878–1960) it remained the official residence of the governor (and later of the high commissioner) and gradually developed to its present size and importance.

★Venetian walls

Construction

The walls, built in 1567–70 by the Venetian military engineer Giuliano Savorgnano, have a total length of just under 5 km. They enclose an oval, with 11 bastions (bearing the names of leading Venetian families). To provide better protection against Turkish artillery the walls were thicker than the previous defences, sloping from the ground

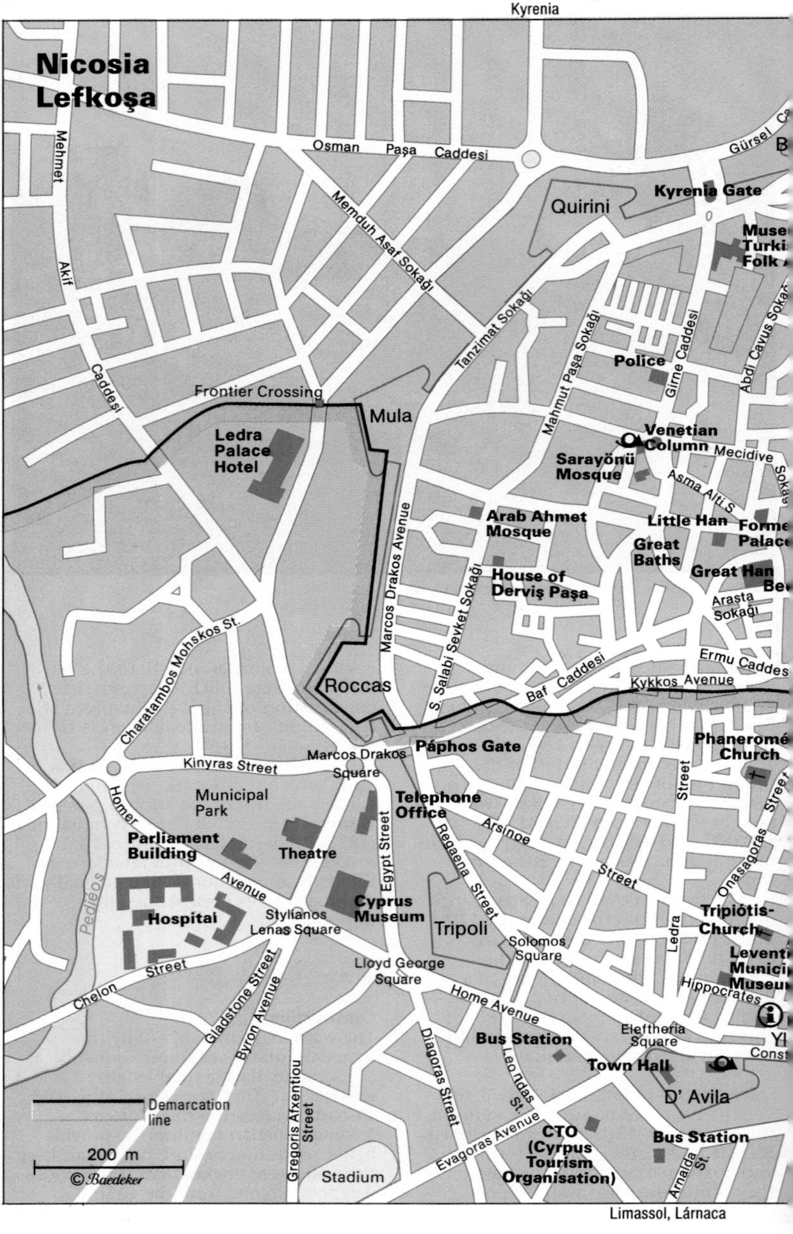
Kyrenia
Nicosia
Lefkoşa
Mehmet
Akif
Caddesi
Osman Paşa Caddesi
Gürsel
Memduh Asaf Sokağı
Quirini
Kyrenia Gate
Tanzimat Sokağı
Mahmut Paşa Sokağı
Girne Caddesi
Abdi Cavus Sokağı
Police
Frontier Crossing
Mula
Ledra Palace Hotel
Venetian Column
Mecidive
Sarayönü Mosque
Asma Alti S.
Arab Ahmet Mosque
Little Han
Great Baths
Great Han
House of Derviş Paşa
Marcos Drakos Avenue
S. Salabi Sevket Sokağı
Arasta Sokağı
Ermu Caddesi
Kykkos Avenue
Baf Caddesi
Charatambos Mohskos St.
Roccas
Marcos Drakos Square
Páphos Gate
Kinyras Street
Municipal Park
Homer
Telephone Office
Parliament Building
Theatre
Egypt Street
Regaena Street
Arsinoe Street
Onasagoras
Avenue
Hospital
Pedieos
Stylianos Lenas Square
Cyprus Museum
Tripoli
Solomos Square
Ledra
Tripiótis-Church
Chelon Street
Gladstone Street
Byron Avenue
Lloyd George Square
Home Avenue
Hippocrates
Bus Station
Diagoras Street
Leonidas St.
Eleftheria Square
Town Hall
D' Avila
Demarcation line
200 m
© Baedeker
Gregoris Afxentiou Street
Stadium
Evagoras Avenue
CTO (Cyprus Tourism Organisation)
Bus Station
Arnalda St.
Tróodos
Limassol, Lárnaca

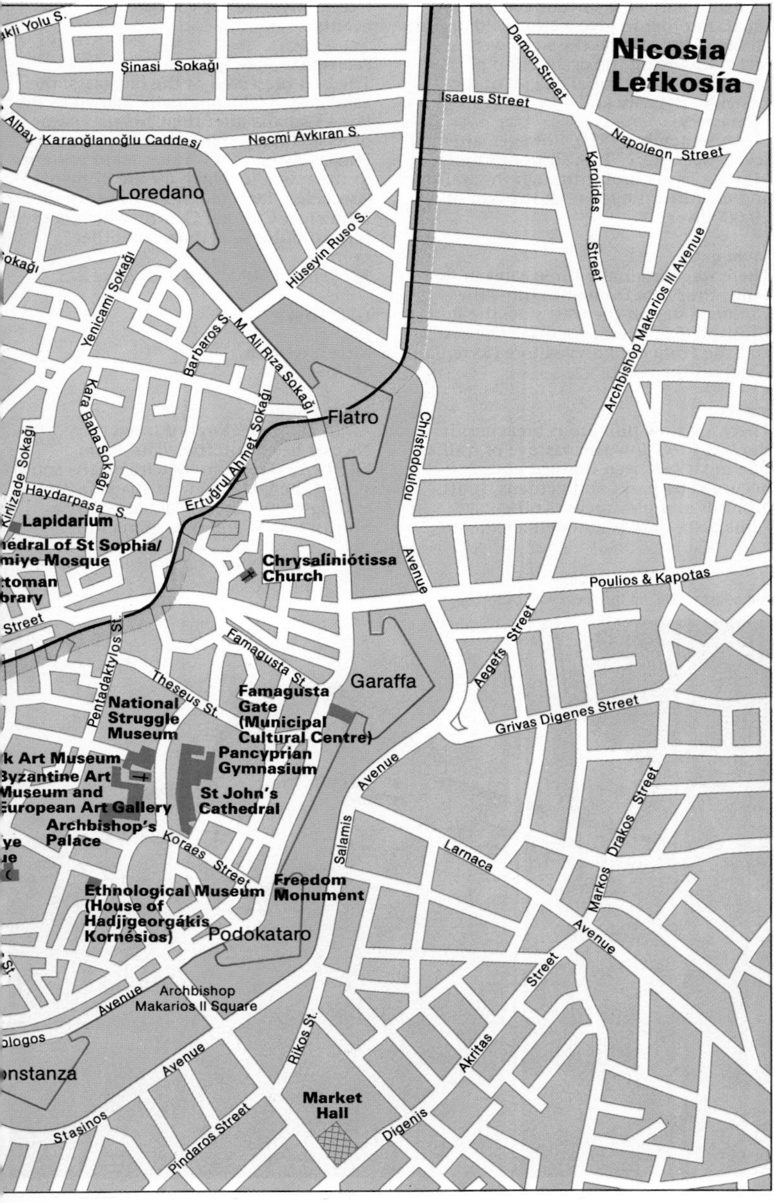
Nicosia
Lefkosía
akli Yolu S.
Şinasi Sokağı
Damon Street
Isaeus Street
Albay Karaoğlanoğlu Caddesi
Necmi Avkıran S.
Napoleon Street
Karolides Street
Loredano
Hüseyin Ruso S.
Archbishop Makarios III Avenue
okağı
Yenicami Sokağı
Barbaros S.
M. Ali Rıza Sokağı
Kara Baba Sokağı
Flatro
Ahmet Sokağı
Christodoulou Avenue
Kirlizade Sokağı
Haydarpaşa S.
Ertuğrul
Lapidarium
hedral of St Sophia/
miye Mosque
ttoman
brary
Chrysalíniótissa Church
Poulios & Kapotas
Street
Aegefs Street
Pentadaktylos St.
Famagusta St.
Garaffa
Theseus St.
National Struggle Museum
Famagusta Gate (Municipal Cultural Centre)
Grivas Digenes Street
k Art Museum
Byzantine Art Museum and European Art Gallery
Pancyprian Gymnasium
St John's Cathedral
Avenue
Archbishop's Palace
Koraes Street
Salamis
Drakos Street
Larnaca Avenue
Markos
ye
ue
Ethnological Museum (House of Hadjigeorgákis Kornésios)
Freedom Monument
Podokataro
St.
Street
Archbishop Makarios II Square
Avenue
ologos
Rikos St.
Akritas
nstanza
Avenue
Market Hall
Stasinos
Pindaros Street
Digenis

upwards, and were surrounded by a moat. In order to give a clear field of fire all buildings outside the walls were razed, involving the destruction of the royal palace, the burial chapel of the Lusignan dynasty and a Dominican monastery.

In September 1570, however, after a seven-week siege, Turkish troops under Mustafa Pasha broke through the walls and captured the town, at the cost of 20,000 lives.

Town gates
There were originally three gates in the walls: the Porta Domenica (now the Páphos Gate) on the west side, the Porta Giuliana (Famagusta Gate) on the east and the Porta del Provveditore (Kyrenia Gate) on the north.

Moat
There are now numerous breaches in the walls to allow the passage of traffic. The moat has been drained and is occupied by parks and gardens, sports grounds and play areas. At the Famagusta Gate is an open-air theatre, frequently used for concerts and other events.

Famagusta Gate
The best preserved of the old gates, the Famagusta Gate, originally known as the Porta Guliana after the Christian name of its architect, stands in Nikiphoros Phokas Avenue. It was the main entrance to the town, to which all the principal streets led. Restored, it now houses the Municipal Cultural Centre, which is used for exhibitions, lectures and other events.
Mon.–Sat. 10am–1pm, 4–7pm.

Old Town

Nicosia – North
See page 204

Ledra Street
All the main features of interest in Nicosia lie within the walls. From Eleftheria (Freedom) Square on the south side of the Old Town the main shopping and business street, Ledra Street, runs northwards to end, like many other

Famagusta Gate, on the town wall of Nicosia

streets, at the boundary with the Turkish-occupied northern half of the town. To the right, just inside the walls, is the **Laïkí Yitoniá** (People's Neighbourhood) quarter, now renovated, with restaurants, souvenir shops and bookshops.

Leventis Municipal Museum
In Hippocrates Street, in the Laïkí Yitoniá quarter, is the Leventis Municipal Museum, Cyprus's first history museum, opened in 1989. Jointly financed by the Leventis Foundation and the city, it occupies a three-storey 19th c. merchant's house in neoClassical style. The ground and first floors illustrate the history of Nicosia with the help of photographs, pictures, coins, clothing and a variety of other exhibits. The displays are arranged in chronological order, from the earliest archaeological finds by way of Byzantine, Frankish and Venetian times, Turkish and British colonial rule, to Nicosia as capital of the Republic of Cyprus. On the second floor are rooms for exhibitions, a reading room and administrative offices.
Tue.–Sun. 10am–4.30pm.

Phaneroméni Church
From Elefthería Square Onaságoras Street runs north-east to the Phaneroméni Church (Church of the Revelation), the largest church in Nicosia, built in 1872 during the period of Turkish rule. Notable features of the interior are the figure of God the Father in a triangular halo (the symbol of the Trinity), the magnificent iconostasis and the large crystal chandeliers.
Daily 6am–noon, 3–5.30pm, and for services.

In the gardens outside the church is a mausoleum containing the remains of Archbishop Kyprianos and other bishops executed by the Turkish governor in 1821 as a deterrent to the movement for Greek independence.

Attached to the church is the Phaneroméni Library, which contains the oldest icons in Cyprus.

Tripiótis Church
North of the Laãkí Yitoniá quarter in Solon Street, once a prosperous residential area, stands the Tripiótis Church, dedicated to the Archangel

Tripiótis Church

Michael, which was built in 1690 on the site of an earlier church of the 15th/16th c. Over the west doorway are architectural fragments from the older church. Even older is a fragment of a frieze over the south doorway depicting a man between vine leaves surrounded by other human figures and birds. The church has a fine iconostasis (17th/18th c.), with icons in gold and silver covers, signs that it was once a society church.

Ömeriye Mosque
From the south-east side of the walled town Ares Street leads to the Ömeriye Mosque. Now run by Syrians, it is the only mosque in the Greek part of Nicosia which is still used for Muslim worship. It was built on the ruins of a 14th c. Augustinian monastery which was destroyed by Turkish gunfire in 1570. The Augustinian house was one of three major monasteries in the Old Town, the others being the Dominican and Franciscan friaries.

The Gothic buttresses of the monastic church can still be seen in the interior of the mosque, and a small vaulted room on the north side, now used as a prayer hall for women, has a beautiful Gothic rose window. From the minaret there is a fine panorama over the town to the Kyrenia hills. Opposite the mosque are the Ömeriye Baths, which are still in use.

Freedom Monument
On the Podokataro Bastion, to the south-east of the walled town, is the large Freedom (Eleftheria) Monument, erected in 1960 after the end of British colonial rule, which symbolises the liberation of the people of Cyprus. Two EOKA fighters are shown raising the iron grille at the gate of a prison, from which men, women, children and priests are emerging. The monument is crowned by a huge figure personifying Freedom.

From the Freedom Monument Koraes Street leads to the Archbishop's Palace, St John's Cathedral, the Byzanatine Museum and Art Galleries and the Folk Art Museum.

★Archbishop's Palace
The neo-Byzantine Archbishop's Palace was built by Archbishop Makarios III between 1956 and 1961. Completed just after Cyprus achieved independence, this magnificent building demonstrates the power and wealth of the Orthodox Church. The palace is open to the public only on special occasions. The former archbishop's palace next to it now houses a folk museum. The monumental bronze statue of Makarios III in front of the palace was erected by Archbishop Chrysostomos in 1987.

Freedom Monument

★St John's Cathedral
St John's Cathedral (Ayios Ioánnis) was built in 1662 during the period of Turkish rule. It is of modest size, since the Ottoman authorities would not allow the building of a large church. The ringing of church bells was also prohibited, and the addition of a bell tower was permitted only in 1858.

The cathedral succeeded an earlier building belonging to a 15th c. Benedictine monastery (later taken over by Orthodox monks), which itself was the successor to a still older church dedicated by the Knights of St John to their patron John the Baptist. The Lusignan king Peter I was buried in the earlier church. Built into the outer walls of the church on the south and west sides are various architectural fragments and a coat of arms of the Lusignan period.

The church has been since 1730 the cathedral of the archbishops of Cyprus, who have been consecrated here since the end of the 18th c.

The church has a barrel vault. The most striking feature of the interior is the magnificent iconostasis, of carved wood covered with gold leaf, with icons of the 18th and 19th c. Below the 18th c. pulpit is an icon of St John the Evangelist, the oldest in the church, painted by Theodóros Poullákis in the 17th c. On the archbishop's throne to the right of the iconostasis is an icon of St Barnabas. On another throne is the double-headed eagle, which is the emblem of the Orthodox church, and in the floor is another large double-headed eagle on which the archbishop stands during his consecration.

The **wall paintings** in the church are 18th c. In the centre of the vaulting is Christ Pantokrator, surrounded by angels, prophets and apostles. On the

Archbishop's Palace

south and north walls are New Testament scenes, from the Annunciation to the Crucifixion. Over the south doorway is the Last Judgment, with the Tree of Jesse to one side.

On the north wall are the Mandílion, the Crucifixion and the scenes from the Passion cycle which usually follow it, the Descent into Hades (Anástasis) and the Ascension. Opposite the Tree of Jesse is a representation of the Creation. At the west end of the church are paintings of Christ's miracles. The most interesting paintings are on the south wall, to the right of the archbishop's throne. They depict the finding of the remains of St Barnabas and their recognition by the Byzantine emperor. This was the event that won autocephaly (independence) for the Church of Cyprus (☛Facts and Figures, Religion).

Mon.–Fri. 9am–noon, 2–4pm, Sat. 9am–noon.

★Icon Museum

The Icon Museum (Byzantine Museum), opened in 1982, occupies the right-hand wing of the former archbishop's palace, next the Archbishop Makarios III Cultural Foundation.

This valuable collection of some 150 icons ranging from the 9th to the 18th c., the finest in Cyprus, brings together icons from churches all over the island. There were undoubtedly many other historic icons in Cyprus, but most of them fell victim to iconoclasts, to the Turks or to fires.

The mosaics which disappeared from the Kanakariá church in Turkish-occupied Cyprus and were recently recovered by the Republic of Cyprus (☛Culture, Heritage under Threat). Six of the lost mosaics are now displayed here in an exhibition of the Evangelists Matthew and John.

Oct.–Apr. Mon.–Fri. 9am–1pm, 2–5pm, Sat. 9am–1pm; May–Sep. Mon.–Fri. 9.15am–1pm, 2–5.30pm, Sat. 9am–1pm.

One of the oldest **icons** in the collection is an encaustic icon of the Mother of God, hung near the entrance. The icon of SS Cosmas and Damian dates from the 10th c. Opposite the entrance is an icon of St John from the church of Asínou which dates from the 12th c., the heyday of icon painting. An icon showing early western influence is a 13th c. Mother of God, painted for Dominican monks, with Latin inscriptions in the marginal scenes.

The Ottoman conquest of Cyprus in 1571 led to a marked decline in the craft of icon painting.

At the end of the main hall in a small room (reconstructed) are 15th c. wall paintings from the church of Ayios Nikólaos tis Stéyis (☛Kakopetriá).

The first floor of the museum houses the **Art Gallery** (same hours), with European paintings (mainly religious themes) by 17th c. Spanish, Dutch and Flemish schools and French pictures of the 17th and 18th c. On the second floor is a collection of prints and drawings illustrating ancient architecture and 19th c. Greek history.

Pancyprian Gymnasium

Opposite the Archbishop's Palace stands the neoclassical Pancyprian Gymnasium, the oldest gymnasium (grammar school) in Cyprus, with the best school library. In the 1950s this was a hotbed of support for the enosis movement. In his book *Bitter Lemons* Lawrence Durrell (☛Introduction, Famous People), who taught for a time in the school, describes the beginnings of the Cypriot rising against British colonial rule. The most notable pupil of the Pancyprian Gymnasium was Archbishop Makarios III.

Folk Art Museum

The Folk Art Museum occupies the ground floor of a 15th c. Gothic building which originally belonged to a Benedictine monastery and from 1730 was the archbishop's palace. The museum was established in 1950 by the Society of Cypriot Studies, but had no suitable premises until 1961, when the archbishop moved to the new palace. In the museum's 12 rooms, which still preserve some Frankish architectural features, are displayed Cypriot costumes, jewellery, woven fabrics, embroidery, everyday objects and old carved chests. A notable feature is the former monastic cloister, surrounded by monks' cells. Room 11 is furnished in traditional Cypriot style, with a painting of a wedding scene by the naive Cypriot painter Michalis Kashialos.

Mon.–Wed., Fri. 8.30am–1pm, 2–4pm, Tue., Thu. 8.30am–1pm, 2–5pm, Sat. 8.30am–1pm.

Between the Folk Art Museum and St John's Cathedral is a bust of Archbishop Sophronios, head of the Church of Cyprus from 1865 to 1900 and a leader of the resistance to British colonial rule. Another marble bust is of Archbishop Kyprianos, who was executed by the Turks in 1821.

National Struggle Museum

In a side wing of the former archbishop's palace, next to the Folk Art Museum, is the National Struggle Museum, established in 1961, which documents the activities of EOKA, the underground organisation which from 1955 to 1959 fought for enosis, the union of Cyprus with Greece (☛History, Cyprus Divided). In addition to photographs, press cuttings, books and other publications the exhibits include weapons, models of home-made bombs, a gallows on which Greek rebels were executed and (in the garden) the car used by Colonel Grivas, the EOKA leader.

In another room are 30 volumes containing the signatures of all the Greek Cypriots who voted for enosis in a referendum held by the Orthodox Church in January 1950.

Mon.–Sat. 8am–2pm, 3–5pm.

Chrysaliniótissa Church

Going along Ayios Ioánnis Street as far as Theseus Street and then turning into Antigonos Street, you come into one of the historic quarters of Nicosia. In Chrysaliniótissa Street is the church of the Panayía Chrysaliniótissa, Our Lady of the Golden Flax (*chrysós*, golden; *linón*, flax, linen); the key can be obtained from the house to the right of the church. The church takes its name from an 11th c. icon painted on linen depicting the Mother of God with a golden hand and wearing a golden crown. The church was built in the 15th c. but incorporates fragments from an earlier church of the 11th/12th c.

The church, with two domes over the nave, has a fine 17th c. iconostasis. In a side room are displayed icons and old Bibles from the 16th and 18th c.

Taht-el-Kale Mosque

Chrysaliniótissa Street and Ymitou Street lead to the little Taht-el-Kale Mosque, in the charming quarter of that name, now

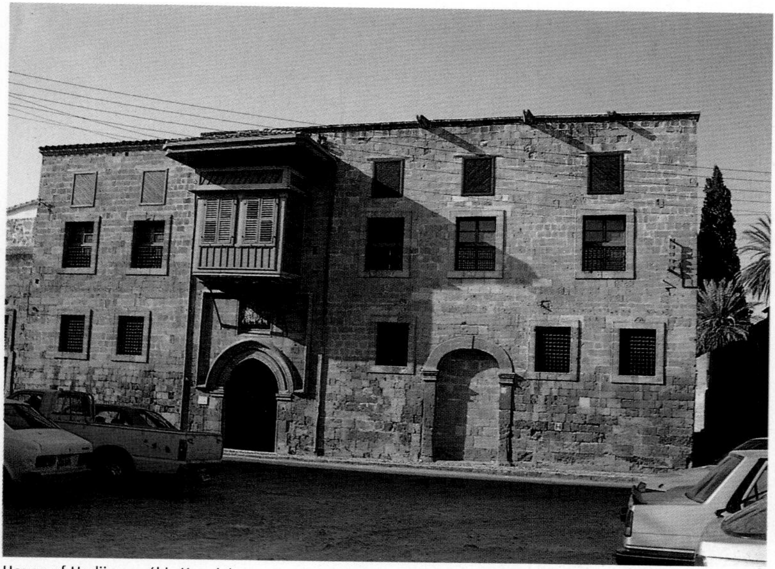
House of Hadjigeorgákis Kornésios

being renovated. The mosque, which has been restored, is no longer used.

★House of Hadjigeorgákis Kornésios
Near the new Archbishop's Palace, in Patriarch Gregorios Street, is the house of dragoman Hadjigeorgákis Kornésios (☛Famous People), a handsome mansion in traditional 18th c. style. In the 18th c. the dragoman was an official who acted as an interpreter and intermediary between the archbishop of Cyprus and the Sultan in Istanbul and whose salary was paid by the Sublime Porte. The archbishop, as representative of the Greek community, was responsible for the collection of taxes but delegated his responsibility to the dragoman, who had the privilege of direct access to the Sultan.

Over the doorway of this three-storey stone house is a marble relief of the Lion of St Mark, a relic of the period of Venetian rule. The use of stone was unusual in 18th c. Cyprus, since stone was expensive and most houses were built of sun-dried brick. Above the lion is a closed wooden balcony, with narrow openings through which the ladies of the household could watch what was happening in the street without themselves being seen. The house is built around three sides of an arcaded courtyard where there is a small Turkish bathhouse. The ground floor was occupied by domestic offices, with a wooden staircase leading to the first floor, which housed the living quarters and state apartments. The rooms are furnished in period style.
Mon.–Sat. 7.30am–2pm.

New Town

In the newer districts of the town outside the Venetian walls are government departments, foreign consulates, office blocks and banks. The principal streets in this part of the town are Evagoras Avenue and Archbishop Makarios III Avenue, with modern shops, restaurants and bars (with or without music). At the end of Demetrios Severis Avenue is the Presidential Palace. In Ayiou Prokopiou Street is the handsome 19th c. mansion (including a church with fine wall paintings) from which Kýkko Monastery administers its extensive properties.

Pottery model of a Bronze Age shrine

★★Archaeological Museum

The principal sight in the newer part of Nicosia, however, is the famous Archaeological Museum (Cyprus Museum) opposite the Municipal Theatre and the Parliament Building.
The museum, exclusively devoted to Cypriot material from the Neolithic period to Byzantine times, gives a comprehensive picture of the cultural history of the island. It was founded in 1882 and moved into its present neoclassical premises, built in memory of Queen Victoria, in 1909. There are plans to move the museum to a larger building. Attached to the museum is an archaeology library.
Mon.–Sat. 9am–5pm, Sun. 10am–1pm. Closed public holidays.

In this section is a brief account of the exhibits displayed in the museum's 14 rooms. On the technical terms used, see introduction, Culture.

Room 1
Neolithic material from Khirokitía: violin-shaped stone (andesite) idols, carnelian necklaces, early comb-decorated pottery. Chalcolithic cross-shaped idols of steatite, red-on-white ware.

Room 2
Bronze Age terracotta figures: the terracotta models of shrines and of various domestic activities are among the most important exhibits in the museum. An early Bronze Age model from Vounoús depicts a religious ceremony in which a priest and a mother and child participate; opposite the entrance to the shrine are three bull-headed creatures, and the ceremony is secretly watched by a man looking over the wall. red polished ware of the early Bronze Age is also represented.

Room 3
Late Bronze Age and Classical period: red-on-black ware, black slip ware, white slip ware. Mycenaean vases, suggesting trading links with the western Aegean. The most important vase, the Zeus Crater (14th c. BC), possibly depicts a scene from the Iliad: Zeus holding the scales of fate before the Greeks set out in their chariots for the battle.

Notable items in the free-standing cases include a faience rhyton of the late Bronze Age and Attic red-figured and black-figured vases. At the far end of the room, to the right, are some fine vases of the Archaic period in the free field style; particularly notable are vases decorated with a bull and lotus flower and a bird holding a fish in its bill.

Room 4
Shrine of Ayía Iríni: a large selection of the 2000 terracotta figures found in this shrine. Most of the figures are armed; some are on carts drawn by oxen (Archaic period).

Room 5
Large sculpture of the Archaic period: since there was no marble on Cyprus, most of the sculpture is in limestone. The exhibits include votive offerings ranging from the Archaic period to Hellenistic times, showing Syrian, Egyptian and Greek influence. Note particularly the female head (3rd c. BC) from the sanctuary of Aphrodite at Arsos, the head of a Kore from Idálion (5th c. BC) and a small figure of Zeus hurling a thunderbolt (ca 500 BC). The Aphrodite of Sóloi (1st c. BC) is one of the most famous items in the museum.

Room 6
The over-life-size bronze statue of Emperor Septimius Severus from Kythréa is an example of the self-glorification of the Roman emperors.

Room 7
Bronze, gold and silver objects: the first part of the room is mainly devoted to bronze articles – weapons, coins, seals and small statuettes. Among the most notable items are the bronze cow from Vouní (5th c. BC) and the horned god from Énkomi (12th c. BC). At the far end of the room is gold and silver jewellery, including a gold sceptre from a tomb at Koúrion (11th c. BC) and a silver dish from Énkomi (14th c. BC).

Room 8
Steps lead down to a lower floor, with reconstructions of tombs (including grave goods) ranging in date from the Neolithic period to the 5th c. BC.

Room 9
Stelae, cippi, urns and sarcophagi, illustrating different burial rites. One stele depicting a woman holding a bird in her hand has an inscription in Cypro-Minoan syllabic script giving her name.

Room 10
Cypro-Minoan syllabic script: tablets from various periods in different scripts illustrate literacy in antiquity. The most important item is a tablet of the 16th c. BC written in the Cypro-Minoan syllabic script, which has not yet been deciphered.

Room 11
Finds from the Tombs of the Kings at Sálamis (see entry). Particularly notable are the grave goods from the magnificent Tomb 79 (8th/7th c. BC). A large bronze cauldron with griffin protomes on an iron tripod, bronze accessories from chariots and harness bear witness to the dead man's wealth. The grave furniture included an ivory chair and bed.

Room 12
Exhibits relating to the mining of copper and the production of bronze reflect the importance of these metals in ancient times. Geological maps show the location of the main sources of metal ores. The reproduction of a copper mine and the explanation of the smelting process illustrate ancient technologies of mining and processing copper.

Room 13
Statues from the Gymnasium, Sálamis, of the Hellenistic and Roman periods, including Apollo with his lyre and figures (2nd c. AD) of Heracles, Nemesis and Hera.

Room 14
Terracotta figures: a bird-headed divinity, plank idols and figures of bulls (Bronze Age); statuettes of divinities and scenes from everyday life, including a birth (Geometric to Classical periods).

Surroundings

Pérakhorio
18 km south of Nicosia, to the left of the motorway to Limassol, lies the village of Pérakhorio, with the little church of the Holy Apostles on a mound (160 m) south-west of the village (key obtainable at No. 12 in the street leading to the church).

The little domed **Church of the Holy Apostles** has wall paintings dating from the late 15th c. The paintings are in poor condition, since the paint was not always applied when the plaster was still wet and the colours therefore did not bind properly into the surface. The peeling paint has revealed the lines sketched out to guide the painter.

The dome has the usual figure of Christ Pantokrator surrounded by angels. In the apse is the Communion of the Apostles, a frequent theme in the Eastern Church which was later taken up by the Protestants. Above this is the Mother of God flanked by Peter and Paul. In the nave is a vivid painting of the Ascension.

Dháli
4 km north-east of Pérakhorio is the village of Dháli. On the road which bypasses the village is a signpost to the site of ancient Idálion, on two hills to the south of the village.

Idálion, in ancient times one of the most important of the city-kingdoms of Cyprus, was founded before the coming of the Achaeans, and was continuously inhabited into the Classical period. In the 5th c. BC it was conquered by the Phoenicians, whose stronghold of Kítion was only a short distance away.

Idálion worshipped Aphrodite and her lover Adonis, who according to legend was killed here by a boar sent by Ares. Excavations have revealed a number of tombs and remains of the town's massive walls (5th c. BC), which stood 6 m high. Few finds of any value were made, since the site had been plundered by tomb robbers, including the American consul Palma di Cesnola, in the later part of the 19th c.

On the outskirts of Dháli, on the road to Potamiá, is the little **Church of Ayios Demetriános** (key from the neighbouring house). Of its wall paintings there survive only an inscription with the date 1317 and portraits of the donor, Michael Katzouroubis, and his wife presenting a model of the church to Christ.

Alámbra
4 km south-west of Pérakhorio, at Alámbra, are the scanty remains of a large Bronze Age settlement. Finds of metal showed that this was once a copper-working centre.

Arkhángelos Monastery
5 km south-west of Nicosia on the road to Páno Dheftera is the Arkhángelos Monastery (key kept by the custodian, who lives at No. 4 in the range of cells). The monastery, now abandoned, dates from the 17th c. and was dedicated to the Archangel Michael. In the narthex of the 12th c. church is the tomb of the founder, Nikiphoros. The iconostasis dates from the 17th c., when the monastery became a dependency of Kýkko Monastery. The monastery now houses the Kýkko Monastery Research Centre.

◄ The Aphrodite of Sóloi, one of the chief treasures of the Cyprus Museum

Káto Dhefterá
14 km south-west of Nicosia, just before Káto Dhefterá, is a cave church, hewn from the rock face, which dates back to the Early Christian period; unfortunately its painted interior is badly damaged. It is dedicated to the Panayía Chrysospiliótissa (Our Lady of the Golden Cave), whose rain-bringing power is celebrated on August 15th, the feast of the Dormition of the Mother of God.

Tamassós
See entry

Monastery of St Heraclidius
See Tamassós

Makherás Monastery
See entry

Páphos G 2

Πάφος
Altitude: 0–150 m
Population: 23,000

Páphos, a town of great historical and artistic interest, lies on the south-west coast of Cyprus. The favourable natural conditions for the construction of a harbour led to the foundation of Nea Páphos (New Páphos) on the site of present-day Káto Páphos (Lower Páphos). The rise of Nea Páphos began with the decline of Palaía Páphos (Old Páphos), 15 km south-east near Koúklia (see entry) – though the shrine of Aphrodite at Old Páphos continued to attract pilgrims.

Káto Páphos
An old Turkish fort guards the picturesque harbour, now occupied only by yachts and fishing boats. The seafront is lined with fish restaurants and souvenir shops and in summer is crowded with visitors.

Immediately adjoining the harbour are the archaeological sites and the hotel district – a relatively quiet and peaceful area, without the high-rise hotels that have defaced Ayía Nápa, Lárnaca and Limassol. The normal population is about 2000, but during the holiday season this increases

Evening light in Páphos harbour

greatly. The building boom in Káto Páphos, once an idyllic fishing village, began with the opening in 1984 of the international airport, 12 km south-east.

Ktíma
2 km inland, on a projecting spur of rock, is a very different part of the town, the district of Ktíma (the word means a country estate: in Frankish times this was royal domain), with a busy shopping quarter, the town market, banks, schools and public buildings. Most of the population of Páphos – Cyprus's smallest district capital – live here. Near the Djami Kebir (Great Mosque) is the old Turkish quarter, now abandoned.

Provincial capital
For many centuries Páphos was a remote and sleepy provincial town. It was only after the partition of the island in 1974 that it was linked with the rest of Greek Cyprus by improved roads and developed into the economic, cultural and administrative centre of a thinly populated region, which depends mainly on agriculture for its subsistence, with plantations of bananas and citrus fruits and vineyards. Because of the numerous sights in and around Páphos, the town has been placed on UNESCO's World Heritage list.

History
According to ancient myth the city of Páphos and the shrine of Aphrodite at Palaía Páphos were founded by king Agapenor of Tegea in Arcadia when he was cast ashore on Cyprus by a storm on his way back from Troy. Material of the Chalcolithic period found at Lemba, Yialia and Souskia, however, show that the first settlements in the area were established as early as the 3rd millennium BC. In later centuries these were overshadowed by the powerful city of Palaía Páphos, which drew hosts of pilgrims to its shrine of Aphrodite the largest in the ancient world.

There is historical evidence for the foundation of Nea Páphos in the 4th c. BC when the last priest-king of Palaía Páphos Nikokles, moved his capital there.

Ptolemaic rule Nea Páphos became a place of some consequence, however, only in the 2nd c. BC, under Ptolemaic rule. The town took over the leading role hitherto held by Sálamis and became capital of the whole island, due to its excellent coastal situation within easy reach of Alexandria and to the huge forests in its hinterland which provided supplies of timber for shipbuilding.

The prosperity of the town in Ptolemaic times is attested by the Tombs of the Kings – tombs not of kings but of wealthy citizens of Páphos.

Roman rule Under the Romans Nea Páphos became the residence of the Roman proconsul and enjoyed its period of greatest prosperity. After an earthquake in the 1st c. BC the town was rebuilt by Augustus in splendid style. Evidence of this prosperity is provided by a series of mansions, named by: archaeologists after their mosaicse the houses of Dionysus, Aion, Theseus and Orpheus. The Romans gave the sacred capital of all Cypriot cities the name of Augusta Claudia Flavia.

Christianisation In AD 46 Paul and Barnabas came to Cyprus on one of their missionary journeys and converted the Roman proconsul, Sergius Paulus, to the Christian faith. After the end of the persecutions of Christians Páphos became the see of a bishop, with one of the largest basilicas on the island.

Arab raids In the 4th c. AD the town was destroyed by earthquakes but was not rebuilt, since Sálamis now became capital of Cyprus. The resultant decline of Néa Páphos was accelerated by Arab raids in the 7th and 8th c.

Later history Under the Lusignans Páphos recovered some of its former importance and became the see of a Roman Catholic bishop. Earthquakes and pirate raids, however, soon led to its abandonment and the foundation of the new town of Ktíma on a higher inland site.

During the period of Turkish rule Páphos was a place of little importance, since towns such as Nicosia and Famagusta lay nearer Turkey.

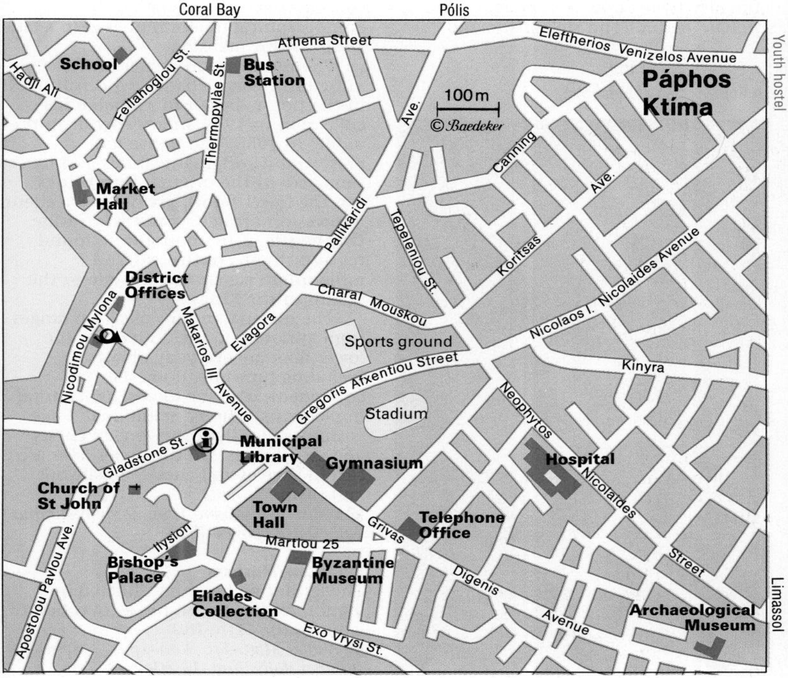

Sights in Ktíma

District Archaeological Museum

Visitors coming from Limassol and entering Ktíma on Grivas Dighenis Avenue pass on the right a series of neoclassical buildings dating from the British colonial period – three gymnasia (grammar schools), the Town Hall and the Municipal Library. One of the few modern buildings in Páphos is the District Archaeological Museum at the near end of Grivas Dighenis Avenue.

The Museum's four rooms display in chronological order finds from Páphos and the surrounding area ranging from the Neolithic period to the Middle Ages. Rooms I and II are mainly devoted to small objects and pottery. The Neolithic period is represented by implements and idols, the Bronze Age by red polished and white slip ware. The black-figured and red-figured pottery of the Archaic and Classical periods indicates contact with Greece. There are also sculpture, funerary reliefs and sarcophagi of the Archaic period. The Hellenistic and Roman periods are represented by votive figures and glassware. A particularly notable item is a Roman torso of Aphrodite, which was found badly damaged on the sea bed off Páphos.

A Roman torso of Aphrodite

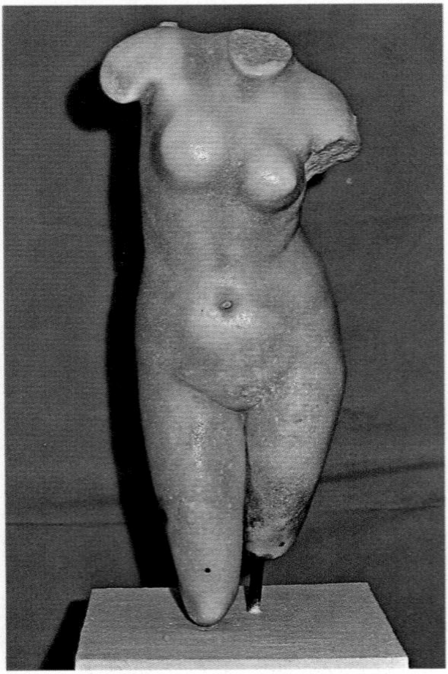

The most interesting of the museum's exhibits are the pottery hot water bottles in the form of arms and legs, which were applied to the appropriate part of the body in the treatment of rheumatism.

Room III displays Hellenistic and Roman domestic pottery from the House of Dionysus.

Room IV is devoted to Byzantine and medieval artefacts. Of particular interest is a Renaissance baldachin supported by four angels (Venetian work), found during the excavation of the Frankish church in the Chrysopolítissa complex.

Mon.–Fri. 7.30am–1.30pm, 3–5pm, Sat., Sun. 7.30am–1pm.

★Ethnological Museum

At 1 Exo Vrysi Street is the private collection of George Eliades, an ethnographical museum housed in a late 19th c. stone mansion.

The founder and owner of the museum, George Eliades, who still lives in the house, began to assemble his collection in 1939 and opened it to the public in 1958. The house has preserved its original features and to some extent the original furnishings (on the lower floor), giving an excellent impression of the Cypriot way of life. On the site of the house were found rock-cut tombs of the 3rd/2nd millennium BC, similar in style to the Tombs of the Kings.

The material in the collection ranges from antiquity to the 20th c. On the lower floor are everyday objects including furniture, domestic equipment, weaving looms, agricultural implements, pottery, traditional costumes, needlework, wooden chests and an oil press. On the upper floor are carved shelves and chests, metalwork and silver.

Winter daily 9am–1pm, 3–5pm; summer daily 9am–1pm, 4–7pm.

Byzantine Museum

The Byzantine Museum, situated in Ioanou Andrea Street, has a collection of icons of the 12th–18th c.

Winter Mon.–Fri. 9am–1pm, 2–5pm; summer daily 9am–12.30pm, 4–7pm.

An old kitchen in the Ethnological Museum

Káto Páphos

★★Roman villas
Between the lighthouse and the harbour are the excavated remains of a number of Roman villas with fine mosaic pavements. Like other places in Cyprus, Nea Páphos was devastated by earthquakes in the 4th c. AD. Most of the houses were destroyed and thereafter were abandoned. In 1962 a peasant's plough uncovered the foundations and mosaics of a Roman house built on the remains of an earlier Hellenistic building of the 4th/3rd c. BC (evidence of its date provided by the discovery of a hoard of 2000 silver tetradrachms of the Ptolemaic period). Since Dionysus featured several times in the mosaics the house became known as the House of Dionysus. Subsequently the remains of other houses in what was evidently an exclusive residential district were discovered nearby, including the governor's palace (the House of Theseus), the House of Aion and the House of Orpheus.
Jun.–Aug. 7.30am–7.30pm; Sep.–May 7.30am–5.45pm.

Mosaics
The technique of mosaicking, which was practised throughout the ancient world, involved extensive preparatory work. After the ground had been levelled and beaten hard several layers of bottoming were laid down and sealed with mortar – first rough stones, then gravel and sherds of pottery. Over this was spread a layer of fine mortar into which small cubes of stone (tesserae) were set to form the mosaic. To ensure the durability of the mosaic it was then scoured with marble dust, sand and lime. The tesserae, usually measuring about 1 cm each way, were mostly of coloured stones, with which Cyprus was well supplied; glass tesserae were used only for certain colours (light orange, yellow, green and blue).

The mosaic pictures were not original creations but were based on designs in pattern books.

★★House of Dionysus

The House of Dionysus, evidently the residence of a prosperous citizen of Páphos, dates from the late 2nd c. AD and covers an area of some 2000 sq m,

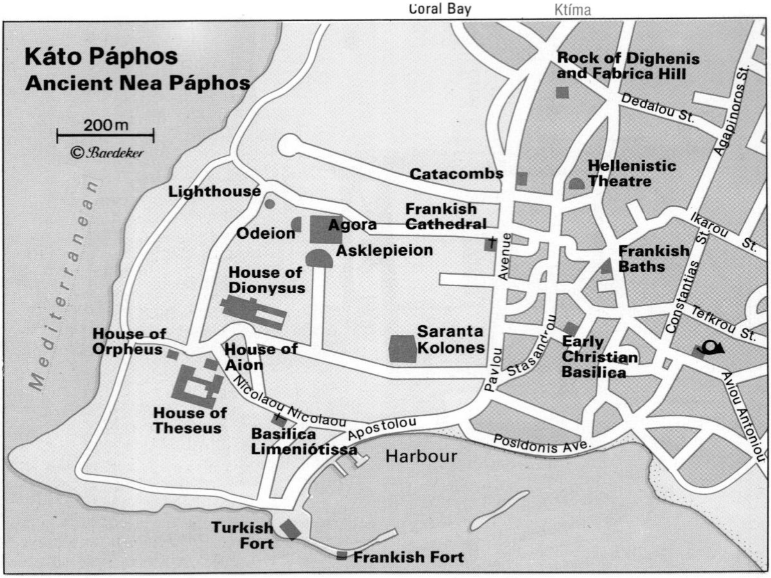

including 556 sq m of mosaic pavements. It is a typical Roman atrium house, built around a colonnaded inner courtyard (atrium) with an impluvium, a basin for collecting rainwater. Opening off the atrium are living rooms, bedrooms and domestic offices. While the main living and reception rooms have mosaic pavements, the bedrooms on the east and north sides of the atrium have plain pebble floors and the domestic offices have floors of beaten earth.

The following description takes account only of the rooms with the finest mosaics.

Scylla mosaic
To the left of the entrance is the oldest mosaic in the villa, the only one to survive from the earlier Hellenistic house. It depicts the sea monster Scylla who Odysseus and his companions encountered in the Straits of Mesina. In contrast to the Roman mosaics, this fine mosaic is composed of plain black and white pebbles.

Narcissus mosaic
Next to this is a mosaic of Narcissus, the youth who fell in love with his own likeness as a punishment for his rejection of the beautiful nymph Echo. When he began to waste away for love of himself Aphrodite took pity on him and turned him into the flower which bears his name.

Four Seasons
The mosaics with personifications of Earth and the four seasons are enclosed in frames consisting of tesserae creating an effect of perspective. The inclusion of a formula of greeting suggests that this was probably the entrance hall of the villa.

Triumph of Dionysus
The largest and most important room in the house, the tablinum, served as a reception room and dining room. The mosaic depicting the triumph of Dionysus shows the god in a carriage drawn by panthers accompanied by his retinue of Satyrs, Silenuses, the god Pan and musicians.

In the centre of the tablinum is a large scene depicting the grape harvest, with peasants cutting the fruit amid vines, birds and hares.

Pyramus and Thisbe
Around the atrium ran a colonnade

paved with a series of mosaics. The first scene depicts the story of Pyramus and Thisbe. The parents of the young lovers opposed their marriage, so they had to meet secretly in a wood. One day when Thisbe went to their meeting place she found a panther there, with blood dripping from its jaws, and fled. Then Pyramus arrived and, seeing the panther with Thisbe's kerchief in its mouth, thought that it had killed her and threw himself on his sword. Thisbe then killed herself to be with him.

Dionysus and Icarius

The next mosaic depicts the first wine drinkers. Dionysus, having been a guest of King Icarius of Attica, showed his gratitude by teaching the king how to grow vines and make wine. In the mosaic Dionysus is depicted on the left drinking wine with the nymph Acme. In the centre of the scene Icarius, delighted with his new skill, offers the drink to two shepherds, the first wine drinkers. They become drunk and, thinking that Icarius is poisoning them, kill him.

Amymone and Poseidon

The beautiful Amymone, one of the 50 daughters of King Danaus, is looking for a spring when she encounters a satyr who tries to ravish her. She is saved by Poseidon, who falls in love with her, presents her with the spring of Lerna and has a son by her, the hero Nauplius. Between Amymone and Poseidon is Eros.

Apollo and Daphne

The last mosaic on the west side of the atrium depicts the unconsummated love of Apollo for the nymph Daphne. Daphne is shown fleeing from Apollo to her father, the river god Peneius. Zeus takes pity on her and turns her into a laurel bush (daphne, from Greek *daphné*) to save her from Apollo. The mosaic shows her legs already turning into the stem of a laurel.

Phaedra and Hippolytus

One of the finest of the mosaics tells the story of Phaedra and Hippolytus. Phaedra, the second wife of Theseus, falls in love with her stepson Hippolytus; but Hippolytus, shown standing on the left of the scene, is wholly devoted to the service of Artemis and to the hunt and rejects her advances. Thereupon Phaedra, her pride wounded, accuses Hippolytus of trying to rape her. Theseus calls on his

Personification of winter from the Four Seasons mosaic

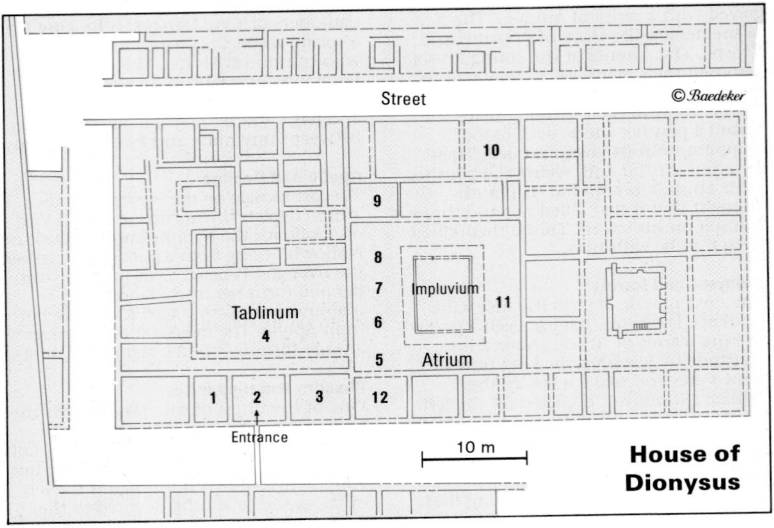

MOSAICS

1 Scylla
2 Narcissus
3 Four Seasons
4 Triumph of Dionysus
5 Pyramus and Thisbe
6 Dionysus and Icarius
7 Amymone and Poseidon
8 Apollo and Daphne
9 Phaedra and Hippolytus
10 Zeus and Ganymede
11 Hunting scenes
12 Peacock

father Poseidon to punish Hippolytus with death. Poseidon sends a wild bull which frightens the horses drawing Hippolytus's chariot, who drag him to his death. Phaedra then kills herself.

Zeus and Ganymede

On the north side of the house is a small mosaic of Zeus and Ganymede. Zeus falls in love with the handsome youth Ganymede and, taking on the form of an eagle, carries him off to Olympus, where he becomes the cup bearer of the gods.

Hunting scenes

Along the north, east and south sides of the atrium are a series of hunting scenes. Among the animals depicted are moufflon, which must have been a favourite species of game in Roman times.

★House of Aion

The House of Aion lies opposite the entrance to the much larger House of Theseus, the Roman governor's palace. The mosaics in this villa, named after the god Aion, who appears in a mosaic in the principal room, were discovered by archaeologists in 1983. The latest mosaics in Páphos, dated to the 4th c. AD, they were probably created after the earthquakes which devastated the town in 332 and 342.

In the entrance hall are five large mosaic panels depicting scenes from Greek mythology in the so-called 'beautiful style', in which the shading of the colours produces a vigorous plastic effect.

Leda and the swan

The first panel (upper left) tells the story of Leda and the swan. In the centre of the scene is Leda, the beautiful queen of Sparta, accompanied by female attendants and personifications of Lacedaemon and the Eurotas river. Zeus is seen approaching her in the form of a swan. From their union are born the twins Castor and Pollux and Helen.

Dionysus and Tropheus
In the second panel (upper right) the boy Dionysus is shown sitting in the lap of Hermes, the messenger of the gods, identified by the small wings on his forehead and feet. Dionysus is being handed over to the care of Tropheus, a Silenus who is to be his protector, and the nymphs who are already preparing the boy's bath.

Cassiopeia and the Nereids
The large central panel depicts the beauty contest between Cassiopeia and the Nereids, which is won by Cassiopeia. She is shown being crowned by Crisis, the personification of justice, on the left, with Helios, Zeus and Athena looking on. In the centre of the scene is Aion, god of time, the judge of the contest. To the right are the Nereids, riding away on a centaur and a triton (personifications of the sea).

Apollo and Marsyas
The fourth mosaic (lower left) depicts the fate of the satyr Marsyas, who had dared to challenge Apollo to a musical contest. The contest is won by Apollo, who is depicted on the right of the scene with his lyre. As punishment for his presumption Marsyas is flayed alive. Two of Apollo's attendants (Scythians) are shown holding Marsyas by the hair.

★House of Theseus

The excavation of the House of Theseus, which dates from the 2nd/3rd c. AD, was begun by archaeologists in 1965. Since it is the largest of the villas (five times the size of the House of Dionysus) it is thought to have been the palace of the Roman governor. Covering an area of almost 9500 sq m, it consists of four ranges of buildings round a large inner courtyard in the tradition of Hellenistic peristyle houses, with rooms for ritual purposes, living and sleeping accommodation and baths (which could be used by the citizens of the town as well as the occupants of the palace). The villa, which was occupied until the 7th c., was richly decorated with wall paintings, marble statues and more than 1400 sq m of mosaic pavements. The mosaics are mostly in geometric designs but include two scenes from Greek mythology.

Theseus mosaic
The first mosaic in the House of Theseus, dating from the 3rd c., is in an apse at the end of the southern colonnade. Circular in form, it depicts the fight between Theseus and the Minotaur in the Cretan Labyrinth; Theseus has just killed the Minotaur, which lies dead at

Apollo and Marsyas mosaic

his feet on the right. To the left of Theseus crouches the bearded god of the Labyrinth. Looking on are two female figures: above, to the right, the personification of Crete, wearing a mural crown; and to the left Ariadne, who gave Theseus the thread which would enable him to find his way out of the Labyrinth. The border of the mosaic with its geometric ornament is also an allusion to the Labyrinth.

Achilles mosaic

A wooden gangway leads to the principal room of the villa, with a mosaic depicting the first bath of the newborn Achilles. His divine mother Thetis, seeking to frustrate the prophecy that he will be killed at Troy, dips her son in the waters of the Styx in order to render him invulnerable; but the heel by which she holds him is not immersed in the water, and this is destined to be the cause of his death. On the right of the scene are the three Fates – Clotho, Lachesis and Atropos – as a reminder that he cannot escape his destiny. Also in the scene are two midwives and Achilles' father Peleus, seated on a throne with his wand of office.

House of Orpheus

To the west of the House of Theseus is another small villa excavated in 1984, named the House of Orpheus after a large mosaic depicting Orpheus seated on a rock with his lyre and surrounded by the animals of the forest who have been attracted by his playing.

Another mosaic – originally discovered by a British soldier in 1942 and covered up again – shows Heracles fighting the Nemean lion.

The third mosaic depicts an Amazon holding a double axe, with her horse.

These three mosaics, dating from the 2nd/3rd c. AD, are similar in style to those in the House of Dionysus. Excavations are still in progress, but the mosaics will be put on show to the public.

Other sights in Káto Páphos

Between the House of Dionysus and the lighthouse are the asklepieion, the agora and the odeion of the 2nd c. AD. The lighthouse stands on the ancient acropolis of Páphos.

Daily until sunset.

Agora

To the right are the remains of the agora, the old market square and place of assembly, an area 95 sq m surrounded by colonnades. On the east side is a three-stepped stylobate; here were found granite columns with marble Corinthian capitals.

Odeion

Opposite the agora is the odeion, which was almost completely destroyed in the earthquakes of the 4th c. and has now been largely reconstructed since it was uncovered in 1972–3. It originally had 25 tiers of seating and could accommodate an audience of 3000. An odeion (or odeum) was a hall for concerts and lectures; like a theatre, it consisted of a semicircular orchestra, a cavea and a stage, but unlike a theatre was usually roofed. Today it serves its original purpose as in summer months it is a venue for ancient Greek drama and musical performances.

Asklepieion

To the left of the odeion are the remains of an asklepieion, a shrine of the healing god Asklepios. It was in three parts, with rooms for sleeping (which was part of the therapy) and for treatment. The asklepieion was linked with the odeion by a long passage.

Some 300 m north are remains of the Hellenistic town walls.

Saranta Kolones

To the east of the Roman villas are the ruins of a medieval castle known as Saranta Kolones (Forty Columns), after the 40 columns of Roman origin used in its construction. The castle was built by the Byzantines about 1100 to protect the coastal region and later was taken over by the Franks. It was destroyed in an earthquake in 1222 and thereafter was used as a quarry for building stone.

The castle, almost square in plan, was surrounded by two circuits of walls, which can be clearly distinguished when it is approached from the west. The outer walls were reinforced by eight bastions of different types, while the inner circuit had four rectangular towers at the corners. The entrance was in the central bastion on the east side. The castle chapel was probably over the barbican at the entrance to the inner stronghold. In the inner courtyard were stables, in

Turkish fort – Páphos harbour

which can be seen feeding troughs formed from Roman columns.

On the north side of the castle are the remains of a mill worked by animal power. Within the large piers supporting the upper floor were latrines. A staircase led to the upper floor.

Early Christian basilica

To the east of the castle of Saranta Kolones, beyond Apostle Paul Avenue, is a large excavation site. To the right are the remains of one of the largest Early Christian basilicas in Cyprus. Built in the 4th c., it originally had seven aisles, with a double apse. In the 6th c. it was rebuilt as a five-aisled basilica with a single apse. At the west end the atrium, ablutions fountain and narthex can still be distinguished. Remains of mosaic pavements indicate that the church was richly decorated. When the crusaders captured Cyprus the basilica was already in ruins.

Frankish church

Nearby, in the street to the left, are the remains of a Frankish church of the late 13th c., dedicated to St Francis. Three aisles can be distinguished, with the remains of twin columns and Gothic pointed arches. In the 16th c. the church was renovated and decorated with Renaissance sculpture, some of which can be seen in the District Archaeological Museum. After the church fell into ruin at the end of the 16th c. the present church of the Ayía Chrysopolítissa was built on the site.

Paul's Column

To the west of the Frankish church is a much worn column at which the apostle Paul is said to have been scourged during his visit to Páphos. The New Testament account (Acts 13,1–13) tells how before converting the Roman proconsul, Sergius Paulus, Paul was involved in a dispute with a sorcerer named Bar-jesus, who he struck with blindness. According to the local tradition Paul was tied to a column and given 39 lashes for preaching Christianity in Páphos. Paul punished the Jewish mayor of the town by making him blind: whereupon the Roman governor, impressed by Paul's power, became a Christian. The column is still visited by numbers of pilgrims.

Frankish baths
In Minoos Street, to the north of Paul's Column, is a Frankish bathhouse, which was roofed with a series of domes during the Turkish period. The medieval masonry still stands 3 m high.

Turkish harbour fort
On the west side of the harbour is a massive Turkish fort. It stands at the point where the ancient town walls ended, at the head of a breakwater. At the end of the breakwater are traces of a small Frankish fortification. The remains of another ancient breakwater can be seen under the water.

The large fort, originally built as a Byzantine fort to protect the harbour, was rebuilt by the Lusignans during the 13th c. In the latter part of the 16th c. the Venetians abandoned the fort and neglected the walls, thereafter concentrating on the defence of Famagusta and Nicosia. In 1592 the Turks rebuilt it, as an inscription records. During the British occupation it was used as a salt store. In the centre of the fort is the square keep of the Lusignan stronghold.
Sep.–May Mon.–Fri. 7.30am–2pm; Jun.–Aug. Mon.–Sat. 7.30am–1.30pm.

Basilica of Panayía Limeniótissa
From the harbour Nikolaou Street runs north-west towards the House of Dionysus. Halfway along this street, on the left, are the remains of the church of the Panayía Limeniótissa (Our Lady of the Harbour), which was built in the early 5th c. and almost completely destroyed by Arabs in the 7th c. Arabic inscriptions on the columns, however, show that the building continued in use. In the 10th c. a new church was built on the ruins, but this was destroyed in an earthquake in the 12th c. The Early

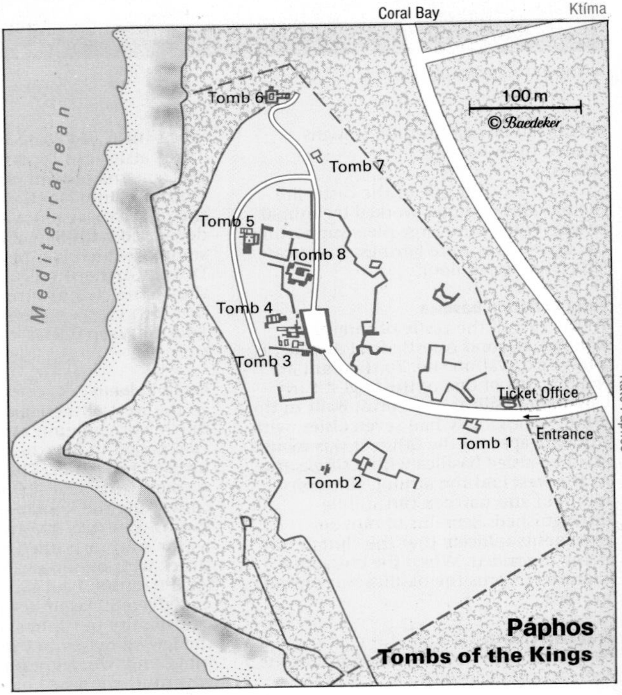

Rock-cut peristyle tomb, Nea Páphos

Christian church was three-aisled, with an apse at the east end and a narthex and atrium at the west end.

Fabrica Hill

At the north end of Apostle Paul Avenue, on the road to Ktíma, is Fabrica Hill, so called because stone masons had their workshop here. The remains of wedge holes show that the hill was used as a quarry – though probably not before Roman times, since Hellenistic tombs were found here. The site of a Hellenistic theatre is being excavated.

This was the scene of a legendary conflict between the Byzantine hero Dighenis and Queen Regaena. The queen had promised to yield to him if he brought her water from the Pentadáktylos hills; but when she broke her promise Dighenis, enraged, flung a gigantic block of stone at her palace.

Regaena responded by throwing a spindle at him. The legend has it that Fabrica Hill is the rock thrown by Dighenis and a granite column found here the queen's spindle.

Catacombs of Ayía Solomoní

Near Fabrica Hill are a group of catacombs in which early Christians sought refuge. Here, where the cave church of Ayía Solomoní now stands, there was once a Jewish synagogue. Solomoní, mother of the seven Maccabee brothers, was killed with them during the persecution of Jews in the reign of Antiochus IV (2nd c.). She is now revered as a martyr and is credited with the power of curing diseases of the eyes. The poorly preserved paintings in the church date from the 12th c. From the inner courtyard a flight of steps leads up to a spring which is believed to have a healing effect on eye conditions.

On the other side of the street, in the direction of the harbour, can be seen the surviving south-west corner of a Frankish cathedral of the 13th c.

★★Tombs of the Kings

2.5 km north of Páphos, reached by way of Tombs of the Kings Street, is one of the most remarkable ancient sights in

Cyprus, the necropolis of ancient Nea Páphos, known as the Tombs of the Kings. The tombs date from the 4th c. BC when Cyprus was held by the Ptolemies and governed from Alexandria. Since there were then no kings in Cyprus Tombs of the Kings is a misnomer. The tombs in fact belonged to the wealthier citizens of Páphos, and give a vivid impression of the town's prosperity under the Ptolemies.

The tombs were used continuously from the 4th c. BC to the 3rd c. AD. Thereafter they provided a refuge for Christians in times of persecution, and during the Middle Ages some of them were converted into houses or were used as prisons. Few grave goods were found by the excavators of the tombs, since they had been systematically pillaged over the centuries, particularly in the 19th c.

Winter daily 7.30am–5pm; summer daily 7.30am–7pm.

Peristyle tombs

The architecture of these peristyle tombs, modelled on the houses of the Ptolemaic period, is particularly striking. Although the idea of constructing underground house-tombs came from Egypt, the architectural details are purely Greek. Opening off a colonnaded inner courtyard (atrium) are the individual tomb chambers, the walls of which were decorated with stucco ornament or paintings. In all the larger tombs were wells. The tomb chambers lead to the small burial recesses (loculi). Architraves with a frieze of triglyphs and metopes are borne on Doric columns.

Tomb 1 Immediately at the entrance to the site is an above-ground chamber tomb with traces of paintings on the walls. It contains two small loculi for children and five larger ones for adults.

Tomb 2 was altered in Roman times, when the original stepped dromos was closed and a new entrance opened up on the south side. Two altars were set up on the north side.

Tomb 3 is entered by a stepped dromos and has a large atrium with a Doric colonnade.

Immediately adjoining this tomb are a number of simple shaft graves surrounded by a wall. These family tombs are thought to date from the Hellenistic period.

Tomb 5 is one of the largest of the tombs, with a dromos over 7 m long and 2.8 m wide. The atrium was surrounded by a colonnade of massive columns, with a well in the centre and the principal tomb chamber on the south side. Built into the tomb was a medieval potter's kiln with a ventilation system. Pottery found here and incised crosses on the walls show that the tomb was in use variously from Hellenistic times into the Middle Ages.

Tomb 8 has no peristyle atrium. The tomb chambers are hewn out of a large block of stone which stands in a rectangular courtyard.

Surroundings of Páphos

Emba

5 km north of Ktíma, off the road to Pólis, lies the village of Emba, in the centre of which is the 12th c. church of the Panayía Chryseleoúsa (Our Lady Blessed with Gold). Originally cruciform, it was later converted into a three-aisled basilica with two domes and a narthex. Of its 15th c. wall paintings only fragments survive. The 16th c. iconostasis has a number of icons, notably one of Christ Antiphonítis (1536) and 16th c. icons of the Mother of God and John the Baptist. A local shopkeeper holds the key.

St Neóphytos Monastery

See entry

Coral Bay

Coral Bay (named after the corals on its beach) is 10 km north of Páphos, and has one of the most popular sandy bays within reach of the town. Once there were only a few restaurants and small hotels here, but since the lifting of the ban on new building the bay has suffered the same fate as other coastal resorts and several large hotel complexes have been built.

At the nearby village of Máa are the remains of cyclopean walls belonging to a fortified Bronze Age settlement of about 1200 BC.

Péyia

18 km north-west of Páphos, at Péyia,

can be found the basilica complex of Ayios Yeóryios, where excavations are in progress. The remains date from the 6th c. when this seems to have been an important episcopal see. In Roman times here below Cape Drepanum there was a town of that name. The foundations of a large three-aisled basilica with three apses, a narthex and an atrium are well preserved. The central apse still has the steps leading up to the bishop's throne. The church had mosaics with geometric designs and representations of birds and fishes, and mosaics of four animals – a boar, a bear, a lion and a bull – can still be seen in the atrium.

North-west of the atrium is a smaller church – probably the baptistery for the diocese, since there is a large immersion font on the south side.

Snake George Exhibition

A special attraction near Peyía is the Snake George Exhibition, where reptiles and amphibians can be seen in an open-air enclosure.

Mon.–Fri. 8am–6pm, Sat., Sun. 10am–5pm.

Lara Bay

Lara Bay, which has a beautiful sandy beach, is best reached by the coastal road. Here the Cypriot fishery authorities are running a project, started in 1976, to protect the turtles, which are now an endangered species.

Peristeróna E 6

Περιστερώνα

Altitude: 200 m

Population: 1200

28 km west of Nicosia on the road to Tróodos is Peristeróna, a village which was a place of some importance in the middle Byzantine period. In the 12th c. it belonged to Kýkko Monastery, and later was handed over to the Frankish counts of Jaffa in Palestine. The main feature of interest is the church of SS Hilarion and Barnabas (key from coffee house next to the church).

Church of SS Hilarion and Barnabas, Peristeróna

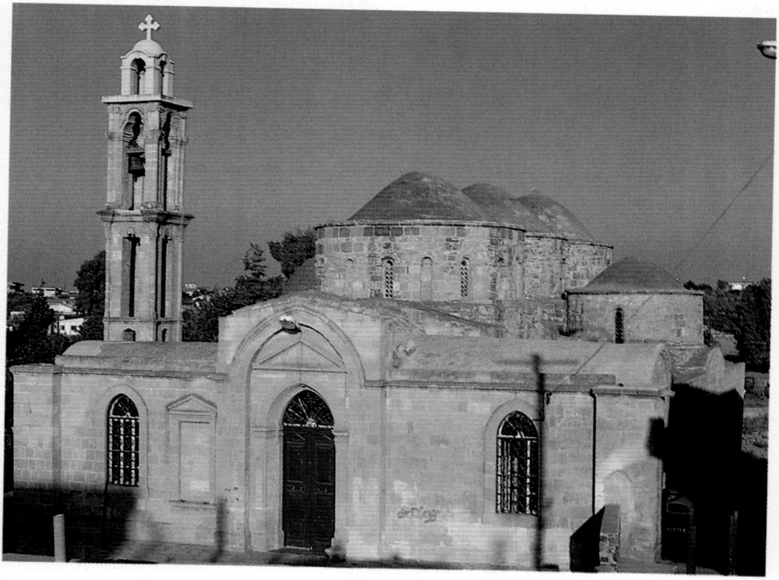

★Church of SS Hilarion and Barnabas

Foundation and legend

The multi-domed church of SS Hilarion and Barnabas – a type rarely found in Cyprus – is one of the most important examples of 11th c. architecture on the island. The two saints to whom the church is dedicated should not be confused with the well known Cypriot saints Barnabas, first bishop of Cyprus, and the hermit Hilarion. These were two young men of Cappadocia (in eastern Anatolia), officers in the Roman army in the time of Theodosius II (5th c.), who on becoming converts to Christianity retired from the army, gave all their possessions to the poor and thereafter lived a life of great piety. Their remains were mysteriously brought to Cyprus and a church was built in their honour.

Church

The basilican church has an imposing effect with its domes and bell tower (a later addition); the five domes are arranged in a cruciform formation (cf. the church of Ayía Paraskeví at Yeroskípos; see entry).

Little survives of the original **interior**. The only relics of the Byzantine period are a 12th c. painting of the Mother of God on the north-east pier and the wooden door of the west doorway. The other paintings (e.g. the figure of David on the north-east pier) date from the 16th c.

In the narthex at the west end of the church – a later addition – are two funerary monuments. Since the burial of the dead within a church was usual only in the Roman Catholic church, it seems that this church was also used by the Franks. This is suggested also by the marble holy-water stoup in the church.

On the 16th c. iconostasis are **icons** of the 16th and 17th c. The most notable is an icon of the Presentation in the Temple (1520), with an inscription naming the donor as Zaphiris, who is depicted kneeling before the high priest. In the north aisle are icons of the 15th and 16th c. depicting St Paul, the Mother of God, Christ and St Barnabas.

Phikárdhou F 7

9 km north-west of Makherás Monastery (see entry) the picturesque little hill village of Phikárdhou (or

House of Katsinioros Phikárdhou

UPPER FLOOR

1 Exhibition room
2 Living room/bedroom
3 Roof terrace
4 Flat roof

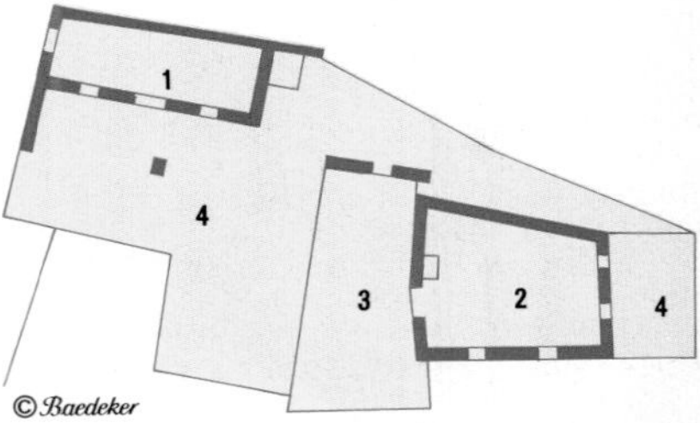

GROUND FLOOR

1 Exhibition room
2 Stall for animals
3 Wine cellar
4 Storeroom

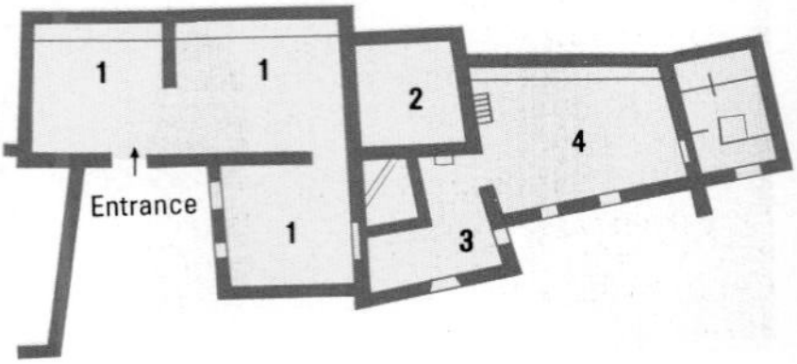

Fikhárdhou) has traditional village architecture, ranging in date between the 18th and early 20th c. This led the Department of Antiquities in 1978 to designate it as a protected historic monument. Since then the village has been systematically restored in cooperation with the house owners. Phikárdhou takes its name from a noble family that had connections with the English court about the year 1500.

Village life
In 1946 the village had a population of 120: now it has fallen to 10, all of whom are older people, still working their land with wooden ploughs and sickles. They are mainly engaged in making wine and distilling brandy (*zivania*), though the grape juice is also used to make the sweets known as *kiofterka* and *soutzouko*. The village's narrow paved lanes are suitable only for pedestrians and animals; the local transport system, therefore, consists of donkeys and mules, which are also used in agricultural work.

Village architecture
Most of the houses are of two storeys, built of limestone and a local coarse stone called sieropetra on foundations of undressed stone. The rooms on the ground floor are usually storerooms and stalls for animals, and there is always a corner for a small wine press. The flat roofs of the lower parts of the building also serve useful purposes (e.g. the drying of grapes); they also serve as verandas, which can be entered from the living quarters on the upper floor. The upper floor usually consists of a single large room, which is divided up by wooden piers. Attached to the house there is usually a small courtyard enclosed by a stone wall.

Houses of Katsinioros and Achilleas Dimitri
The two most important houses in the village, the Katsinioris House on the northern outskirts and the Achilleas Dimitri House beyond it, partly dating from the 16th c., have been restored, and with their original furniture and furnishings, photographs and other exhibits offer a glimpse of traditional Cypriot village life
⌚ *Daily.*

Platanistása F 6

Πλατανιστάσα
Altitude: 900 m

The village of Platanistása lies in the eastern Tróodos massif 30 km south-east of the little town of Tróodos. 5 km north-west of the village is the church of the Stavrós tou Ayiasmáti (key from the village priest).

★Church of the Stavrós tou Ayiasmáti

The church of the Stavrós tou Ayiasmáti (Holy Cross of Ayiasmáti) probably takes its name from the little town of Ayiasmáti in Asia Minor, for according to the local legend refugees from there came to Cyprus after the fall of Constantinople in 1453 and founded a monastery. This barn-roofed church (☛Culture, Art and Architecture) of the late 15th c. has wall paintings showing Western influence.

Inscriptions over the north and south doorways give the name of the donor as

St Mamas, Platanistása

Peter, son of Peratis, and that of the painter as Philip Goul, who was also responsible for the paintings in the church of St Mamas at Louvarás. On the outside of the south wall is a painting of the donor and his wife presenting a model of the church to Christ.

Wall paintings
The paintings in the interior of the church are in two zones. In the upper zone are scenes from the life of the Virgin and the life of Christ; in the lower zone are figures of saints, notable among them St Mamas on his lion (☛Sights from A to Z North Cyprus, Mórphou) and St George.

The New Testament cycle begins on the **south wall**, near the iconostasis, with Elizabeth and Zacharias (parents of John the Baptist), followed by the evangelists Matthew and Luke, the Birth of the Virgin, her Presentation in the Temple, the Nativity of Christ, the Presentation of Jesus in the Temple, the Baptism of Christ, the Raising of Lazarus, the Entry into Jerusalem and the Transfiguration. An interesting feature is the inclusion of genre scenes, including the milking of the ewes, in the Nativity. A common detail in Byzantine representations of the Baptism is a figure personifying the Jordan river: here he is shown at Christ's feet pouring water from a jar.

On the **west wall** are the Crucifixion, the Descent from the Cross, the Last Supper, the Washing of the Feet, Christ in the Garden of Gethsemane, the Betrayal and Christ before Annas and Caiaphas.

The cycle continues on the **north wall** with Peter's Denial, Christ before Pilate, the Mocking, the Lamentation, Doubting Thomas, the Ascension, the Descent of the Holy Ghost (Pentecost), the Dormition of the Mother of God and the evangelists Luke and John. The Dormition includes the figure of the Jew Jephonias, who tries to touch the Virgin's bier but has his hands cut off by the Archangel Michael.

In a recess on the north wall are 10 small scenes depicting the discovery of the True Cross by Helen, mother of Constantine the Great. The series begins with the declaration by a Jew named Judas that he has learned from his forefathers the whereabouts of the Cross. In the second scene he denies any knowledge, and is punished by being confined for three days in a dry well. In the third scene he is released after revealing where the Cross is hidden. The next scene shows him praying on Golgotha and being told in a divine revelation the exact position of the relics (including the other two crosses). The sixth scene depicts the discovery of the relics, which are then taken to St Helen in a triumphal procession. In the eighth scene the True Cross is identified by a dying woman. Judas, converted to the Christian faith, is appointed bishop of Jerusalem. He discovers the nails used in Christ's crucifixion, and in the last scene he is shown taking them to Helen, who sinks to her knees in reverence.

Apse In the vault of the apse is the Mother of God Blacherniótissa with her hands raised in prayer, flanked by the Archangels Michael and Gabriel. Below this are the Communion of the Apostles and eight prelates.

Palekhóri

Church of the Metamóphosis tou Sotíros
10 km south-east of Platanistása, in the picturesque little village of Palekhóri (or Palächori), is the church of the Metamórphosis tou Sotíros (the Transfiguration of the Saviour; key held by priest). The walls of the early 16th c. church are completely covered with paintings, which show affinities with the paintings in the churches of Platanistása and Louvarás and the church of the Archangel Michael in Galáta. Here too western influence is evident.

In the upper zone of the walls are New Testament scenes, also figures of saints of the Eastern Church.

The cycle begins on the south wall with the death of St Mary the Egyptian, a repentant harlot who, after her conversion to Christianity, lived as a hermit in the desert. This is followed by the Three Youths in the Fiery Furnace, the Nativity of Christ, the Presentation in the Temple, the Baptism of Christ, the Raising of Lazarus, the Entry into Jerusalem and the Transfiguration. In the Baptism figures personifying the Jordan

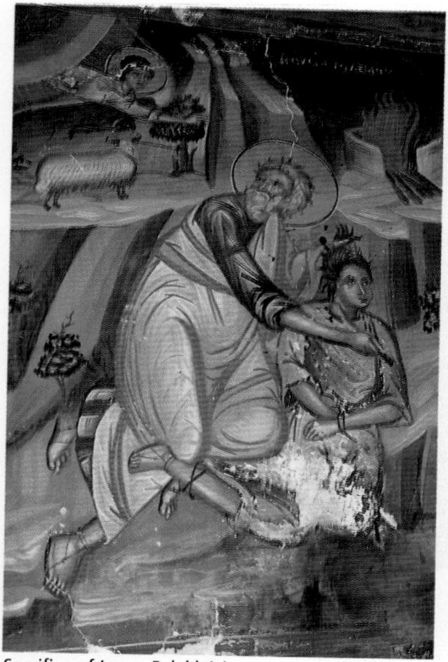

Sacrifice of Isaac, Palekhóri

river (a bearded man) and the sea (a woman riding on a fish) are seen at Christ's feet, fleeing before him (cf. the church of Ayía Paraskeví, Yeroskípos).

On the west wall the cycle in the upper zone begins with the Last Supper, the Washing of the Feet, Christ on the Mount of Olives and the Betrayal. Below this is Christ before Annas and Caiaphas, followed by Christ before Pilate, Peter's Denial and the Mocking.

In the vault of the apse is the Mother of God with her hands raised in prayer, flanked by the Archangels Michael and Gabriel. Below this is the Communion of the Apostles, with Judas (far left) spitting out the bread, and below this again are Fathers of the Church. On the side walls are the Sacrifice of Isaac and the Hospitality of Abraham.

Church of Panayía Chrysopantanássa
In the main street of the village stands the small three-aisled basilica of the Panayía Chrysopantanássa, which also dates from the 16th c. The wall paintings are poorly preserved and unrestored. They include scenes from the life of the Virgin, a figure of St Nicholas and the story of the discovery of the True Cross.

Pólis E 2

Πόλις
Altitude: sea level
Population: 1800

The little town of Pólis (City) lies in Khrysókhou Bay on the north coast of Cyprus, on the site of the ancient city-kingdom of Márion. It has beautiful beaches along the coast, but its remote situation has largely preserved it from the high-rise hotels and numbers of tourists of the more easily accessible resorts. The visitors who come here are mostly backpackers, who can find cheap accommodation in private houses, or in the campsite north of the town close to the beach. To the east of Pólis are old copper mines, long since closed down.

History
The ancient settlement of Márion is believed to have been founded in the late Bronze Age by Achaean incomers. By around 1000 BC a city-kingdom had been established here, though one of no great importance. In the 5th c., however, copper mining brought the town a degree of prosperity.

During the conflict between Greeks and Persians Márion was initially on the Persian side, but in the 4th c., together with other city-kingdoms, it ceased to pay tribute to the Persians. During the fight for the succession of Alexander the Great Márion supported Antigonus, and after the victory of his rival Ptolemy I, at the end of the 4th c., the town was razed. It was later rebuilt by Ptolemy II and renamed Arsinoe.

In Byzantine times the town became known as Pólis tis Khrysókhou, the City of the Land of Gold.

During the fighting between Greeks and Turks in the 1960s Pólis suffered severe damage in Turkish air attacks.

Surroundings

Lakhí
A few kilometres west of Pólis is the village of Lakhí, once a picturesque fishing port with brightly coloured boats, but now filled with innumerable tavernas where coaches deposit tourists for an evening of live Cypriot entertainment.

Akámas peninsula
To the west of Pólis is the Akámas

Baths of Aphrodite, near Pólis

peninsula, with the most north-westerly point on the island, Cape Arnaúti. The peninsula takes its name from Akámas, son of Theseus, who is said to have landed here on his way back from Troy. This uninhabited area, one of the most beautiful parts of Cyprus, with ideal walking country, was declared a nature reserve in 1989, and it is hoped to make it a national park; but since it is used by the British forces on Cyprus as a training area it is occasionally closed to the public. On the peninsula, near the Baths of Aphrodite, are four nature trails (including the Aphrodite and the Adonis Trails) laid out by the Cyprus Tourism Organisation (CTO).

In spite of opposition from environmentalists, the former foreign minister Aleco Michaelides pushed through his plan to build a luxury hotel on the peninsula: the Anassa was opened in 1998, threatening the survival of the Mediterranean's last colonies of green turtle.

★Baths of Aphrodite

8 km north-west of Pólis are the Baths of Aphrodite (Loutra tis Aphroditis). From a shady recess in the rock water flows into a small pool where, it is said, Aphrodite used to bathe under a fig tree. Here she was surprised one day by Theseus' son Akámas and the two fell in love. But they were discovered and betrayed by an old woman (the personification of calumny), and Aphrodite was forced to return to Olympus.

Fontana Amorosa

In a sandy bay 8 km beyond the Baths of Aphrodite, in the direction of Cape Arnaúti, is the Fontana Amorosa, Aphrodite's Fountain of Love. According to local tradition (though there may be some confusion with the Baths of Aphrodite) anyone who drinks from the spring will be filled with youthful amorous ardour. The spring can by reached only on foot or by boat from Lakhí. There is a beautiful footpath from the Baths of Aphrodite.

Droúsha

10 km south of Pólis on a minor road to Páphos, picturesquely situated on a hill (700 m), is Droúsha, a village with traditional houses. From here there is a

magnificent view of the bay in which Pólis lies.

Pyrgá – Royal Chapel F 8

Πυργά
Altitude: 160 m

In the village of Pyrgá 32 km to the west of Lárnaca near the Limassol-Nicosia motorway, is the so-called Royal Chapel, a name of fairly recent origin (key available from the coffee shop nearby).

The chapel, which is dedicated to St Catherine, was built during the period of Frankish rule, as is shown by the Gothic architecture, the Lusignan coat of arms on the vaulting, and the Frankish figures and French inscriptions in the wall paintings. The coats of arms and the figure of King Janus of Lusignan which appears in one of the paintings suggest that this was a royal foundation.

Built in 1421, the simple chapel has three doorways. Only fragments of the paintings that once covered the walls have been preserved. The figures of King Janus and his wife Charlotte of Bourbon appear in the Crucifixion scene. Below this is the Lamentation, in which a Western bishop, presumably the second founder, appears. The paintings are still very much in the Byzantine style, but the representation of the Mother of God Hodigitría shows Italian features.

Surroundings

Kórnos
To the west of Pyrgá, beyond the motorway, is the village of Kórnos, which is famed for its pottery, made by traditional methods. The coarse red ware with anthropomorphic designs is shaped on simple potters' wheels and fired in kilns reminiscent of Corinthian kilns of the 6th c. BC.

St Neóphytos Monastery F 2

Μονή Αγίου Νεοψύτου
Altitude: 400 m

10 km north of Páphos, on the slopes of Mount Melissovounos, is the monastery of St Neóphytos. Outside the monastery are the cave and the cave chapel

Royal Chapel, Pyrgá

(Enkleistra) hewn from the rock by St Neóphytos in the 12th c. A large monastery was built close to the Enkleistra in the 15th c., and the saint's remains were transferred to it in the 18th c. The monastery has extensive ranges of guest rooms and attracts large numbers of visitors on holidays and feast days.

St Neóphytos
St Neóphytos was born in 1134 in Káto Drys near Léfkara. At the age of 18 became a novice in the monastery of Ayios Chrysóstomos, where he taught himself to read and write. A planned journey to the Holy Land ended with his arrest in the harbour of Páphos, and after his release he withdrew to the desolate hill region inland from Páphos, where he hewed a cell and a small chapel from the rock of the hillside. The piety and learning of the saintly recluse soon attracted large numbers of pilgrims and disciples.

Neóphytos wrote treatises on the Old and New Testaments, hymns and songs which mark him out as one of the great spiritual writers of the 12th c. He also composed a caustic account of the capture of Cyprus by crusaders. He died in 1214 at the age of 80 and was buried in the tomb which he had himself prepared in the Enkleistra.

★Enkleistra

Neóphytos founded a monastery in 1170 and drew up a rule for it. He enlarged the cave chapel by the addition of a nave, the original chapel becoming the sanctuary of the church. The numbers of his disciples continued to increase, and in 1196 he withdrew to a new retreat above the church, from which he could listen to services through a hole in the roof of the church.

The Enkleistra is entered through the naos of the church, to the right of which, separated from it by the iconostasis, is the sanctuary (bema). In the bema is a small stone altar. Beyond this is the saint's cell, with a bench and a table hewn from the rock and the tomb which he had constructed for himself.

The **wall paintings** in the Enkleistra were commissioned by the saint himself between 1170 and 1200. They are unique in showing Neóphytos among the saints while still alive. The earlier paintings are the work of Theodoros Apseudes; the painter of the scenes in the second phase, more than ten years later, is unknown.

Particularly notable are the paintings in the saint's cell, above his tomb. In the Descent into Hades (Anástasis) Christ is shown liberating Adam and Eve, watched by David and Solomon as representatives of the Old Testament. In the representation of the Déesis (the Virgin and St John interceding with Christ for mankind) Neóphytos is shown kneeling at Christ's feet.

In the bema is a 16th c. painting of Christ Pantokrator. Of particular note is the representation of Neóphytos between the Archangels Michael and Gabriel. An inscription expresses his hope that he will be enrolled among the angels.

Some of the paintings in the naos were overpainted and renewed in the 16th c. They depict scenes from Christ's Passion: the Last Supper and the Washing of the Feet (both painted about 1503), the Betrayal, Christ before Pilate and the Crucifixion (all 12th c.). The

The Enkleistra, with the saint's cell and rock-cut church

Wall paintings in the cave church of St Neóphystos Monastery

Hospitality of Abraham on the south wall dates from the 16th c.

Monastic church

The monastic church opposite the Enkleistra was built in the 15th c. to replace the cave church, then too small. The nave is separated from the aisles by columns with Corinthian-style capitals and is roofed by a large dome. The saint's remains are in a wooden sarcophagus to the left of the iconostasis; his skull is preserved in a silver reliquary. On the 16th c. iconostasis is a 19th c. icon of St Neóphytos holding a silver cross.

The surviving **wall paintings** date from the early 16th c., when Cyprus was under Venetian rule. In the south aisle are scenes from the life of Anne and Joachim, who are shown presenting gifts to the high priest Zacharias, in the hope of fulfilling their desire for a child.

In the north aisle is the cycle of the Acathist Hymn, 24 scenes dedicated to the life and glorification of the Virgin. The hymn is thought to have been composed by the patriarch of Constantinople in the 7th c. Among the scenes depicted are the Annunciation, the Visitation, the Nativity and the Flight into Egypt.

Stavrovoúni Monastery F 8

Μονή Σταυροβουνίου
Altitude: 690 m

Stavrovoúni has the richest tradition of all Cyprus's monasteries and is the most austere. It is reached by turning off the Limassol–Nicosia motorway shortly before Kórnos and continuing on a steep and winding road that passes the monastery of St Barbara (Ayía Varvára), now an annexe of Stavrovoúni. Beyond this, visible from afar – indeed a landmark for passing ships – is the monastery of Stavrovoúni, perched on a conical crag. From the monastery there are breathtaking views of the Tróodos massif, the south coast of Cyprus (Lárnaca) and in clear weather as far as Nicosia. The monastery's name, Hill of the Cross (from *stavrós*, cross, and *vounó*, hill), refers to the relics of the True

Stavrovoúni Monastery

Cross, which led to the foundation of the monastery.

In this arid region the supply of water is a problem. In earlier times the monastery depended on water collected during the winter in four underground cisterns. Water is now pumped up from a spring at the foot of the hill.

Closed noon–3pm. Only men are permitted to enter the monastery.

Legend

According to legend the monastery was founded in the 4th c. at the behest of St Helen, mother of Constantine the Great. When returning from the Holy Land in AD 327 with the relics of the True Cross she was driven ashore on Cyprus by a storm. The site of the present monastery was then occupied by a pagan temple of Aphrodite. An angel told Helen in a dream to build a church on Cyprus. Then when she awoke on the following morning the relics had disappeared and the pagan altar on the hill was engulfed in flames. The relics were found in the fire, unscathed: whereupon Helen resolved to found a monastery on the spot and left it some of the relics. Thereafter, it is said, a long period of drought on Cyprus came to an end.

History

During the period of Lusignan rule the monastery was occupied by Benedictine monks. In the 15th c. it was pillaged by the Mamelukes, who are thought to have been responsible for the disappearance of the relics of the True Cross (some fragments of which are allegedly preserved in a silver cross in the church). The present fortress-like monastery was built in the 17th and 18th c. on the remains of earlier buildings.

The monastery

The domed church, in the centre of the ranges of cells, contains a valuable 15th c. wooden cross decorated with scenes from the life of Christ. On the north side of the monastery was discovered a secret crypt in which the monks took refuge in times of danger. It now contains a chapel dedicated to SS Constantine and Helen.

Tamassós — E 7

Ταμασσός
Altitude: 150–200 m

20 km south-west of Nicosia, at Politikó, are the excavated remains of ancient Tamassós (Roman Tamassus), one of the oldest city-kingdoms in Cyprus.

The road approaching the site runs past curious flat hills, evidence of the copper mining that once brought the city wealth and power. Two tombs and the remains of a temple are all that can be seen today.

The site was first investigated by the German archaeologist Max Ohnefalsch-Richter in the 19th c. Systematic excavations were begun in 1970.

Jun.–Aug. Tue.–Sun. 9am–noon, 4–7pm; Sep.–May Tue.–Sun. 9am–1pm, 2–4.30pm.

History

Tombs of the 3rd millennium BC are evidence of the earliest occupation of the site, and other finds have shown that it was continuously inhabited in the following millennia. In the *Odyssey* (I,184) Athena speaks to Telemachus of a city named Temesa that could be reached by sea, where she desired to exchange iron for copper. This was probably the Cypriot town of Tamassós, which was known in Homer's time for the mining and processing of copper. In the 7th c. BC the town enjoyed its first great period of prosperity.

At the beginning of the 5th c. BC Tamassós was destroyed, probably as a consequence of its involvement in the Ionian rebellion against the Persians. Thereafter it was rebuilt and established trading contacts with mainland Greece. There is historical evidence for the cult of Aphrodite, Zeus, Dionysus and Heracles and of the building of temples to these divinities. In the 4th c. BC King Pasikypros sold Tamassós to the city-kingdom of Kítion (Lárnaca). After the expulsion of the Persians the city was again destroyed, probably during the fighting between Alexander the Great's successors.

After being once again rebuilt Tamassós had a further period of prosperity. In the 1st c. AD Paul and Barnabas came to Tamassós in the company of Heraclidius (see below), a Cypriot, who then became the first bishop of Tamassós. There is believed to have been a bishop of Tamassós in the Middle Ages, but thereafter the town declined into insignificance.

Sights

★Royal tombs
The two large dromos tombs of the 7th c. BC found at Tamassós are thought on the basis of their rich grave goods to have been the tombs of the local kings. The decorative stone mouldings and the roof structure point to an imitation of the timber buildings which were then normal.

Tomb 11 The first tomb is approached by a narrow stepped dromos. On either side of the entrance are half-columns topped by carved capitals with volutes. The tomb chamber containing the sarcophagus is entered through a pedimented doorway in which the stone is cut to resemble wooden panels.

Tomb 5 The second tomb is also entered by a stepped dromos, the walls of which are faced with finely dressed stone. The

In the monastery of St Heraclidius

doorway of the tomb chamber is richly decorated in the same way as a house or temple, flanked on both sides by pillar-like blocks of stone in which are carved large capitals with volutes. Over the doorway is a frieze of dentils, another imitation of timber construction.

The doorway leads into an antechamber with recesses carved from the rock in the likeness of doors, blind windows and friezes of volutes and palmettes. The antechamber and the tomb chamber both have gabled roofs, with stone beams again imitating timber prototypes.

Temple of Aphrodite
Some 200 m south of the royal tombs are the scanty remains of a sanctuary whose origins go back to the Archaic period. The excavators interpreted this as a temple of Aphrodite, together with dwellings and copper workshops. Here as at Kítion (Lárnaca) cult and copper working were closely associated. The temple consisted of a forecourt, the main temple and the holy of holies.

Monastery of St Heraclidius (Ayios Iraklidhíos)

1.5 km west of Tamassós, at Politikó, is the monastery of St Heraclidius. Founded about 400, it was abandoned in the 18th c. but in 1962, on the initiative of Archbishop Makarios III, was reoccupied by a community of nuns.

Legend
St Heraclidius, the son of a pagan priest, accompanied the apostles Paul and Barnabas on their missionary journey to Tamassós, and on the way there was baptised in the Pedhiéos river. After thorough instruction he was appointed by Paul to be the first bishop of Tamassós. There he served the large Jewish community, together with 'Mnason of Cyprus, an old disciple' (Acts 21,16), and built a small basilica.

Heraclidius is credited with numerous miracles, including the raising of the dead and the control of floods. During the absence of St Mnason he suffered a martyr's death in the market square of Tamassós and was succeeded as bishop by Mnason.

History
About AD 400 a three-aisled basilica was built over the graves of the two saints. Remains of mosaics, columns and capitals from this church survive in the present monastery. The original church was destroyed by Arabs in the 9th c. and later replaced by a new one. The present two-aisled church was built in the 15th/16th c. on the ruins of its predecessor.

Monastery
In the southern aisle of the church, which is dedicated to St Heraclidius, are pillars and wall paintings of the 10th/11th c. from the earlier churches.

In the 17th and 18th c. the monastery had a great reputation as a school of icon painting and a number of 18th c. wall paintings in the church are by a monk named Philaretos, who worked in this school. The iconostasis in the southern aisle is 18th c. The northern aisle was added in the 16th c. and became an independent church dedicated to the Trinity. Its iconostasis is 17th c., as are the icons of Christ, the Mother of God and John the Baptist.

The church's greatest treasure is the skull and a bone from the hand of St Heraclidius, which are wrapped in cloth of gold.

Reliquary chapel
On the south side of the church is a small domed chapel built in the 14th c. over the supposed tomb of the saint. It contains a number of stone sarcophagi of the Roman period. Built into the high stone iconostasis are fragments with Early Christian designs and symbols. In the 15th c. the iconostasis was painted with figures of saints; it was restored in the 18th c.

Burial vault
To the east of the church are steps leading down to a burial vault, said to have been the first resting place of the saint's remains.

Makherás
See entry

Tróodos Massif E–G 3–7

The Tróodos massif, which lies wholly within the Greek Republic of Cyprus and covers almost a third of the island, has

A remote village in the Tróodos massif

some of the most beautiful scenery in Cyprus. The successive ranges of hills within the massif are separated by deep valleys. To the west the mountains merge into an extensive upland region in which vines and fruit are grown. The northern part of the massif, in which there are many abandoned copper mines, is almost uninhabited. There are hotels in the little towns of Tróodos (see below), Páno Plátres, Pródhromos, Pedhoulás and Kakopetriá (see entry).

Mount Ólympos
The highest peak in the Tróodos massif, and in the whole island, is Mount Ólympos (1951 m), on the summit of which is a British radar station. A viewing platform affords a magnificent panorama of the range, extending in clear weather as far as the coast. Around Mount Ólympos are four waymarked nature trails (see below) laid out by the Cyprus Tourism Organisation (CTO).

On the east side of Mount Ólympos is Páno Amíandos, where until recently asbestos was mined in opencast workings. As a result of the carcinogenic qualities of asbestos the mine has now been closed down. In order to obviate the danger of soil erosion there are plans to plant two million trees in this area.

Skiing on Mount Ólympos
The good snow cover which can be expected on Mount Ólympos from January to March allows skiing in this area. With Austrian help, four ski lifts have been installed and a ski school established. In addition to short descents through the forests and some rather bumpy pistes there are two langlauf trails.

Holidays in the hills
During the last decade some of the remoter mountain villages have increasingly been abandoned as young people have left the country for the towns. Life returns to these villages only during the hot summer months, when relatives and friends come to visit the surviving villagers. The mountains are a popular holiday area with the people of Cyprus, who like to spend their holidays – almost invariably in August – in the cooler hill regions. Since the hotels are soon fully booked and there is only one campsite (at Tróodos), many Cypriots

bring their tents and domestic equipment and camp on their own. Throughout the region there are beautifully situated and well maintained picnic areas.

Flora and fauna
The slopes of the hills are mainly covered with Aleppo pines and at higher levels black pines. There are also cypresses, Cypriot cedars (Cedar Valley: ☛Kýkko Monastery), holm oaks, pines, strawberry trees and mulberries. Fruit trees and vines grow up to 1200 m.

Of the hundreds of species of birds the most typical is the bare-necked griffon vulture. Walkers should beware of the adder and the green, black-spotted koúfi viper.

In the remoter mountain regions moufflon can occasionally be glimpsed. This national animal of Cyprus more easily found in the moufflon enclosure at the Stavrós tis Psókas forestry station (☛Kýkko Monastery; Facts and Figures, Nature).

★Monasteries and churches
Over many centuries the mountains offered hermits and monks the seclusion and solitude they sought, and as a result there are numbers of medieval monasteries in the Tróodos, for example Kýkko (see entry), Troodhítissa and Ómodhos (see below), and Makherás (see entry). Scattered among the hills are nine small Byzantine barn-roofed churches, all included in UNESCO's list of World Heritage Sites. They are famed for their magnificent wall paintings (☛Asínou, Kalopanayiótis, Kakopetriá, Lagoudherá and Platanistása).

During the 1950s the mountains offered refuge for the EOKA freedom fighters, who were able, with the support of the monasteries, to carry on their underground struggle against British colonial rule.

Nature trail on Mount Ólympos

★Walking in the Tróodos massif

On military rules there are no walking maps of the Tróodos massif. Walkers should always carry a compass with them, since very few footpaths are waymarked: two exceptions are the walk in Cedar Valley (2 hours) and the path from Politikó to Makherás monastery (5 hours).

The four nature trails around Mount Ólympos all start from Tróodos. Each trail is numbered and given a name (see below). The paths are well made, with numbered signs drawing attention to particular species of plants. At the end of each trail, under the arched timber gateways, walkers can obtain leaflets describing the route; if stocks have run out, as they frequently do, the leaflets can be obtained from the CTO.

Nature Trail 1 (Atalante)
The Khromion trail (9 km) begins at a wooden gate near the post office in Tróodos (at the roundabout) and encircles Mount Ólympos at a height of about 1700 m to end on the Tróodos–Pródhromos road 4 km north-west of Tróodos. It affords magnificent views of the mountains, extending down to the coast.

Nature Trail 2 (Persephone)
The Makria Kontarka trail (3 km) starts from a wooden gate at the Civic Restaurant in Tróodos. It too offers magnificent views.

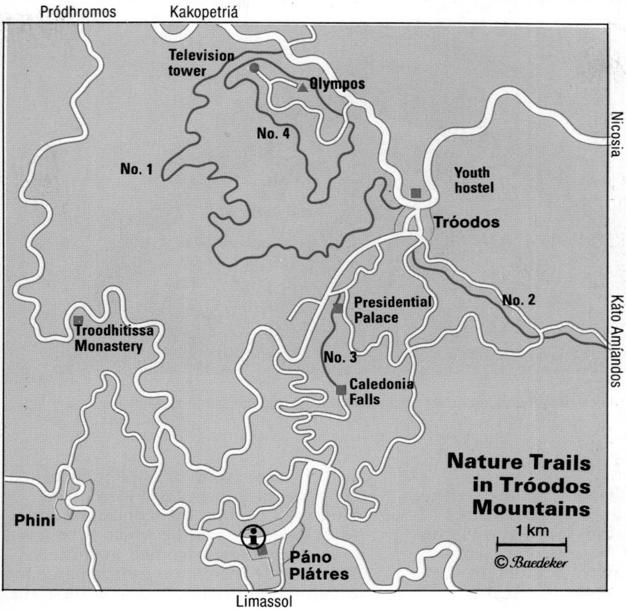

Nature Trail 3 (Kaledonia)
The Krýos Potamós trail (2 km) begins 2 km south of Tróodos on the Páno Plátres road (near the presidential residence) and runs along a green and shady valley to the Kaledonia Falls, ending above Páno Plátres at the Psiló Déndro trout farm, where walkers can rest in the shade of tall trees and have a meal of freshly caught trout.

Nature Trail 4 (Artemis)
The Khionístra trail (7 km), which is not yet completely waymarked, begins 1.5 km north-west of Tróodos on the road leading to Mount Ólympos, just after the turn-off for Pródhromos. At various points there are extensive views of the majestic mountain landscape.

Sights

Tróodos
Tróodos, the highest town in Cyprus (1700 m) and an important road junction, lies below the summit of Mount Ólympos, 50 km from Limassol and 80 km from Nicosia. In truth the town consists solely of tourist facilities including grill restaurants, two hotels, souvenir shops, a filling station and a post office. Not surprisingly, therefore, it has a rather deserted village air in the low season, when no cars or tourist buses stop here. During the summer street traders and roadside stalls add to the bustle of activity in the town, and horses can be hired for treks in the surrounding area. All the nature trails described above start from or near Tróodos. There is also a very pleasant walk along the Krýos Potamós (Cold River) to the Kaledonia Falls, which are something of a miracle on this arid Mediterranean island. Tróodos is also a hive of activity when the skiing season begins in January (runs until March).

Outside the town on the Páno Plátres road is the summer residence of the president of Cyprus. On the palace, which was built for the British governor of Cyprus in 1880, is a plaque recording that the French poet Arthur Rimbaud (then a deserter from the Dutch army) worked on the construction of the house.

Mother of God with her wonder-working girdle (main doorway of Troodhítissa Monastery)

Páno Plátres

7 km south of Tróodos, on the southern slopes of the hills, is Cyprus's most popular mountain resort, Páno Plátres (alt. 1000–1200 m; pop. 600), with excellent facilities for visitors. In addition to numerous hotels, restaurants and coffee houses there are many holiday houses belonging to wealthy Cypriots and Lebanese. Even the last king of Egypt, Farouk, had a sumptuous villa here. Through the town flows the Krýos Potamós (Cold River), the only watercourse in Cyprus which has a flow of water – though sometimes not very much – throughout the year.

Troodhítissa Monastery

On a hill (1300 m) 10 km north of Páno Plátres is the Troodhítissa Monastery, which has not been open to the public for several years. Legend attributes its foundation in the 10th c. to the discovery by two shepherds of the icon of the Mother of God of Tróodos, which had earlier been hidden by a monk to save it from iconoclasts. In later centuries the icon miraculously survived a series of fires. During the period of Turkish rule the monastery became a Christian school. It is now the summer residence of the bishop of Páphos.

The oldest part of the present monastery is the 18th c. church, successor to an earlier church of the 13th c. As in the past, the monastery attracts large numbers of pilgrims to venerate the silver-plated icon of the Mother of God on the iconostasis and a wonder-working girdle which is believed to enable childless women to conceive. This may be the reason for the name by which the monastery is also known, the Panayía Aphrodítissa.

Phiní

From Troodhítissa it is 90 min. walk to the hill village of Phiní (alt. 900 m), in a valley 6 km west of Páno Plátres. For centuries Phiní has been famed for its unglazed pottery – though here, as elsewhere in Cyprus, the traditional craft is slowly dying out. In the past the men of the village made pitharia, large storage jars for grain, wine or oil, 1.5–2 m high, which were set into the floors of the village houses. The local pottery is now mainly made by women who produce smaller pots of various kinds. There is a small museum displaying the different types of local ware.

Phiní also makes the finest hand-made basketwork chairs on the island, using branches from the local holm oaks.

Ómodhos

10 km south-west of Páno Plátres is the pretty hill village of Ómodhos (alt. 850 m), with the monastery of the Holy Cross (Stavrós). The village's main source of income is wine, but the women also make beautiful lace.

According to local legend the monastery was founded to house a fragment of the True Cross (brought to Cyprus by St Helen in the 4th c.; ☛Stavrovoúni) and the hemp rope with which Christ's hands were bound, now preserved in two silver crosses on the iconostasis of the church. The monastery also possesses the skull of the apostle Philip, presented by one of the Byzantine emperors, with the stamps of four emperors to vouch for its authenticity.

The present monastic buildings are modern, with fine hand-carved cedar ceilings; the ceiling of the former chapter house is particularly sumptuous. There is also a small EOKA museum, commemorating the underground movement for the liberation of Cyprus, which was supported by the monastery.

Yeroskípos G 2

Γεροσκήπος
Altitude: 50 m
Population: ca 1800

4 km south-east of Páphos lies the village of Yeroskípos, whose name is derived from the classical Greek Hierós Képos (Sacred Garden). In all probability this was the site of the gardens of the sanctuary of Aphrodite at Palaía Páphos (☛Koúklia). The fragments of ancient masonry found scattered about the churchyard suggest that there may have been a small shrine of Aphrodite in Yeroskípos itself. The pilgrims who landed at Páphos perhaps made their way up through the sacred gardens to the much venerated sanctuary at Palaía Páphos.

Silkworm culture

Until the second world war Yeroskípos, with its numerous mulberry trees, was a centre of silkworm culture. It owes its present prosperity to its proximity to the busy tourist centre of Páphos; it is famed for its pottery and for its Turkish delight (*loukoumia*), now sold all over South Cyprus.

★Church of Ayía Paraskeví

In the centre of the village is the little five-domed church of Ayía Paraskeví, with 15th c. wall paintings (key in the shoemaker's shop opposite the church). The church, which dates from the 10th/11th c., is one of only two five-domed churches in South Cyprus (the other at Peristeróna; see entry). The model for the multi-domed church derives from the 6th c. church of St John at Ephesus. The church of Ayía Paraskeví, which is three-aisled, has three domes over the nave and one over each of the aisles. On the south side of the apse is a small domed chapel. The bell tower was built in the 19th c., the western part of the church as recently as 1931.

Legend

Ayía Paraskeví (St Friday), to whom the church is dedicated, is credited with the power of curing eye complaints. Paraskeví is said to have been born on Cyprus in the 2nd c. AD and to have been named Friday because she was born on that day to parents who had hitherto been childless. After the death of her parents she gave all her possessions to the poor, went to Rome and lived in a Christian community there. She was martyred during the persecutions in the reign of Antoninus Pius.

Wall paintings in Ayía Paraskeví

Church of Ayía Paraskeví

Wall paintings
The wall paintings mostly date from the 15th c., but during restoration paintings of the 10th and 12th c. also came to light. In the east dome, over the altar, was found a cross with floral and geometric decoration, evidently dating from the iconoclastic period (8th–9th c.). The church must therefore be one of the oldest in Cyprus apart from the Early Christian basilicas, now destroyed. Among the 12th c. paintings is a representation of the Dormition of the Mother of God on the north wall, below the central dome, which was overpainted in the 15th c. by a Crucifixion. The 15th c. paintings depict scenes from the life of the Virgin and the life of Christ, with a profusion of figures reflecting western influence.

In the central dome is the Mother of God with her hands raised in prayer, in the western dome Christ Pantokrator. Particularly notable is the painting of the Baptism of Christ on the south wall, below the central dome. At Christ's feet is a small figure of a bearded man, a personification of the Jordan, who turns to flee before Christ. To the right is an old woman in a boat drawn by two sea monsters, representing the sea. The reference is to Psalm 114, 3: 'The sea saw it and fled: Jordan was driven back.'

Double icon
On the north wall of the nave, immediately in front of the painting of Ayía Paraskeví, is a double icon of the 15th c., hung behind glass, which was formerly on the iconstasis. On one side is the Mother of God with the Child, on the other the Crucifixion.

★Folk Art Museum

The little Folk Art Museum near the church in Athens Street illustrates the domestic life and folk art of the district of Páphos.

It occupies the house of the British consul in western Cyprus, which was acquired by the Department of Antiquities in 1978. The house was built in 1799 by Andreas Zimboulakis, an immigrant from Greece who became British consular agent.

The rooms of this typical Cypriot house are entered from a courtyard with a wooden gallery on the upper floor. The exhibits include a fully equipped kitchen, spinning and weaving equipment, agricultural implements and a wedding room with fine old chests, needlework, pottery and traditional costumes.

Sep.–May Mon.–Fri. 7.30am–2pm, Sat. 7.30am–1pm; Jun.–Aug. Mon.–Fri. 7.30am–1pm, also Tue. 4–6pm.

Sights from A to Z North Cyprus

To make it easier to locate the places listed in the Sights from A to Z section of the guide, their coordinates on the fold-out map are shown at the head of each entry.

Bellapais/Bellabayis D 8

Altitude: 300 m

Bellapais Abbey lies at the foot of the Pentadáktylos hills in the village of Bellapais, 6 km south-east of Kyrenia. The name of the abbey, one of the most beautiful Gothic monastic ruins in the Mediterranean area, is derived from the Greek *epískopos* (bishop) by way of Lapais and Abbaye de la Paix (Abbey of Peace). *Daily 8am–5pm.*

Lawrence Durrell

The writer Lawrence Durrell lived in the village of Bellapais in the 1950s. In his book *Bitter Lemons* he describes the abbey in these words: 'I was prepared for something beautiful, and I already knew that the ruined monastery of Bellapais (now Beylerbeyi) was one of the loveliest Gothic survivals in the Levant, but I was not prepared for the breath-taking congruence of the little village which surrounded and cradled it against the side of the mountain.' He also refers to the 'Tree of Idleness' in front of the abbey, which still survives. He was warned by one of his Cypriot friends, if he intended to try and work, never to sit under the Tree of Idleness: 'its shadow incapacitates one for serious work.'

History

The abbey, dedicated to Our Lady of the Hill, was founded in 1205 by Augustinian monks who had fled to Cyprus from Jerusalem after its conquest by Saladin in 1187. The Lusignan king Hugo I granted it extensive properties. In the 13th c. the abbey passed to Premonstratensian monks who had also fled from the Holy Land. Bellapais then became known as the White Abbey after the white habit of the Premonstratensians. The abbots were under the jurisdiction of the archbishop of Nicosia, with whom they frequently came into conflict.

The present church was built in the reign of Hugo III (1267–84) and the other buildings date from the 14th c. The king granted the abbot special privileges: he was permitted, for example, to wear an episcopal mitre during mass and when outside the abbey to wear a sword and gilded spurs. Thanks to generous gifts and donations the abbey grew rich and powerful.

Decline set in during the 16th c., when the strict rule of the abbey was increasingly disregarded and the monks broke their vow of chastity. The Venetian authorities were about to take measures to restore order when Cyprus was captured by the Ottomans and the monks fled from Bellapais.

★★Abbey

Church

In accordance with the usual layout of medieval monasteries, all the buildings are set around a cloister. The present entrance to the abbey is on the west side. It leads through a courtyard into the narthex of the church (locked; the key is with the keeper). In the walls of the narthex are recesses for tombs, and there are remains of 15th c. wall paintings. The church, which lies on the south side of the cloister, has a nave with side aisles and a square choir at the east end. In the north wall of the church is a staircase leading up to the monks' dormitory (which no longer survives); the monks came down these stairs to attend services during the night. On the north side of the choir is a small sacristy.

Cloister

The cloister, in late Gothic style (14th c.), has pointed arcades and remains of flamboyant tracery. On the

Bellapais Abbey

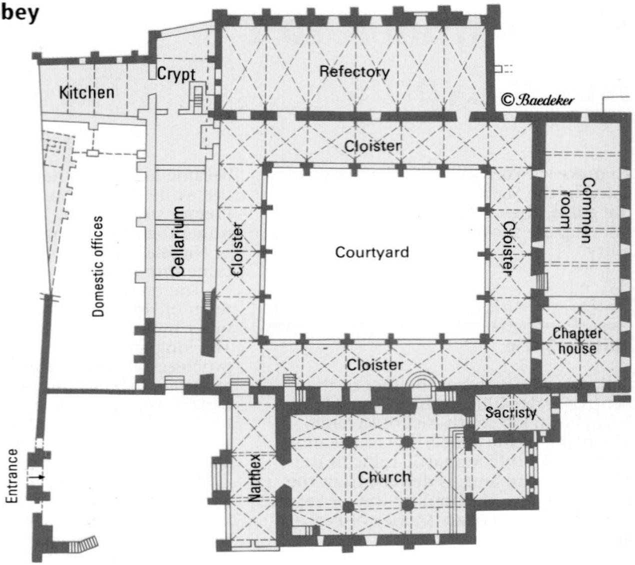

lawn in the centre of the cloister are four tall cypresses.

Chapter house

At the south-east corner of the cloister is the chapter house, with a single column in the centre which supported the vault. The corbels on which the ribs of the vault rested show traces of the former magnificent relief decoration. The daily meeting of the monks was held here, presided over by the abbot.

Common room

The long room adjoining the chapter house was originally barrel vaulted and is thought to have been the monks' common room, or possibly a scriptorium for the writing and copying of books. Over these two rooms was the monks' dormitory.

Refectory

On the north side of the cloister stands the refectory. In front of the entrance is a Roman sarcophagus decorated with masks and genii carrying garlands, which was used to contain water. Over the doorway are the arms of the Lusignans as kings of Cyprus and Jerusalem.

The refectory, with a groin vault, is preserved intact. Measuring 30.4 × 11.5 × 11.5 m high, it is one of the largest refectories of its time. On the north side steps lead up to a pulpit with rich tracery from which one of the monks read sacred texts during meals. There are six windows, from which there are fine views of the town of Kyrenia on the coast below. Under the refectory was a storeroom reached by a staircase.

There are only scanty remains of the buildings on the west side of the cloister, probably the kitchen and other domestic offices.

Surroundings

Vounoús/Taskent

From Bellapais an unmade road runs south through the hills, coming in 10 km to Vounoús/Taskent, with the excavations of an early Bronze Age necropolis. Here, in addition to a variety of pottery, were found the two famous clay models of a ploughing scene and a circular shrine in which some religious ceremony is being performed; both are now in the Archaeological Museum on

Bellapais Abbey

the Greek part of Nicosia (☛Sights from A to Z South Cyprus, Nicosia).

Buffavento Castle D 8

Altitude: 954 m

Buffavento Castle (the Italian name means defier of winds) is perched on a precipitous crag in the Pentadáktylos hills south-east of Bellapais. To reach it from Nicosia, take the Famagusta road and shortly before Trakhóni/Demirhan turn into a road on the left which runs up to a pass; then from the summit of the pass (view of Mount Pentadáktylos 740 m) take a dirt road on the left which comes in 6 km to a car park below the castle (28 km). From here it is a 30 min. climb to the castle. Buffavento can be reached from Kyrenia by leaving on the Famagusta road and at its highest point (view of the Mesaória plain) taking a road on the right (24 km).

In contrast to the two other castles in northern Cyprus, St Hilarion and Kantara (see entries), there are only slight remains of Buffavento. It does, however, offer superb views of the north coast (Kyrenia), the Mesaória plain and the castle of St Hilarion.

History

Like Kantara and St Hilarion, Buffavento was built in the 10th c. and later refortified by the Lusignans. Lying between the other two, it was an important link in the island's signalling system. The Lusignans also used it as a prison. At the end of the 15th c., after the Venetians gained control of Cyprus, the castle was demolished.

Castle

There are only scanty remains of the castle, which was built of undressed local stone. It consisted of a lower ward, the foundations of which can still be identified, and an upper ward some 20 m higher up. The lower ward looks down on the Mesaória plain; from the upper ward, on the summit of the hill, there is a fine panorama. The lower ward was occupied by the soldiers' living quarters and guardrooms, stables and storerooms. In the upper ward there are traces of a number of rooms facing west and two cellars.

The castle is in the present-day military zone and not often open to the public.

Surroundings

Monastery of Ayios Ioánnis Chrysóstomos
Below the castle, 3 km away, is the monastery of Ayios Ioánnis Chrysóstomos (St John Chrysostom; alt. 570 m), in which St Neóphytos is said to have been a novice at the age of 18 (☛Sights from A to Z South Cyprus, St Neóphytos Monastery).

The monastery has two churches standing side by side. The older one, to the south, was originally built in the 11th c. and was one of the few examples in Cyprus of a church with a dome carried on corner squinches. After its collapse it was replaced by a new church in the 19th c. The other church, which dates from the 12th c., has wall paintings of that period. Since the monastery lies in a military area and is used as a barracks, it cannot be visited.

★★Famagusta/Gazimağusa E 11

Altitude: sea level
Population: 20,000

Famagusta (Turkish Gazimağusa, or Mağusa for short), the second largest town in North Cyprus and formerly the island's principal port, lies 60 km east of Nicosia. The Greek name of the town, Ammóchostos (buried in sand), refers to its situation on the beaches of golden sand that extend along the east coast of Cyprus. It consists of two very different parts, the Old Town within the Venetian walls, which have been preserved intact, and the New Town (Yeni Mağusa or Maras) outside the walls. Before 1974 the Old Town was inhabited solely by Turks, the New Town (then known as Varósha or Maras) by Greeks.

Varósha
Before 1974 Varósha was the tourist quarter of Famagusta, well equipped with high-rise hotels, banks, shops, markets and restaurants. Famagusta then had a total of some 10,000 hotel beds – more than the rest of the island put

The old town of Famagusta, with St Nicholas's Cathedral

together. Varósha is now a depressing sight. The hotels, damaged by bombing in 1974, lie in a closed military area and are steadily falling into ruin. From the luxury Palm Beach Hotel, one of the few still open in Famagusta, there is a view of what is now a ghost town.

Port
The port of Famagusta, once the largest in Cyprus, has also declined. Before 1974 it was the only port in Cyprus with modern facilities and accordingly handled most of the island's trade. Now it is one of only two commercial ports in North Cyprus the other being Kyrenia.

University
The Eastern Mediterranean University, in which tuition is in English, was founded in 1986. It has departments of engineering and other vocational subjects. The Gothic church of Ayios Exorinós now serves as its Cultural Centre.

Tourism
Famagusta has begun to redevelop its tourist trade within the last few years, and is now the second most important tourist centre in North Cyprus. New hotels have been built along the beautiful sandy beaches north-east of the town, generally low-rise developments with their standard of amenity below that of the Greek Cypriot hotels. The efforts of the government of North Cyprus to boost tourism have been effective and it is the fastest growing sector of the North's economy.

Old Town
The Old Town with its narrow streets, ruined Gothic churches, street traders, fruit stalls and shoeshine boys has a rather Oriental air. The many little shops and boutiques offer a tempting range of goods.

History

The history of Famagusta begins in the 3rd c. BC with the foundation by the ruler of Egypt, Ptolemy II, of the town of Arsinoe to the south of the ancient city of Sálamis (Constantia). In the 7th c. AD the inhabitants of Constantia fled before the Arabs to the neighbouring town of Arsinoe, which had long been a city of ruins half buried under drifting sand.

The town was now rebuilt and became known as Ammóchostos (buried in sand), since the new city was still threatened by the destructive power of the sand. It continued to be harassed by Arab raids, and achieved a measure of prosperity only in the 12th c., after an influx of Armenians. Then, following the conquest of Cyprus by Richard I, king of England, in 1191, Ammóchostos became known under the Lusignans as Famagusta.

Medieval heyday
In 1291 Acre, the last Christian stronghold in the Holy Land, fell to the Muslims. Many crusaders, monks and merchants fled to Cyprus, bringing goods and money with them, and settled in Famagusta. The port became a major centre of trade between East and West, and merchants from many countries set up their businesses in the town. In the 13th and 14th c. it was one of the most flourishing and wealthiest towns in the whole Mediterranean area. The population grew to 70,000, and the streets were lined with sumptuous noble mansions. The kings of Jerusalem were now crowned in Famagusta, which was said to have more than 365 churches.

Venetian rule
In 1374 there was a bitter dispute between the Genoese and the Venetians in Cyprus, when the Genoese were denied their traditional privilege of holding the right-hand rein of the king's horse during the ceremonies of a royal coronation. They then captured and pillaged Famagusta and compelled the king to pay tribute. In 1489 the Venetians recovered the town and strengthened its defences in anticipation of a Turkish attack.

Turkish rule
In 1571, however, the Turks succeeded in taking the town after a 10-month siege. During the peace negotiations a dispute arose between the negotiators: the Venetian commander, Marcantonio Bragadino, was killed for failing to honour his promise to spare the lives of 50 Turkish prisoners of war. The Christian population fled from Famagusta but were allowed to live outside the town. Since then the Old Town of Famagusta has remained Turkish, as the Turkish name Gazimağusa (unconquered city) indicates.

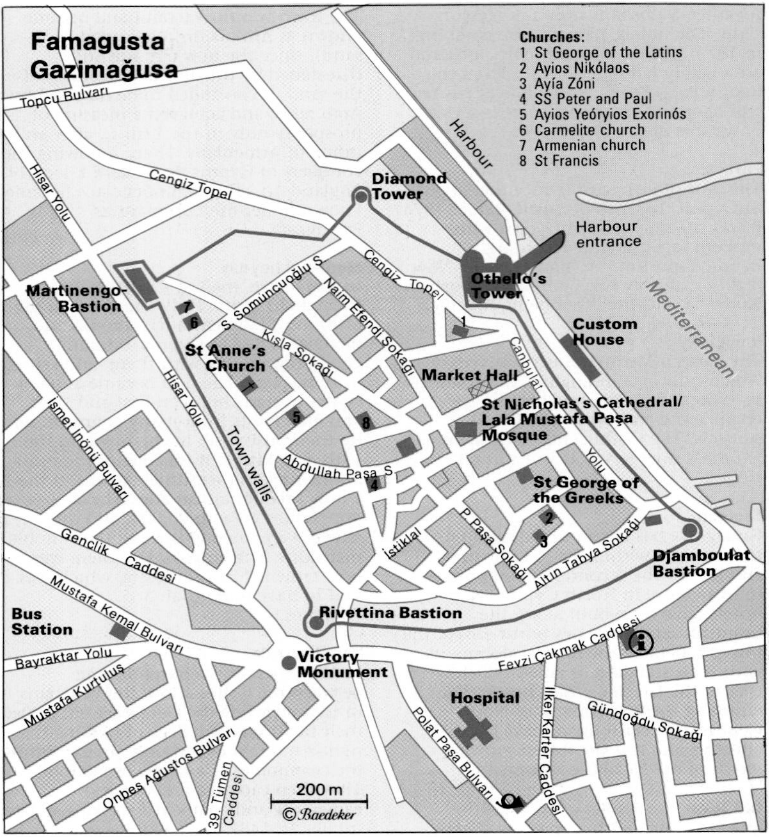

19th and 20th centuries

After the Turkish conquest Famagusta declined into a town of little consequence, but in the 19th and 20th c. its importance revived with the development of the port. The Turkish Cypriots continued to live in the Old Town, with Greeks and Armenians in the outer districts. In 1974, after heavy fighting, Famagusta fell to the Turkish forces.

Sights

Victory Monument

At a roundabout on the south side of the town, just outside the walls, is the Victory Monument erected by the Turks in honour of those who died in the civil war. It is a dynamic work of sculpture with scenes of battle and of flight, topped by the figure of Atatürk, the founder and first president of modern Turkey. Just beyond the roundabout a road on the left leads through the Land Gate (the Rivettina Bastion or Ravelin) into the Old Town.

Town walls

The walls of Famagusta, still excellently preserved, were built at the end of the 15th c. on the remains of older walls erected by the Lusignans. As the Turkish

Othello's Tower

threat grew steadily greater the city commissioned a Venetian architect, Giovanni Girolamo Sanmichele, to build larger and stronger walls. The new walls, in the form of an irregular polygon with a total circuit of 3.5 km, were 18 m high and up to 9 m thick. On the seaward side they were reinforced by the Diamond Tower, the Citadel (Othello's Tower) and the Djamboulat Bastion. The land walls, which were surrounded by a moat, were given additional protection by the Martinengo and Rivettina bastions. There were originally only two entrances to the town, the Sea Gate and the Land Gate; others were opened up during the period of British colonial rule.

★Othello's Tower/Othello Kalesi
The Citadel, popularly known as Othello's Tower, is a square structure with fortified round towers at the corners, built by the Venetians in 1492 on the remains of a smaller Lusignan stronghold. Two sides are on the sea, while the two landward sides were protected by a moat. An inscription under the Lion of St Mark at the main entrance gives the date of construction and names the builder as Niccolò Foscarini. In the inner courtyard of the Citadel are remains of a square Gothic tower and a large hall of the Lusignan period. Visitors can climb to the wall walk, from which there are good views of the harbour and the Old Town with its numerous churches.
Mon.–Sat. 8am–5pm.

Since Shakespeare's **Othello** is set in a seaport in Cyprus, the Citadel has been identified as the scene of the drama and has become known as Othello's Tower. The Venetian vice-governor has been cast as the Moor of Venice, since his name was Cristoforo Moro, in allusion to his dark skin. According to another theory Othello was Francesco di Sessa, who was exiled to Cyprus and, being also dark skinned, was known as the *capitano moro*. Shakespeare himself was never in Cyprus, but took his plot from a story by a Venetian writer, Giraldo Cinzio.

Djamboulat Bastion
The Djamboulat Bastion (modern

Turkish spelling Canbulat) houses a small museum as well as the tomb of a Turkish cavalry officer, Canbulat Bey, who during the siege of Famagusta in 1570 rode his horse on to a wheel covered with knives with which the Venetians had protected the entrance and by his sacrifice enabled the Turks to take the town. His tomb is still honoured. The museum's collection includes Bronze Age pottery, Turkish domestic tools and clothing (including wedding garb) and weapons of the 17th–19th c.
Mon.–Fri. 8.30am–1pm, 2.30–5pm.

Opposite the Djamboulat Bastion is a military cemetery commemorating the Turks who fell during the defence of Famagusta in 1963.

Martinengo Bastion
The Martinengo Bastion, completed about 1550, is named after Hieronimo Martinengo, who died on his way to Cyprus to command the Venetian troops. The most massive of Famagusta's bastions, with walls up to 6 m thick, it was designed to protect the town against attack from the landward side. Inside the bastion are two large underground chambers which offered shelter for 2000 men or could be used as ammunition stores.

Church of St George of the Latins
Opposite Othello's Tower are the ruins of the little church of St George of the Latins, one of the oldest Gothic buildings in Famagusta, dating from the late 13th c. Richly decorated, in a style reminiscent of the Sainte Chapelle in Paris, it provided the model for St Catherine's Church in Nicosia.

Church of St George of the Greeks
From the Land Gate Istiklâl and M Ersu streets lead to the ruined Gothic church of St George of the Greeks, built in the late 14th c. as the Orthodox counterpart to the Roman Catholic cathedral of St Nicholas. The architectural decoration and the pointed arches show Gothic influence, while the domed roof of the nave recalls Byzantine models. In the choir apse there are remains of wall paintings. Unfortunately much of the church was destroyed over time.

The ruined church of St George of the Greeks

St Nicholas's Cathedral Lala Mustafa Paşa Mosque

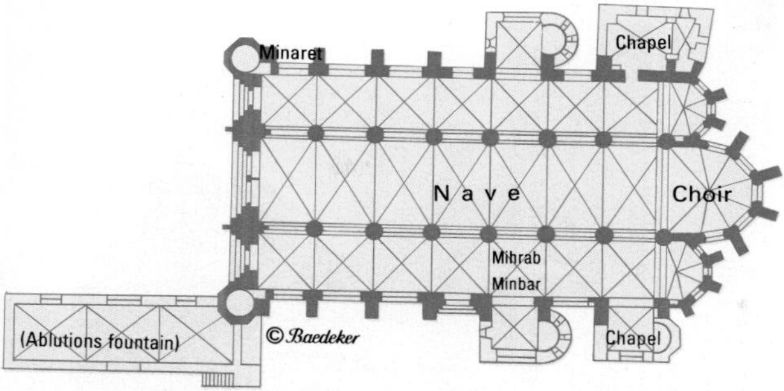

Ayios Nikólaos and Ayía Zóni
To the east of St George of the Greeks are two small Orthodox churches. The two-aisled 15th c. church of Ayios Nikólaos is now a ruin. Adjoining it is the well preserved Byzantine domed cruciform church of Ayía Zóni (the Holy Girdle of the Mother of God), which dates from the 14th c. (no access).

★★St Nicholas's Cathedral/Lala Mustafa Paşa Mosque
From St George of the Greeks Naim Efendi Street runs north-west to St Nicholas's Cathedral in Namík Kemal Square, which dominates the skyline of Famagusta. This Roman Catholic cathedral is one of the best-preserved Gothic buildings on the island. It was begun in 1298 under the direction of Baudouin Lambert and consecrated in 1326, at the same time as St Sophia in Nicosia. This was the coronation church of the kings of Jerusalem – for the Lusignans were not only kings of Cyprus and Armenia but also nominally kings of Jerusalem, though that city was now held by the Turks. The last Lusignan queen, Catherine Cornaro, signed her abdication document here, and her husband James II was buried in the cathedral.

St Nicholas's Cathedral, the most Gothic church in Cyprus, shows affinities with the French cathedrals in the Île de France. When it was converted into a mosque in the 16th c. the sculpture was removed and the paintings covered with whitewash, and a small minaret was built on the north tower of the facade.

The **facade**, which is preserved up to the third stage of the towers, is a masterpiece of Gothic architecture. The three doorways are topped by crocketed gables with delicate tracery. The second stage has a large and beautiful rose window flanked by two blind windows. The towers, now reduced to stumps, have Gothic windows crowned by gables. The walls of the church are supported by massive buttresses. At the left- and right-hand ends of the facade are two small polygonal staircase towers giving access to the external gallery on the west front, on which the kings showed themselves to the people after their coronation.

The **interior** of the church is three-aisled and five bays long. The arches of the vault rest on massive columns; the clerestory has large Gothic windows. For its present function as a mosque the walls are whitewashed and the floor is covered with carpets, and there are a mihrab and a minbar on the south side. At the east end of the nave is the polygonal apse; there is no ambulatory. The windows of the choir have fine tracery and externally are topped by gables. The aisles end in small apsidal chapels. In the apse of the north aisle (now the women's part of the mosque), set into the floor, is a medieval gravestone with a figure of St Nicholas with his episcopal mitre and crosier.

On the south side of the square in front of the church are the remains of a Venetian **loggia**, now housing an ablutions fountain.

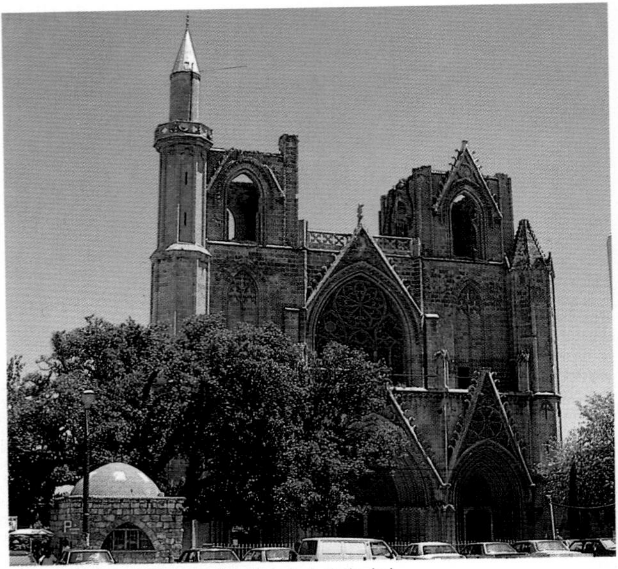

The richly decorated facade of St Nicholas's Cathedral

Ancient tree
In the square in front of the church is a 600-year-old sycomore fig tree (a native of North Africa) planted during the period of Lusignan rule.

Palazzo del Provveditore
In Namík Kemal Square, opposite the cathedral, are the remains of the Palazzo del Provveditore, the Venetian governor's palace. There was a royal palace here in the 13th c., in which the Lusignan kings resided after their coronation. The Venetians enlarged the palace, giving it a monumental Renaissance doorway, which still survives, together with some fragments of walls. The doorway, in rusticated stonework, has three arched entrances giving access to the interior of the palace, which is now a car park. In front of the doorway four large granite columns from ancient Sálamis support a cornice. Over the central round-headed arch are the arms of the Venetian governor, Giovanni Renier (1552). Beyond the doorway, to the left, are the remains of a building which in Turkish times was used as a state prison. The Turkish national poet Namík Kemal was confined here from 1873 to 1876 for writing a play which was considered to be seditious. There is a monument to him on the north side of the square in front of the cathedral.

Church of St Francis
To the north of the Palazzo del Provveditore stand the ruins of a Gothic church belonging to a Franciscan friary founded by the Lusignan king Henry II in the 13th c. It now houses the Old Town Discothèque.

Cafer Paşa Baths
Round the apse of the church is a disused public bathhouse built in 1601 by the Turkish governor, Cafer Paşa, who also constructed an aqueduct to bring water to Famagusta. In Namík Kemal Square is the Cafer Paşa Fountain.

Church of SS Peter and Paul
From Namík Kemal Square Abdullah Paša Street leads to the early Gothic church of SS Peter and Paul, built in the 14th c. at the expense of Simone Nostrano, a wealthy merchant, for the use of the merchants' guild.

This three-aisled basilica, excellently preserved, is purely Gothic. The nave is separated from the aisles by low pointed arches on columns and is lit by simple clerestory windows. The nave leads directly into the apse, and there are two small lateral apses at the east end of each aisle. The nave and aisles are spanned by vaulting with carved bosses.

After the Ottoman conquest in 1571 the church was converted into the Sinan Paša Mosque, and thereafter was used as a potato and grain store. After renovation in the 1960s it now houses the Municipal Library.

Ayios Yeóryios Exorinós

Continuing along Abdullah Paşa Street to the town walls and turning right, you come to the Nestorian church of Ayios Yeóryios Exorinós, built in 1359 by one of the wealthiest merchants in Cyprus. The original church was three bays long with a semicircular apse, but soon after it was built it was enlarged by the addition of two short aisles, only two bays long, ending in small apsidal chapels. In Turkish times it was used as a camel stable, but in the early 20th c. it was taken over by Orthodox Christians and dedicated to Ayios Yeóryios Exorinós (St George the Exile).

The church has remains of wall paintings (which originally covered the whole of the interior) and inscriptions dating from its occupation by the Nestorians. It now houses the Cultural Centre of the Eastern Mediterranean University.

Other churches and Icon Museum

An Armenian church dedicated to the Mother of God, a Carmelite church and the little church of St Anne all lie within a military area near the old town walls and cannot be visited. Also within the prohibited zone is an Icon Museum (ask outside the area).

Surroundings

Énkomi–Alasia, Tuzla

See Sálamis

Monastery of St Barnabas

See Sálamis

Sálamis

See entry

★Kantara Castle C 11

Altitude: 680 m

Kantara Castle is reached from Nicosia by taking the road which runs via Kythréa/Değirmenlik and Lefkóniko/Geáitkale to Tríkomo/Iskele and then turning left into a road signposted to Árdhana/Ardahan (86 km). From Famagusta take the coast road; then at Perivólia/Baháeler turn left into the road to Tríkomo/Iskele and continue from there to Kantara (43 km).

Kantara (meaning bridge, arch) is the most easterly of the three medieval castles in the Pentadáktylos hills, built to defend the island's northern approach. From the castle there is a superb panorama of the north coast and Famagusta Bay.

History

The three castles of Kantara, St Hilarion and Buffavento (see entries) were built by the Byzantines in the 10th c. to provide protection against Arab raids.

Kantara commanded an extensive area ranging from Famagusta to Buffavento. The Lusignans enlarged and strengthened the castle, now known as Le Candaire, and it played an important part during the Lusignan king Henry I's conflict with Emperor Frederick II. Frederick landed in Cyprus on his way to the Holy Land in the Fifth Crusade and claimed possession of the island.

Although Henry gave way, the Cypriot nobility rose against Frederick's forces, who then withdrew to the safety of the castles. In 1230 the Cypriot lords compelled them to surrender; two years later Kantara was recaptured by the emperor's forces, but soon afterwards it was finally regained by the Lusignans. At the end of the 14th c. the castle was further strengthened during the conflict with the Genoese. In the 16th c. its walls were slighted by the Venetians, and in subsequent centuries it fell into ruin.

Castle

A flight of steps goes up to the gateway of the castle, flanked by two towers. This leads into the outer ward. The surviving masonry dates mainly from the 14th c. Beyond this is the main front of the castle, flanked by two towers. From here the upper ward is entered through the left-hand tower. Within this area are various buildings, a cistern and, on the

View of the coast from Kantara Castle

highest point, a large watchtower, with a fine window on the lower floor. To the south is a horseshoe-shape tower with a sally port.

★Karpasía/Kırpaşa Peninsula A–C 12–15

The Karpasía peninsula (Karpas for short; Turkish Kırpaşa) is the long panhandle at the north-eastern end of Cyprus, with the foothills of the Bešparmak range extending to its furthest tip. From Nicosia it is some 145 km to Cape Andréas at the end of the peninsula, from Famagusta 115 km.

Landscape

The peninsula, 80 km long and up to 15 km across, is a lonely region of great scenic beauty. The village people live mainly by farming, growing corn, vegetables and tobacco. Until 1985 the peninsula was a closed military area and has therefore remained largely untouched by tourism. After the partition of Cyprus in 1974 and the departure of the Greek inhabitants of the peninsula the abandoned villages were reoccupied by Turkish Cypriots fleeing from the south and returning from abroad. There are still, however, some 360 Greeks who refused to leave their homes in 1974. United Nations troops now watch over the maintenance of peace between the Greek and Turkish populations. As the ruins of many early Christian churches show, the peninsula was densely populated in Byzantine times but was increasingly abandoned after repeated Arab raids.

In the following description distances are reckoned from Famagusta.

Tríkomo/Iskele (20 km)

The village of Tríkomo, to the north of Famagusta, was the birthplace of the EOKA leader Colonel Grivas. In the centre of the village stands the little 15th c. church of Ayios Iákovos. Of greater interest, however, is the principal church, dedicated to the Panayía Theotókos, which dates from the 11th c. and has 12th c. wall paintings showing

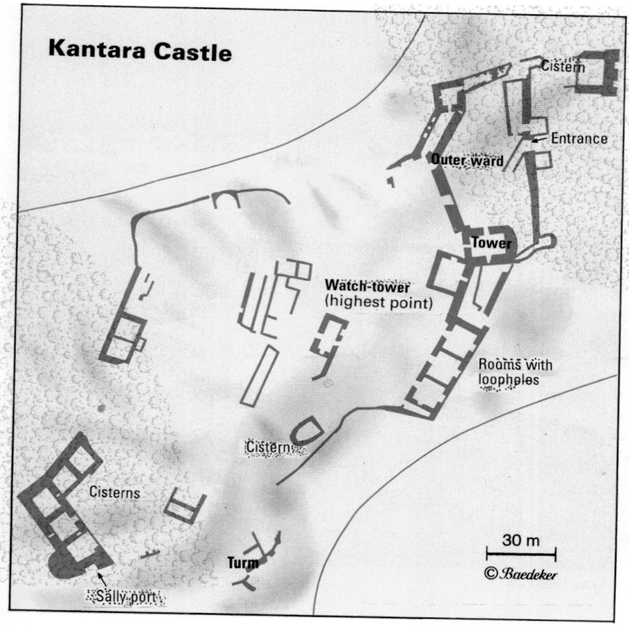

stylistic affinities with the paintings in Asínou church. The surviving paintings depict scenes from the life of the Virgin; in the dome is Christ Pantokrator.

Livádhia/Sazlıköy (38 km)
From the turn-off for Tríkomo the coast road continues to Ayios Theódhoros/Çayírova, from the far end of which a road goes off on the left to Livádhia (3 km). In this village, opposite the mosque, a narrow dirt road goes off on the left to the abandoned church of the Panayía Kyra, standing alone in a field. This little domed cruciform church was built in the 10th/11th c. on the remains of an Early Christian basilica and originally belonged to a monastery. Before 1974 there was a mosaic of the Mother of God in the apse (☛Heritage under Threat).

Lythrángomi/Boltaşli (56 km)
The main road continues to Leonárisso/Ziyamet, from which a road on the right leads to Lythrángomi, with the fine church of the Panayía Kanakariá, which originally belonged to a monastery. This three-aisled domed church was built in the 12th c. on the remains of a 6th c. Early Christian basilica; the south aisle with its doorway was added in the 13th c.

The apse of the original church had a fine 6th c. mosaic of which fragments were still in position in 1974. Thereafter it was stolen and disappeared, finally turning up in the United States (Indianapolis) in 1989. An American art dealer had bought the mosaic from a Turk for US$1.2 million and offered it to the Getty Museum in Malibu, California, for US$ 20 million. When the Church of Cyprus heard this it claimed the mosaic as church property, and an American court finally directed that it should be returned to Cyprus. The mosaic has been restored and is now on show in the Icon Museum in Nicosia (☛Sights from A to Z South Cyprus, Nicosia).

The church contains badly damaged remains of wall paintings of the 10th–16th c. South of the church are

Church of the Panayía Kyra, Livádhia

ruins of the monastery buildings, which are now used as stables.

Ayía Triás/Sipahi (65 km)
From the turn-off for Lythrángomi the main road continues to Yialoúsa–Yenierenköy, where a road goes off on the right to Melánarga/Adaáay. The first little road opening off this road on the left leads to the village of Ayía Triás/Sipahi, at the far end of which, on the left, are the remains of the Early Christian church of Ayía Triás. In this large excavation site are the foundations of a three-aisled basilica of the 7th c., with a few columns or their bases indicating its plan. There is a well preserved mosaic pavement with geometric patterns. Associated with the church was an extensive complex of buildings, including a small baptistery with a baptismal chapel on the south side of the apse containing an immersion font for the baptism of adults.

Rizokárpaso/Dipkarpaz (86 km)
Rizokárpaso, the most easterly village on the peninsula, was the see of an Orthodox bishop in the 13th c. The former cathedral of Ayios Synésios, now much altered, is still used by the Greek community living in Rizokárpaso.

Monastery of Ayios Andréas (115 km)
30 km east of Rizokárpaso is the monastery of Ayios Andréas, which before 1974 attracted crowds of pilgrims every weekend; the key is held by the custodian, who lives in the cell block. According to the local legend the apostle St Andrew, while sailing along the coast of Cyprus, saved a ship's captain who was dying of thirst by directing him to a spring on Cape Andréas. The captain expressed his gratitude by the gift of a valuable icon, to house which the monastery was founded. Thereafter St Andrew became the patron of seafarers.

The monastery buildings date from the 19th and 20th c. The monastery is still in Greek hands, and on special feast days like the Dormition of the Mother of God (August 15th) and St Andrew's Day a service is conducted by the Rizokárpaso priest.

There is a Turkish Cypriot police post here.

On the shore below the monastery is

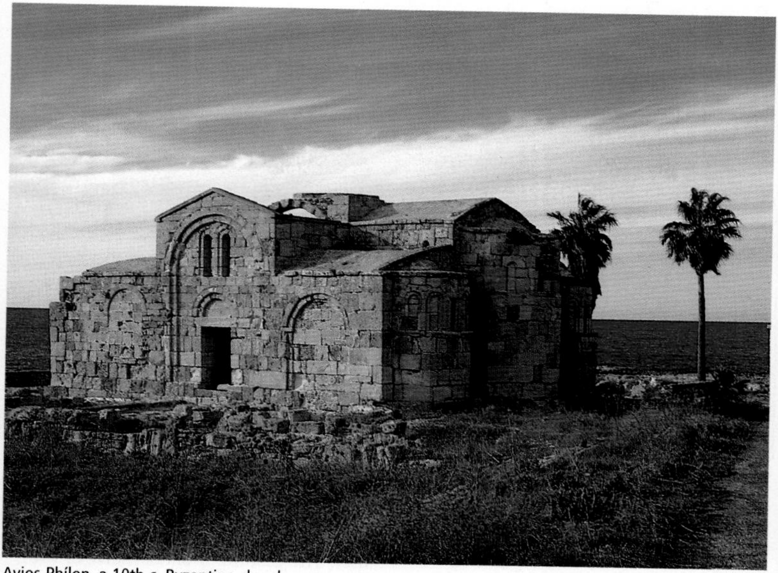

Ayios Phílon, a 10th c. Byzantine church

a small square Gothic chapel (15th c.) built over St Andrew's Spring, with a central column supporting the vault.

Cape Andréas
From the monastery it is another 5 km to the cape, on which the site of a Neolithic settlement has been found. At the end of the 12th c. Isaac Comnenus, fleeing from Richard I, king of England, was taken prisoner here. Off the cape are the Klídhes (Keys) Islands.

Ayios Phílon
On the way back from Cape Andréas, shortly before the church, take a road which runs up on the right and comes in 4 km to the ruined church of Ayios Phílon, overlooking the coast. Near here was the ancient city of Karpasía, destroyed by Arabs in the 9th c.

The church of Ayios Phílon was built in the 10th c. on the remains of a small Early Christian church. With its fine stonework it is a magnificent example of 10th c. Byzantine church architecture. The church is three-aisled, with a narthex and an atrium. On the south side are the baptistery, a cistern and a font.

Aphendriká
About 8 km east of Ayios Phílon are the three Early Christian basilicas of Aphendriká – all that is left of a once important city destroyed by Arabs. The churches were rebuilt in the 10th c. The best preserved of the three is the three-aisled church of the Panayía Asomatos.

★Kyrenia/Girne C/D 7/8

Altitude: 0–30 m
Population: 7000

Kyrenia, on the north coast of Cyprus, is one of the most idyllic little towns on the whole island. The small horseshoe-shape harbour with its yachts and fishing boats is surrounded by old houses and tavernas. Immediately south of the town are the Pentadáktylos hills.

Kyrenia is reached from Nicosia on an excellent road (26 km). Coming from

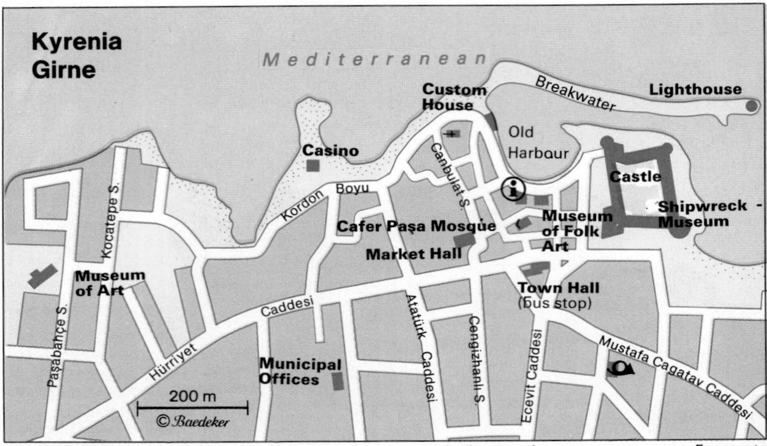

Lápithos (Lapta) St Hilarion, Nicosía Famagusta

Famagusta, turn off the Nicosia road just after Demirhan into a road on the right (73 km).

Tourism
Kyrenia is now the principal tourist centre in North Cyprus, with beautiful sandy beaches east and west of the town and good walking in the nearby Pentadákylos hills. The majority of North Cyprus's hotels are situated in or around Kyrenia. Small hotels and guest houses, such as the long-established Dome Hotel, are located in the centre of town or on the harbour while larger hotels are slightly away from the town centre. Most of the visitors come from Turkey. There are also some British-owned holiday and retirement houses in and around Kyrenia, which was a favourite British resort during the colonial period.

★Harbour
The little harbour, dominated by the massive bulk of the castle to the east, is suitable only for small boats. In the centre of the harbour basin is a small medieval tower, from which a chain could be spanned to the shore to close the harbour to an enemy. Beyond the castle is a modern harbour (military port) used by freighters and ferries.

Old Town
Kyrenia has a well preserved Old Town of narrow streets and handsome houses with romantic balconies. Notable features are the Cafer Paşa Mosque and the neighbouring Turkish baths (still in use). The ground floors of many of the old houses on the harbour have been converted into attractive restaurants.

History
Antiquity The area was first settled in Neolithic times. In the Bronze Age the population increased, and there were close contacts with the coast of Asia Minor. After the Hellenisation of the island by the Achaeans Kyrenia became one of the Cypriot city-kingdoms, which in 312 BC came under the control of the powerful city of Sálamis. At the end of the 4th c. BC Kyrenia, in common with the other cities of Cyprus, was incorporated in the empire of the Ptolemies. In the 4th c. AD it became the see of a bishop.

Middle Ages The town suffered repeatedly from Arab raids and in the 7th c., when the Roman fortifications were still standing, the Byzantines built a citadel at the harbour entrance. When the harbour was again fortified in the 10th c. the work was confined to the enlargement and strengthening of the citadel, and the town walls were abandoned.

During the conflict between Emperor Frederick II and the Cypriot nobility in the early 13th c. the imperial forces entrenched themselves in the castle but were compelled in 1233 to surrender. Thereafter the castle was rebuilt, and in the 14th c. it became the favourite residence of the Lusignan king James I.

In 1460 Kyrenia was the scene of a struggle for the succession between the heiress to the throne, Carlotta, and John II's illegitimate son James the Bastard, who claimed the throne for himself. The conflict was won by James, who starved Carlotta out in Kyrenia and later married Caterina Cornaro, the last Lusignan queen of Cyprus.

During the period of Venetian rule the castle was much altered. After the Turkish conquest of Nicosia in 1570 Kyrenia surrendered without more ado.

Sights

★Castle

The castle lies in the north-east of the town, protecting the entrance to the harbour. Its origins go back to the citadel built in the 7th c., which was enlarged and strengthened in the 10th c. The Lusignans made further changes and the north and east wings were completely rebuilt. The Venetians reinforced the castle by building stronger towers. In 1570 it passed into the hands of the Turks. During the period of British colonial rule it was used as a prison. In 1959 it was assigned to the Department of Antiquities, and it now houses the Shipwreck Museum (see below).

The castle, roughly square in plan, is flanked by three large corner towers. Within the castle are some remains of its Byzantine predecessor, a rectangular structure with small round towers. A 12th c. Byzantine chapel dedicated to Ayios Yeóryios (St George) has also been preserved. Behind this is a large circular bastion built by the Venetians. From the Frankish period dates the guardroom in the western range, which now contains the tomb of Sadík Paşa, commander of the Turkish fleet, who was killed in 1570. There are fine views of the harbour and the hills from the walls, which mostly date from the Frankish period.

The harbour of Kyrenia, one of the principal attractions of North Cyprus

On the east side of the castle is a range of Frankish living apartments: two of these are now occupied by the Shipwreck Museum (see below). From the wall at the south end there is a view down into the courtyard, at the south-east corner of which can be seen the remains of a horseshoe-shape Byzantine tower.

Mon.–Sat. 8am–1pm, 2–5pm.

Shipwreck Museum

In the Shipwreck Museum, opened in 1976, are displayed the remains of an ancient cargo ship of the 4th c. BC complete with its cargo. A series of photographs document the recovery of the ship by a team of American archaeologists in 1968. The wreck, lying 1.5 km off the coast at a depth of 33 m, was discovered by a sponge diver. It is one of the oldest wrecks ever found in the Mediterranean. The archaeologists were able to trace the course of the ship's voyage, from Samos by way of Kos and Rhodes to Cyprus. The ship, which was some 80 years old when it went down, was 14 m long, built of timber from Aleppo pines, using copper nails. The cargo included over 400 amphoras, 29 millstones and numbers of jars containing almonds. Among the other objects found were four wooden spoons and cups, suggesting that the vessel had a crew of only four men, who lived on the fish they caught and the almonds they carried with them.

In the early 1980s a group of archaeologists from Texas built replica of the ship, *Kyrenia II*, which in 1986 sailed along the coasts of Cyprus.

Museum of Folk Art

On the harbour is the Museum of Folk Art, in a traditional Cypriot house of the 18th c. The basement originally served as a barn and a granary. On the first floor are displayed agricultural and domestic equipment, including oil presses, ploughs and weaving looms; on the second floor is the old living room; and on the third floor is a display of crochet work and embroidery.

Mon.–Sat. 8am–1pm, 3–5pm.

Cafer Paşa Mosque

In the street immediately behind the harbour front is a mosque built by Cafer Paşa in 1580 and restored in the 1970s. The minaret is a picturesque landmark on the town's skyline.

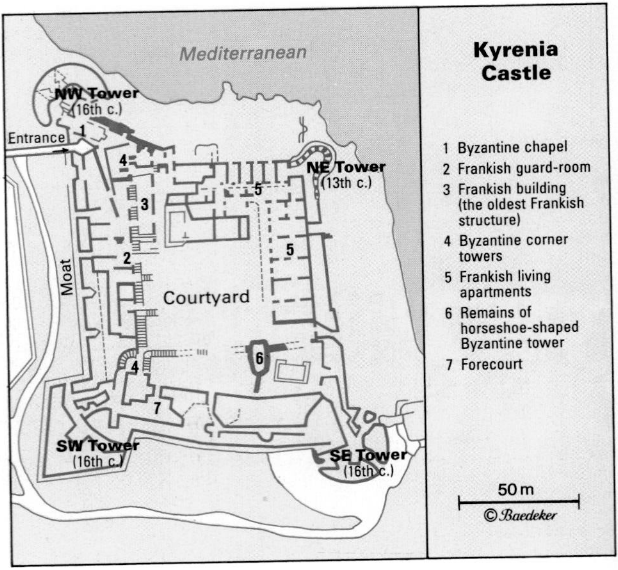

Kyrenia Castle, with the Shipwreck Museum

Art Museum
To the west, a little way from the town centre, is the Museum of Art, with a collection of European paintings, Chinese and European porcelain and needlework from the Far East.
Mon.–Sat. 8am–1pm, 2–5pm.

Byzantine harbour
A road that goes off on the left from the Famagusta road just before the hospital leads to an ancient quarry and the Byzantine harbour (beyond which is the new naval harbour). Here are remains of a rock-cut Byzantine chapel.

Surroundings

Ayios Epíktetos
10 km east of Kyrenia is Ayios Epíktetos/Catalköy. In the Club Acapulco holiday village is the site of a Neolithic settlement.

Sourp Magar monastery
Further east a road branches off the coast road on the right shortly before Ayios Amvrósios/Esentepe and runs south to the ruined Armenian monastery of Sourp Magar (alt. 500 m; 35 km from Kyrenia). The monastery, dedicated to the 4th c. hermit Makarios, was founded by Copts in the 12th c. and taken over by Armenians in the 15th c. In the 19th c. it became a place of refuge and an orphanage for the Armenian community in Turkey; the present church dates from that period. The monastery is still a favourite place of pilgrimage for Armenians living in Cyprus.

Antiphonitis monastery
From Ayios Amvrósios a road goes south-east to the beautifully situated Antiphonitis monastery (30 km from Kyrenia), now abandoned, which dates from the 12th c. The church is the last surviving example in Cyprus of the type with a dome carried on squinches. The narthex was added in the 14th c., the loggia on the south side in the 15th. There are some remains of the wall paintings that once covered the interior.

Kármi/Karaman

10 km south-west of Kyrenia lies the pretty village of Kármi/Karaman. Mainly consisting of new houses, it is a holiday resort and retirement retreat for many British people. Just before the village are the excavations of a group of Bronze Age chamber tombs.

Peace and Freedom Museum

8 km west of Kyrenia on the Mórphou road, on the right, is the Peace and Freedom Museum. In the courtyard of the museum are military vehicles and armour captured from Greek Cypriot troops. The museum illustrates the intervention of Turkish troops in 1974 and commemorates those who fell. Unfortunately all the explanations are in Turkish.

A short distance further along the road is the monumental concrete Peace Memorial, commemorating the Turkish intervention on July 20th 1974.

Lamboúsa

10 km west of Kyrenia, at the village of Karavás/Alsancak, are the excavated remains of ancient Lamboúsa, which lie in a closed military area and cannot be visited. In the 8th c. BC Lamboúsa was a splendid royal capital. In the Early Christian period it was a place of considerable importance, the see of one of the leading Cypriot bishops, but in the 7th c. it was destroyed by Arabs. Here in the 1960s was found a famous hoard of Early Christian silver, part of which can now be seen in the Archaeologial Museum in Nicosia (☛Sights from A to Z South Cyprus, Nicosia).

Lápithos

A few kilometres inland from Lamboúsa is Lápithos/Lapta, the site of an ancient city founded in Achaean times, where there is said to have been a sanctuary of Aphrodite. Excavations have discovered geometrically shaped tombs.

Mórphou/Güzelyurt D 5/6

Altitude: sea level
Population: 12,000

The little town of Mórphou (beautiful country in Turkish), lies 50 km from Kyrenia at the western tip of the Turkish-occupied part of Cyprus, in a fertile alluvial plain bordering the wide sweep of Mórphou Bay. The town's economy depends mainly on the huge citrus plantations that surround it. The agricultural development of this area began in the Frankish period, when the Lusignans promoted the growing of sugar cane and cotton.

Until 1974 the mines at Skouriótissa and Mavrovouní also made a contribution to the town's economy, producing copper, iron ore and pyrites. Nowadays the soft drinks industry is of some importance.

History

The Mórphou plain was first settled during the Bronze Age. Artefacts recovered in this area suggest that it was occupied by incomers from western Anatolia. Down the centuries Mórphou Bay always played an important part in the economy. The town established here, however, never developed into a large city-kingdom, probably because it was overshadowed by its powerful neighbour, Sóloi/Soli.

Sights

Church of St Mamas

The church of St Mamas (key in adjoining Archaeological Museum) was built in the 18th c., the successor to Byzantine and Frankish churches on the site and probably also to an ancient temple of Aphrodite. Since 1974 it has been a Museum of Greek Orthodox Art.

The **interior** of the church, which is three-aisled, with a high dome, incorporates fragments of Gothic work. The columns in the nave have Gothic ornament, and the two small marble columns in the west window and the tomb of St Mamas are other relics of the medieval building. The north and south doorways also show Gothic features.

The carving on the iconostasis is 17th c. work, and in the lower part is finely carved relief decoration of the Venetian period (16th c.). The royal doors in the centre of the iconostasis are flanked by two small marble columns with Gothic capitals. On the columns at the east end of the nave are paintings of SS Peter and Paul.

On the north wall, under a Gothic arch, is the Byzantine sarcophagus of St Mamas, and above it is a series of painted scenes from his legend. The story they tell is that the saint's sarcophagus was washed ashore in Mórphou Bay, found by a peasant and, in accordance with instructions given in a vision, taken to a particular spot where a monastery was built in the saint's honour.

Legend St Mamas, one of the saints most venerated in Cyprus, gained the reputation of a tax rebel and now ranks as the patron saint of tax evaders. He is said to have lived as a hermit in a cave near Mórphou. The Byzantine governor called on him to pay his taxes, and when Mamas refused he sent two soldiers to bring him to the capital, Nicosia. On the way there they encountered a lion, which Mamas tamed, and he then rode into the town on the lion. The governor was so impressed that he exempted Mamas from payment of any taxes in future.

Museum of Archaeology and Natural History
The former residence of the Orthodox bishop of Mórphou is now occupied by the small Museum of Archaeology and Natural History. The ground floor is mainly devoted to natural history, with a collection of stuffed animals, including many species of birds, fishes, turtles and tortoises, snakes and foxes.

On the upper floor are antiquities from private collections, including material from the excavation of a Bronze Age settlement at Toúmba tou Skoúrou (near Mórphou), pottery of the Bronze Age and the Geometric and Archaic periods, idols and Hellenistic and Roman oil lamps, as well as Byzantine pottery. The most interesting exhibit is a statuette of the Ephesian Artemis – with her numerous breasts evidently a fertility symbol – which was recovered from the sea off Sálamis in 1980.
Daily 8am–6pm.

Surroundings

Ayía Iríni/Akdeniz
23 km north of Mórphou are the excavations of Ayía Iríni/Akdeniz. The site (in an area which is sometimes closed to the public on military orders) is reached by turning off the main road to

Church of St Mamas, Mórphou, now a Museum of Greek Orthodox Art

Kyrenia at Dhióris/Tepebasí into a minor road heading towards the coast.

In a sanctuary on this site were found 2000 terracotta figures of varying size dating from the Archaic period, some of which can now be seen in the Archaeological Museum in Nicosia (☛Sights from A to Z South Cyprus, Nicosia).

Mýrtou-Pigádes
17 km north-east of Mórphou is the Bronze Age shrine of Mýrtou-Pigádes, which is reached by taking a road on the right 1 km beyond Mýrtou/Çamlıbel. Here in a courtyard is a stone altar with large bulls' horns. Evidence was found of connections with Minoan Crete during this period, so it seems likely that the bull cult was derived from there.

Philiá/Serhadköy
At Philiá, 10 km east of Mórphou, are the excavated remains of an early Bronze Age settlement. Pottery found here suggested connections with western Anatolia. This is regarded by archaeologists as a site of particular importance in the chronology of early Cypriot cultures.

Sóloi/Soli
See entry

Vouní/Bademliköy
See entry

★Nicosia/Lefkoşa D/E 7/8

Altitude: 165 m
Population: 45,000

On the situation and importance of Nicosia, the Green Line through the divided city, the frontier crossing point, the history of the city and the Venetian walls see Sights from A to Z South Cyprus, Nicosia.

The Turkish part of Nicosia can be reached either by way of the frontier crossing point at the old Ledra Palace Hotel (☛Practical Information South Cyprus, Frontier Crossing) or by travelling direct to North Cyprus by way of Turkey.

Sights

Kyrenia Gate
The Kyrenia Gate, formerly known as the

Museum of Archaeology and Natural History, Mórphou

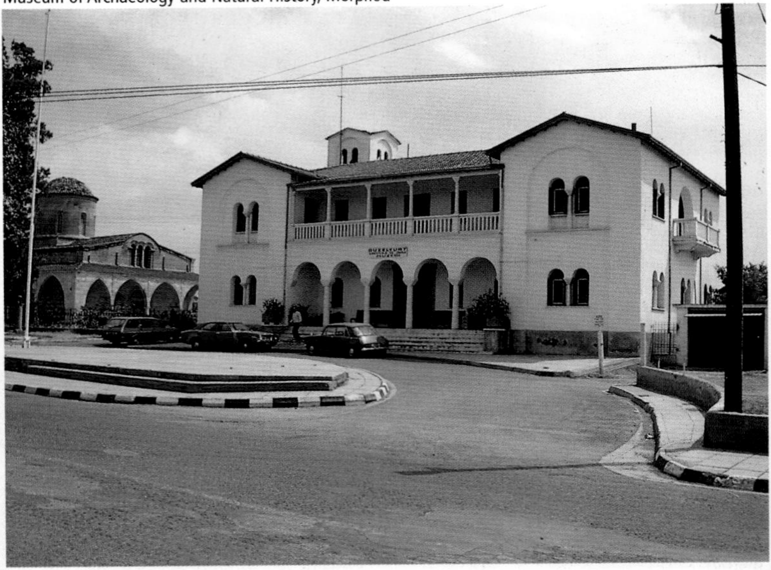

Kyrenia Gate

Porta del Provveditore, is a short distance from the frontier crossing point along Selim II Street. The gate, built in the 16th c. as part of the walls, is the most northerly of the three original gates. The square tower on top of the gate was added during restoration work in 1821. During the British colonial period the central opening was closed and traffic was directed to left and right of the gate.

Mevlevi Tekke/Museum of Turkish Folk Art
At the near end of Girne Caddesi (Kyrenia Street), which runs south from the Kyrenia Gate, is the Museum of Turkish Folk Art, which since 1963 has been housed in the former monastery (*tekke*) of the Whirling Dervishes. The order of Whirling Dervishes, founded in the 13th c. by Mevlâna Jelâleddin Rumi (1202–73), was banned by Kemal Atatürk in 1925 on account of its reactionary views. The dervishes sought by dancing and singing to achieve a state of ecstasy which would bring them closer to Allah.

In the former prayer hall are displayed traditional dervish costumes and musical instruments (red flutes, small drums), precious fabrics, pewter, furniture and illustrated manuscripts of the Koran. In a long corridor roofed with domes are 16 identical sarcophagi belonging to leaders of the dervish community. In the courtyard are Ottoman gravestones.
Mon.–Sat. 8am–1pm, 2–5pm.

Venetian Column
Girne Caddesi leads into Atatürk Square, in the centre of which stands the tall Venetian Column. This grey granite column was brought to Nicosia from ancient Sálamis in the 16th c., set up on a hexagonal base and decorated with the coats of arms of leading Venetian families. The Lion of St Mark that originally topped the column was replaced during the British colonial period by a copper globe.

Sarayönü Mosque
To the west of the Venetian Column, beyond a row of houses, can be seen the minaret of the Moorish-style Sarayönü Mosque, built in 1820d in the time of Ali Paşa, as a prayer hall for the Turkish

View of Nicosia from the south

governors. At the beginning of the 20th c., after its destruction in an earthquake, it was restored by a British architect. The interior has horseshoe arches formed from stones of different colours. Since 1964 the mosque has been used only for marriages.

Arab Ahmet Mosque
From Atatürk Square, Saraÿnü Street to the right runs into Mahumet Paşa Street. Along this street to the left is the Arab Ahmet Mosque.

It was built in the 17th c. in honour of Arab Ahmet, a general who had distinguished himself during the conquest of Cyprus in the 16th c. The mosque, which was restored in 1845, is the only domed mosque in Nicosia. It is set in beautiful gardens, originally an Islamic cemetery. It contains a number of historic tombs, including that of Grand Vizier Kamil Paşa (1833–1913), the only Cypriot to attain that rank.

House of Derviş Paşa
From here Salahi Sevket Street joins Beliğ Paşa Street, along which to the left is the recently restored House of Derviş Paşa. This 19th c. mansion, in what was formerly the Armenian quarter of the town, was built by Derviş Paşa, publisher of the first Turkish Cypriot newspaper, *Zaman* (The Times), which began to appear in December 1891.

This two-storey house is in a style typical of the houses of well-to-do Turkish families in the 19th c. The ground floor is built in stone, the upper floor in sun-dried brick. The ground floor rooms, with the servants' quarters and the kitchen, open off the central

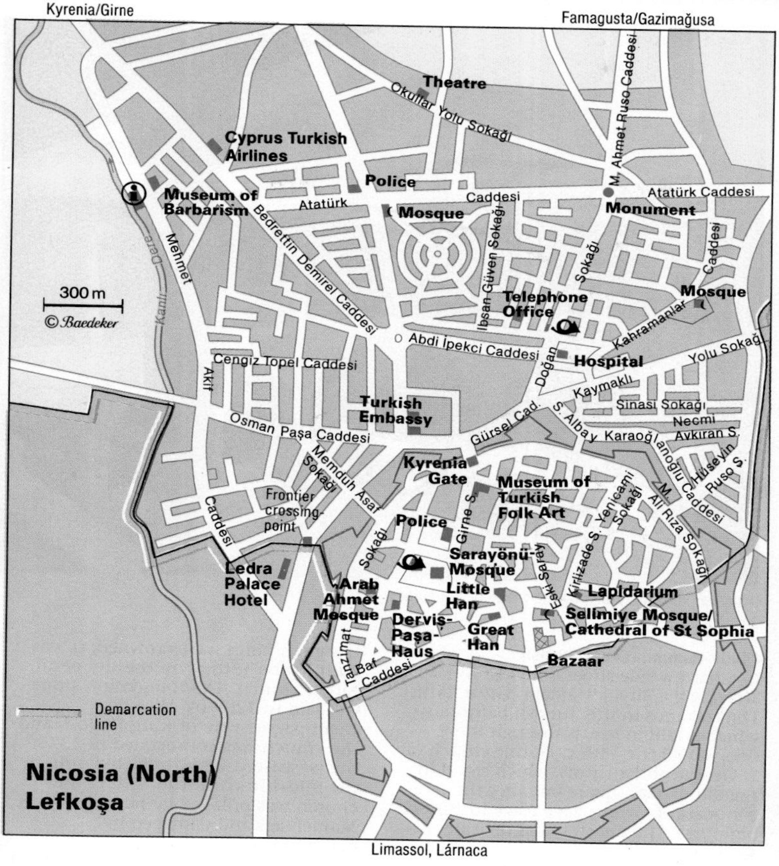

courtyard; they now display domestic equipment, porcelain and weaving looms.

The decoration and furnishings of the family rooms on the upper floor, including the bride's room, the bedrooms and the dining room, have been preserved in their original condition, and with their display of costumes and fabrics give a picture of Turkish life in the 19th c.

Daily 8am–1pm, 2–4.45pm.

★ Büyük Han (Great Han)

From Beliğ Paşa Street Kyrenia Street (Girne Caddesi) leads to Arasta Street, in which is the Büyük Han (Great Han), an old caravanserai. Built by Mustafa Paşa in the 16th c., it provided accommodation for travelling merchants. In the 19th c., under British colonial rule, it was used as a prison, and was later occupied by poor Turkish families. Its most striking features are the octagonal chimneys. In the centre of the spacious inner courtyard is a small Islamic chapel (*mescit*), a prayer hall for the merchants. On the ground floor were stables and storerooms, on the upper floor living rooms and bedrooms.

The building is being restored to house a Museum of Turkish and Islamic Art.

Little Han, now occupied by the Office of Antiquities

Büyük Hamam (Great Baths)
In a narrow side street off Asma Altí Street is the Büyük Hamam (Great Baths). The entrance to this Turkish bathhouse, which is still in use, is through the doorway of the 14th c. Gothic church of St George of the Latins, which stood in the old market square but after the conquest of Cyprus gave place to Turkish buildings. The doorway has delicate sculpture.

★Kumarcílar Han (Little Han)
On the right-hand side of Asma Altí Street is the 17th c. Kumarcílar Han (Gamblers' Han) or Little Han, now occupied by the Turkish Cypriot Office of Antiquities. It was laid out round a courtyard, now a lawn surrounded by flower beds. The former guest rooms are on the upper floor.

★★Cathedral of St Sophia/Selimiye Mosque
Asma Altí Street runs into Arasta Street, which leads direct to the former Cathedral of St Sophia, now the Selimiye Mosque. The largest Gothic church in Cyprus, in which the Lusignan kings were crowned, it was built in the 13th c. on the site of an earlier church. The foundation stone was laid in 1209 by Alice de Champagne, wife of King Hugo I, and the church was consecrated in 1326; the west front was completed only in the mid-14th c. In the 15th c. the church was pillaged by raiding Mamelukes and damaged by earthquakes.

After the Turkish conquest in 1571 the cathedral was converted into the Aya Sofya Mosque. The unfinished west towers were topped by minarets, the Gothic sculpture was removed and the paintings in the interior covered with whitewash. The medieval gravestones set into the floor are now covered by carpets, and a mihrab (prayer niche) marks the direction of Mecca. The mosque was renamed the Selimiye in 1945 in honour of Selim II, Sultan at the time of the conquest of Cyprus.

The three-aisled **basilica** is rather squat in appearance but is reminiscent of French Gothic cathedrals. Like Reims

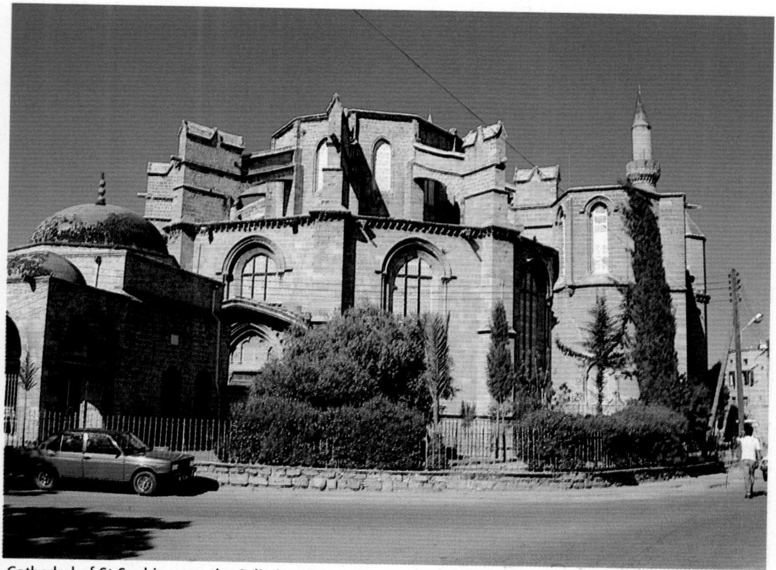

Cathedral of St Sophia, now the Selimiye Mosque

and Amiens cathedrals, it has an ambulatory round the choir, but it lacks the ring of choir chapels, the transept and the triforium of the French cathedrals.

The vaulting of the nave is borne on round columns. The ribs of the vaulting end at the top of the columns and are not carried down to the ground in the manner usual of French cathedrals. In the apse are four antique columns.

In the second bay on the south side is the Chapel of St Thomas Aquinas, who dedicated his work *Of the Rule of Princes* to one of the Lusignan kings. The porch at the west end of the church, with its slender columns and beautiful capitals, is French in character. Here are the remains of figures of kings and saints, destroyed by the various conquerors. Over the porch is a gallery on which kings and great personages received the homage of the people.

The nave and aisles have the flat

Cathedral of St Sophia Selimiye Mosque

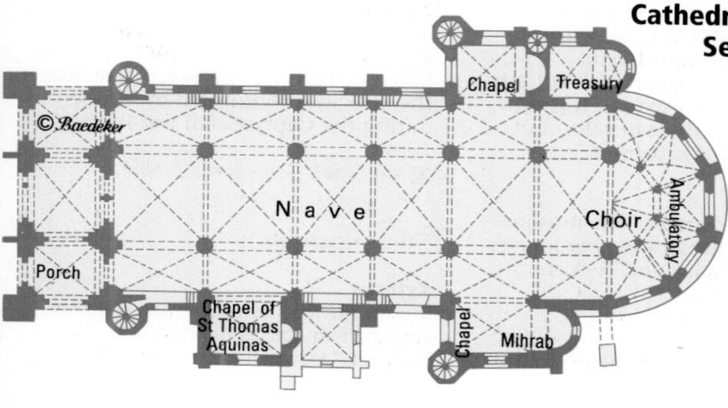

roofs typical of Cyprus. Great buttresses help to withstand the thrust of the vaults.

The custodian of the Bedesten, the Ottoman Library, the Lapidarium and St Catherine's Church can be found in a small room adjoining the Library or in the Office of Antiquities in the Little Han.

Bedesten
To the south of the Selimiye Mosque are the ruins of the Bedesten (Covered Market), originally the church of St Nicholas of the English, which shows both Byzantine and Gothic features. Of the original 12th c. church there survive the two aisles on the south side and wall paintings depicting St Andrew. In the 14th c. the church was enlarged: a north aisle was added, the nave was reroofed with a dome borne on a drum, the choir was extended by a five-sided apse and the large and richly decorated doorway on the north side was surmounted by a gable. Over the doorway are a statue of a saint and six coats of arms added in the Venetian period. On a small subsidiary doorway is a relief of the Dormition of the Virgin.

The church contains medieval gravestones and reliefs. During the period of Venetian rule it was the seat of an Orthodox bishop. In the Turkish period it was used as a grain store and later as a cloth market. Facing the church on the south side is the present market hall.

Archbishop's Palace
On the north side of the Selimiye Mosque stands the former palace of the Roman Catholic archbishop, built in 1329, which was connected with the cathedral of St Sophia by an underground tunnel. After the Turkish conquest the upper floor was rebuilt in Turkish style. In 1821 it became the official residence of the Turkish governor, and during the British colonial period it was used as a school. It is now the headquarters of the Association of Turkish Cypriot Municipalities.

Chapter house
At the south-east corner of the mosque the medieval chapter house now houses a collection of firearms and Turkish gravestones.

Ottoman Library
To the east of the mosque can be found the Ottoman Library, built in 1829 in honour of Sultan Mahmut II (1784–1839), which has a valuable collection of old Turkish, Persian and Arabic books and manuscripts. Many of its treasures came from the palace library in Istanbul. Above the bookcases, in gold letters, is a poem by the mufti of Cyprus, Hilmi Effendi, addressed to the Sultan.
Sun.–Fri. 8am–1pm, 2–4.45pm.

★Lapidarium
50 m east of the mosque is the Lapidarium, also known as Jeffery's Museum after its founder. Housed in a 15th c. Venetian building, the museum displays a collection of medieval architectural fragments, gravestones and furniture. A large late Gothic traceried window is believed to have come from the palace of the Lusignan kings. Of particular interest are a sarcophagus of the Dampierre family and the gravestone of the Frankish general Adam of Antioch.

St Catherine's Church/Haydar Paşa Mosque
From the Lapidarium Kirlizade Street leads to St Catherine's Church, the most important Gothic church in Nicosia after the Cathedral of St Sophia. Built in the 14th c., it probably belonged originally to a monastery. This narrow church has a vaulted nave and a triangular apse. After the Turkish conquest in 1571 it was converted into a mosque (named after a noted Turkish general) and equipped with a minaret.

Museum of Barbarism
Outside the Venetian walls, in Mehmet Akif Street (the road to Kyrenia), is the Museum of Barbarism. The museum occupies an old Turkish house in which the wife and three children of a Turkish doctor and officer, Nihat Ilhan, were murdered in December 1963 by Greek EOKA/B fighters. Photographs document the atrocities committed by Greeks during the Cypriot civil war in the 1960s.
Mon.–Sat. 8am–1pm, 2–5pm.

Surroundings

Kythréa
15 km north-east of Nicosia, near the road to Famagusta, is the town of Kythréa/Değirmenlik, on the site of

ancient Chytri, which according to legend was founded in the 12th c. BC by Chytros, son of Akamas. Excavations here found a Bronze Age necropolis and slight remains of the acropolis and a temple of Aphrodite. The find of a bronze statue of Emperor Septimius Severus (☛Sights from A to Z South Cyprus, Nicosia, Archaeological Museum) shows that the site was continuously occupied into the Roman imperial period.

Nearby is the spring of Kephalovryson, from which a 60 km aqueduct carried water to ancient Sálamis.

★St Hilarion Castle D 7

Altitude: 721 m

St Hilarion Castle is reached from Kyrenia by taking the road to Nicosia and turning into a road on the right shortly before the summit of the pass (11 km from Kyrenia, or 15 km from Nicosia). The road runs through a military area in which photography is forbidden.

St Hilarion, the most westerly and the best preserved of the castles in the Pentadákylos hills, is perched on a crag with twin peaks, affording magnificent views of the hills extending down to Kyrenia on the coast. The ruins bear witness to the one-time splendour of this Castle of the Thousand Rooms, as it is popularly known.

Daily 8am–5pm.

History

The castle is named after St Hilarion, a 6th c. Syrian hermit who spent the last years of his life in a cave in the Pentadákylos hills. A chapel was built in his honour and then, in the 10th c., a monastery. In the 11th c. the Byzantines built a castle on the site, incorporating the monastic buildings; remains of the 10th c. church can still be seen. Under the Lusignan kings the castle was strongly fortified and was given the name of Dieu d'Amour, a garbling of the Greek word Didymoi (Twins) – referring to the twin peaks of the hill.

Frankish rule In the 13th c. the castle played an important part during the

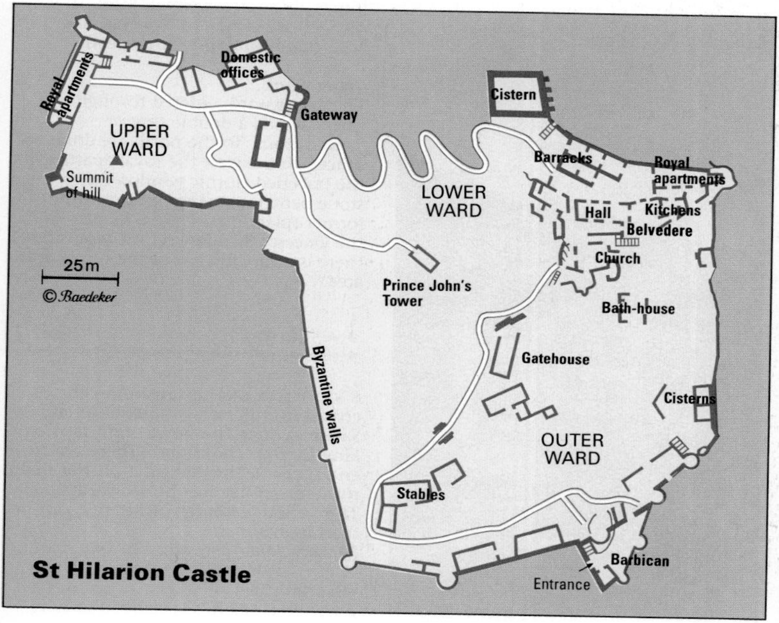

conflict between the Cypriot nobility and Emperor Frederick II, who claimed possession of the island. Frederick's forces withdrew to the castle but in 1232, after a long siege, were forced to surrender it to the Lusignans, who thereafter made it a summer residence.

In the 14th c. St Hilarion was again involved in a conflict for control of Cyprus. When the Lusignan king Peter I died in 1369 his son Peter was not recognised as his successor by the nobility, who preferred his uncle, Prince John of Antioch. Peter I's widow, Eleanor of Aragon, mustered her forces against Prince John who sought safety in St Hilarion. Then, doubtful of the loyalty of his own Bulgarian bodyguard, he had them thrown from a tower of the castle to their death. Finally, however, he lost the struggle for the throne, and Peter II succeeded his father.

The present ruins date mainly from a rebuilding of the castle in 1391. In Venetian times St Hilarion was abandoned.

Ruins of St Hilarion Castle

Sights

Outer ward
The castle is in three sections: the outer, lower and upper wards. The outer ward is entered through a gateway with a barbican, from which a stepped path leads up to the outer ward, passing a large cistern, stables and living quarters for the garrison.

Lower ward
Passing through a gatehouse, once approached by a drawbridge, you enter the lower ward. Beyond this is the 10th c. Byzantine church, the only relic of the former monastery. The church originally had a dome on squinches. To the north of the church are steps leading down to a large hall, probably the former refectory. To the east is the Belvedere, a vaulted loggia. Adjoining this are the apartments in which the royal family lived before the completion of the upper ward.

Prince John's Tower
To the left of the path leading to the upper ward, standing by itself, is Prince John's Tower, from which John of Antioch is claimed to have had his bodyguard thrown to their death.

Upper ward
The upper ward, entered through a gateway, had a double ring of fortifications. To the north are domestic offices, to the west the royal apartments; the traceried Gothic windows with their stone benches give some idea of the former splendour of these rooms. From the Queen's Window on the west side there is a superb view of the surrounding area.

★★Sálamis D 11

8 km north of Famagusta, on the coast, are the excavations of ancient Sálamis, once the most important city-kingdom on the island. There are two entrances to the site, one on the main road, the other on the seaward side. The various features of interest can be seen by car.

Daily 8am–7pm, winter to 5pm.

History
The city of Sálamis is claimed to have

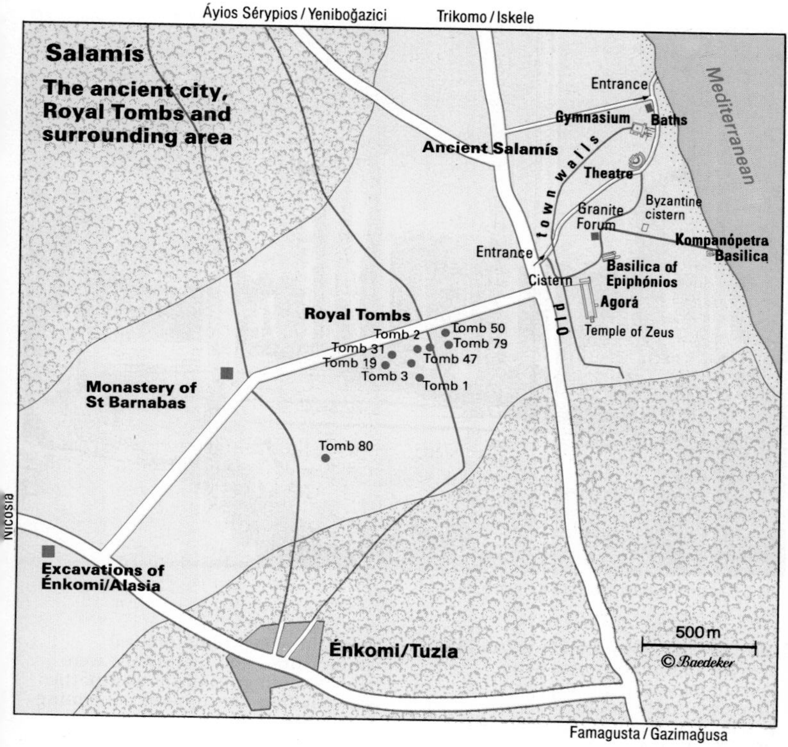

been founded in the 12th c. BC by Teukros (Teucer), a hero of the Trojan War, son of the Greek king Telamon of Sálamis. In the 11th c. Sálamis took the place of the neighbouring city of Alasia (see below), which was destroyed in an earthquake, and thereafter became, economically and politically, one of the leading cities in Cyprus, with a population in its heyday of 100,000. It owed its predominance to its excellent situation in a large bay within easy reach of the East and to the quality of its kings.

In the 8th c. BC Sálamis was the most powerful city-kingdom in Cyprus, with trading contacts with Cilicia, the Phoenicians and Egypt. Outside the city was a large necropolis. At the end of the 8th c., however, Sálamis together with the rest of Cyprus was compelled to pay tribute to Assyria. Under Egyptian rule Sálamis became predominant over the other city-kingdoms. The first coins minted in Cyprus were issued by King Euelthon of Sálamis (560–525 BC). During the struggle between the Greeks and the Persians there were repeated rebellions in Sálamis. The expansionism of king Euagoras I in the 5th c. BC brought Sálamis into conflict with the Persians, but in 323 BC, with the help of Alexander the Great, the city broke free from Persian control.

In the Ptolemaic period the city-kingdoms of Cyprus were dissolved, and thereafter Sálamis lost its predominant position to Páphos. In the 4th c. AD the city, now largely Christianised, was devastated by an earthquake and a tidal wave, after which it was rebuilt and renamed Constantia. In the early 5th c. Constantia became capital of the island. Then in the 7th c., after continuing Arab

The palaestra at Sálamis, part of the gymnasium

raids, the town was abandoned and the new city of Ammóchostos (later Famagusta) was founded a few kilometres to the south.

The surviving remains of ancient Sálamis date mainly from late antiquity and the Byzantine period.

Sights

To the right of the seaward entrance to the site are the gymnasium and the baths.

Gymnasium

The gymnasium, which was discovered in 1882, dates from the 4th c. AD. It replaced an earlier building destroyed in the earthquake.

In ancient times this was a place of both physical and intellectual training. Physical exercises were practised in the palaestra, an open court, originally sanded. In the centre was a fountain basin, and later also a statue. Round the court were four porticoes, off which opened various rooms – changing rooms, work rooms and other rooms in which philosophical conversations and discussions were held. At both ends of the east portico were pavilion-like annexes containing rectangular pools.

Latrine At the south-west corner of the gymnasium is a communal latrine with 44 seats. In Roman times the latrine had a clear view of the palaestra, but in the Christian period it was closed off by a wall.

Museum The annexes to the east portico house a small museum displaying sculpture found during the excavations. Some of the antique statues lack their heads, struck off in Christian times.

Baths

From the east portico we enter the baths. The first room is one of the two frigidaria (cold baths), with an octagonal pool in the centre. Between this and the other frigidarium is the sudatorium (sweat bath), with a recess containing a painting which shows Hylas, Heracles' companion, raising his spear against a water nymph.

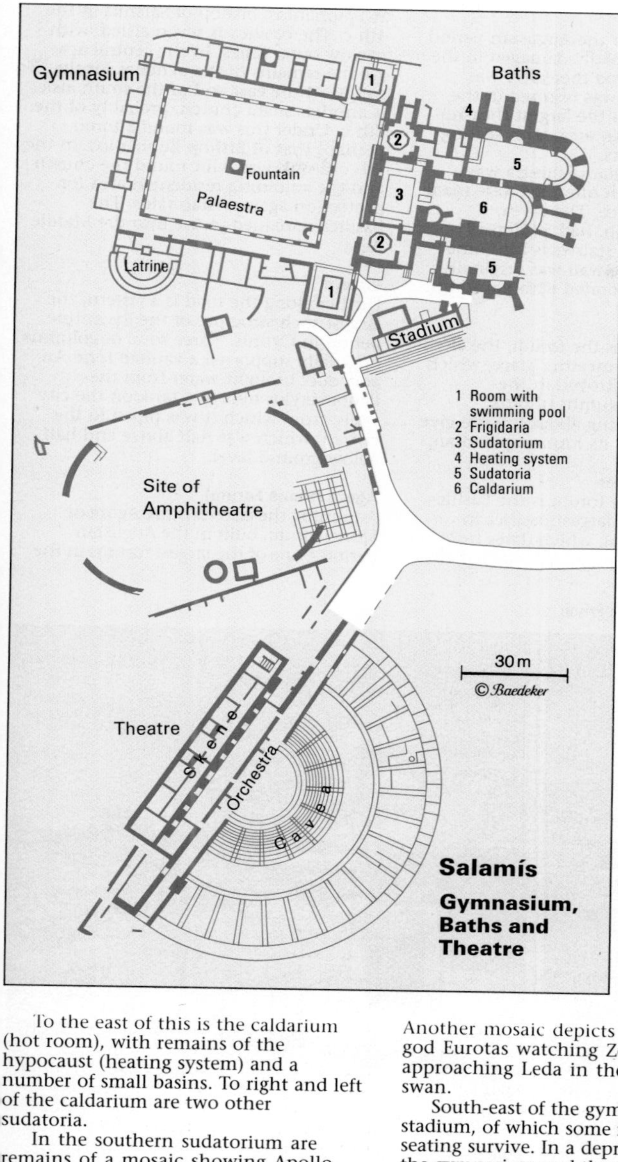

To the east of this is the caldarium (hot room), with remains of the hypocaust (heating system) and a number of small basins. To right and left of the caldarium are two other sudatoria.

In the southern sudatorium are remains of a mosaic showing Apollo and Artemis killing Niobe's children. Another mosaic depicts the old river god Eurotas watching Zeus approaching Leda in the form of a swan.

South-east of the gymnasium was the stadium, of which some remains of the seating survive. In a depression between the gymnasium and the theatre is the site of the amphitheatre.

Theatre
The theatre, built in the Augustan period (31 BC–AD 14), was badly damaged in the 4th c. earthquake and thereafter was used as a quarry. It was restored in the 1960s. It was one of the largest theatres in the Mediterranean area, with seating for 17,000 spectators.

In the semicircular orchestra was a small altar on which offerings were made before a performance. The cavea, originally 20 m high, had 50 tiers of seating, divided by stairways into nine segments. The stage wall was originally 40 m long and decorated with paintings.

Granite Forum
In this area also was the forum, the city's market square and meeting place, which was completely destroyed in the earthquake. The columns of pink Egyptian granite lying about the site give some indication of its former splendour.

Basilica of Epiphánios
To the south of the forum is the Basilica of Epiphánios, the largest basilica in Cyprus (58 × 42 m), which dates from the end of the 4th c. AD. It is named after St Epiphánios, bishop of Sálamis in the 4th c. The basilica is seven-aisled, with narrow outer aisles. In the central apse are the remains of the benches for the clergy. At the east end of the south aisles is another small church, probably of the 7th c. Under this was found a tomb, perhaps that of Bishop Euphánios. In the 7th c. a wall was built round the church and the adjoining residential area for protection against Arab raids. The basilica remained in use into the Middle Ages.

Cistern
Further along the road is a cistern, the largest such structure of the Byzantine period in Cyprus. Three rows of columns originally supported a vaulted roof. An aqueduct brought water from the Pentadákylos hills to a tank on the city walls, from which it was piped to the cistern, which was half above and half below ground level.

Agora (Stone Forum)
Adjoining the cistern is the Agora or Stone Forum, built in the Augustan period – one of the largest forums in the

Tomb 50, St Catherine's Prison

Tomb 50 (reconstruction), St Catherine's Prison

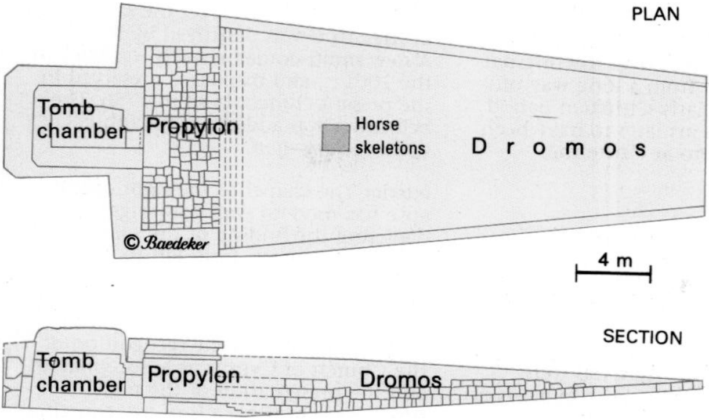

Roman world (55 × 228 m). On the north side was a long portico, which was originally lined with shops.

Temple of Zeus
On the south side of the Agora was the temple of Zeus, a small podium temple which was presumably dedicated to Zeus Salaminios. It was approached by a broad flight of steps and surrounded by colonnades. The slight remains of the podium date from the Augustan period.

Kampanópetra Basilica
Unusually, the Kampanópetra Basilica has two atria (forecourts). The larger one is at the west end, leading into the narthex, which has an apse at each side. The smaller atrium on the east side opens on to the seashore. In the west atrium is an octagonal fountain for ritual ablutions before services. Flanking the aisles of the basilica are katekhouména for the catechumens, the unbaptised members of the community.
Daily 8am–5pm.

★Royal Tombs

The Royal Tombs lie a few hundred metres west of Sálamis on the road to the monastery of St Barnabas. The ticket kiosk is on a side road to the left.

The necropolis of Sálamis, the largest cemetery area on the island, extending for a total length of 5.2 km, dates from the 8th/7th c. BC. In this area the kings and nobles of Sálamis were buried in underground chambers, some of which have been preserved.

All the tombs are of the same type. A long walled dromos (entrance passage) ran down to the tomb, widening as it approached the entrance. From the end of the dromos steps led down to the propylon, a paved forecourt on the far side of which was the doorway of the tomb chamber. After the burial the dromos was filled in and a mound was built up over the grave.

The rich grave goods found in the tombs, as well as demonstrating the wealth of their owners, yielded information on burial rites. In the forecourt of several graves were the skeletons of horses and humans, suggesting that the dead man's servants were sometimes sacrificed as well as his horses. Beside the skeletons were items of harness, a chariot and vessels filled with food for the dead man. Many of the grave goods show Assyrian or Egyptian influence.
Daily 8am–4pm.

Tomb 79
The finest of the tombs is No. 79, in which were found horse skeletons, remains of chariots, two thrones decorated with ivory, a bed 1.89 m long by 1.11 m wide and two bronze cauldrons with animal protomes in Egyptian style – all now in the Archaeological Museum in Nicosia (☛Sights from A to Z South Cyprus, Nicosia).

Tomb 50

Lying near the road is Tomb 50, known as St Catherine's Prison, its vaulted roof (added in Roman times over the original gabled roof) visible from a long way off. It was used in the Early Christian period as a prison, and seems later to have been a chapel dedicated to St Catherine; hence its name.

Tomb 3

Tomb 3, on the other side of the access road, is covered with a high mound which attracted 19th c. tomb robbers. It is approached by a dromos 24.6 m long and 5.2 m wide, lined by walls of sun-dried brick. The tomb chamber itself is built of dressed stone. Here too were found horse skeletons and the remains of chariots. Traces of a funeral pyre on the floor of the dromos point to a fire burial.

Cellarka tombs

Near the royal tombs is the Cellarka complex of simple shaft tombs belonging to humbler members of the community. Something like a hundred of these tombs, which lie just below the surface of the ground and have short dromoi, have been excavated. Many are evidently family tombs, separated from their neighbours only by a low wall.

Monastery of St Barnabas

2 km west of the Sálamis excavations lies the former Monastery of St Barnabas. In 1992 the church was restored, the altar rebuilt and the interior walls decorated with icons. Around the inner courtyard in the former communal rooms of the monastery there is an archaeology museum (with among other things, finds from Sálamis).

Legend

St Barnabas is the patron saint of Cyprus. A native of the island, he sailed to Cyprus with the apostle Paul and helped him in his missionary activity. During a later visit to Cyprus he was stoned to death near Sálamis by the Jews. He was buried by a companion, but the place of his burial remained unknown until the 5th c., when Archbishop Anthemios of Cyprus, guided by a vision, found the saint's tomb and thus enabled the Church of Cyprus to attain autocephaly (☛Facts and Figures, Religion).

Monastery

The monastery built over the saint's tomb in the 5th c. was destroyed by the Arabs. A new multi-domed church was built in the 10th c., and its plan is preserved in the present church, built in 1756. The bell tower was added in the 20th c.
Daily 8am–4pm.

Interior The chapel to the right of the apse has modern wall paintings depicting the finding of the saint's tomb in four sequences: from left to right Anthemios's dream; the finding of the tomb and the Gospel which it contained; Anthemios presenting the Gospel to Emperor Zeno; and the recognition of the Church of Cyprus as autocephalous and the presentation of the new privileges. On the walls of the church, which is otherwise without sculptural decoration, are antique capitals.

Separate from the church is a modern **burial chapel** containing the tomb of St Barnabas (key from custodian of monastery).

Enkomi/Tuzla – Alasia

A few kilometres south of the monastery of St Barnabas (10 km north-west of Famagusta), near the village of Énkomi/Tuzla, are the excavated remains of ancient Alasia, whose origins go back to the 2nd millennium BC. The earliest evidence of settlement at Alasia dates from the 17th c. BC, when the town began to grow wealthy through the working and export of copper. Between the 15th and 12th c. Alasia played an important part as an intermediary in trade between the Middle East and the Aegean, and Minoan merchants, later followed by Mycenaeans, came to Cyprus. Opposite Alasia on the coast of Syria was the city of Ugarit, where excavations have brought to light a Cypriot quarter with goods from Alasia.

Copper working

In its heyday the city was surrounded by walls and had a population of between 10,000 and 15,000. As at Kítion (Lárnaca) there was a close association between cult and copper working. The smelting ovens lay within the bounds of the city, frequently near temples.

Monastery of St Barnabas ➤

Excavations

Excavations have revealed the foundations of the ancient city of the 13th and 12th c. A main street traversed the settlement from north to south, with side streets dividing it into separate quarters. Remains of the town walls, dwellings and a number of temples were also discovered. The first excavators found skeletons and rich grave goods: gold jewellery, ivories, bronze and silver objects, pottery, and the famous 12th c. statue of a horned god now in the Archaeological Museum in Nicosia (☛Sights from A to Z South Cyprus, Nicosia).

Sóloi/Soli E 4

Altitude: 30 m

The excavations of ancient Sóloi lie on the slopes of a hill above Karavostási (landing stage, Turkish *Gemikonağí*), which in antiquity was the port of Sóloi. The harbour was used in the 20th c. for the shipment of ore from copper mines at Skouriotissa, which is now on the other side of the Green Line. The disused conveyor belts for loading the ore still reach far out to sea.

Daily 8am–6pm, winter to 5pm.

History

Legend recounts that Sóloi was founded by Akámas, son of Theseus and the lover of Aphrodite. According to Strabo (64/63 BC–AD 23) the city was rebuilt on its present site about 600 BC on the advice of Solon, one of the Seven Sages. In gratitude for this excellent advice king Philokypros named the new city after Solon.

City-kingdom At the end of the 6th c. BC Sóloi ranked after Koúrion and Amathoús as one of the leading city-kingdoms on the island. Herodotus (V, 115) tells us that the city distinguished itself in repeated rebellions against the Persians. The palace of Vouní (see entry) was built by the pro-Persian king of Márion (Pólis), Doxandros, to give him better control of Sóloi. In Roman times Augustus (31 BC–AD 14) granted the copper mines of Sóloi to Herod the Great, king of Judaea, and many Jews came to Sóloi to work in the mines. In

Swan mosaic in the Early Christian basilica, Sóloi

Remains of the palace of Vouní

the 7th c. Sóloi suffered from repeated Arab raids. In spite of this the remains of temples and houses seem to have survived into the 18th c. Thereafter the site was used as a quarry.

Excavation
Excavation of the site began in the 1920s, revealing remains of a Roman theatre and an Early Christian basilica.

Sights

Theatre
The theatre of Sóloi (reconstructed), which dates from the 2nd c. AD, is considerably smaller than the theatres of Koúrion and Sálamis. The cavea is 52 m in diameter, the semicircular orchestra 17 m. From the theatre there is a magnificent view of the sea (though in ancient times this would be blocked by the stage wall).

Temple of Aphrodite and cemeteries
Remains of a temple of Aphrodite were found on the hill behind the theatre. A number of cemeteries round the site bear witness to a large population in the Geometric period, continuing into Roman times.

Aphrodite of Sóloi
The excavations of the site recovered the famous marble statue, the Aphrodite of Sóloi, which is now one of the principal treasures of the Archaeological Museum in Nicosia (☛Sights from A to Z South Cyprus, Nicosia).

Early Christian basilica
At the foot of the hill are the remains of a 5th c. Christian basilica, with three apses at the east end, on the foundations of which a new church was built in the Middle Ages. Excavations have revealed the Early Christian mosaic pavements that originally covered the whole area of the basilica. A number of representations of animals have survived, including in particular a fine swan.

Vouní/Bademliköy
See entry

Palace of Vouní

1 Entrance hall
2 Living apartments
3 Domestic offices
4 Kitchens
5 Bath-house
6 New entrance in 3rd phase

1st phase
2nd phase
3rd phase

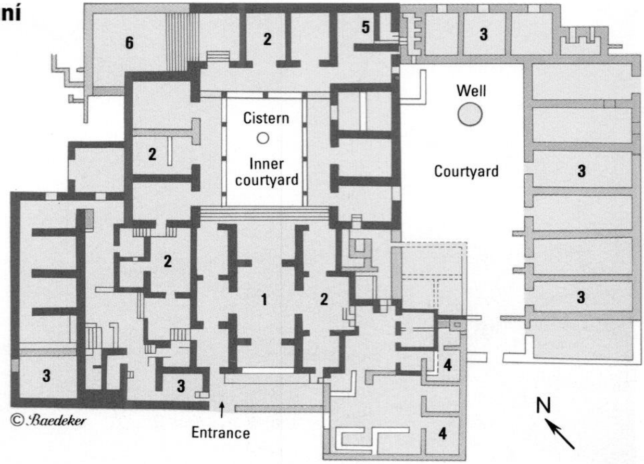

Vouní/Bademlıköy E 4

Altitude: 255 m

5 km from Sóloi, at the western tip of North Cyprus, are the remains of the palace of Vouní. A winding road leads up to the top of the hill (*vouní*), from where there are fine views of the coast. The palace, excavated from 1928 onwards, lies on the highest point of the hill. *Daily 8am–4pm.*

History

The palace of Vouní had only a short life. Built in the early 5th c. BC, it was destroyed by fire about 380 BC. It is believed to have been built by the pro-Persian king Doxandros of Márion to control the pro-Greek city of Sóloi.

Three building phases have been identified, suggesting that the palace was altered and enlarged by different owners at different times. Above the palace are a temple of Athena and treasuries of the 5th c. BC.

Sights

First phase

Approaching the palace from the south you come into a long room divided into three sections, presumably the entrance hall. From here a flight of steps leads down to a courtyard surrounded on three sides by porticoes. In the centre of the courtyard are the remains of a cistern, with a stele on the east side which would have supported a windlass for raising water.

Around the courtyard are living apartments, some of them originally of two storeys. The arrangement is reminiscent of the Persian type of *liwan* house. To the east are the remains of baths, which are among the oldest to have survived from antiquity.

Second phase

During the second phase various store-rooms were added on the east side of the palace, laid out round a courtyard containing a well.

Third phase

In the final phase the original entrance was walled up and a new one built on the north side of the palace, on the pattern of the Greek megaron house.

Temple of Athena

On the southern slopes of the hill (the side opposite the custodian's house) are the remains of a temple of Athena. Here was found the famous Cow of Vouní, a small bronze statuette which is now in the Archaeological Museum in Nicosia (☛Sights from A to Z South Cyprus, Nicosia).

Practical Information A to Z

Practical Information from A to Z South Cyprus

Arriving

By air

The quickest and easiest way to get to Cyprus is by air. Cyprus is linked with the international network of air services, and in recent years has increasingly become a connection for the Middle East and the Gulf states.

Direct flights from London to Lárnaca International Airport are operated by British Airways and Cyprus Airways. The airport at Páphos is used mainly by charter flights.

The flight from London to Lárnaca takes around 4½ hours.

By sea

There are services run by Poseidon Lines throughout the year from Athens (Piraeus) to Limassol via Iraklion (Crete) and Rhodes; the journey takes about two days. Cyprus also has connections with Israel (Haifa), Syria (Latakia), Lebanon (Beirut) and Egypt (Alexandria).

Shipping lines in Greece:

POSEIDON LINES SHIPPING CO. SA
Akiti Miaouli Street 35–39, Piraeus
☎ *(01) 4292046, fax (01) 4292041, email info@greekislands.com*

SALAMIS LINES LTD
Filellinon Street 9, Piraeus
☎ *(01) 4294325, fax (01) 4294557, email info@cruisecyprus.com*

Shipping lines in Cyprus:

POSEIDON LINES (CYPRUS) LTD
Franklin Roosevelt Street 124, Limassol
☎ *(05) 745666, fax (05) 745577*

SALAMIS LINES LTD
28th October Avenue, Limassol
☎ *(05) 355555, fax (05) 364410*

Accommodation

See Camping, Hotels, Youth Hostels

Monasteries

Some monasteries provide free accommodation for tourists (a donation for the monastery is however expected). They include the following:

Neóphytos Monastery and Chrysorroyiátissa Monastery, both near Páphos
Kykko Monastery in the Tróodos massif (only for Cypriots and needy foreigners)

Airlines

Cyprus Airways
21 Alkeos Street, Nicosia
☎ *(02) 751996*
203 Archbishop Makarios III Avenue, Limassol
☎ *(05) 373787*
37 Gladstone Street, Páphos
☎ *(06) 233556*

British Airways
Lárnaca Airport
☎ *(04) 643288*

Beaches

The coast of Cyprus consists mainly of shingle beaches, small sandy bays and bizarrely shaped cliffs. The most beautiful beaches and the finest sand are in the south-east of the island at Ayía Nápa. The west coast has a mixture of sand and shingle beaches and rocky coasts. A wellknown sandy beach is the Lady's Mile Beach to the west of Limassol. Popular bathing beaches are the Ayía Nápa beaches in the south-east and Koúrion Bay and Coral Bay on the west coast.

The bathing season begins in April and lasts until the end of November. Even in winter the temperature of the water never falls below 16°C. Water quality is in general excellent.

Many beaches belong to hotels and are closed to non-residents. They are well maintained and equipped with all necessary facilities. On popular beaches not belonging to hotels – including particularly the beaches outside Ayía

Nápa and on the coast to the west of Páphos and Pólis – there is usually a restaurant which hires out sun umbrellas and loungers.

Nudism is officially prohibited and offends Cypriot morality, which visitors should respect. Unofficially there are a number of small beaches (e.g. in Pólis Bay) where nude bathing is tolerated. Topless bathing is now allowed on many beaches, particularly hotel beaches.

The following is a selection of the best known bathing beaches.

Lárnaca
Beach below the seafront promenade (usually overcrowded)
Mackenzie Beach, at the airport
Beaches to the east of the town (mainly hotel beaches)
Cape Kíti, 17 km west via Perivólia (sand and shingle)

Limassol
Town (Dassoudi) beach, opposite the Municipal Gardens
Lady's Mile Beach, to the south-west, beyond the new harbour (sand and shingle)
Governor's Beach, 22 km east, just beyond the road to Ayios Yeóryios convent (sand and shingle)

Pissoúri
Pissoúri Beach, a beautiful sandy beach reached from the road to Columbia Pissoúri Beach Hotel

Páphos
Tourist Beach, to the south of the town, a well cared for beach run by the Cyprus Tourism Organisation (can also be reached from Yeroskípos)
Timi, a long sandy beach south of Páphos
Coral Bay, 10 km north, a popular bathing beach with tavernas
Pétra tou Romíou, 21 km south, a shingle beach near the Rock of Aphrodite

Pólis
Lakhí, 5 km west of Pólis, with sand and shingle beaches extending to the Baths of Aphrodite.

Camping

Camping outside designated sites is prohibited and those who practise it are liable to prosecution.

Official camping and caravanning sites (below) are equipped with washing facilities, shops and tavernas.

Lárnaca
Forest Beach Camping
8 km east on the beach
Apr.–Oct.
(04) 622414

Limassol
Governor's Beach Camping
20 km east
All year.
(05) 632300

Páphos
Feggari Camping
13 km north near Coral Bay, at Pegeia
All year
(06) 621534

Yeroskípou
Yeroskípou Zenon Gardens Camping
3 km east of Páphos harbour, east side of Yeroskípou Tourist Beach
Apr.–Oct.
(06) 242277

Pólis
Pólis Camping
In a eucalyptus grove on the beach
Mar.–Oct.
(06) 321526

Tróodos massif
In a pinewood 2 km from Tróodos Hill Resort on the Kakopetriá road
May–Oct. (weather permitting)
(05) 421624

Car Rental

Since most visitors to Cyprus come by air, car rental is often a good option for getting around. There are offices or agencies of car rental firms in all the larger towns and at Lárnaca airport. In addition to the well known international firms (Avis, Hertz, Europcar, Budget) there are numerous local firms from which cars, motorcycles, mopeds and even bicycles can be hired.

The driver of a rented car must possess a national driving licence and be at least 21 years old. The wearing of seat belts is obligatory for drivers and front-seat passengers, with a substantial fine for non-compliance. (See also Motoring)

Car rental firms at Lárnaca airport:

AVIS
☎ *(04) 6431120*
BUDGET
☎ *(04) 629170*
EUROPCAR
☎ *(04) 645590 (town); 515157 (airport)*
HERTZ
☎ *(04) 643388 (airport); 655145 (town)*

Conversions

To convert metric to imperial multiply by the imperial factor; e.g. 100 km equals 62 mi. (100 × **0.62**).

Linear measure

1 m	**3.28** ft
	1.09 yds
1 km (1000 m)	**0.62** mi.

Square measure

1 sq m	**1.2** sq yds
	10.76 sq ft
1 ha	**2.47** acres
1 sq km (100 ha)	**0.39** sq mi.

Capacity

1 litre (1000 ml)	**1.76** pints
	2.11 US pints
1 kg (1000 grams)	**2.21** pounds
1 tonne (1000 kg)	**0.98** ton

Temperature

°C	°F	°C	°F
–5	23	20	68
0	32	25	77
5	41	30	86
10	50	35	95
15	59	40	104

Currency

The Cypriot unit of currency is the Cypriot pound (C£), also called the lira, which is divided into 100 cents.

Cypriots frequently still count in shillings (*sillíngia*), of which there were 20 to the pound; a shilling is thus equivalent to 5 cents.

There are banknotes for 1, 5, 10 and 20 pounds and coins in denominations of 1, 2, 5, 10, 20 and 50 cents.

Changing money

Exchange rates are subject to fluctuation. They can be obtained from banks and tourist offices and are also published in national newspapers.

It is advisable to change money in Cyprus itself, where the exchange rates are better than outside the country.

Import and export of currency

There are no restrictions on bringing in foreign currency in banknotes or traveller's cheques, but sums in excess of 1000 US dollars or the equivalent in other currencies must be declared on arrival. There is a limit of C£100 on the amount of Cypriot currency that may be taken out of the country.

Cheques and credit cards

Traveller's cheques and Eurocheques are accepted by all banks. There are also plenty of cash dispensers accepting Eurocheque cards. The main international credit cards (Visa, Diners' Club, American Express, Access, Eurocard) are accepted by most shops, restaurants and hotels.

Banks

There are both local and international banks in Cyprus. Traveller's cheques, Eurocheques and credit cards are accepted (☛Opening Hours).

Customs Regulations

In addition to personal effects visitors may take the following items into Cyprus duty-free: 200 cigarettes or 250 grams of cigars and tobacco; 75 **centilitres** of wine; 1 litre of spirits; 30 **centilitres** of perfume and toilet water and other goods to the value of C£50 (excluding jewellery). They may also take their own car without payment of duty for three months (extendable).

The import into Cyprus of drugs, weapons and plants (flowers, fruit, bulbs, seed) is prohibited.

Antiques may be exported only with an authorisation from the Ministry of Transport. The export of historic icons is prohibited. For information:
CYPRUS DEPARTMENT OF ANTIQUITIES
PO Box 2024, CY 1516 Nicosia

Cycling

In the major tourist centres bicycles can be hired from hotels or from car and motorcycle rental firms (☛Car Rental).

If you want to take your own bicycle to Cyprus, most airlines will carry it within the normal free baggage allowance of 20 kilograms. For longer tours of Cyprus, you should be prepared for some rough riding since the minor country roads on which there is less motor traffic tend to be hilly and are unsurfaced.

Cyprus Cycling Federation
The Federation is glad to answer any questions. It also runs cycle races in spring and autumn. For information:
CYPRUS CYCLING FEDERATION
Viziinos Street, Nicosia
☎ *(02) 663341*

Electricity

Electricity is 240 volts AC. Power sockets in most new buildings take British-style three square-pin plugs. Almost all hotels have 110 volt sockets for electric razors.

Embassies and Consulates

Offices of the Republic of Cyprus

United Kingdom
High Commission of the Republic of Cyprus
93 Park Street, London W1Y 4ET
☎ *(020) 7499 8272/4*

United States
Embassy of the Republic of Cyprus
2211 R Street North West, Washington DC 20008
☎ *(202) 4625772/0873*

Offices in Cyprus

British High Commission
Alexander Pallis Street, Nicosia
☎ *(02) 473131/7*

United States Embassy
Metochiou and Ploutarchou Streets, Nicosia
☎ *(02) 476100*

Emergencies

In the larger towns dial 199 for police, fire or ambulance services. The fire service and police can also be reached by dialling 112.

Police stations
Nicosia
☎ *(02) 305115*
Lárnaca
☎ *(04) 630200*
Limassol
☎ *(05) 330411*
Páphos
☎ *(06) 240140*
Pólis
☎ *(06) 321451*
Agrós
☎ *(05) 521136*
Plátres
☎ *(05) 421351*
Ayía Nápa
☎ *(03) 721553*
Pedhoulás
☎ *(02) 952648*
Paralímni
☎ *(03) 821211*

Health
See entry

Excursions

Many travel agencies in Cyprus operate coach tours (usually half-day or day trips) taking in the most interesting sights – archaeological, artistic or scenic – on the island, with a knowledgeable English speaking guide. They also organise walking tours and boat trips. Excursions can be booked either in the agencies themselves or in hotels, which will have posters advertising the various agencies' programmes.

Food and Drink

Food

Times of meals
Lunch is eaten between 12.30 and 2pm. Dinner does not usually begin before 8pm, though hotels have adjusted to the habits of foreign visitors and often serve dinner earlier.

Cuisine
Hotel restaurants offer a predominantly international cuisine, adapted to British and French tastes, but Greek Cypriot cooking can be found in the tavernas.

Cypriot dishes are tasty and substantial, highly spiced but not sharp. Much use is made of parsley, garlic, coriander and lemon juice. The sweets show Arabic influence.

Mezedhes

Characteristic of Greek Cypriot cuisine are the *mezedhes* (singular *mezé*) – a choice of appetisers or hors d'oeuvre offered as an accompaniment to a drink or at the beginning of a meal. They may amount to a meal in themselves, with anything from 16 to 32 different items, either hot or cold.

The following are some of the things that may be included as *orektiká* (hors d'oeuvre):

dolmádhes = stuffed vine leaves
féta = ewe's cheese
haloúmi = hard, salty goat's cheese which may be eaten raw, roasted or fried
hiroméri = smoked ham
hoúmous = purée of chick peas, sesame, olive oil and lemon
loúnza = smoked pork tenderloin
manitária = mushrooms
marídhes = fried whitebait
tahina = sesame paste
talattoúri, tsatzíki = sliced cucumber and garlic in yoghurt
taramosaláta = pink dip made from cod's roe

Other dishes

Salads (salátes)

horiátiki = country salad of cucumbers, tomatoes, greens, olives and *féta*
kapári = tender caper shoots in salt and wine vinegar
melintzanosálata = aubergine salad
patatasaláta = potato salad

Soups (soúpes)

psarósoupa = fish soup
soúpa avgolémono = chicken soup with egg and lemon juice
soúpa hoúmi = chick pea soup

Meat dishes (kréata)

afélia = cubes of pork stewed in red wine with coriander
arní me fasólia = lamb with beans
keftédhes = fried meat balls
kléftiko = lamb roasted in aluminium foil in a sealed oven or earthenware pot
kotópoulo lemonáto = chicken boiled in a lemon sauce
kounéli stifádo = rabbit stew with onions
koupépia or *dolmades* = vine leaves stuffed with rice and minced meat
moussaká = layers of fried aubergine and fried sliced potatoes interspersed with minced meat and covered with a bechamel sauce
paidákia = grilled lamb cutlets
pastítsio = noodles with minced meat and potatoes
piperés yemistés = stuffed peppers
pítta = flat unleavened bread, often filled with kebabs of shredded veal
sheftaliá = grilled spice sausage
soúvla = large pieces of grilled meat (usually lamb)
souvlákia = kebabs of lamb or pork grilled on a spit
stifádo = beef stew with onions
tavás = lamb or beef cooked in a sealed earthenware pot with onions
tomátes yemistés = stuffed tomatoes

Fish (psária)

astakós = lobster
barboúnia = red mullet
garídhes = prawns
kalamári = squid
oktapódhi = octopus
péstrofa = trout
tónnos = tunny

Vegetables

Potatoes (*patátes*) are almost invariably served with meat, often in the form of chips. Rice (*rísi*) may be served as an alternative. A particular speciality is sweet potatoes (*kolokási*).

Sweets (glyká)

baklavá = layers of filo pastry filled with ground almonds in a cinnamon-flavoured syrup
dáktyla = finger-shaped filled pastry
flaoúnes = small Easter cakes filled with cheese and peppermint
loukoumádhes = honey puffs
skámali = semolina pudding sprinkled with almonds
soutzoúko = almonds soaked in grape juice
vasilópitta = New Year cake containing a coin which brings luck to the finder

Recipes

Soúpa avgolémono

Ingredients (6 to 8 people): 8 cups of chicken stock, 1 cup of rice, 6 egg yolks, half a cup of lemon juice, salt and pepper to taste.

Boil the rice in the chicken stock until cooked. Remove from the heat. Whisk the egg yolks with the lemon juice, slowly adding 1 or 2 cupfuls of the stock. Then gradually pour the egg mixture into the stock and continue to stir. Add salt and pepper to taste.

Dolmádhes
Ingredients: 300 grams of fresh or dried vine leaves, 1½ cups of oil, 3 cups of finely grated onions, 2 cups of rice, 2 cups of hot water, half a cup of pine kernels, 3 tablespoons of finely chopped dill, 3 tablespoons of parsley, half a teaspoon of finely grated mint, salt, pepper, 1 teaspoon of sugar, 2 lemons, 2 cups of boiling water.

Lightly brown the onions in half the oil, add the rice and cook slowly for 10 minutes in a closed pan. Add the hot water, pine kernels, herbs and spices. Steam in the closed pan until the water has evaporated. Take off the cooker and allow to cool. Wash the vine leaves and boil for 2–3 minutes in salted water until they are soft; then stuff them with the rice, put them in a pan and pour the rest of the oil, the lemon juice **and the boiling water** over them. Cover with a plate, put the lid on the pan and steam for 45 minutes.

Minced meat may be added to the rice if desired.

Stifádo
Ingredients: 1 kg beef, ½ kg of small peeled onions, 4 finely chopped cloves of garlic, 1 cup of oil, 3 laurel leaves, black pepper, cinnamon, ½ kg of grated tomatoes, 2 cups of hot water, half a cup of vinegar, salt and pepper.

Cut the meat into small pieces. Lightly brown the onions in a casserole, then remove the onions and cook the garlic in the casserole until it is soft. Add the meat and brown on a low heat then add the vinegar; when this is boiling add the tomatoes, salt, pepper, laurel leaves, cinnamon and hot water. Cook for about 2½ hours on a low heat – thirty minutes before the meat is done add the onions.

The last two recipes are from the book by Nearchos Nicolaou, *Dishes from Cyprus, the Island of Aphrodite.*

Drinks (potá)

Coffee, tea
A Cypriot meal always ends with a cup of coffee. Cypriots usually drink mocha coffee, either without sugar (*kafés skéttos*), with a little sugar (*kafés métrios*) or very sweet (*kafés glykós*). Tea (*tsái*) is also a popular drink.

Soft drinks
Popular non-alcoholic drinks are milk (*gála*), orange juice (*portokaláda*), almond juice (*soumáda*) and other common soft drinks.

Wine
See entry

Fortified drinks and spirits
Oúzo (an aniseed-flavoured spirit), brandy and sherry are made in Cyprus. Country people make a marc brandy (*dzivaniá*), the sale of which is officially prohibited.

Brandy sour
A favourite long drink in Cyprus is brandy sour, which also appeals to visitors. This refreshing drink is a mixture of brandy, lemon juice, angostura and soda water.

Beer (bíra)
A local firm, Keo, brews a light and digestible beer. Carlsberg beer is also brewed locally.

Frontier Crossing

Visitors to the Greek part of Cyprus can (though this is not encouraged by the Cypriot government) make day trips into the Turkish-occupied area in the north between 8am and 6pm (sometimes 4.30pm). The only frontier crossing point is in Nicosia at the end of Markos Drakos Avenue. There, by the old Ledra Palace Hotel, is the Greek passport control, and between this and the Turkish frontier control is the United Nations buffer zone. At the Turkish control point a one-day visa costing C£1 will be issued. It is not permitted to spend the night in the Turkish zone or to take a car over the frontier.

For an excursion into North Cyprus visitors can either rent a car or use public transport; but in view of the short time allowed the best plan is to see the principal sights by taxi. A reasonable price for the day can be negotiated. Visitors must be sure to return to South Cyprus by 6pm at latest.

Visitors to North Cyprus are not allowed to cross into the Greek Republic of Cyprus. (☛Sights from A to Z South Cyprus, Nicosia.)

Guides

In Cyprus there are licensed guides qualified to take visitors around archaeological sites and other places of artistic and historical interest.

Information about such guides can be obtained from the central organisation to which all licensed guides belong:

Cyprus Tourist Guides Association
4 Phohopoulas Street, Nicosia

Health

Medical care

Since there is no medical school in Cyprus all Cypriot doctors have been trained in Europe or the United States, and most of them speak English.

For inpatient treatment there are public General Hospitals, in which emergency treatment is free. For serious illnesses, however, it is advisable to go to private hospitals, which have a better clinical facilities.

Bills for medical treatment, either by general practitioners and specialists or in hospitals in the private sector, and the cost of medicines usually have to be paid on the spot. It is essential, therefore, to take out temporary medical insurance before leaving home.

Consulting hours

Mon.–Sat. 8am–1pm, 4–7pm.

Emergencies

Dial 199 for ambulance service.

Hospitals

There are public hospitals (General Hospitals) in:
Ayía Nápa; 12 Leoforos Kryou Nerou;
☎ *(03) 721796*
Lárnaca; Vasileos Pavlou Square;
☎ *(04) 630312*
Limassol: 15 Spyrou Araouzou Street;
☎ *(05) 330777*
Nicosia; Laiki Yitonia
☎ *(02) 801400*
Páphos; 3 Gladstone Street
☎ *(06) 240111*
Plátres
☎ *(05) 421316*
Pólis; Agiou Nikolaou Street
☎ *(06) 322468*

Chemists

There are chemists (Greek *pharmakíon*) in all towns of any size. They are identified by a red cross on a white ground and, usually, the English word Pharmacy. Most of the common international medicines and drugs are available in Cyprus.

Opening hours

See Opening Hours.

Out-of-hours service

Medicines can be obtained outside the normal hours by dialling 192 or the emergency number 199. The addresses of chemists providing out-of-hours services on a rota basis are shown on a notice in the window of all chemists and are listed in newspapers.

Hotels

In general hotels in Cyprus are of high quality, in line with international standards. The main tourist centres – Ayía Nápa, Lárnaca, Limassol and Páphos – have large numbers of hotels and the hill regions and the smaller towns along the coast are well equipped with accommodation.

CTO

Hotel standards are monitored by the Cyprus Tourism Organisation (CTO), which annually fixes minimum and maximum tariffs for the different categories of hotels, with regard to the standard of comfort and amenities provided.

Apartments

Holiday apartments are divided into three categories, from A to C. Establishments below these categories are called boarding houses. There are very few rooms to let in private houses.

Hotel categories and prices

Hotels in Cyprus are divided into five categories. The rates for each room must be displayed in the room. The five-star hotels meet the most exacting requirements.

The price ranges per person for a double room with breakfast in the various categories of hotel are as follows:

*****	C£80–160
****	C£50–100
***	C£35–60
**	C£25–50
*	C£15–30

In the low season (Nov.–Mar. in the coastal regions, Oct.–Jun. in the hills) prices are between 20 per cent and 50 per cent lower, the biggest reductions being in January and February.

Hotel and restaurant bills include a 10 per cent service charge, plus 8 per cent Value Added Tax (VAT). In addition waiters expect a further tip.

During the high season advance booking is advisable. Information about hotels and complete hotel lists can be obtained from the Cyprus Tourism Organisation (☛Information).

Hotels (selection)

Agrós

*****Rodon**
☎ *(05) 521201, fax (05) 521235,*
email rodon@spidernet.com.cy
155 rooms. Modern hotel on the slopes of the Tróodos massif with views of the surrounding hills and of the village of Agrós; well-equipped rooms, a swimming pool and a piano bar.

Ayía Nápa

*******Grecian Bay**
PO Box 30006
☎ *(03) 721301, fax (03) 721307,*
email grecian@grecian.com.cy
240 rooms. This large luxury hotel on a white sandy beach near Ayía Nápa has one outdoor and two indoor swimming pools and a fitness centre complete with sauna, Turkish bath and whirlpool.

******Grecian Sands**
PO Box 21630
☎ *(03) 721616, fax (03) 722691*
137 rooms. Only a 15-minute walk from the town centre, of this comfortable hotel is set in attractive grounds, with a pool and several restaurants.

*****Nissi Park**
PO Box 30400
☎ *(03) 721121, fax (03) 722196,*
email nissi@spidernet.com.cy
80 rooms. This friendly hotel in the style of a Cypriot monastery is on the western side of the lively resort of Ayía Nápa.

*****Napa Mermaid**
PO Box 404
☎ *(03) 721608, fax (03) 721909,*
email mermotel@cytanet.com.cy
130 rooms. On the edge of the holiday village of Ayía Nápa, the hotel's rooms either look onto the sea or the fishing harbour, and are all equipped with TV, refrigerator, telephone and safe.

Coral Bay

*******Coral Beach**
PO Box 2422, Coral Bay
☎ *(06) 621711, fax (06) 621742,*
www.coral.com.cy
304 rooms. The traditional Cypriot-style hotel lies about 10 km north of Páphos, by the idyllic Coral Bay. With its sandy beach, yacht harbour, several restaurants and retail outlets, this luxury hotel is ideally suited for an exclusive seaside holiday.

Droúsha

*****Drousha Heights**
☎ *(06) 332351, fax (06) 332353*
40 rooms, 12 studios. 10 km from Lakhí and Pólis, on the edge of the mountain village of Droúsha, this friendly hotel has a fine view of the Akámas peninsula.

Kakopetriá

*****Hellas**
4 Andreou Manantos Street
☎ *(02) 922450, fax (02) 922227*
An older mid-range hotel, with a fine view of Kalkopetriá

****Hekali**
Above the village square
☎ *(02) 922501, fax (02) 922503,*
email hekalihotel@cytanet.com.cy
Friendly hotel with good service and a rustic restaurant.

Lárnaca

*******Golden Bay**
Lárnaca–Dhekélia road
☎ *(04) 645444, fax (04) 645451*
About 200 rooms. 10 km from Lárnaca is the finest and most expensive hotel in the area, with a magnificent lobby two storeys high and a restaurant of distinction.

******Lordos Beach**
Lárnaca–Dhekélia road
☎ *(04) 647444, fax (04) 645847,*
email administration@lordosbeach.com.cy

There is a fine view of the hotel's bathing area from the sun terrace of this comfortable mid-range hotel. A variety of sporting activities, a sauna and Turkish bath, and live music with your dinner are further attractions.

***** Four Lanterns Sunotel**
19 Athens Avenue
☎ *(04) 652011, fax (04) 626012, email crown@cytanet.com.cy*
56 rooms. The oldest hotel in the town, dating from the British colonial period, it is situated on the promenade.

***Pavion**
St Lazarus Square
☎ *(04) 656688, fax (04) 658165*
10 rooms. You can stay very cheaply in this simple guest house in the centre of the **old town**, which is particularly popular with young holidaymakers.

Léfkara

****Agora,**
On the main street
☎ *(04) 342901, fax (04) 342905*
This old house, in whose courtyard a market used to be held, has been converted into a simple but friendly hotel.

Limassol

*******Amáthus Beach**
Amáthous
☎ *(05) 321152, fax (05) 327494, email amathus@spidernet.com.cy*
244 rooms. About 10 km east of Limassol, near the ruined site of Amáthous, is 'one of the leading hotels of the world', which offers every conceivable luxury that you might expect from a five-star hotel.

*******Hawaii Grand**
Amáthous
☎ *(05) 634333, fax (05) 311888, email hawaii@hawaii.com.cy*
255 rooms. As soon as you step into the very grand lobby, it is clear that this hotel is intended for upmarket clientele. The picture is completed with elegant rooms, gourmet cuisine and first-class service.

*****Aquamarina**
139 Spyros Araouzos Street
☎ *(05) 374277, fax (04) 374086*
70 rooms. On the shore road as you leave the old town is this modern mid-range hotel, which is particularly popular with tourist parties.

***Luxor**
101 Agios Andreas Street
☎ *(05) 362265*
15 rooms. On the old town's most important shopping street is this basic guest house, which is suitable for young holidaymakers.

Nicosia

******Churchill Nicosia**
1 Achaeans Street
☎ *(02) 448858, fax (02) 445508*
52 rooms. On the way out to Engomi you come to this town hotel; with its superior decor and air conditioning it is equally popular with tourists and business people.

*****Cleopatra**
8 Florina Street
☎ *(02) 671000, fax (02) 670618*
About a 10-minute walk south of the centre in a rather unattractive built-up area, this hotel nonetheless surprises visitors with its welcoming bedrooms and fine bathrooms.

****Averof**
11 Averof Street
☎ *(02) 773447, fax (02) 773411*
25 rooms. This modern but friendly hotel with rustic decor is on the west bank of the Pediéos, near the demarcation line.

Páphos

******Annabelle**
Poseidon Avenue
☎ *(06) 238333, fax (06) 245502, email the-annabelle@thanos.hotels.com.cy*
198 rooms. Right on the shore and within walking distance of Páphos harbour, this top hotel is very popular with discriminating tourists. The bathing facilities are particularly attractive with a cave and waterfalls.

******Páphos Beach**
Poseidon Avenue
☎ *(06) 265555, fax (06) 266370*
190 rooms. Only 5 minutes from Páphos harbour, this fine hotel has a sandy beach and beautiful gardens, as well as a tennis court and a variety of other sports facilities.

******Avanti**
Poseidon Avenue
☎ *(06) 250000, fax (06) 244511*
This modern hotel in the centre of Páphos has a large outdoor pool complex, as well as an indoor pool, three tennis courts and a fitness centre.

*****Paphian Bay**
Poseidon Avenue
☎ *(06) 264333, fax (06) 264870, email molnager@paphian-cbh.com*
219 rooms. The hotel has tastefully furnished rooms and many sports facilities (tennis court, water-sports complex). Entertainment is provided by Cypriot evenings and a nightclub.

****Kinyras**
91 Makarios III Avenue
☎ *(06) 241604, fax (06) 242176, email kinyras@spidernet.com.cy*
16 rooms. A simple, older hotel in the old town with an attractive courtyard containing a fountain and a good restaurant.

***Kings**
Tombs of the Kings Road
☎ *(06) 233497, fax (06) 245516*
A hotel with a family atmosphere which was thoroughly refurbished a few years ago, situated about halfway between the old town and the harbour.

Paralímni/Protarás

*******Grecian Park**
PO Box 487, Paralímni
☎ *(03) 832000, fax (03) 832870, email grecian-park-hotel@cytanet.com.cy*
226 rooms. Attractively set in a luxuriant green landscape above a sheltered bay with a sandy beach, this spacious luxury hotel has every conceivable facility.

******Capo Bay**
Protarás
☎ *(03) 831101, fax (03) 831110, email into@capobay.com.cy*
225 rooms. This large hotel on the so-called Fig Tree Bay has a large range of sports, and particularly water-sports facilities.

******Odessa**
PO Box 497, Protarás
☎ *(03) 831645, fax (03) 832146*
Here are all the extras you expect from a four-star hotel: landscaped pool complex, water-sports facilities (water skiing, windsurfing, diving), fitness centre, a stylish restaurant and several bars.

Pedhoulás

***Jack's**
☎ *(02) 952817*
A simple guest house in the mountain village of Pedhoulás.

Pissoúri

******Columbia Beach**
☎ *(05) 221201, fax (05) 221505, email columbia@cytanet.com.cy*
129 rooms. A top hotel on the rather remote bay of Pissoúri, popular with tourists.

***Bunch of Grapes Inn**
☎ *(05) 221275, fax (05) 252210,*
11 rooms. An old stone-built hotel with character and atmosphere, formerly a large farmhouse. The romantic inner courtyard is the setting for a restaurant in the summer.

Plátres

******Forest Park**
☎ *(05) 421751, fax (05) 421875, email forest@cytanet.com.cy*
140 rooms. The grand drive leading to the best hotel on the Tróodos massif is itself impressive, and the mountain hotel itself set amidst peaceful pinewoods retains a British character.

*****New Helvetia**
6 Helvetia Road
☎ *(05) 421348, fax (05) 422148, email helvetia@spidernet.com.cy*
25 rooms, 8 suites. Up above the village of Plátres on the Tróodos massif, with a friendly atmosphere and rustic character, this hotel has been owned by the same family since 1929.

***Minerva**
☎ *(05) 421731, fax (05) 421075, email minerva@cylink.com.cy*
An older, basic guest house with a luxuriant planted terrace. The owner is an amateur botanist and can take visitors on guided walks.

Pólis

****Bougainvillea**
☎ *(06) 322201, fax (06) 322203,*
11 studios/apartments. A small complex of apartments in bungalows close to the centre of Pólis.

Tróodos

****Jubilee**
☎ *(05) 420107, fax (05) 673991*
37 rooms. This simple hotel is on the road to Pródhromos; useful as a base for hikes on the Tróodos massif.

Information

Internet

www.kypros.org
Information about Cyprus can be obtained from the following offices of the Cyprus Tourism Organisation (CTO):

United Kingdom
Cyprus **Tourist Office**
213 Regent Street, London W1R 8DA
☎ *(020) 7349822*

United States
Cyprus Tourism Organisation
13 East 40th Street, New York NY 10016
☎ *(212) 6835280*

Cyprus
Cyprus Tourism Organisation
PO Box 4535, CY1390 Nicosia
☎ *(02) 337715, fax 331644, email Cytour@cto.org.cy*

Local tourist offices in Cyprus
Ayía Nápa
12 Leoforos Kryou Nerou
☎ *(03) 721796*
Lárnaca
Vasileos Pavlou Square
☎ *(04) 654322*
Airport Lárnaca
☎ *(04) 643000*
Limassol
15 Spyros Araouzos Street
☎ *(05) 362756*
Limassol Harbour
☎ *(05) 343868*
Nicosia: Laiki Yitonia
☎ *(02) 674264*
Páphos
3 Gladstone Street
☎ *(06) 232841*
Páphos Airport
☎ *(06) 422833*
Plátres
☎ *(05) 421316, in summer (03) 721796*

Publications

Information about events, theatre programmes, festivals and sporting occasions is published in the Cyprus Tourism Organisation's *Diary of Events* or *Monthly Events, Cyprus Time Out, Nicosia This Month* and *Seven Days in Cyprus*.

Insurance

Visitors are strongly advised to take adequate insurance cover including loss or damage to luggage, loss of currency and jewellery. As Cyprus is not a member of the European Union it is also advisable to take out adequate medical insurance before leaving home.

Language

As a result of Cyprus's 80 years of British colonial rule visitors can usually find some local people with a knowledge of English. But in the remoter parts of the country it is helpful to have at least a smattering of modern Greek.

Modern Greek

Modern Greek is considerably different from ancient Greek though it is surprising how many words are still spelled the same as in classical times. Even in such cases, however, the pronunciation is very different.

Greek alphabet

Greek	Name	English equivalent
Α, α	alpha	a
Β, β	beta	b
Γ, γ	gamma	g, y before e or i
Δ, δ	delta	d, as in 'the'
Ε, ε	epsilon	e, as in 'egg'
Ζ, ζ	zeta	z
Η, η	eta	e, semi-long
Θ, θ	theta	th, as in 'thin'
Ι, ι	iota	i
Κ, κ	kappa	k
Λ, λ	lambda	l
Μ, μ	mu	m
Ν, ν	nu	n
Ξ, ξ	xi	x
Ο, ο	omicron	o, semi-long
Π, π	pi	p
Ρ, ρ	rho	r, lightly rolled
Σ, σ	sigma	s
Τ, τ	tau	t
Υ, υ	upsilon	u
Φ, φ	phi	ph
Χ, χ	chi	kh, ch as in 'loch', kh/sh before e or i
Ψ, ψ	psi	ps
Ω, ω	omega	o, semi-long

There is no recognised standard system for the transliteration of the Greek into the Latin alphabet and many variations are found.

Accents

The position of the stress in a word is

very variable, but is always shown in the Greek alphabet by an acute accent.

The diaeresis (¨) over a vowel indicates that it is to be pronounced separately, and not as part of a diphthong.

Punctuation

Punctuation marks are the same as in English, except that the semicolon (;) is used in place of the question mark (?) and a point above the line (·) in place of the semicolon.

Numbers

Cardinals

0	midén
1	énas, myá, éna
2	dió, dío
3	tris, tría
4	tésseris, téssera
5	pénde
6	éksi
7	eftá
8	okhtó
9	enneá
10	déka
11	éndeka
12	dódeka
13	dekatrís, dekatría
14	dekatésseris, dekatéssera
15	dekapénde
16	dekaéksi, dekáksi
17	dekaäftá
18	dekaokhtó, dekaoktó
19	dekaënneá, dekaënnéa
20	íkosi
21	íkosi énas, myá, éna
22	íkosi dió, dío
30	triánda
31	triánda énas, myá, éna
40	saránda
50	penínda
60	eksínda
70	evdomínda
80	ogdónda, ogdoínda
90	enenínda
100	ekató(n)
101	ekatón énas, myá, éna
153	ekatón penínda tris, tría
200	diakósi, diakósies, diakósia
300	triakósi, -ies, -ia
400	tetrakósi, -ies, -ia
500	pendakósi, -ies, -ia
600	eksakósi, -ies, -ia
700	eftakósi, -ies, -ia
800	okhtakósi, -ies, -ia
900	enneakósi, -ies, -ia
1000	khíli, khílies, khília
5000	pénde khiliádes
1,000,000	éna ekatommírio

Ordinals

1st	prótos, próti, próto(n)
2nd	défteros, -i, -o(n)
3rd	trítos, -i, -o(n)
4th	tétartos, -i, -o(n)
5th	pémptos
6th	éktos
7th	évdomos, evdómi
8th	ógdoos
9th	énnatos, ennáti
10th	dékatos, dekáti
11th	endékatos, endekáti
20th	ikostós, -i, -ó(n)
30th	triakostós, -i, -ó(n)
100th	ekatostós, -i, -ó(n)
124th	ekatostós ikostós tétartos
1000th	khiliostós

Fractions

¼	tétarton
½	misós, -i, -ó(n), ímisis

Days, months, festivals

Week (evdomáda)

Sunday	Kiriakí
Monday	Deftéra
Tuesday	Tríti
Wednesday	Tetárti
Thursday	Pémpti
Friday	Paraskeví
Saturday	Sávato(n)

Months (mines)

January	Yanuários, Yennáris
February	Fevruários, Fleváris
March	Mártios, Mártis
April	Aprílios
May	Máios, Máis
June	Yoúnios
July	Yoúlios
August	Ávgustos
September	Septémvrios
October	Októvrios, Októvris
November	Noémvryos, Noémvris
December	Dekémvrios

Festivals

New Year's Day	Protokhroniá
Easter	Páskha, Lámbra(i)
Whitsun	Pendikostí
Christmas	Khristoúyenna

Everyday expressions

General

Good morning/day!	Kaliméra!
Good evening!	Kalispéra!
Good night!	Kalí níkhta!
Goodbye!	Kalín andámosi(n)!
Do you speak …	Omilíte …
English?	angliká?
French?	galliká?
German?	yermaniká?
I do not understand	Den katalamváno
Excuse me	Me sinkhorite
yes	né, málista (nod)
no	ókhi (nod upwards)
please	parakaló
thank you	efkharistó
yesterday	khthes
today	símera, símeron
tomorrow	ávrio(n)
Help!	Voíthia!
open	aniktó
closed	klistó
When …	Poté …
single room	domátio me éna kreváti
double room	domátio me dío krevátia
room with bath	domátio me loutro
How much?	Póso káni?
Waken me at 6	Ksipníste me stis éksi
Where is …	Pu iné
the lavatory?	to apokhoritírion?
a pharmacy?	éna farmakíon?
a doctor?	enas yatrós?
a dentist?	énas odondoyatrós?
… Street?	i odós (+ name in genitive)?
… Square?	i platía (+ name in genitive)?

Travelling

aircraft	aeropláno(n)
airport	aerolimín
arrival	erkhomós
bank	trápeza
boat	várka, káiki
bus	leoforíon, búsi
bus stop	stásis
change	allásso
departure (by air)	apoyíosis
(by boat)	apóplous
(by train)	anakhórisis
exchange (money)	saráfiko
ferry	férri-bóut, porthmíon
flight	ptísis
hotel	ksenodokhíon
information	pliroforía
lavatory	apokhoritírion
luggage	aposkevá
luggage check	apódiksis ton aposkevón
non-smoking compartment	dya mi kapnistás
porter	akhthofóros
railway	sidiródromos
restaurant car	vagón-restorán
ship	karávi, plíon
sleeping car	vagón-li, klinámaksa
smoking compartment	dya kapnistás
station (railway)	stathmós
stop (bus)	stásis
ticket	bilyétto
ticket-collector	ispráktor
ticket window	thíris
timetable	dromolóyion
train	tréno
waiting room	éthusa anamonís

Post office

address	diéfthinsis
air mail	aeroporikós
express	epígousa
letter	epistolí
letter box	grammato-kivótio(n)
parcel	déma, pakétto
postcard	takhidromikí kárta
poste restante	post restánt
post office	takhidromíon
registered	sistiméni
stamp	grammatósimo(n)
telegram	tileghráfima
telephone	tiléfono(n)

Maps

Road maps

The Cyprus Tourism Organisation supplies, free of charge, a map on the scale 1:400,000 (not entirely accurate).

Other maps available in Cyprus (and possibly through specialised map shops outside Cyprus) include the following:

Cyprus Topographical Map, 1:100,000 (available from MAM bookshop in Nicosia)

Other maps may be found in petrol stations, bookshops and souvenir shops in Cyprus.

Walking maps

On grounds of security no detailed maps for walkers are available.

Media

Radio

Radio programmes are broadcast by the Cyprus Broadcasting Corporation (CBC), by the British Forces radio, and by private stations. CBC transmits programmes in English Mon.–Fri. 10–10.30am, 1.30–2.30pm and 7.30–9pm. There is news in English at 7.30pm (Channel 2, 603 kHz and VHF 94.8 MHz). On the same channel a tourist programme – *Welcome to Cyprus* – is broadcast Mon.–Fri. 8–8.30am.

The British Forces Broadcasting Service (BFBS) transmits programmes 24 hours a day (Channel 1, MW 1503 kHz and VHF 89.9 MHz).

Television

Cypriot Television transmits only on one channel. The news bulletin at 6pm includes items in Greek, English and Turkish.

Motoring

Road network

Cyprus has an excellent network of roads serving all its towns and villages and many of the roads are asphalted. There is a four-lane motorway from Nicosia to Limassol and Lárnaca. A wide road runs along the coast from Páphos to Ayía Nápa, and in the Tróodos massif also numerous roads have been surfaced, so that there are only a few difficult dirt roads left.

Most signposts and road signs are in English as well as in Greek. On dirt roads, however, they are sometimes only in Greek.

Regulations

Vehicles travel on the left, as in Britain. On roundabouts traffic coming from the right has priority. Road traffic regulations are in line with international custom.

The maximum speed in built-up areas is 50 kph, on main roads it is 80 kph and on motorways 100 kph.

Seat belts must be worn in the front and back seats of a car; the penalty for not doing so is a fine. Children under five must not sit in the front seats.

Motorcyclists must wear helmets.

Drinking and driving

It is an offence, with heavy penalties, to drive with a blood-alcohol content of over 90 milligrams.

Number plates

Rented cars always have a red number plate; Cypriot private cars have yellow or white plates. Official cars have green plates, United Nations vehicles blue ones.

Filling stations

Petrol (regular and unleaded) and diesel are usually sold by the litre (☛Opening Hours).

Breakdown assistance

Cyprus Automobile Association (CAA)
12 Chrysanthou Mylonas Street, Nicosia
☎ *(02) 313233, fax (02) 313482, www.cyprus.com*

The CAA, provides breakdown assistance and will suggest reasonably priced towing and repair services.
☎ *(02) 313131.*

Visitors driving their own car can also obtain information from the CAA on third-party insurance.

Overseas breakdown assistance and insurance is also available from AA Five Star Europe.
☎ *(0800) 0852840, www.theAA.com.*

Car rental

If you want to hire a car, it is best to go to one of the major international car-rental firms, where you can rely on the safety standards. Take out additional insurance where your usual cover is not adequate for third party, theft and accident risks.

Note that many rental firms give a discount if you have proof of membership of a national motoring organisation. And a credit card can be used in place of a cash deposit.

Accidents

If involved in an accident do not get angry; be polite and keep calm. Then take the following action:

1. Warn oncoming traffic by switching on the car's warning lights and setting a warning triangle some distance before the scene of the accident.
2. Look after anyone who has been injured, calling an ambulance if necessary.
3. Inform the police.
4. Write down names and addresses of others involved in the accident, also the make and registration number of other vehicles, the names of their insurance companies and policy numbers. It is also

Distances (km) between towns in South Cyprus

	Nicosia	Limassol	Páphos	Lárnaca	Tróodos	Ayía Nápa	Pólis
Nicosia	-	86	163	51	77	88	205
Limassol	86	-	77	69	46	123	106
Páphos	163	77	-	146	120	182	42
Lárnaca	51	69	146	-	123	37	160
Tróodos	77	46	120	123	-	160	104
Ayía Nápa	88	123	182	37	160	-	197
Pólis	205	106	42	160	104	197	-

important to record the time and location of the accident and the address of the police station informed.
5. Gather evidence by writing down the names and addresses of witnesses (independent witnesses are particularly important). Draw a sketch of the accident and if a camera is available take photographs of the scene.
6. Make no admission of responsibility for the accident, and above all do not sign any document in a language you do not understand.
7. In foreign countries there are often different regulations for settling claims and in legal matters relating to accidents. The laws that apply are those of the country concerned, the assessment of damage usually takes longer than in the UK, and often not everything is replaced.

Nightlife

Among the most popular places of entertainment for visitors are the bouzouki bars where performances of folk music and dancing can be enjoyed. These are to be found in the four large towns (Nicosia, Limassol, Lárnaca and Páphos) and in some of the smaller tourist centres like Plátres and Pólis. In addition there are numerous discotheques, night bars and cabarets in the tourist centres and main towns.

Information about what is on in Nicosia can be obtained from *Nicosia This Month* (available only in Cyprus).

Opening Hours

Banks
Mon.–Sat. 8.30am–12.30pm. Many open also in the afternoons.

Chemists
Mon.–Fri. 7.30am–1pm, 3–7pm, closed Wed. and Sat. afternoons.

Filling stations
Summer Mon.–Fri. 6am–7pm, Sat. 6am–4pm; winter Mon.–Sat. 6am–6pm., Sat. 6am–4pm. Closed pub. hols.

Government offices
Mon.–Fri. 7.30am–2.30pm; Thu. 8am–6pm.

Museums and archaeological sites
See Sights from A to Z for individual sights. The main museums or sites are open on most public holidays, but all are closed on major religious festivals and national holidays (☛Public holidays).

Post offices
Mon.–Fri. 7.30am–1.30pm, also Thu. 3–6pm, Sat. 7.30am–2pm. Some larger post offices are also open (except Wed.) May–Sep. 3.30–5.30pm; Oct.–Apr. 4–6pm.

Shops
May–Sep. Mon.–Sat. 8am–1pm, 4–7pm; Oct.–Apr. Mon.–Sat. 8am–1pm, 2.30–6pm. Shops are closed Wed. and Sat. afternoons.

Photography

Archaeological sites and places of historical and artistic interest can usually be photographed, but flash photography is forbidden in some of the Byzantine churches in the Tróodos massif and in most museums (though photography may be allowed in a museum on written application for permission). Permission should always be asked before photographing people. Most Cypriots do not mind being photographed.

It is strictly forbidden to take photographs of military installations, the demarcation zone between the Greek and Turkish parts of Cyprus and guard posts on the Green Line.

Reputable brands of **film** can be bought all over Cyprus, though prices are rather higher than at home. It is advisable, therefore, to take sufficient films for the holiday. Photographic shops in the large towns can supply accessories and carry out repairs to cameras.

Post

Postal rates

Postage on a postcard to the UK is 26 cents and on an airmail letter 31 cents; they take about 5 days to arrive.

Head post offices

Nicosia: Central Post Office, Eleftheria Square
☎ *(02) 303231*
Limassol: Central Post Office, Gladstone Street and Themis Street
☎ *(05) 330190*
Lárnaca: Post Office, Paul Zenon Kitieus Street
☎ *(04) 630181*
Páphos: Post Office, Apostolos Pavlos Avenue
☎ *(06) 240223*

Public Holidays and Festivals

Official holidays

On the following public holidays shops (except in resort areas) and banks are closed:

January 1st: New Year's Day
January 6th: Epiphany
March 25th: Greek Independence Day
April 1st: Cypriot National Day (the beginning of the fight for independence from British rule)
May 1st: Labour Day
August 15th: Dormition of the Mother of God
October 1st: Independence Day (foundation of the Republic of Cyprus)
October 28th: Greek National Day ('Ókhi Day', commemorating Greece's 'No' to the Italians in 1940)

Pillar box – a relic of colonial times

December 25th–26th: Christmas

Movable festivals

Green Monday (Monday of Shrovetide): Carnival (great carnival parade in Limassol); Festival of St Lazarus in Lárnaca, when the icon of the saint is carried through the town during Holy Week.

Easter: The Greek Orthodox Easter is not at the same time as the Catholic and Protestant Easter; it is celebrated on the first Sunday after the first full moon after the beginning of spring (March 21st). On Good Friday shops are open in the morning and on Easter Saturday all day. On Easter Day and Easter Monday they are closed all day. In 2002 Easter is on May 5th.

Whitsun: Kataklysmos festival in Lárnaca on Whit Monday, 50 days after the Orthodox Easter (all shops closed).

See also Introduction, Culture, Folk Traditions.

Local religious festivals

January 17th: St Anthony's Day (Nicosia and Limassol)

January 24th: St Neophytus' Day (monastery of St Neóphytos)

February 2nd: Presentation of the Virgin in the Temple (festival in Chrysorroyiátissa monastery)

April 23rd: St George's Day (Lárnaca)

June 29th: SS Peter and Paul (solemn religious service in Káto Páphos, with the archbishop of Cyprus)

September 14th: Festival of the Holy Cross in Stavrovoúni and Ómodhos

October 4th: Festival of St John Lampadistes in Kalopanayiótis

October 18th: Festival of St Luke in Nicosia and Palekhóri, Koúklia

Other festivals

May: Anthestiria Festival (Flower Festival) in Lárnaca, Limassol, Páphos and Paralímni

July: Limassol Festival (folk events, exhibitions, circus, drama)

Beginning of August: Pampaphia Folk Festival in Páphos

End of August/beginning of September: Dionysia (wine festival, with music and dancing) at Stroumbí, near Páphos

Beginning of September: Limassol Wine Festival, a 12-day festival held in the Municipal Gardens, which attracts thousands of visitors who on payment of a small entrance charge can sample all the wines of Cyprus.

September/October: Cypria International Festival in Nicosia (music, dance, theatre)

◄ Procession on the feast of the Epiphany

Public Transport

The forms of public transport available in Cyprus are buses, service taxis (shared taxis) and ordinary taxis. There are no railways or tram services.

Buses

Service buses – the cheapest form of transport in Cyprus – operate between towns and villages and also between the larger towns and nearby beaches. There is usually only one bus a day to villages in the hills and the buses do not always keep to their timetable. Services between villages mostly use old Bedford buses which carry mail and luggage as well as passengers. Each village has its own bus to take people to work and children to school.

Most bus services are run by the two large companies, Lefkaritis and KEMEK. Information about services can be obtained from local bus offices and tourist information offices.

Bus services from Nicosia

Nicosia–Lárnaca: Lefkaritis, 6 Stasinos Avenue
☎ *(02) 442566*

Nicosia–Limassol: KEMEK, 34 Leonidas Street
☎ *(02) 463989*

Nicosia–Plátres, Kalopanayiótis, Pedhoulás: KEMEK, Leonidas Street/Homer Avenue
☎ *(02) 463989*

Nicosia–Tróodos and Kakopetriá: Solea Bus, Costanza Bastion, near Eleftheria Square

Nicosia–Kýkko Monastery: Kambos Bus, Leonidas Street/Homer Avenue

From Lárnaca

Lárnaca–Nicosia, Limassol: Lefkaritis, Athens Street
☎ *(04) 625440*

Lárnaca–Ayía Nápa: EMAN, Athens Street, opposite Sun Hall Hotel

Lárnaca–Paralímni (via Dherínia): Paralímni Bus, Athens Street

Lárnaca–Léfkara: St Lazarus Square

Old Bedford buses

Lárnaca–Airport: Athens Street, at Four Lanterns Hotel, Bus 21
Airport–Lárnaca: Bus 21

From Limassol
Limassol–Nicosia, Páphos: KEMEK, enosis Street/Irene Street
☎ *(05) 363241*
Limassol–Lárnaca: Lefkaritis, Spyros Araouzos Street/Hadjipavlou Street
☎ *(05) 362670*
Limassol–Plátres: Karydas, 21 Thessaloniki Street
☎ *(05) 362061*
Limassol–Plátres: Plátres Bus, 50 Eleftheria Street
☎ *(05) 362907*
Limassol–Plátres, Pródhromos, Pedhoulás: G Demos, enosis Street/Irene Street
Limassol–Agrós: Agros Bus, enosis Street/Irene Street

From Páphos
Páphos–Pólis: Fontana Amorosa Bus, Pallikarides Street
☎ *(06) 236740*
Páphos–Limassol: KEMEK, Fellahoglou Street
☎ *(06) 234255*
Páphos–Pyrgos: Pyrgos Bus, Karavella car park, near Ev. Pallikarides Avenue
Páphos–Coral Bay: ALEPA Bus, Karavella car park, by the Zena cinema (near Ev. Pallikarides Avenue)

From Pólis
Pólis–Páphos: Fontana Amorosa Bus
☎ *(06) 321115*

Service taxis

Service taxis (shared taxis) are large Mercedes taxis which can seat up to seven people. They run at half-hourly intervals on fixed routes between the larger towns, from 6am to 6pm (7pm in summer).

Service taxis can pick up passengers by arrangement at any particular point on their route and will drop them at any desired point at their destination.

Fares
The fares are reasonable, normally ranging between C£1 and C£1.50 depending on distance. The fare is the same whatever the number of passengers

Offices
Nicosia–Lárnaca: Acropolis, 9 Stasinos Avenue
☎ *(02) 472525*
Nicosia–Lárnaca, Limassol: Kyriakos, 27 Stasinos Avenue
☎ *(02) 444141*
Nicosia–Lárnaca: Makris, 11 Stasinos Avenue
☎ *(02) 466201*
Nicosia–Limassol: Karydas, 8 Homer Avenue
☎ *(02) 462269*
Nicosia–Limassol: Kypros, 9 Stasinos Avenue
☎ *(02) 464811*

Lárnaca–Limassol, Nicosia: Acropolis, Kalogreon Street/Makarios Avenue
☎ *(04) 655555*
Lárnaca–Limassol, Nicosia: Makris, 13 King Paul Street
☎ *(04) 652929*
Lárnaca–Nicosia: Kyriakos, 2 Hermes Street
☎ *(04) 655100*

There are no service taxis to Ayía Nápa, into the Tróodos massif (except Limassol–Plátres) and to the airport. For Páphos, change in Limassol.

Limassol–Nicosia, Páphos: Karydas, Thessaloniki Street
☎ *(05) 362061*
Limassol–Nicosia, Páphos: Kypros, 49 Sp.Araouzos Street
☎ *(05) 363979*
Limassol–Nicosia, Páphos: Kyriakos, Thessaloniki Street
☎ *(05) 364114*
Limassol–Lárnaca: Makris, 166 Hellas Street
☎ *(05) 365550*
Limassol–Lárnaca: Acropolis, 49 Sp.Araouzos Street
☎ *(05) 366766*

Páphos–Limassol: Karydas, 29 Ev. Pallikarides Street
☎ *(06) 232459*
Páphos–Limassol: Kypros, 134 Makarios Avenue
☎ *(06) 232376*

For Lárnaca or Nicosia, change in Limassol.

Taxis

The ordinary taxis have meters. Fares, which are fixed by the government, are reasonable. The charge is increased by about 10 per cent for journeys outside the towns. For journeys at night (between 11pm and 6am) there is approximately a 15 per cent increase. For every first piece of luggage weighing over 12 kg there is a supplementary charge. Taxi drivers usually expect a tip.

Restaurants

Cypriots like eating out in parties of family and friends. Not surprisingly, therefore, Cyprus is particularly well equipped with restaurants and eating places in every category of price and quality, ranging from sandwich stalls by way of modest tavernas to speciality restaurants serving French cuisine. Even in remote little villages there are modest but excellent family-run tavernas, and there are bars and pubs in all places of any size.

Coffee house (kafenion)
The local coffee house (*kafenion*) is a popular meeting place and social centre. In addition to coffee and other drinks it serves a variety of sweets.

Prices
Prices are controlled by the Cyprus Tourism Organisation (CTO), and restaurants are required to display their tariffs. 13 per cent is usually added to the bill, of which 10 per cent is the service charge and 3 per cent go to the CTO.

Tipping
Hotel and restaurant bills include a 10 per cent service charge, plus 8 per cent Value Added Tax (VAT). In addition waiters expect a further tip.

Menus
Menus are usually written in English as well as in Greek.

Restaurants (selection)

Ayía Nápa
Oleander
10 Nero Avenue
A cosy taverna with a wide range of grills. Open from 6pm.

Taverna Napa
On the road to Paralímni
This taverna has a long tradition and offers good value for money. Open from 6pm.

Kakopetriá

Maryland
There is a fine panorama from this old building alongside a former watermill, which houses a top restaurant.

Lárnaca

Archontissa
Athens Avenue
This decidedly expensive restaurant in a beautiful old building is near the middle of the promenade.

Zephyros Beach Tavern
Psarolimano
The taverna is by the fishing harbour; it can satisfy a discriminating palate and is relatively expensive. Open lunch and dinner.

Psarolimano
By the fishing harbour
Locals eat here, which means that you can rely on the freshness of the fish.

Limassol

Ladas (Old Harbour)
Agias Theklis Street
Traditional fish taverna at the western end of the old harbour.

Fiesta
Potamos Germasogias, George A Avenue
About 500 m east of the Amathus Beach Hotel, you can enjoy the sunset from the terrace of this superb restaurant while savouring a juicy steak or the succulent mezé dishes.

The Old Neighbourhood
14 Odos Angyras (Ankaras)
You can meet many locals here, enjoying the plain fare in this unpretentious little taverna in the old town.

There are numerous restaurants in the hotel district and on the seafront promenade, and many modest little tavernas round the old market hall. It is also worth going out to the village of Yermasóyia for its friendly tavernas, such as the Flogera Tavern, where bouzouki players provide atmosphere.

Nicosia

Astakos Fish Tavern
6 Menelaos, Engomi
This is a good seafood restaurant where you can eat lobster, crayfish, mussels and superior fish dishes, but it is not cheap.

Acropolis
12 Leonidas Street
This old-fashioned taverna close to the Old Town offers good mezé dishes and wine from the wood.

Mattheos
Lefkonos Street
Close to Phaneroméni Church, this simple taverna has a wide range of cooked dishes on offer. Open 10am–6pm.

Xefoto
Laiki Yitonia
One of the most popular restaurants in the Old Town, with outstanding mezé dishes. It really starts to swing after 9.30pm, when you can sing and dance to live music.

Páphos

Pelican
The best and most expensive of the many seafood restaurants on Páphos harbour. Its mascot (a pelican) is much photographed.

Demokritos
Agios Antonios Street
In the Páphos hotel district is this large taverna, which offers traditional music from 8pm.

Paralímni

Working Man's Club
On Church Square in the town centre
The food in this simple taverna is good value. The lamb chop with mint sauce is particularly good.

Plátres

Psiló Dendro
Trout Farm in Pano Plátres
The best thing to order in this top restaurant, with its open fire and large shady garden, is trout from their own trout farm.

Pólis
Karouzis
On the road to the campsite
The best taverna in the place, with a good selection of mezé dishes.

Shopping

In the towns there are shops of all kinds selling both home-produced and imported goods, and in the old quarters of Limassol and Lárnaca visitors will still find traditional craft workshops selling their own products. Prices are, in general, fixed, though in individual cases there may be scope for bargaining.

Clothing, jewellery, lace

Shoes are a particularly good buy since Cyprus has a considerable shoemaking industry. Textiles and leather goods can also be bought at very reasonable prices. Silver jewellery, often based on ancient artefacts, can be found in Limassol, Nicosia and Páphos and in the little village of Léfkara. Lace made in traditional fashion can be bought not only in Léfkara and Ómodhos where it is made but also in all tourist centres. Páphos is famed for its woven fabrics.

Pottery, sponges, sweets, drinks

Pottery and basketry are produced in the Páphos area and the villages of Kórnos and Phiní are also noted for their pottery. Natural sponges are fished off the west coast near Páphos; they are relatively expensive, since they are now found only in areas difficult of access.

Various kinds of sweets, in particular Turkish delight, are popular souvenirs of a visit to Cyprus, and Cyprus brandy and Commandaria, the sweet dessert wine which is one of the oldest wines in the world, also offer good value.

Craft centres

In order to promote the production and sale of traditional craft goods the Cyprus Handicrafts Service has established craft centres in a number of towns in which visitors can buy a range of traditional articles such as pottery, embroidery, leather, copper and batik.

There are craft centres in Nicosia, Limassol, Lárnaca and Páphos.

Bookshops

Books in Cyprus tend to be expensive. In some of the larger towns there are bookshops with books in English, French and German:

KP Kypriacou
57 Anexartisia Street, Limassol
☎ *(05) 37511*

A Ioannides & Co.
30 Athens Street, Limassol
☎ *(05) 362204*

MAM (The House of Cyprus Publications)
Laiki Yitonia, Nicosia
☎ *(02) 472744 (archaeology and art)*
Bridgehouse
Shop 13, Byron Avenue, Nicosia
☎ *(02) 443297*

Sport

Cycling

Bicycles can be rented in all the larger towns and in tourist centres (☛Cycling).

Diving

There are excellent diving grounds off the coasts of Cyprus, particularly in a number of small bays on Cape Gréco, near Ayía Nápa. Diving equipment can be hired in the main tourist centres. Information from:
Cyprus Federation of Underwater Activities
PO Box 1053, Nicosia
☎ *(04) 477757*

Fishing

A number of private lakes and artificial lakes are stocked with freshwater fish such as trout, carp and grayling. Fishing permits can be obtained from:
Head of Fisheries Department, Ministry of Agriculture and Natural Resources
☎ *(02) 303526.*

Angling equipment can be bought in the large towns and there are also hotels which hire out equipment.

Golf

There are currently only three golf courses (all 18 holes):
Tsada Golf Club
8 km north of Páphos
☎ *(06) 642774, fax (06) 642776*
Secret Valley Golf Club
Near the Aphrodite Rock (18 km east of Páphos)
☎ *(06) 642774, fax (06) 64 27 76*
Elias Golf Course
Pareklissia near Limassol
☎ *(05) 325000*

Riding

Although riding is not a widely popular sport in Cyprus a number of riding clubs have been established in recent years.

Lapatsa Sporting Centre
Dhefterá (12 km outside Nicosia)
☎ *(02) 621021*
Elias Beach Horse Riding Centre
On Limassol–Nicosia road, Limassol
☎ *(05) 325000*
Flamingos Riding Club
☎ *(04) 655660*
Riding Centre
Near the Tombs of the Kings, Páphos
☎ *(06) 633966*
Lucky Horse Ranch
In Skoulli, 5 km from Pólis Chrysochous
☎ *(06) 413278*

Sailing
There are marinas at Lárnaca, Limassol, Páphos and Ayía Nápa; the most modern of these, the Lárnaca Marina (☎ *(04) 653110, fax (04) 624110)*, has moorings for 450 boats. The St Raphael Marina at Limassol (☎ *(05) 321100)* has 227 moorings and facilities for boat hire. Both the Lárnaca and the Limassol marinas have repair, cleaning and supply facilities for fuel, electricity and drinking water, as well as showers.

Skiing
Skiing is possible in the Tróodos massif in winter. There are four ski lifts and two cross-country ski trails on their highest peak, Mount Ólympos (1951 m; ☛Sights from A to Z South Cyprus, Tróodos Massif). The Cyprus Ski Club hires out skiing equipment.

Tennis
There are public tennis courts in all the larger towns, and many hotels and apartment complexes have courts on which non-residents can also play. Below is a selection:

Champs Elysées
Archangel Street, Nicosia
☎ *(02) 353188*
Eleon Tennis Club
3 Plutarch Street, Nicosia
☎ *(02) 449923*
Field Club
Egypt Avenue, Nicosia
☎ *(02) 452041*
Lapatsa Sporting Centre
Dhefterá (12 km outside Nicosia)
☎ *(02) 621201*

Lárnaca Tennis Club
10 Kilkis Street, Lárnaca
☎ *(04) 656999*
Famagusta Tennis Club
3 Mesaorias Street, Lárnaca
☎ *(05) 335952*
Limassol Sporting Club
11 Olympion Street, Tsiflikoudia, Lárnaca
☎ *(05) 359818*

On Yeroskípos tourist beach (4 km east of Páphos)
☎ *(06) 234525*

Walking
Cyprus offers ideal walking country. In the Tróodos massif and on the Akámas peninsula at the Baths of Aphrodite there are nature trails laid out by the Cyprus Tourism Organisation. Stout footwear is advisable since many paths are narrow and stony; hiking boots also provide protection against snakes. You can also join organised walking tours.

Windsurfing
Waterskiing
Many hotels and private agencies offer facilities for various water sports, including windsurfing, waterskiing and surfing, as well as surfboard hire.

Equipment for windsurfing, sea canoeing, diving and snorkelling, as well as for sailing and motor boats, can be hired from the water sports school:
Jalos Sports
Pólis
☎ *(06) 322494, 321089*

It also organises boat trips.

Telephone

Local, long-distance and international telephone calls can be made from payphone kiosks, from hotels or from the offices of the Cyprus Telecommunications Authority (CTA). Cheaper rates operate between 8pm and 7am for long-distance calls and between 10pm and 8am for international calls. Payphones are operated by coins or phonecards. There are cellular phone connections with Greece, the United Kingdom and Germany.

There are CTA offices in the larger towns:
Nicosia: 1 Museum Avenue
Limassol: Athens Street (corner of Markos Botsaris Street)
Lárnaca: Lord Byron Street
Páphos: Grivas Dighenis Street

International dialling codes
United Kingdom to Cyprus: 00 357
United States or Canada to Cyprus: 011 357

Cyprus to the United Kingdom: 00 44
Cyprus to the United States or Canada: 00 1

Local dialling codes
When telephoning from abroad the initial zero of the local code should be omitted. The most important codes are:

Nicosia: 02
Ayía Nápa: 03
Paralímni/Protaras: 05
Lárnaca: 04
Limassol: 05
Plátres: 05
Páphos: 06
Pólis: 06

Time

Cyprus observes Eastern European Time, 2 hours ahead of Greenwich Mean Time. Summer Time, 3 hours ahead of GMT and 2 hours ahead of British Summer Time, is in force from the last weekend in March to the last weekend in September.

Travel Documents

Visitors from the United Kingdom, the United States, Canada and many other countries require only a passport, without visa, for a stay of up to 3 months. For a longer stay a residence permit must be obtained; further information from the Chief Immigration Officer in Nicosia.

No vaccinations are required.

Visitors with a North Cyprus stamp in their passport will not be admitted to the Republic of Cyprus (nor will they be allowed into Greece).

Notes
When hiring a self-drive car it is sufficient to present a national driving licence.

Weights and Measures

Although Cyprus adopted the metric system in 1987, Cypriots still often use British Imperial measures among themselves. Petrol is however seldom still sold by the gallon, although distances are sometimes given in miles and weights measured in *okes* (1.268kg).

When to Go

Summer
Cyprus has some 340 sunny days per year (☛Introduction, Facts and Figures, Climate). It gets very hot in summer, with temperatures ranging between 30°C and 40°C on the coast and in inland areas, but visitors who are not afraid of heat will enjoy a bathing holiday during the summer months. Only in the hills is it rather cooler.

Spring and autumn
The most pleasant months are in spring (April and May) and autumn (September to November). During these months it is not so hot, though with Cyprus's perennial mild climate the water is still warm enough for bathing. In spring the island is covered with trees in blossom and is particularly attractive for walkers. There may be occasional light showers of rain both in spring and in autumn.

Winter
In the mild winter months Cyprus is ideal for a restful holiday, without the hustle and bustle of the main holiday season. Since the temperature of the sea never falls below 16°C, bathing is still possible. In winter there is snow in the hills and modest facilities for skiing on Mount Ólympos (four ski lifts).

Wine

Cyprus is one of the oldest wine-producing countries in the world, and is still a world leader in terms of production per head. Its success in maintaining this position over the last 20 years is largely due to the introduction of modern wine-making techniques.

A third of the agricultural population is engaged in viticulture. The most important wine-producing areas are the relatively rainy southern slopes of the Tróodos range, followed by the coastal plains.

Vineyards in western Cyprus

Grapes
The native grapes – never affected by phylloxera – are Mavron, Maratheftiko and Ophthalmo (black) and Xynisteri and Alexandria Muscatel (white).

Commandaria
The oldest wine on the island was made by the Knights of St John in the 12th c. and named Commandaria after their commandery of Kolóssi (☛Sights from A to Z South Cyprus, Kolóssi). Commandaria is made from the black Mavron and white Xynisteri grapes in the proportion of nine to one. The heavy sweetness of this dessert wine is the result of the sun-dried grapes. Eleven villages, including Yerasa and Kalokhoria, are entitled to call their wine Commandaria.

Wineries
The bulk of Cyprus's wide range of white wine (*áspro krasí*), red wine (*kókkino krasí*) and sherry-type wines comes from four large wineries in Limassol – Keo, Sodap, Etko and Loel. Visits to these, which are all on the harbour, can be made in the mornings. For times inquire at your hotel or the tourist office.

Country wines
The country wines made by the growers themselves are also of good quality, and as a rule rather heavier. The villages of Ómodhos, Plátres and Kiláni are noted for their wine. Like many monasteries in the rest of Europe, Chrysorroyiátissa Monastery in the gently rolling hills in the west of the island also produces excellent red and white wines.

White wines
The dry white wines can be particularly recommended. Among the best known are Aphrodite, Palomino, White Lady, Keo Hock, Thisbe and Arsinoe 62. Rather sweeter are St Hilarion and Blonde Lady.

Red wines
The most popular dry red wines are Othello, Afames, Keo Claret, Dark Lady, Hermes, Negro and Olympus.

Youth Hostels

Youth hostels in Cyprus are open to holders of the International Youth Hostel Association card. Beds can be booked in advance through:
Cyprus Youth Hostel Association
PO Box 1328, Nicosia
☎ *(02) 442027*

Youth hostels
Lárnaca
27 Nikolaos Rossos Street
☎ *(04) 621188*
Nicosia
5 Hadjidakis Street
☎ *(02) 674808, fax (02) 672896*
Páphos
37 Eleftherios Venizelos Avenue
☎ *(06) 232588*
Stavrós tis Psókas Forest Station
☎ *(06) 722338*
Tróodos
In the pinewoods near the village
☎ *(05) 420200*

Practical Information from A to Z North Cyprus

Arriving

Visitors can travel to North Cyprus either by air or by sea, but entering it from South Cyprus is subject to restrictions of the Greek Cypriot authorities (☛Frontier Crossing).

By air
Since the Turkish Republic of North Cyprus is not recognised under international law, no international airlines fly to North Cyprus apart from Turkish Airlines, Cyprus Turkish Airlines, Istanbul Airlines and Onur Airlines, which use the Turkish Cypriot airport of Ercan (24 km east of Nicosia). These airlines cannot fly direct to Ercan from Britain and other countries and flights therefore always make an intermediate stop in mainland Turkey (usually Istanbul); there are also flights from Izmir, Ankara, Antalya and Adana. Visitors can of course fly to Istanbul by other airlines and get a connecting flight from there to Ercan on one of the Turkish airlines.

The flight from Britain, allowing for the stop in mainland Turkey, takes about 6 hours.

By sea
The only shipping services to North Cyprus are from the Turkish ports of Taşucu (west of Silifke), Mersin, Antalya and the Israeli port of Haifa.

From Tašucu the fast MV *Barbaros* (the Kíbrís Express) sails daily (except Saturdays) in summer to Kyrenia (Girne); the crossing takes 2–3 hours. The *Fatih Feribotu* sails three times weekly between Taşucu and Kyrenia, the *Girne Sultan* four times weekly, taking about 8 hours.

Shipping offices:

TAS TUR
Atatürk Caddesi 82, Tašucu
☎ *3241334*

◀ Traditional lace makes a good present or souvenir

SEA BIRD CO. LTD
Iskenderun Caddesi 40/4, Girne
☎ *8153554*

From Mersin there is a ferry to Famagusta three times weekly. The crossing takes about 10 hours.

TURKISH MARITIME LINES
Liman Binasí, Kat 2, Mersin
☎ *2318828*
ÇELEBI HAN
Istikll Caddesi 127, Sok. 2, Mersin

Note
On arrival in North Cyprus it is advisable to ask the immigration officer not to put a stamp in your passport (request a separate entry visa to be stamped instead), since this would make it difficult on a future occasion to enter South Cyprus and would likely cause difficulty in entering Greece.

Accommodation
See Camping, Hotels

Beaches

Some of the finest beaches on the island are in North Cyprus, such as the wide bays with beaches of fine sand at Famagusta and the little sand and shingle bays at Kyrenia.

Beaches belonging to hotels are equipped with sun umbrellas and loungers and can be used by non-residents on payment of an admission charge.

Topless bathing and nudism are not permitted in North Cyprus and would seriously offend the morals of local Muslims.

Famagusta
Beach on the south side of the town, at the Palm Beach Hotel
Long beaches to the north of the town
Sálamis Beach, at the excavations of ancient Sálamis

Karpasía peninsula
Beautiful lonely sandy beaches

Kyrenia
Many of the beaches to the west of Kyrenia belong to hotels.
Riviera Beach, 4 km west: good for snorkelling
Golden Rock Beach, 8 km west (restaurants)
Mermaid Beach, to the west of the town, at the Deniz Kízí Hotel
Mare Monte Beach, 12 km west, at the Mare Monte Hotel
Karakum Beach, 4 km east
Acapulco Beach, at the Club Acapulco holiday village
Twelve Mile Beach, 20 km east: the longest sandy beach on the coast.

There are other beaches in Mórphou (Güzelyurt) Bay.

Camping

Camping outside designated sites is permitted, but the local people should always be asked for permission. There are three official camp sites with sanitary facilities:
Onur Camping
North of Sálamis, opposite the Gíranel Bay Hotel

Riviera Camping
6 km west of Kyrenia (restaurant, private beach)

Lara Camping
15 km east of Kyrenia

Car Rental

The driver of a rented car must possess a national or international driving licence and be 25 years or over with at least 2 years driving experience.

Rental charges in North Cyprus are very reasonable, and are reduced still further in the off season. The charge usually includes third party insurance and unlimited mileage.

Conversions

See Practical Information South Cyprus, Conversions.

Currency

The currency of North Cyprus is the Turkish lira (TL). There are banknotes for 20,000, 50,000, 100,000, 250,000, 500,000, 1 million and 5 million TL and coins in denominations of 50, 100, 500, 1000, 2500, 5000, 10,000, 25,000 and 50,000 TL.

The Turkish lira is liable to rapid inflation. It is advisable, therefore, to check the current exchange rate through a bank or travel agency before leaving home and to change only as much money as is likely to be required for immediate needs.

Exchange rates are better in Turkey or North Cyprus than in other countries. Major European currencies and the US dollar, traveller's cheques and major credit cards are also welcome.

Banks in North Cyprus will change cash, traveller's cheques and *Eurocheques*. Many shops, restaurants and hotels accept credit cards (Eurocard, Visa, Diners' Club).

Customs Regulations

In addition to personal effects visitors may take into North Cyprus, duty-free, 2 bottles of wine or 1.5 litres of spirits, 400 cigarettes or 500 grams of tobacco.

The export of antiques from North Cyprus is prohibited.

Cycling

Hitherto there have been practically no facilities for hiring bicycles in North Cyprus. As part of the effort to promote tourism, however, a bicycle hire agency has recently been opened on the harbour promenade in Kyrenia.

Electricity

Electricity is 240 volts AC. Power sockets take British-style plugs, usually three pins.

Embassies and Consulates

North Cyprus is not recognised officially, and the only diplomatic mission is the Turkish embassy. To look after the interests of British residents, however,

the British high commissioner or his representative is available at a small office behind the post office in Kyrenia (Girne) on Saturday mornings. The consular section of the High Commission maintains an office in:
Mehmet Akif Street, Nicosia
Mon.–Fri. 7.30am–1pm
2274938
For American citizens there is the American Centre in:
Güner Türkmen Street
Mon.–Fri. 8am–5pm
2272443

Emergencies

Police
Nicosia/Lefkoşa: Atatürk Square, Girne Caddesi
2283311
Famagusta/Gazimağusta: at St Nicholas's Cathedral and in Ilker Karter Caddesi
3665389
Kyrenia/Girne: at Castle
8152111
Mórphou/Güzelyurt
7142200
Léfka/Lefke
7287423
Tríkome/Iskele
3712333
Lápothos/Lapta
8218512

Excursions

Local travel agencies operate coach tours (usually day trips) to the main sights in North Cyprus, with English speaking guides. They also organise walking tours and boat trips. Excursions can be booked either in the agencies themselves or in hotels.

Food and Drink

Food

The food and drink of North Cyprus are broadly similar to those of the Greek part of the island, though some dishes have different names and show the influence of mainland Turkey. *Mezedhes* are also popular in North Cyprus, but exclude pork.

The times of meals are as in South Cyprus. The hotels also generally serve international cuisine; many tasty local dishes, however, can be found in Turkish restaurants.

North Cypriot dishes
Balík = fish
biber dolmasí = green peppers stuffed with rice
biftek = beefsteak
cacík = cucumber salad with yoghurt and garlic (Greek tsatzíki)
ekmek = bread
günür áorbasí = soup of the day
imam bayíldí = 'The imam fainted', aubergines with onions and tomatoes
köfte = meat balls
lahmacun = Turkish pizza with highly spiced minced meat
omlet = omelette
piliá = chicken
pirzola = lamb chop
šeftali = a spicy lamb sausage
šiš kebab = pieces of meat grilled on a spit
tarama = a paste made from spiced cod roe
tavuk = chicken
yaprak dolmasí = stuffed vine leaves
yešil salata = green salad

Drinks

Since practically no grapes are grown in North Cyprus most of the wine (*šarap*) in this part of the island is imported from Turkey. Well-known brands are Villa Doluca and Kavaklídere (both red and white). Selim and Son's winery produces a dry white wine named Aphrodite.

Raki is a spirit similar to the Greek ouzo.

Beer (*bira*) also comes from Turkey. Two popular light beers are Turkish-brewed Efes and Tuborg. A locally brewed beer is called Gold Fussel.

Coffee (*kahve*) and tea (*áay*) are drunk in the coffee houses. As in South Cyprus there are three degrees of sweetness – sweet (*šekerli*), medium sweet (*orta*) and without sugar (*sade*).

A favourite non-alcoholic drink is *ayran* (yoghurt diluted with water).

Recipe

Imam bayíldi ('The imam fainted')
Ingredients: 2 onions (chopped), 3

spoonfuls olive oil, 2 tomatoes (diced), 2 spoonfuls chopped parsley, garlic, the juice of half a lemon, salt, 3 aubergines (medium size), 2 cups water.

Preheat the oven to 180°C. Cook the onions in oil for 5 minutes and pour them into a dish with the tomatoes, the garlic, the parsley and the lemon juice. Add salt and stir well. Cut the stalks off the aubergines. Peel half of each aubergine with a potato knife, leaving the other halves in their skins, and lightly cook them in the oil from the onions. Then cut the aubergines lengthwise, take out the flesh and fill them with the tomato, onion and parsley stuffing. Cook for 45 minutes in an ovenproof dish, and garnish with parsley.

Frontier Crossing

Visitors to North Cyprus cannot enter the Greek part of Cyprus, which regards a visit to the Turkish part of the island as an illegal act. Visitors to South Cyprus may, however, make day trips into the Turkish area – though this is not encouraged by the Greek Cypriot authorities (☛Practical Information from A to Z South Cyprus, Frontier Crossing).

Health

Medical assistance

Since there is no medical school in North Cyprus, all the doctors have been trained in other countries, most of them in Turkey. Many doctors speak English.

Hospitals
There are both public hospitals and private clinics. Visitors receive free emergency treatment in public hospitals, otherwise hospital treatment must be paid for. It is therefore advisable to take out temporary medical insurance before leaving home.

The following are the largest hospitals:

Kyrenia/Girne: Cumhuriyet Caddesi
☎ *8152266*
Mórphou/Güzelyurt
☎ *7142125*
Famagusta/Gazimağusa: Polatpaša Bulvarí
☎ *3662876*

Emergency aid
Nicosia/Lefkoşa
☎ *2285441*
Kyrenia/Girne
☎ *8152266*
Famagusta/Gazimağusa
☎ *3665328*
Tríkomo/Iskele
☎ *3712319*
Léfka/Lefke
☎ *7817757*
Karavostási/Gemikonağí
☎ *7717322 or 7717351*
Lápithos/Lapta
☎ *2818322*

Chemists

The word for a chemist shop is *Eczane*. Since not all common medicines can be obtained in North Cyprus visitors who require particular drugs should take a supply with them.

Opening hours
See Opening Hours

Hotels

Categories
North Cyprus has a wide range of hotels and bungalow complexes, covering a great variety of quality and price categories (from one to five stars). The Ministry of Tourism supervises hotel standards and tariffs. North Cyprus is particularly popular with visitors from Turkey.

Selection

Nicosia/Lefkoşa
***SARAY
Girne Caddesi
☎ *2283115, fax 2284808*
Situated in the Old Town near Atatürk Square. The rooms have air-conditioning, and there are occasional performances of folk music and dancing.

Famagusta/Gazimağusa
*****PALM BEACH
Kemal Servet Sokagí
☎ *3662000, fax 3662002*
108 rooms. The hotel is right by the beach, on the outskirts of the town. There are tennis courts and a sandy beach with loungers and sunshades.

******Park**
8 km out of town at Sálamis excavations
☎ *3788213*
89 rooms. The hotel, built in the style of a country house, is situated by a long, gently sloping sandy beach. Restaurant and casino, as well as sports and entertainment facilities; there is also a reading room with an open fire.

*****Mimoza**
☎ *3788219*
52 rooms. The hotel is about 11 km north of Famagusta, on the wide Bay of Salamis. The beach has excellent facilities for bathing and water sports of all kinds. Occasional evening entertainments.

Kyrenia/Girne

******Dome**
☎ *8152453, fax 8152772*
170 rooms. The hotel is right on the seafront and only a few minutes from the town centre. The rooms have air-conditioning, a minibar and balcony. On a small spit of land are a freshwater swimming pool, a natural pool and a sun terrace.

******Lapethos Club**
☎ *2287630, fax 8218966*
103 rooms. The complex situated 13 km west of Kyrenia comprises the hotel and several two-storey villas that are ideal for families. There is a restaurant with a panorama of the sea and a casino.

Olive Tree
☎ *8244201*
This well-cared for bungalow holiday village outside Kyrenia is flanked on one side by the mountains and on the other by the Mediterranean. Bar, restaurant and swimming pool. During high season there is occasional live music.

*****Acapulco**
☎ *8244110*
This holiday village (hotel and bungalows) on a fine beach is about 10 km east of Kyrenia (bus service). Facilities include a sauna, fitness studio and table tennis room; also a restaurant, casino and disco.

***** Mare Monte**
☎ *8218310*
Hotel with 16 rooms and 76 bungalows. About 10 km west of Kyrenia (shuttle service) is this family hotel. Visitors can relax on the bathing beach (snack bar). There are souvenir shops and an open-air disco.

****British**
☎ *8152240, fax 8152742*
18 rooms. Situated in the centre of Kyrenia, most rooms have a balcony with a fine view. The many cafes, shops and restaurants around it are very inviting.

Pia Bella
☎ *8155321, fax 8155324*
34 rooms and 2 suites. This small town hotel has a restaurant and a swimming pool with bar set in a beautiful garden. There are plenty of entertainments and walks in Kyrenia and the surrounding area.

Top Set
☎ *8222204, fax 8222478*
58 rooms. Situated about 14 km west of Kyrenia, this hotel has a restaurant on a terrace with Cypriot and Turkish cuisine.

Information

Information about North Cyprus (brochures, map, list of hotels and tour operators) can be obtained from:

United Kingdom
The Tourism Counsellor
Office of the London Representative
Turkish Republic of Northern Cyprus
28 Cockspur Street, London SW1Y 5BN
☎ *(020) 79305069, 78394577*

United States
Office of the Representative
Turkish Republic of Northern Cyprus
821 United Nations Plaza, 6th Floor, New York NY 10017
☎ *(212) 5575612*

Office of the Representative
Turkish Republic of Northern Cyprus
1667 K Street, Suite 690, Washington DC 20006
☎ *(202) 4625772*

Canada
Dr Ezel Örfi (Honorary Representative)
The Office of The Honorary Representative in Canada of the Turkish Republic of Northern Cyprus 300 John Street, Suite 330, Thornhill, Ontario L3T 5W4
☎ *(416) 9058848604*

North Cyprus
Ministry of Tourism and Social Assistance
Mersin 10, Nicosia/Lefkoša

Local tourist offices in North Cyprus
Nicosia/Lefkoşa: Mehmet Akif Caddesi (outside town walls),
Mon.–Fri. 8.30am–noon, 2–4pm.
Famagusta/Gazimağusa: Fevzi Çakmak Caddesi (in New Town),
Mon.–Fri. 9am–noon, 2–4pm.
Kyrenia/Girne: on harbour promenade (below the mosque),
Mon.–Fri. 9am–12.30pm, 1.30–5pm.
Ercan Airport
(371) 4703

Language

The official language of North Cyprus, and the language spoken by most of the population, is Turkish. In the tourist centres, however, many people speak English.

Alphabet

Turkish	Pronunciation
a	a
b	b
c	j
á	ch as in 'church'
d	d
e	e
f	f
g	g (hard, as in 'gag')
ğ	barely perceptible; lengthens preceding vowel
h	h (emphatically pronounced, approaching c in 'loch')
í	uh sound, as in the last syllable of 'over'
i	i
j	zh as in 'pleasure'
k	k
l	l
m	m
n	n
o	o
ö	eu, as in French *deux*
p	p
r	r
s	s
ş	sh
t	t
u	u
ü	as in French *une*
v	v
y	y, as in 'yet'
z	z

Numbers

Cardinals

0	sífír
1	bir
2	iki
3	üá
4	dört
5	beş
6	altí
7	yedi
8	sekiz
9	dokuz
10	on
11	on bir
20	yirmi
21	yirmi bir
30	otuz
40	kírk
50	elli
60	altmíş
70	yetmiş
80	seksen
90	doksan
100	yüz
200	iki yüz
1000	bin
2000	iki bin

Fractions

½	yarím
¼	áeyrek

Words and expressions

General

Good morning!	Günaydín!
Good day!	Merhaba!
Good evening!	Iyi akšamlar!
Good night!	Iyi geceler!
Goodbye!	Allah aísmarladík!
Have a good trip	güle güle
yes	evet
no	hayír
please	lütfen
thank you	mersi
open	aáík
closed	kapalí
exit	áíkís
Is there . . .	Var mí . . .
How much?	Bu kaáa?
Where . . .	Nerede . . .
When . . .	Ne zaman . . .
men	erkekler
women	kadínlar
letter	mektup

chemist	eczane
bookshop	kitapái
post office	postahane

Topography

island	ada
garden	baháe
town hall	belediye
petrol station	benzin istasyonu
street, road	cadde(si)
mosque	cami(i)
market	áarşí(sí)
fountain	áeşme
hill, mountain	dağ
sea	deniz
house	ev
bathhouse	hamam
inn, caravanserai	han
castle, fortress	hisar
landing stage	iskele
gate	kapí
caravanserai	kervansaray
direction of Mecca	kíble
church	kilise
bridge	köprü
pavilion, kiosk	köšk
village	köy
tower	kule
library	kütüphane
harbour	liman
square	meydan(í)
prayer niche in a mosque (marking the direction of Mecca)	mihrab
pulpit in a mosque	minber
museum	müze(si)
room	oda
school	okul
bus stop	otobüs durağí
park	park
beach	plaj
police	polis
ablutions fountain	şadírvan
palace	saray
town	şehir
street	sokak (sokağí)
water	su
repair garage, workshop	tamirhane
dervish convent	tekke
hill	tepe
tomb	türbe
ship	vapur
road	yol

Media

The Bayrak Broadcasting and Television Corporation (Bayrak Radio ve Televizyon, BRT), with two radio and television channels, transmits brief news bulletins in English.

Greek Cypriot and British Forces programmes and the BBC World Service can also be received in North Cyprus.

Motoring

Road network

North Cyprus has an excellent road network and all towns and villages can be reached by car. Only minor roads, for example on the Karpasía peninsula or in the hills, are unsurfaced though they can easily be negotiated by cars.

Regulations

Road traffic regulations are in line with international standards. Vehicles travel on the left, with overtaking on the right; vehicles on roundabouts have priority.

You may find that often distances on signposts and road signs are given in miles (☛260).

The speed limit in towns is 48 kph, outside built-up areas it is 80 kph.

Fuel

Petrol is still sold by the gallon in North Cyprus. Standard grade petrol is not available: only premium and diesel: It is considerably cheaper than in western Europe.

Petrol stations, generally located in town centres, are open daily 6am–6pm (sometimes later).

Maps

Most of the maps of Cyprus (☛Practical Information South Cyprus, Maps) give only the Greek names of places in North Cyprus which now have Turkish names.

There is a free North Cyprus Tourist Map (1:330,000), obtainable from the Offices of the Representative, Turkish Republic of Northern Cyprus (☛Information), and at tourist offices in North Cyprus.

Nightlife

There are a number of discos, bars and casinos in the three principal towns of North Cyprus.

Discos

Nicosia:

Distances (km) between towns in North Cyprus

	Nicosia	Famagusta	Mórphou	Kyrenia	Rizokárpaso	Sóloi
Nicosia	-	61	40	26	123	54
Famagusta	61	-	94	73	80	108
Mórphou	40	94	-	48	158	12
Kyrenia	26	73	48	-	133	60
Rizokárpaso	123	80	158	133	-	184
Sóloi	54	108	12	60	184	-

Picnic Hotel, outside the Old Town
Saray Hotel, Girne Caddesi (Atatürk Square)

Famagusta:
Palm Beach Hotel, Kemal Servet Sokağí
Old Town Disco and Pub, west of St Nicholas's Cathedral

Kyrenia:
Dome Hotel, in the town centre by the sea
Rooks, opposite the Dome Hotel
Moonlight Disco, on the Famagusta road
Hippodrome, in the town centre, opposite the Town Hall

Casinos
There are casinos in Nicosia (Sabri's Oriental Hotel), Famagusta (Sálamis Bay Hotel, Palm Beach Hotel) and Kyrenia (Hotel Liman, Dome Hotel, Celebrity Hotel). French and American roulette, baccarat and blackjack are played under international rules. The casinos are usually open 9pm–4am.

Opening Hours

Banks
Summer Mon.–Fri. 8am–2pm; winter Mon.–Fri. 8.30am–noon.

Chemists
Summer Mon.–Sat. 7.30am–1pm, 4–6pm; winter Mon.–Sat. 8am–1pm, 2–6pm.

Government offices
Summer Mon.–Fri. 7.30am–2pm; winter Mon.–Fri. 8am–1pm, 2–5pm.

Museums
The opening hours of museums and archaeological sites vary from place to place (☛Sights from A to Z). On major religious festivals like the Sugar (Eid-l Fitr) Festival and the Festival of Sacrifice museums and sites are closed.

Public holidays
See entry

Post offices
Mon.–Fri. 7.30am–2pm, 4–6pm, Sat. 7.30am–2pm.

Shops
May–Sep. Mon.–Sat. 7.30am–1pm, 4–6pm; Oct.–Apr. Mon.–Sat. 8am–1pm, 2–6pm.

In rural areas many shops stay open later in the evening and are also open on Sundays. In some tourist areas shops do not close for lunch and may stay open until 8pm.

Photography

It is forbidden to take photographs of military installations, but there are no restrictions about photographing features of tourist interest. Photography is also permitted in most museums. Before photographing people you should ask their permission.

Films are expensive in North Cyprus, and not all brands are available. It is advisable, therefore, to take an adequate supply of films from home.

Post

Postal services
There are post offices in all towns of any size, which can be recognised by the sign 'PTT'. Since North Cyprus is not internationally recognised, all its mail goes via Mersin, a Turkish provincial town. As a result of the detour mail addressed to western Europe is likely to take at least 8–10 days to arrive. Mail for

North Cyprus should have Mersin 10, Turkey after the name of the town.

Post offices
See Opening Hours

Head post offices
Nicosia:
Saraýnü Sokaǧí, near Atatürk Square
Famagusta:
Near St Nicholas's Cathedral
Kyrenia:
Cumhuriyet Caddesi

Public Holidays

Official holidays
Since Atatürk's reforms in the 1920s the weekly day of rest in Turkey has been Sunday and not, as in other Islamic countries, Friday. The holidays and festivals celebrated in North Cyprus are broadly the same as in Turkey. During both fixed holidays and movable festivals all shops and public institutions are closed.

January 1st: New Year's Day
April 23rd: National Sovereignty Day, Children's Day
May 1st: Labour Day
May 19th: Youth and Sports Day, Atatürk Memorial Day
July 20th: Peace and Freedom Day (anniversary of the landing of Turkish troops in 1974)
August 1st: TMOUNT Day (Turkish Endurance Organisation)
August 30th: Victory Day (commemorating Turkey's victory in the war with Greece in 1922)
October 29th: Turkish National Day (commemorating the proclamation of the Republic of Turkey in 1923)
November 15th: Proclamation of the Turkish Republic of Northern Cyprus, 1983

Movable festivals
Ramadan is the month of fasting. It moves back 11 days each year (i.e. occurs 11 days earlier). The 24th day of Ramadan is a public holiday.

Seker Bayramí (Sugar Festival): a three-day festival at the end of Ramadan, when gifts of sweets are exchanged.

Kurban Bayramí (Festival of Sacrifice): a 3-day festival on which animals are killed and shared with the poor (☛Culture, Folk Traditions). It also moves back 11 days each year.

Local festivals
Mid-July: Festival of Tourism in Kyrenia/Girne
May/June: Orange Festival in Mórphou/Güzelyurt
Mid-July: Festival of Tourism in Famagusta/Gazimağusa
Beginning of August: Wine Festival in Famagusta/Gazimağusa

Public Transport

Buses

Buses run regular services, usually at hourly intervals, between all the places of any size in North Cyprus; fares are low. The timing of services can be found by enquiry at bus stations.

Nicosia
The bus station is in Kemal Aşík Caddesí. From here there are buses and service (shared) taxis to Kyrenia, Famagusta and Mórphou/Güzelyurt. There are also buses to Kyrenia starting from Girne Caddesi (in front of the Museum of Turkish Folk Art in the Mevlevi Tekke).

Famagusta
The bus station is outside the town walls in Mustafa Kemal Bulvarí (Levkoşa Yolu), near the Atatürk Monument.

Kyrenia
The bus station is in the town centre, at the point where the Nicosia road begins.

Restaurants

Nicosia
There are a number of restaurants offering local specialities in Girne Caddesi.

Amasyali
This restaurant north of Atatürk Square offers Turkish cuisine.

Eniste
94 Mehmet Akif Caddesi
Grills are the speciality of this white-tiled restaurant

Famagusta
There are good restaurants near the Palm Beach Hotel.

Dernek
On the road to Sálamis, the Dernek serves excellent local cuisine and has a tea garden.

Petek Pastanesi
This cake shop near Othello's Tower is recommended, with its tempting assortment of cakes, pastries and sweets. It will also serve breakfast on request.

Viyana Restaurant
This garden restaurant is in the town centre near the Cathedral. Before ordering be sure to check the price, otherwise you may get a shock.

Kyrenia
A midday break is best spent in one of the restaurants by the picturesque harbour.

Harbour Club
You have a fine view of the harbour from the attractively laid out dining areas. Fish dishes as well as French and international cuisine are on the menu.

Lemon Tree
5 km east of Kyrenia. There are fish dishes on the menu and live music.

Kybele
It is well worth making the trip out to this restaurant by the ruins of Bellapais Abbey; fine view of the coastal plain.

Set Fish
A harbourside restaurant with delicious fish dishes.

Set Italiano
This restaurant near the mosque is for any lover of Italian food and drink, especially pasta.

Shopping

In the larger towns leather goods and items of clothing can be bought at reasonable prices. Popular souvenirs are beautiful woven fabrics and basketwork, pottery, alabaster and copper articles. A wide range of gold and silver jewellery can be seen in Kyrenia and Famagusta.

Bookshop
Rüstem's Bookshop in North Cyprus sells foreign (mostly English) books:
Rüstem's Bookshop (Rüstem Kitabevi)
26 Girne Caddesi, Nicosia (near Atatürk Square, opposite the Saray Hotel)
☎ *2071418*

Sport

North Cyprus, like the southern part of the island (see Practical Information South Cyprus, Sport), caters for a range of sports. Many hotels have their own tennis courts and facilities for a variety of water sports.

Sailing
Lack of wind in summer months and military restrictions around parts of the coastline make sailing difficult. The old harbour of Kyrenia provides moorings.

Dolphin Sailing operates sailing, para-sailing, speed boat and aqua-rocket trips from Deniz Kízí beach (Kyrenia) from May to October. Sailing dinghies and catarmarans can also be hired from Palm Beach and Sálamis Bay Hotels in Famagusta.

Waterskiing
Waterskiing is operated from the hotels Club Acapulco, Chateau Lambousa and Mare Monte in Kyrenia; and Deniz Kízí, Palm Beach and Salámis Bay in Famagusta.

Windsurfing
Sailboards can be hired from the hotels Celebrity, Club Kyrenia, Chateau Lambousa and Mare Monte in Kyrenia; and Palm Beach, Park, Sálamis Bay, Cyprus Gardens, Long Beach and Mimoza in Famagusta.

Diving
Kyrenia Diving Centre
21 Philecia Court, Kyrenia
☎ *8156087*

Fred Dive Ltd
7 Kemal Ašík Caddesí, Nicosia
☎ *8151743*

Tennis
In Kyrenia there are tennis courts at the Celebrity, Chateau Lambousa, Mare Monte and Club Acapulco hotels, Jasmine Court Hotel Apartments, LAS Holiday Centre, Olive Tree Holiday Village and Riverside Holiday Village.

In Famagusta the Cyprus Gardens, Palm Beach, Park, Sálamis Bay and Sea Side hotels have tennis courts.

Riding
Tunal Riding Club (a stud)
3 km west of Kyrenia, at Karaoğlanoğlu

Walking
The Bešparmak Hills are good walking country. There are no waymarked routes.

Telephone

Telephone calls can be made from hotels but these are very expensive: it is better to use telephone kiosks or telegraph offices. Payphones are operated by tokens (jetons), obtainable in post offices and telegraph offices.

All international calls are routed via Mersin in Turkey.

Telegraph offices
Nicosia: Telecommunication Office, in the Yenišehir district
Famagusta: Polatpaša Bulvarí
Kyrenia: Cumhuriyet Caddesi

International dialling codes
North Cyprus to the United Kingdom: 00 44
North Cyprus to the United States or Canada: 00 1
United Kingdom to North Cyprus: 00 90 392
United States or Canada to North Cyprus: 011 90 392

Tipping

It is customary to give a tip of about 10 per cent in hotels and restaurants, also to hairdressers and taxi drivers.

Travel Documents

Visitors to North Cyprus must have a valid passport, and children should be entered in the passport. The passport will be stamped by the North Cyprus immigration officers on entry and exit. Since a North Cyprus stamp in a passport will prevent the holder from entering the Greek Republic of Cyprus, and also from visiting Greece, it is advisable to ask to have the stamps put on a separate inserted page.

Weights and Measures

See Practical Information South Cyprus, Weights and Measures

When to Go

See Practical Information South Cyprus, When to Go

Index

Source of Illustrations

Front and back covers: AA Photo Library (A Kouprianoff)

AA Photo Library: 8, 76 (A Kouprianoff); 224 (M Birkitt)
Archiv für Kunst und Geschichte: 48 (3×); Archaeological Museum, Nicosia: 54, 146, 148, 152; Couteau: 94; dpa: 44; Feltes-Peter: 2, 3 (2×), 13, 14, 17 (2×) 18 (2×), 27, 29 (left), 30, 41, 55, 58, 59, 62, 65, 72, 79, 87, 88, 90, 93, 99, 103, 109, 112, 119, 120, 123, 127, 128, 130, 133, 135, 137, 140, 141, 142, 143, 145, 153, 155, 157, 168, 169, 172, 176, 178, 179, 180, 189, 192, 194, 203, 204, 205, 209, 212, 214, 219, 220, 221, 254
Guenther: 11, 96, 125: Hartmann: 182
IFA-Bilderteam: 52; Lade, Helga: 19
Peters/Strub: 21, 29 (right), 33, 63, 64, 69, 73, 84, 86, 91, 100, 105 108, 114, 116, 118, 150, 159, 161, 163, 165, 167, 170, 173, 175, 185 186, 190, 196, 197, 199, 201, 206, 208, 216, 245, 246
Pierides Museum: 124; Schapowalow: 253
Troodhitissa-Kloster: 22; Zavallis: 38/39

Imprint

183 photographs, 54 maps and plans, 1 large fold-out map

German text: Astrid Feltes-Peter, Barabara Peters, Dr Wolfgang Hasselpflug (climate)
Cartography: Franz Huber, München; Mairs Geographischer Verlag (large fold-out map)
General direction: Rainer Eisenschmid, Baedeker Ostfildern
Editorial work German edition: Baedeker-Redaktion (Astrid Feltes-Peter)

English translation: James Hogarth, Alec Court, Robin Sawers
Editorial work English edition: g-and-w PUBLISHING, Wina Gunn
Design: The Company of Designers, Basingstoke, Hampshire, UK

4th English edition 2001

Published by AA Publishing (a trading name of Automobile Association Developments Limited, whose registered office is Norfolk House, Priestley Road, Basingstoke, Hampshire RG24 9NY; registered number 1878835).

Distributed in the United States and Canada by:
Fodor's Travel Publications, Inc.
201 East 50th Street
New York NY 10022

A CIP catalogue record of this book is available from the British Library.

Licensed user: Mairs Geographischer Verlag GmbH & Co., Ostfildern

Typeset by Fakenham Photosetting Ltd, Fakenham, Norfolk, UK
Printed in Italy by G Canale & C SpA, Turin

ISBN 0 7495 2965 2

Only a selection of hotels and restaurants can be given; no reflection is implied therefore on establishments not included.

In a time of rapid change it is difficult to ensure that all the information given is entirely accurate and up to date, and the possibility of error cannot be eliminated.

Although the publishers can accept no responsibility for inaccuracies and omissions, they are constantly endeavouring to improve the quality of their guides and are therefore always grateful for criticisms, corrections and suggestions for improvement.

Notes

Notes

Notes

Notes